ERRATUM

On page 219, the last phrase in the top paragraph should read as follows:

". . . ; similarly the few Jewish cutlery firms in Sheffield were absorbed, only Viner's and Harris Miller & Co continuing independently."

Economic History
of the Jews in England

THE LITTMAN LIBRARY OF
JEWISH CIVILIZATION

EDITORS
David Goldstein
Louis Jacobs
V. D. Lipman

For the love of God
and in Memory of
JOSEPH AARON LITTMAN

"Get Wisdom, get understanding:
Forsake her not and she shall preserve thee"

Economic History of the Jews in England

Harold Pollins

Rutherford • Madison • Teaneck
Fairleigh Dickinson University Press
London and Toronto: Associated University Presses

Associated University Presses, Inc.
4 Cornwall Drive
East Brunswick, N.J. 08816

Associated University Presses Ltd
27 Chancery Lane
London WC2A 1NS, England

Associated University Presses
Toronto M5E lA7, Canada

Library of Congress Cataloging in Publication Data

Pollins, Harold.
  Economic history of the Jews in England.

  (The Littman Library of Jewish civilization)
  Bibliography: p.
  Includes index.
  1. Jews—Great Britain—Economic conditions.
2. Great Britain—Economic conditions. 3. Great
Britain—Ethnic relations. I. Title.   II. Series:
Littman library of Jewish civilization.
DS135.E5P64   330.941'0089924   80-70683
ISBN 0-8386-3033-2   AACR2

Printed in the United States of America

For Joe, Debbie, Karen
and in Memory of Percy Pollins
and Dora Pollins

Contents

List of Tables

Preface

This book is an investigation of the economic pursuits of Jews in Britain from the seventeenth century to the present day. An introductory chapter deals with the brief period when a medieval Jewish community existed in England and which came to an abrupt end in 1290 with the expulsion of the Jews. It looks too at the 'middle period' between that episode and their readmission in 1656; the main study starts at that point.

Its purpose is to describe Jewish economic activities and to suggest reasons for any patterns which are displayed. It follows the historian's conventional interests by asking: what happened? why did it happen? Apart from a brief excursus in the final chapter it does not attempt to enter the grand theories, which have been put forward from time to time, which assay a specific role for Jews in economic history, in particular in the development of capitalism. However intellectually exciting they may be they all suffer from insecure factual foundations. In any case it is a curious irony that such studies have so little to say about Britain, the world's first industrial capitalist society. The country was well able to develop commercial and financial institutions and expertise when Jews were either not present—between 1290 and 1656 (except for a handful for short periods)—or were in Britain in small numbers in the eighteenth century during her economic emergence.

In place of grand theory this book is an exercise in middle range theories, but the laudable objective of providing information and analysis at that level is no straightforward matter. Sundry difficulties attend the task of collecting relevant data—problems of definition and of scarcity of information. They are not all unique to Jewish history: occupational titles are often ambiguous so that a tailor may be employed or he may be an employer, and a merchant is not necessarily engaged in overseas trade. A minor problem is to do with the geographical area covered. Although most Jews in Britain in the last three centuries have lived in or near London, there are references in this book to virtually the whole of the British Isles. Where precision is necessary I have used the appropriate term: United Kingdom, Great Britain, England, Wales, Scotland, Northern Ireland, Ireland, etc. But to avoid such clumsy terms as 'Jews of the British Isles' I have sometimes loosely referred to 'Anglo-Jewry' or

'Britain'. I am conscious that this is a dangerous step. I understand that, following pressure from Jews living in the Celtic fringe, the English Zionist Federation was forced to change its name to the Zionist Federation of Great Britain and Northern Ireland. I am aware that the Jewish Lads' Brigade in Glasgow has a kilted, pipe band; and that the upbringing and education of Jews in the Irish Republic has provided them with a view of British history markedly different from that which British Jews would normally understand.

Similarly the use of the phrase 'Jewish community' is no more than a shorthand convention for Jews living in the country or a particular area of it. One of the major contrasts in modern Jewish history between a few countries like Britain and others in Europe was the former's greater liberalism, and Jews were not administered politically through their defined geographical-religious groupings. And while Jews are normally associated in local religious communities, there may be several of them in the same district. The use of the phrase certainly does not extend to a discussion of the financial and economic aspects of communal organisations.

'Economic history' here refers mainly to types of occupations and types of industry. But even if details of that kind were comprehensively available—and they are not—they would not tell us much about Jewish economic life unless we were to be satisfied with lists of facts. While the prime consideration in the book is the economic life of Jews in Britain, that has to be put within the context of both Jewish history in general and British history, especially economic history. And I have not hesitated to pursue particular points in social and political history where such excursions seemed desirable. A discussion of Jewish trade unions must necessarily be related to British labour history as well as to the particular Jewish features of the period.

Two matters—one of definition, the other of the supply of information—are closely related, and are a consequence of the position of Jews in British society, notably since the readmission in the seventeenth century. The extensive freedom they enjoyed, compared with the Jews of most other countries, meant that they have not been recorded as Jews in official records. There are no accurate figures of such basic matters as population numbers let alone economic categories. Much effort has to be devoted by researchers into establishing whether 'Moses Samuel' is Jewish or a Welsh nonconformist. And when we do have more information than just a mere name we have to decide whether or not to include a person if, say, he marries a non-Jew or, more ambiguously, appears to have nothing to do with the Jewish religious community. In Jewish history it has not been unusual for individuals consciously to embrace Christianity in order to be able to pursue occupations which were closed to Jews: it was common in nineteenth-century Germany for example, as the conversion of Karl Marx's father testifies. But there is not much evidence that Jews in Britain followed that course. Benjamin Disraeli's father left the community because of a conflict with the synagogue; and most Jews who 'seceded' did so for their own personal reasons.

Problems of this kind make the task harder but by no means impossible and it is to be hoped that the broad outline which this book provides will be expanded and corrected by future studies. For a relatively brief work for such an extended historical coverage has to be based on the researches of other people. Anyone entering this field is conscious of a profound debt to the numerous scholars whose extraordinarily meticulous investigations into many areas of Anglo-Jewish history have provided a wealth of materials and lines of thought. In the course of writing this book I have also sought, usually successfully, information from many historians as well as from people in the non-academic world. I acknowledge their help individually in the notes. Among those who have been especially helpful are Father Frank McHugh, Dr Joseph Buckman, Professor George Bain (particularly on trade union history), Bill Williams (whose later history of Manchester Jewry is awaited) and P. L. Cottrell. Dr Vivian Lipman, whose wide-ranging researches have been used extensively, read a draft of the work and suggested both changes in detail and important structural improvements. I am especially grateful to him.

My colleagues at Ruskin College collectively deserve thanks. All, at some stage, have been pestered for ideas and for references. Some, usually re-signedly, have found themselves listening to extracts just written; usable comments have sometimes ensued, as they did from lunchtime sessions at the Nag's Head with Peter Donaldson, Roy Moore and assorted extras. Victor Treadwell has counselled wisely and provided the benefit of his wide biblio-graphical knowledge. David Horsfield, the College librarian, obtained many items for me. Raphael Samuel has been enthusiastic. The late Paul Brodetsky supplied literature and many important pointers. Bill Cooke read some of the chapters in draft. I deeply regret that the late Gerald Harrison did not have the chance to read what I made of his generously-given knowledge of seventeenth-century literature.

Lionel Kochan suggested that I should write this book, and I acknowledge his continuing interest and his expertise in Jewish and European history which he allowed me to exploit.

A brief version of chapters 7 and 9 was delivered to the conference of the Urban History Society in 1975, and an earlier draft of chapter 10 was given to the Jewish Historical Society of England in 1976.

This book is for my children. They did not know my parents, whose memory I salute for many reasons but especially for the laudable anxiety they induced in me about certain features of economic theory by their refusal to behave according to the assumptions in the textbooks.

Ruskin College, Oxford   Harold Pollins

Acknowledgments

Table 3 is taken from V. D. Lipman, *Social History of the Jews in England: 1850–1950,* published by C. A. Watts in 1954, reprinted by permission of Pitman Publishing Ltd.

Table 6 is reprinted by permission of the World Jewish Congress.

Table 7 is reprinted by permission of the Jewish Welfare Board.

Tables 9 and 10 are reprinted by permission of The London School of Economics and Political Science.

Table 11 is reprinted by permission of Dr Cyril Hershon.

Tables 12, 13 and 14 were first published in the *Jewish Journal of Sociology* (vol. 14, no. 2, December 1972, and vol. 17, no. 1, June 1975), and are reprinted by permission of the Editor of the *JJS*.

Introduction
The Earlier Communities

The modern Jewish community in England dates from 1656. In that year a small group of people in London were permitted to establish a synagogue for prayer and a place for the burial of their dead: two essential institutions for their religious life. Since then there has been a continuous history of Jewish life in the British Isles: its economic aspects are the main themes of this book.

This year of 1656 is rightly called the date of 'resettlement' or 'readmission': Jews had been known in England well before the seventeenth century. Some historians have suggested there were very early contacts but it is generally agreed that the medieval settlement began after the Norman Conquest of 1066–71. 'The first Jews of medieval England were Norman imports',[1] who presumably accompanied others from northern France who crossed the Channel in the wake of William.

Very little is known about the earliest pioneers, why they came, who they were and how many they numbered: on such matters the few records are unhelpful. It is most likely that more arrived as a result of the First Crusade of 1096. In Jewish history the march of the Crusaders to the Holy Land was a disaster, the route along the Rhineland marked by massacres of Jewish communities; for although the Crusade was a confrontation with Islam, the nearest infidels were the Jews. Northern France did not experience these physical attacks, except in one place, Rouen,[2] which became 'the undoubted recruiting ground for the first generations of medieval English Jews'.[3] Perhaps, too, the great fire in that town a few years later, which began in the Jewish quarter,[4] impelled some to move to England. Although later on some Jews came from the Rhineland and even further afield, medieval Anglo-Jewry was essentially French in language and culture, and remained so even after England lost her possessions in France in the early years of the thirteenth century.[5]

If the beginning of Anglo-Jewish settlement is somewhat vague, the end was definite and unequivocal. In 1290 Edward I expelled all professing Jews from the kingdom, thus concluding dramatically just two centuries of the community's existence. Probably about 2,500 to 3,000 Jews were forced to leave the country (only a few chose conversion to Christianity instead)—a population which had fallen from a peak of perhaps 5,000 in the early thirteenth century. At its height Anglo-Jewry amounted to one-quarter of 1 per cent (0.025) of the population of England.[6]

They were not distributed evenly throughout the country, but congregated in the towns, London being the first and remaining the main settlement. From about 1130 groups settled in some twenty to twenty-five other places, generally in the more prosperous south and east, notably at Norwich, Canterbury, Oxford, Cambridge, Exeter and Lincoln. The relative importance of these provincial communities varied from time to time, and in some towns the settlements were brief. The most northerly settlement was at Newcastle-upon-Tyne; none reached Scotland, but some found their way to Ireland (also under Norman rule).[7] Jews may also have lived elsewhere: it has been suggested that they may have resided—albeit in isolation and only sporadi-cally—in as many as two hundred places.[8] But this is doubtful: it is more likely that 'the Jews whose names associate them with places outside the large country towns were those who had an occasional rather than permanently sedentary connection'[9] with them.

Yet Jews never became an integral part of the local population. They were not members of the *commune* of the town, but of a separate Jewish *commune*, and they undertook few of the characteristic functions of townspeople. We do not find them as craftsmen or retailers, or as merchants engaged in exporting or importing (apart from London they did not live in port-towns). Their main economic activity—the best-documented one—was moneylending—and this too was not to merchants or to burgesses. The Jews supplied the financial needs of people living in the country.[10] Obviously they did not live in an enclosed or self-sufficient community. They were not cut off from the surrounding non-Jewish world and while they generally lived near to each other, near a market or royal castle, it was not uncommon for Jewish and non-Jewish residences to be intermingled: there was no ghetto.

Very few records survive to throw light on their day-to-day lives: England seldom enters the rabbinical *Responsa,* the rulings and judgments given by rabbis to all manner of questions which are a major source of information on Jewish life and conditions.[11] On the other hand an abundance of documents exists about Jewish finance in this period, mostly of an official kind, state or ecclesiastical. 'The relationship between medieval anglo-Jewry and the State . . . was dominated by the fiscal purposes of the Crown.'[12] Unique adminis-trative procedures were arranged for the revenue the king claimed from the Jews, handled from the 1190s by the *Scaccarium Judaeorum* or Exchequer of the Jews, headed by Justices or Keepers of the Jews. It acted in three main ways: it handled the royal revenue from the Jews, acted judicially in certain cases affecting them, and controlled the *archa* system whereby, in various defined towns, all debts owed to Jews and their settlements were registered. This administrative machinery originated with the need to deal with the immense and complex estate of Aaron of Lincoln, who died in 1186. By law the property of a dead Jew could pass to his heir, usually on payment to the king of one-third of the estate. In this case 'the heirs did not, or were not permitted to, succeed',[13] and Henry II seized Aaron's possessions. The arrangements made to handle them became formalised as the Exchequer of the Jews.

The documents that survive from these various sources provide much information about individuals, such as the wealthy Jurnet family of Norwich, one of the more important provincial centres,[14] and sufficient details exist about Rabbi Elijah of London (d. 1284) for a virtual biography to be written.[15] Elijah, described as being a member of 'the most distinguished Anglo-Jewish family of the Middle Ages', was a leader of the community, a rabbi, a physician, a writer on religious matters and a financier. This combination of functions was by no means uncommon, the wealthiest Jews of England often carrying on these various activities, including a not inconsiderable body of intellectual work.[16]

The financial activities of Elijah were characteristic of those of the few major Jewish moneylenders of the time. Although based on London, he made loans in many parts of the country 'from Cumberland in the north to Devon in the south'. He sometimes formed partnerships or consortia with other Jews such as Benedict of Winchester, Gamaliel of Oxford and Aaron fil' Vives. (Wives also were often associated with these business dealings.) Elijah's clients, it is said, 'included nobles, commoners, burghers and monasteries, not to mention the royal family—for example, the queen mother, Eleanor of Provence, to whom he advanced 600 marks in 1275'.[17]

A statement of that kind needs qualifying. Although an individual member of the royal family might borrow, the Crown did not (except for a few years in the twelfth century): obviously the king preferred to tax rather than to have the obligation of repaying a loan.[18] Moreover the Jews' debtors were not men of the highest social ranking, but rural gentry whose borrowings were for consumption, not to improve production.[19] Against the debt they would pledge chattels or land, and, if the debt was not repaid, the land found its way to a third party. In an important sense the peculiar legal status of the Jews was a major feature of the land market. If a Jew came into the possession of land, he could not acquire a freehold interest in it but could dispose of it. No other specific group of creditors was in this position. 'This circumstance, and their predominance for a time as private moneylenders, caused the Jews to become the vehicle—though not, of course, the sole vehicle—for the transfer of land.'[20]

Details of this kind are quite familiar to students of English history, but they raise many questions which deserve to be examined. Why have the researches of many scholars been able to uncover only a few other occupations of Jews in medieval England? We come across those who served the religious needs of the community; some were employed by rich Jews as clerks, agents or domestic servants; doctors, vintners, two cheesemongers, and a fishmonger are mentioned; some traded in goods, and others were pawnbrokers. We have the

names of a few soldiers, Abraham, the crossbowman, and 'John, the Jew', a
serjeant-at-arms; these may have been converts to Christianity, who possibly
had been soldiers before their conversion.[21] In a period of two centuries these
few examples do not amount to very much: otherwise the evidence points only
to moneylending. Is this because of the nature of the surviving documents?
Since most of them are concerned with finance, they do not enlighten us about
other Jewish activities. The records show quite clearly that there was a
comparatively small number of great Jewish magnates, those whose names
occur frequently and for large amounts of money. A second group of middling
moneylenders was somewhat larger, but a third group appears only occasionally in the records as moneylenders, and for small amounts. A detailed,
plausible analysis of the Jews of Norwich during the period 1220–40 shows that
of perhaps 150 individuals 10 (of one extended family) were very wealthy; 30
were 'upper-middle-class'; 60 were 'ordinary middle-class'; and 50—i.e.,
one-third—were poor.[22]

About the poor only occasional scraps of information come our way. The
records of a court case of 1230 provide one example. It concerned two Flemish
merchants who laid a complaint against three Jews. The Jews offered to sell
them a maple-wood cup and the transaction ended with the merchants being
accused of offering base money and being attacked physically by the Jews. It is
very likely that these Jews were not engaged in legitimate trade: the cup may
have been an unredeemed pledge for a loan, or it could have been stolen. The
case is 'a reference to three Jews of the half-world', and the general conclusion
could be that 'the proletarian Anglo-Jew of the Middle Ages [scraped] a living
by occasionally negotiating a loan, taking articles on pledge, and then furbish-
ing up and hawking a miscellaneous collection of unredeemed pledges.'[23]

The concentration of Jews on moneylending was not unique to England. It
was already an important activity for the Jews of Rouen in the eleventh
century;[24] it was common among the Jews of many Continental countries. The
main reason for this speciality must have been the nature of medieval Christian
society which barred Jews from numerous occupations. The guilds, for example, controlled entry into the major handicrafts and trades, but since they were
as much religious fraternities as economic institutions, Jews were not admitted.
Only one example is known of a Jew is England being accepted by a guild.[25]
There was little left for them but moneylending. But no one accepts the
argument that Jewish moneylending emerged because the Church forbade
Christians to charge interest on money, that if Christians were not allowed to
supply the funds needed in a money economy, the Jews could: they were not
forbidden doctrinally to lend money to Christians. In practice, loans were
supplied by Christians too.

A recent study of the debts of Canterbury Cathedral priory for the period
1215–95—the first detailed examination of the total borrowings by a single
person or institution—illustrates the point.[26] The priory required large sums
for the conduct of its business at the papal court, to pay taxes to the pope and

the king and to meet the heavy cost of electing a new Archbishop of Canterbury. Jews lent only small amounts, 'as the treasurers usually borrowed from Jews when they needed a ready supply of coin to take on journeys or to pay for provisions at a fair'.[27] The main sources were Italians—the money often borrowed in Rome—and various Christians in England, including some members of the clergy. The records clearly show that interest was paid on some of the loans, sometimes openly stated, at other times disguised. As the thirteenth century progressed, and the Church tried to insist on the prohibition of usury, acceptable devices such as the exaction of penalties for the late repayment of debts were used.[28]

Although providing further evidence of the existence of Christian moneylenders,[29] whether charging interest on loans or not, the Cathedral priory's records cannot be used to generalise about Jewish and non-Jewish moneylending in England. They may or may not reflect their relative contributions to the English money market. The significance of Jewish finance is more apparent in fiscal matters. The Jews were a small, separately administered group, on whom special taxes (tallages) could be imposed by the Crown. The taxable income came from the interest they charged on loans, in turn obtained from Christian borrowers, the Jews being, in effect, indirect tax-collectors for the king. During the thirteenth century, beginning perhaps with the notorious 'Bristol' tallage of 1210—preceded by the imprisonment of Jews throughout England—severe financial demands were made upon them.[30] Moreover, their resources were greatly depleted by the civil wars of the mid-thirteenth century, and they were therefore of less service to the Crown as a source of revenue. This situation could be remedied in two ways: their economic role could be changed, or their property could have been confiscated and the Jews expelled. Both were in fact done.

The first measure was the *Statutum de Judeismo* of 1275, which was an attempt 'to turn the Jews from moneylending into other occupations'.[31] The statute forbade Jews to lend money at interest, and in return they were to be allowed to be merchants and artisans. This did not work. The Jews could not become guild members, and they argued that they could not deal in goods because they could not travel the country easily. In fact they continued their usurious practices although disguised as commodity transactions, repayments being stipulated in goods, not in money. Clearly this experiment in occupational diversification did not succeed, neither did it provide the Jews with the income from which the king could exact revenue. Whereas tallages on the Jews were frequent, almost annual, after 1267 only one further imposition was made, in 1287, before the expulsion. Possibly their resources had been denuded when substantial amounts were obtained by the Crown in 1278–9 through forfeiture of Jewish property and from fines following accusations of debasing the coinage by clipping. Many Jews (and non-Jews) were arrested for the offence: Jews' houses were plundered by the mob and some of the arrested Jews were ordered to be hanged. Others, against whom the evidence was uncertain, were fined and released. Many had to forfeit their property to pay a fine instead. The result must have been further to diminish the Jews' assets.[32]

The official reasons for the expulsion, which came three years after the tallage of 1287, was that the Jews had continued with their usurious practices despite the prohibition of 1275.[33] The king, Edward I, was certainly keen to uphold Church doctrine on the evils of lending at interest, and it may also be that his financial innovations reduced his need for the Jews. The imposition in 1275 of a duty on the export of wool and leather, together with the more regular collection of taxes on personal property, improved his revenue receipts. The special arrangement he made with the Italian society of Riccardi, which advanced ready cash in advance of revenue receipts, aided the Crown's liquidity.[34] These and other foreign financiers, such as the Cahorsins, were performing banking services for the Crown, whereas the Jews had been a source of taxation.

The expulsion of 1290 followed the confiscation of the Jews' property, a year after the king had done the same to his Jewish subjects in Gascony. He needed the money to pay the large ransom for his cousin Charles of Salerno, captured by Aragon. In both cases the Jews' physical property was confiscated and sold for the benefit of the king, and debts owed to them came into his possession. The king remitted the interest which was due on them, but collected the principal sums from the debtors. Having taken their property, Edward I expelled the Jews.[35]

Expulsions of unwanted groups are not unknown throughout history: a limited, parochial view of the removal of the Jews from England in 1290 has to be avoided. At the same time it would be improper to confine a discussion about the abrupt ending of medieval Anglo-Jewry within an economic context. It is necessary indeed to look at the relationship between the Jewish and Christian worlds, for the nature and the effects of those contacts did much to determine the scope and range of Jewish economic activity. Despite the special features of English history, the position of the Jews was very similar to that of their co-religionists in many other European countries during the medieval period. The Jews were distinctively an 'outside' group. As well as being alien, they followed a religion different from, and to some extent in opposition to, the prevailing Christian beliefs. At a time when religion was a pervasive influence on men's conduct, the possession of different beliefs was crucial. Other, non-Catholic, religions experienced the obloquy of the Church but they had few adherents in medieval Europe, and the Jews, in any case, inhabited a special residence within the universe of non-Christians.[36] To Christians, the Jews were the people who denied the Messiahship of Jesus and had·thus broken the Covenant with God. The Jews for their part asserted the opposite—they had maintained the Covenant—but since they were always in a minority and political power rested with the Gentiles, they were always at a disadvantage. Wherever the Jews resided they lived on sufferance, and on the Continent, even before the establishment of the medieval Anglo-Jewry, they were regarded in practice as *servi camerae,* in effect the property of the king (or ruler of the state). From him they derived the only rights they had, and were dependent on his protection: much of Jewish history in the middle ages in England turns on the relation between the Crown and the Jews. For example, they generally lived near a royal castle where in time of trouble they could seek refuge.

What happened in practice depended on the circumstances of the time. A strong king might protect the Jews, but a weak one did not, and the conflicts between contenders for the Crown, or between barons and Crown, were not conducive to strong government.[37] Moreover the teachings of the Church were extremely relevant in determining the attitude towards Jews. 'The papal view can be summarised thus: Jews ought to be repressed on account of Jewish crimes, but they should not be harmed since their eventual conversion was required as a sign of—possibly a prerequisite for—the Second Coming.'[38] Yet the more popular view of the Jews equated them with the Devil and with all manner of obnoxious acts—usury, blasphemy, magic, as well as cheating and sharp practice. It would indeed be very easy to portray medieval Anglo-Jewish life in all the horrors of pogrom and persecution, tempered admittedly by official protection. The first known murder libel concerned William, a boy whose body was found at Easter time in 1144, the Jews being accused of killing him. William of Norwich became a *cause célèbre,* his story incorporated into local folklore and his remains enshrined in the cathedral, 'down to the time of the Reformation . . . venerated as those of a saint and martyr'.[39] The accusation gave rise to much local feeling, and at a synod of the clergy a priest (an uncle of the dead boy) demanded that the Jews be brought to justice. They were summoned to appear before the synod, but the sheriff acted on their behalf, reminding the clergy that the ecclesiastical courts had no jurisdiction over Jews. They were the king's property and in the charge of the sheriff, who took them back to the castle for safety, where they stayed until the immediate danger had passed.

Much more devastating were the outbreaks of violence in 1189–90. Richard I, who had just come to the throne, was an enthusiast for the Crusades and we can reasonably associate the greater religious fervour of those years with attacks on Jewish communities, despite the king's efforts to safeguard them. The worst was at York in 1190, an event so enshrined in Jewish history that even today some orthodox families 'actively discourage their children from coming to settle—or even to study—in the city'.[40] The whole community, perhaps some 150 souls, was besieged but could not escape the mob—in this case the royal protection did not work—and the majority committed suicide. As always, it is very difficult to decide whether the attack was a consequence of religious antagonism or because of the Jews' hated role as moneylenders. The events at

York, it has been suggested, were 'led by indebted gentry and needy crusaders, who in a fine blend of religious prejudice and financial self-interest had finished by burning the bonds of the Jews in the middle of the Minster.'[41]

These were some of the highlights, and it is noteworthy that the deterioration in the Jews' condition during the thirteenth century coincided with the stricter attitude of the Church towards them—the hostility towards usury, for example, and the requirement to wear a distinctive badge. But the expulsion ought not to be seen as the culmination of two centuries of growing anti-semitism. Alongside the more abundant evidence of hostility towards them can be placed examples of amicable relationships between Jews and Gentiles.[42] The explanation for the expulsion has to be sought in a combination of political and economic circumstances in which anti-Jewish sentiment was only one factor.

Besides England's distinction of being the first country in which the ritual murder accusation was made, it was the pioneer in banning Jews from the whole kingdom. The next country was France in 1306, and the English Jews who had settled there after 1290 found themselves on the move again.[43] The material for historians of Anglo-Jewry, studying the next two centuries, is a residue of a small number of converts, including the occasional flamboyant figure such as the converted Portuguese Jewish soldier of fortune Duarte Brandão (subsequently Brandon or Brampton). During the Wars of the Roses in the late fifteenth century he advanced in the military and naval hierarchy, became governor of the island of Guernsey and received a knighthood.[44] But such personalities are merely of some antiquarian interest. It is much more realistic virtually to withdraw England after 1290 from Jewish history until events in Spain and Portugal produced another stream of refugees, some of whom made a brief mark on the country in the sixteenth and early seventeenth centuries.

The Jews of the Iberian peninsula—the Sephardim—were, and are, distinguishable from those of northern Europe—the Ashkenazim—mainly in terms of religious ritual, tradition and language. The differences are not theological. Their history also separates them, for whereas the Ashkenazim of the middle ages experienced a form of life not too dissimilar from that of the medieval English Jewry—restrictions, massacres, expulsions—the story of Spanish Jewry is the one bright spot in Jewish history books. There we read of 'the golden age' when, despite some restrictions, there was a remarkable flowering of Jewish intellectual and creative activity, and Jews in Spain were able to enjoy a much wider range of occupations, including craftsmanship.

Yet Spain and Portugal were the site of the greatest tragedy in Jewish history since the time of the Crusades. A great pogrom in Seville in 1391 was followed by what the Ashkenazim would have found unbelievable—many Jews converted to Christianity. Even earlier there had been conversions—out of sincere religious conviction, perhaps, or out of opportunism because Christianity opened the door to previously unavailable jobs. Now fear was an important motive. Whatever the reason for their actions, they were now legally able to enter occupations previously barred to them: they were full Christians. In the fifty years after the pogrom they moved into 'important positions in royal, urban and ecclesiastical administration and government',[45] apparently without much opposition, but in the second half of the fifteenth century the tide turned against them, beginning with an uprising in Toledo in 1449. Subsequently, in a period of general social dislocation, other outbursts against converts and Jews culminated in massacres in at least twelve places in 1473.[46]

Eventually in 1492 the Jews (and the Moors), unless they agreed to convert, were expelled from Spain. Four years later they were ordered to leave Portugal, but before the date fixed for leaving many were forcibly converted to Christianity, and at first not permitted to emigrate.

As in Spain the immediate result was a widening of opportunities, and Portugal also adopted the Spanish system of separately identifying the converts. From 1550 to 1773 the official term was 'christão novo' or 'new Christian', and all were forced to recognise their origins even if many generations away from the original conversion, and even if sincere in their beliefs. One of the functions of the Inquisition was to tease out the truth, for there was some basis for suspecting the genuineness of the converts. Despite the obvious attractions of being members of the Church, many of the converts secretly practised Judaism while outwardly carrying out the full Christian requirements. They passed down increasingly garbled versions of Jewish prayers, ever fearful of denunciation to the Inquisition and ever ready to deny, even under torture, that they were secret Jews.* Many of them emigrated.

As might be expected, there is considerable discussion among historians about the causes of these events in the Iberian peninsula, which affected the Moors in the same way. Some emphasise economic matters. 'The problem of anti-semitism was linked to other aspects of popular movements and . . . in general popular violence was related to a deterioration in economic conditions.'[47] More generally, it is argued, the expulsions of Jews from Spain and Portugal were a consequence of the pressure of population in those countries.[48] Other explanations stress the role of religion rather than of economics. 'It is possible to state that the elimination of religious dissent was due to an unalterable desire to maintain orthodoxy over and above all material concerns.'[49]

Although most *conversos* and Jews settled in Mediterranean countries, a few went elsewhere, to South America and—more important for us—to north-west Europe. Unlike those who ended up in Italy or Greece, who seem to have been relatively poor, the settlers further north were men of substance. Settlements came into existence at ports and trading centres such as Hamburg, Rouen and

---

*I shall use the term *conversos* to denote these secret or crypto-Jews, following the practice of Professor Haim Beinart, the specialist in the subject, rather than the more familiar *marranos*, which has unfortunate derogatory connotations.

the great commercial and financial city of Antwerp, where the family of Mendes, with extensive trading and financial connections, lived from 1512 to the 1540s. The *conversos* there were harassed by the Inquisition, and since Antwerp was in decline in the second half of the century, they moved on to the city that replaced it, Amsterdam.[50]

A few, but only a few, came to England. In the very decade of the Spanish expulsions some were in London, apparently not hiding their Judaism: that, at any rate, was the complaint made to the king, Henry VII, by Ferdinand and Isabella of Spain.[51] Perhaps they were only temporary residents, for there are no further references to them or to other Jews in England until the 1530s.[52]

For this period the main source of knowledge is the records of the Inquisition, especially of the commissions which sat in Zeeland in 1539, in Milan in 1540 and in Antwerp in 1539 and 1543. In these archives at least sixty-nine *conversos* including wives and children are stated to be living in England, all in London. Many are described as merchants—a rather vague term—several as physicians, two or three as agents of Antwerp *conversos* and one as a perfumer. No occupation is given for many of them. One of them, Gaspar Lopes, a cousin of Diego Mendes of Antwerp, went to Italy in 1539, presumably on business for the Mendes firm, and after his arrest as a Jew by the Inquisition turned informer. On interrogation he described the house of a London *converso*, Alves Lopes, which was used as a secret synagogue and also as an office for giving relief and advice to Portuguese *conversos* fleeing from the Portuguese Inquisition.

As a result of these deliberations, which were communicated to England, the government issued orders in 1541 for the arrest of certain persons who were suspected of being secret Jews. Nothing came of the charges and the prisoners were released,[53] but the London *converso* group apparently declined rapidly in the 1540s, presumably because the Mendes house in Antwerp—probably their economic base—came to an end in that decade. Nevertheless, according to evidence given to the Lisbon Inquisition in the 1550s,[54] some remained. This testimony mentioned *conversos* living in London and Bristol during the period 1545–55, only twenty-two people in all, but the lists are obviously incomplete—wives and children are omitted, and other known *conversos* are not included. Again we read of merchants and physicians, including the head of the Bristol community, Dr Henrique Nunes, in whose house the *conversos* assembled for prayer, and Dr Hector Nunez of London, subsequently associated with Sir Francis Walsingham, Secretary to Queen Elizabeth, in his diplomatic activities.

The *conversos* in England, as in Antwerp, not surprisingly, passed as Protestants, but it was not a safe cover. The marriage of Mary Tudor to Philip II of Spain in 1554 necessarily led to action against English Protestants. Protestant refugees were expelled, and presumably some at least of the *conversos* also found it expedient to leave. But under Elizabeth I a number came to

London.[55] The records of the Inquisition produce between eighty and ninety individuals, and 'probably also not a few humble Jewish refugees who are still unidentified'.[56] The known names suggest that many of them belonged to a small number of families. Ferdinando Alvarez had twelve relations: Dunstan Añes twenty-two; Dr Rodrigo Lopez, physician to the queen, eleven. These and other families were interconnected by marriage.

The life of these *conversos* is analogous to that of the contemporary 'church papists', those Roman Catholics who outwardly conformed to the Protestant religion. Historians of both groups have similar problems of identification and of knowing, even when names are uncovered, whether the individuals really followed their ancient faith or were genuine members of the church to which they publicly belonged. Thus of these eighty or ninety *conversos*, undoubtedly of Jewish origin, it is impossible—naturally—to know if they regularly practised Judaism in secret. Some contemporary reports stated unequivocally that they were not afraid to assert their Jewishness openly. Solomon Cormano, on a diplomatic visit to London, 'availed himself of his diplomatic privilege to hold Jewish services in his house'. It was reported that 'he and all his trayne used publickely the Jewes rytes in prayinge, accompanyed wth divers secret Jewes resident in London.'[57] Other documents assert that some were known to be Jews.[58]

Several of them were able to supply useful intelligence to the authorities through their contacts with Spain and Portugal, where they had business connections. Dunstan Añes for example acted in this way for Secretary Walsingham, and even more information was supplied by Dr Hector Nunez through whose connections with Flanders the government was aware in 1587 and 1588 about preparations for the Armada. A brother of Dunstan Añes, Francisco, held a command in the garrison at Youghal in Ireland, subsequently becoming its mayor and a member of the Irish parliament. Dunstan's son-in-law Dr Rodrigo Lopez, convicted of plotting to poison Queen Elizabeth, was executed.[59]

By the end of the sixteenth century there were very few Jews indeed in England. It is not at all clear what happened to the Elizabethan community, apart from the deaths of leading characters such as Hector Nunez in 1591 and Dunstan Añes in 1594—the Añes family remained in England but were completely absorbed into the general population. Others are said to have left for the Levant or to have joined the newly-established Amsterdam community. During the first decade of the seventeenth century no more than half a dozen heads of families can be traced. A quarrel among them led to one party denouncing their opponents as Judaisers. By an order of 1609 all Portuguese merchants living in London who were suspected of being Jews had to leave the country. The event is somewhat obscure, and it seems that some 'secret Jews' remained.[60]

The group who were to inaugurate the new community in England in 1656 were therefore relative newcomers, the majority arriving in the 1650s; the earliest was Antonio Fernandez Carvajal, who came from Rouen in the 1630s when the *converso* settlement there was broken up.[61]

It is a pleasingly neat conclusion to this introduction that he should come from northern France and from the same town as his English forebears five and six centuries before. That is the only similarity. He lived as a Catholic, even being fined for not attending church, and the other Sephardim who followed him came from a great variety of places, but rarely from France. Their culture was Spanish and Portuguese and they were children of a different tradition, one of secrecy and the denial of their Jewishness. What needs to be discussed is why they thought it expedient in 1656 to throw off their mask and announce that they were Jewish. What had changed in Britain to encourage them to do so?

Economic History
of the Jews in England

I
Readmission, 1656

It all took place within six months. In the autumn of 1655 a petition was presented to Oliver Cromwell, the Lord Protector, requesting the readmission of the Jews to England. The petitioner was Menasseh ben Israel, a Sephardi rabbi of Amsterdam, not—it is important to note—the London *conversos*. They were associated neither with it nor with the subsequent conference which examined the question. It was not until March 1656 that the *conversos* publicly announced, in another petition, that they were Jews and asked for certain religious rights.

This was the essence of the readmission, a brief episode but full of problems for historians, not least the complete absence of any document recording the authorities' response to the March 1656 petition. No one knows exactly what happened; a gap in knowledge which in the past led to dates other than 1656 for the resettlement. Much more important and difficult are explanation and interpretation. Why did the readmission take place in the seventeenth century?

One matter is certain: this was a very different world from the middle ages. After the Reformation, religious hostility was directed against Roman Catholicism, equated by some Protestants with deeds of the Devil. For the moment, in rankings of antagonism, the Jews did not occupy the top position; on the contrary, they were granted by some Puritans a special place of consideration and praise. The Old Testament became more generally available through the translation of the Bible into English, and with it came a new appreciation and understanding of Judaism. In these old writings it was common to find analogies with current political and social controversies; the objectionable features of the middle ages and the monarchy were compared with the past world they could read about, to the advantage of the latter. 'Many Puritans regarded themselves as the chosen people . . . [they looked back] to the customs and traditions of a tribal society, still relatively egalitarian and democratic; its standards and myths could be used for destructive criticism of the institutions that had been built up in medieval society.'[1] In literature as well as in politics the universe of discourse was informed by the Old Testament.[2]

But it is not sufficient to point to these matters, or to the introduction of Hebrew studies in the universities, or to the fact that some Puritan sects went so far as to adopt certain religious practices from Judaism such as keeping Saturday holy, and were probably called 'Jews', to the confusion of researchers.[3]

The extraordinary religious argumentation which the Reformation produced resulted in a proliferation of sects who, with difficulty and with many setbacks, had in the long run to live with each other, to accept each other's existence. This religious pluralism was not necessarily extended to Catholics or to non-Christians, but it was obviously a considerable change from the monolithic medieval church. At least it permitted the possible peaceful co-existence of diverse groups. Perhaps this attitude helps to explain why an occasional voice from within the Puritan ranks asked for tolerance for the Jews. In the euphoria in the late 1640s at the beginning of the Interregnum there was a slight chance it might happen. The Council of Mechanics in 1648 passed a resolution in favour of universal toleration for all religions, 'not excepting Turkes, nor Papists, nor Jews'. The final document, the Agreement of the People, did not go as far as that and spoke of toleration only for Christians.[4]

Perhaps the most remarkable aspect of the new atmosphere was the role of the Jews within the numerous eschatological disputations and prophecies. In recent years many writers have drawn attention to, indeed insistently emphasised, the widespread diffusion of millenarian ideas in many countries at this period. In England they became part of the political discussion of the day. What to many may seem absurd—the literal analysis of biblical passages as the basis of future events—was by no means the property of an eccentric fringe. John Napier is said to have invented logarithms 'in order to help him understand the mysteries of the Apocalypse'.[5] Numerous arithmetical calculations were made to determine when Christ's kingdom would be established: one popular date was 1656, but there were many others. Our interest is in the prominence given to the Jews within these millenarian expositions. There was much talk of the 'restoration' of the Jews; their conversion to Christianity was expected as an essential preliminary to the millennium; some argued for their return to the Holy Land then under Turkish rule; others advocated their readmission to England. A major strand was conversion, as an expression of a kind of equality—Jews and Christians together would enter the new world—a qualitative difference from the old attitude that the Jews were in some sense evil and should be converted for that reason.[6]

Many millenarian ideas had a long history, but it is important that they were propagated especially in the 1630s and 1640s. One explanation for their efflorescence was the dismay caused by the defeat of Protestantism by the counter-Reformation in the 1620s.

> From Gibraltar to Danzig, from the Channel ports to Hungary, the ideological enemy struck down every citadel of Protestantism in turn. . . . Amid such a series of catastrophes the whole climate of opinion in Protestant

Europe was convulsed. It was the end of an era, perhaps the end of an illusion. . . . Armageddon had arrived. How, in these last convulsions of the world, could men breathe the atmosphere or think thoughts of the past, even the immediate past? Was it not time to count the few remaining days of the world, to expect the conversion of the Jews, to listen to the last, or at least the penultimate Trump, to calculate the abstruse and fugitive number of the Beast?[7]

How pleasant it would be to conclude at this point; to state that, given this background, the Puritan Interregnum of 1649–60 was exactly the right moment for the Jews to be readmitted. Now was the victory of the godly people; here was a political system in which many at the centre of power were millenarians; some had advocated readmission. It was not as simple as that—as is not unusual in British history, developments had their source in *ad hoc* responses to immediate problems rather than in profound ideological theorising.

The traditional accounts of the readmission, it is true, emphasise diplomatic activity rather than millenarianism, a central role being assigned to Menasseh ben Israel, a Dutch Sephardi rabbi. He published *Spes Israelis* in Latin and also in Spanish, the pamphlet being translated into English in 1650 by Moses Wall, a friend of John Milton and a millenarian. By 1652 it had gone into two editions and a reprint. The pamphlet is certainly part of the public discussion about readmission. It was answered almost immediately by Sir Edward Spenser, a Member of Parliament, *An Epistle to the Learned Menasseh ben Israel, in Answer to his, Dedicated to the Parliament* (London, 1650), who argued that if the Jews were to be readmitted it should be under certain severe conditions, to make them aware of their sins and to make them convert to Christianity. Moses Wall added a section to the second English edition arguing that the Jews would convert. Similarly it is clear that Menasseh ben Israel was in close contact with such well-known Interregnum figures as John Dury and, especially, John Thurloe, Cromwell's Secretary of State from 1652.

Moreover, as part of Menasseh's motives was the fact of a large body of Jewish refugees. The Portuguese Inquisition was flourishing, and the Thirty Years' War in central Europe was a disaster for Jews and many streamed westward. England was a possible refuge. There is no doubt that he used his connections with important English politicians during the 1650s to press his case.

But it is clear that his 1650 pamphlet, *The Hope of Israel,* did not advocate Jewish settlement in Britain. Although it was dedicated to parliament, it has very few references to Britain and no mention at all of readmission. In fact he wrote it as a response to the published views of English millenarians who had invoked his name in their efforts to obtain support to convert American Indians to Christianity—there being a theory that the Indians were descendants of the lost ten tribes of Israel. Menasseh could not allow his name to be associated with efforts aimed at conversion, and the pamphlet, whose Spanish edition was dedicated to the officers of the Amsterdam Sephardi community, was primarily an essay of consolation to the Sephardim, telling of the imminence of the Messiah because of the virtual completion of the Jewish dispersal. The central place allotted in the traditional account to *The Hope of Israel* is clearly misconceived.[8]

The story gets going in 1654 and concerns Cromwell, the Lord Protector. Two petitions were presented in that year by David Abrabanel, otherwise Manuel Martinez Dormido, a refugee from Brazil following the Portuguese conquest. Dormido asked Cromwell to make representations to the Portuguese for the restitution of his property, and also requested the readmission of the Jews to England: he described himself as a Jew. The petitions were endorsed: 'His Highness is pleased in an especiall manner to recommend these two annexed papers to the speedy consideration of the Council that the Petition may receive all due satisfaction and with all convenient speed.' The Council of State, the appropriate body to deal with the matter under the constitutional arrangements of the Interregnum, decided to take no action. Cromwell, however, did and addressed a letter to the king of Portugal demanding compensation.[9] This inconclusive episode is interesting: far from Dormido's admission that he was a Jew attracting sanctions, Cromwell took the case up and pressed it, even though Dormido was a new arrival and not a citizen. His petitions appear to be the earliest open admission that any Jews were living in England. Another was Simon de Caceres, but the remainder—Antonio Fernandez Carvajal ('the first English Jew'), and those who came in the 1650s— were outwardly Catholic. Although Carvajal was a contractor for the parliamentary army and in the mid-1650s acted as an 'intelligencer', supplying foreign news to Cromwell, no evidence exists to support the view—put forward by some historians—that Cromwell knew they were secret Jews.

At any rate the London *conversos* at first took no part in the more rapid series of events which began in 1655. After the end of the war with Holland, Menasseh ben Israel arrived in London. He brought a new pamphlet, *The Humble Addresses*, written in a different tone: 'the case for Readmission being argued almost exclusively on grounds of political expediency'.[10] Much of it is devoted to considering 'How Profitable the Nation of the Jewes are'. Thus:

> My third Motive is grounded on the Profit that I conceive this Common wealth is to reap, if it shall vouchsafe to receive us; for thence, I hope, there will follow a great blessing from God upon them, and a very abundant trading into, and from all parts of the world, not onely without prejudice to the English Nation, both in Importation, and Exportation of goods.[11]

He presented Cromwell with a comprehensive petition, asking that the Jews be admitted on terms of equality with the native population; that they should have public synagogues, the free observance of their religion, and a cemetery. They should also have their own tribunals to determine disputes according to Mosaic law.

The whole matter was submitted to the Whitehall conference of prelates, politicians, lawyers and merchants held in December 1655. It considered two questions. The first was swiftly answered: there was no legal objection to Jews entering England. No comparable response was given to the second question: on what conditions should they be admitted? From the existing incomplete account of the conference, there must have been a great deal of opposition to the idea of re-entry: the London merchants, at least, were afraid of competition from the immigrants. Among the differing opinions expressed by the theologians at the conference was the strong feeling that the Jews would not convert. The only positive support for readmission came from Cromwell. He made a closing speech to the conference, of which there is not a full report but only one by a person 'who was, or professed to have been, present, told in later years and coming to us at second-hand.'[12] Cromwell, addressing the clergy,

> desired to be informed by them whether it was not their opinion, that the Jews were one day to be called into the church? He then desired to know, whether it was not every Christian man's duty to forward that good end all he could? . . . This silenced the clergy. He then turned to the merchants. . . . He then fell into abusing the Jews most heartily, and after he had said everything that was contemptible and low of them: 'Can you really be afraid,' he said, 'that this mean despised people should be able to prevail in trade and credit over the merchants of England, the noblest and most esteemed merchants of the whole world!'[13]

Another account refers to him saying 'that since there was a Promise of their Conversion, means must be used to that end, which was the preaching of the Gospel, and that could not be had unless they were permitted to reside where the Gospel was preached.'[14]

Cromwell did not get his way. The conference ended with nothing beyond the definite statement that Jews were not legally excluded. But since nothing was decided on the right to practise their religion, the possibility of residence was no greater than before. At this point some historians' narratives of these matters wander into fantasy, with talk of Cromwell privately telling the Jews they could have their request. Cecil Roth, the Anglo-Jewish historian, stated in a 1956 lecture that 'it was at one time believed that he [Cromwell] gave an affirmative reply to the petition (if only by word of mouth) at the beginning of February, and the romantic Anglo-Jewish antiquarians of half a century ago introduced a new commemmorative anniversary into their Calendar on 4 February as "Resettlement Day".' He continues: 'It is certain he did nothing positive at this stage.'[15] But matters came to a head the next month, when the London *conversos* at last took a hand.

The whole group were placed in jeopardy because of the war between Spain and England which broke out in the autumn of 1655. In March 1656 the Council of State ordered that goods belonging to subjects of the Spanish Crown would be seized, and two ships and other property belonging to a *converso* merchant, Antonio Robles, were impounded. Almost all the *conversos* might have suffered the same, except for Antonio Carvajal, who had recently been 'endenizened'—a form of naturalisation. Two petitions were presented at the end of March. In one, Robles asked for the restoration of his goods on the ground that he was not a Spaniard and a Catholic but a Portuguese Jew who had come to England to escape the Inquisition. In May the Council ordered his goods to be restored, thus *de facto* permitting Jews to live in Britain and to hold property.

The second petition was submitted by Menasseh ben Israel and six *conversos* and acknowledged the 'Manyfold favours and Protection' which Cromwell had granted the Jews, enabling them to meet privately for religious purposes. They asked for two things: a written assurance that they might continue in the same way without fear of molestation; and a licence to permit them to bury their dead. The requests were very limited. There was nothing about readmission, nor for equal rights with natives: only for limited favours for those already in the country.

No written record of a response to the second petition exists: the relevant page in the minutes of the Council of State is missing. We do not know whether it was discussed, and, if it was, what the answer was. The only certainty is that late in 1656 a lease was obtained on a house in Cree Church Lane to be used as a synagogue, and early in 1657 arrangements were made for a plot of land in Mile End, east London, to be used as a place of burial. These actions imply that the response must have been favourable, but the argument that it was formal and written (and was lost when some unknown person cut out the page from the Council of State's minutes)[16] is not convincing. A recent imaginative examination of the evidence plausibly suggests that the petitioners were told by Cromwell, or by someone on his behalf, 'you had better do bravely what you suggest, and if you act with discretion the public will grow accustomed to these things and the Protector will see you come to no harm'.[17]

This was the substance of the 'readmission' of 1656, so-called despite the absence of any statement about immigration. It was right for the Anglo-Jewish community to celebrate its tercentenary in 1956, commemorating the establishment of the oldest Jewish congregation in Britain, the Spanish and Portuguese synagogue. No charter set out Jewish rights or listed any obligations, each aspect with its own dangers. The Jewish presence could have been questioned in the future, and the dependence on the word of a ruler was very similar to the position of the Jews in many medieval countries. A head of state might change his mind, or a new one might have an opposite attitude towards the Jews. The absence of obligations was the more important feature. There were no limitations on the choice of residence, no special taxes, no impediments to economic activities; that is, they were not specifically restricted *as Jews*. They were equal, in the sense that any obstacles to complete freedom were those they shared with others of like quality: as aliens, as non-members of the Church of England, or as non-Christians. There were no laws devoted only to them.

It is curious, nevertheless, that the high hopes of 1649–50 should so quickly have evaporated. Why was there so much difficulty; why was there so much opposition? The conversion issue was obviously important. Jews, it was realised, would not willingly be converted to Christianity. Moreover, there was a reaction against millenarianism, partly because of the extreme views being propagated by the numerous sects. And Judaism was not being held in such high esteem as before. Whereas the Barebones Parliament of 1653 had received a proposal to replace the existing political institutions by a body fashioned after the Jewish Sanhedrin, now people wrote of the cruelty of Mosaic law, and of the undesirability of introducing it into England. A more mundane development was a widespread disillusionment with the regime, and hostility towards it. It was 'as if all incipient as well as overt Puritan hostility to the Protector found the "Jewish Question" an opportune means of safe opposition.'[18]

If we include the obvious opposition of the merchants, there is no great difficulty in understanding what happened. But there is much less certainty when we examine Cromwell's motives for his persistent support. This Jewish episode is only one of the many features of Cromwell and the Cromwellian period which have attracted various and often conflicting interpretations. Contemporary documents and publications are plentiful, but not explicit statements of the reasons for particular policies. Inferences have to be made from the sources; their acceptability depending on their plausibility.

Only one full-scale examination of the readmission affair has been written: Lucien Wolf's account published in 1901. He reproduced many documents in this book and in separately published articles, and his work has formed the basis for later studies, usually within works on Cromwell or the Civil War and Interregnum periods. Wolf was a lucid writer: primarily a journalist, his knowledge of politics and politicians added much to his understanding of men's behaviour. But his imagination led him to interpretations often based on no evidence at all. Subsequent research has amended and extended some of his findings, but not all writers have been aware of the corrections. For example, Antonia Fraser's ten-page account in her recent life of Cromwell is greatly marred by the use of some of Wolf's early work.[19]

Such details need not concern us. The views of the various writers can be considered under three classifications.

Readmission as Part of Cromwell's General Economic and Political Policies

Wolf argued that the Jews were known as important traders and financiers; they were to be attracted to London to help Britain's economic development. If they came from Amsterdam, their legal position in England would have to be regularised. The Swedish historian E. F. Heckscher more broadly stated that the toleration extended to Jews in western European countries 'was determined primarily by commercial considerations' (although he adds that 'financial requirements' were relevant, as was religion).[20] Another argument is that readmission was connected with Cromwell's South American exercise of 1655 onwards, and that he needed the Jews familiar with that part of the world.[21]

Cromwell's Need of Money

The Protectorate was short of money in the 1650s. The Jews, it is said, would supply this if they were admitted. The great American historian W. C. Abbott wrote, somewhat vaguely, after a lifetime of study: 'It seems not improbable that this question may have entered into the discussions of the Council on the subject. Whether it did or not . . .'[22] It was at one time said that Cromwell even brought Jews to Britain as early as 1643 'with the specific object of supplying the pecuniary needs of the new administration', but this was a misreading of a document.[23]

Religious Toleration and Millenarianism

Most writers acknowledge the relevance of religion in the discussion of Cromwell's policies. Only Wolf dismissed it in his discussion of Cromwell and the Jews. Christopher Hill, for example, states after detailing various millenarian views: 'These expectations played their part in Cromwell's decision to readmit the Jews to England in 1656'.[24] Robert S. Paul emphasises Cromwell's religious toleration, and thinks that there is little in the economic argument. Cromwell had more to lose materially through the opposition of the London merchants than from the admission of the Jews. Presumably this is in line with those who emphasise Cromwell's religious tolerance.[25]

Perhaps the most judicious statement is the one that combines several explanations:

> Was this because the Old Testament had taught him to think of them as God's chosen people, or was it for commercial reasons and because they worked for his intelligence service? His mind worked to and fro between the City, Whitehall and the Holy Land without a sense of incongruity; the probability is that all three considerations influenced him.[26]

Which leaves us where we were, for no student of Cromwell nowadays denies that his policies were an amalgam of politics, economics and religion. The question each time is to know, in any particular circumstance, which aspect loomed largest in his mind. At least we can dismiss the simplistic mercantilist approach which assumes some kind of consistency of policy: that we should expect seventeenth-century politicians to be more capable of pursuing a single-minded set of policies than present-day rulers is somewhat curious.[27]

Two pieces of contemporary evidence from John Thurloe's papers are helpful in coming to a conclusion; both date from the Whitehall conference of December 1655. One, from Major-General Whalley, appears to be the only statement made by someone in Cromwell's circle which referred directly to the economic aspects of readmission.

> It seems to me, that there are both politique and divine reasons; which strongly make for theyre admission into a cohabitation and civill commerce with us. Doubtlesse to say no more, they will bring in much wealth into this commonwealth; and where we both pray for theyre conversion, and beleeve it shall be, I know not why wee should deny the meanes.

The second is a letter to Nieupoort, the Dutch ambassador, from Thurloe, reporting a visit by Menasseh ben Israel: 'and he did assure me, that he doth not desire any thing for the Jews in Holland, but only for such as sit in the inquisition in Spain and Portugal.'[28] This was undoubtedly his response to the anxiety of the London merchants, who feared competition if Jewish merchants were to enter the country: he would not encourage those in Amsterdam to come to London. It is very likely that while possibly a political ploy, it was also the truth. Behind all the millenarianism and his economic argument for admission, Menasseh was really looking only for a home for Jewish refugees, a time-honoured activity of renowned Jews throughout the ages. If so, this puts it into proper perspective. Past interpretations have been too great for the evidence to bear. The readmission was important for Jewish history, but not for British history. It was just one item among many facing the politicians of the day; it happened to receive some attention because of the particular form of contemporary religious discussion.

The uncertainty in our understanding of the reasons for the readmission appropriately parallels the absence of a written document. In one sense its non-existence was an advantage. In the immediate aftermath of the restoration of the monarchy in 1660, the Jews might have suffered during the reaction against the Protectorate: Cromwell's policy might have been reversed. The Corporation of the City of London petitioned Charles II for their expulsion; Thomas Violet issued a virulent pamphlet. Although no action was taken by the authorities, it is no wonder that the Sephardi congregation collectively forgot about their origin for some 250 years during which they maintained that their community had begun after the Restoration in 1660. This assertion occurs in what was the earliest history of the Jews in England, D'Bloissiers Tovey, *Anglia Judaica; Or the History and Antiquities of the Jews in England,* published in 1738. The congregation used to have 'a special ritual for the commemoration of the re-admission of the Jews under Charles II,'[29] no doubt because the first written document proferring them rights is dated 1664. Indeed

W. C. Abbott was clearly mistaken in saying that 'Cromwell took his place among the great heroes of the Jewish people.'[30] Until writers such as Lucien Wolf in the late nineteenth century examined the subject, the role of Cromwell was not known in this history. Moreover there is some evidence that the absence of synagogue records for the very early years was due to their conscious destruction by the congregation 'as part of a general policy which seems to have been decided at an early date, to draw a veil over the awkward truth that the origins of the Synagogue lay under the Commonwealth.'[31]

Expediency was sensible in the early uncertain years of the Restoration. The absence of a written residence statute made it more difficult for the new regime to reverse the readmission policy if it had wanted to. In the event it did not; on the contrary, when the presence of the Jews was questioned on a number of occasions in the late seventeenth century, the royal response was favourable.

The various religious policies which came into operation under the later Stuarts did not refer to Jews, but could be interpreted to do so indirectly. Charles II's Declaration of Indulgence of 1662, intended to modify the Act of Uniformity passed earlier that year, enabled groups outside the Church of England to engage in public worship. It is possible that the Jews interpreted it as applying to them.[32] It was a short-lived novelty.

The Conventicles Act of 1664 (16 Car. II, c.4), aimed at nonconformists, made illegal 'an assembly conventicle or meeting under colour or pretence of any exercise of any religion in other manner than according to the liturgy and practice of the Church of England'. Later that year the Earl of Berkshire claimed the power of 'supervising' the Jews, and unless they made an arrangement with him he would prosecute them and seize their property.[33]

The London Jews petitioned Charles II asking that 'untill they shall receive from your Majesty some significacon of your Royall pleasure that they should depart the Kingdome they may remaine heere under the like protection with the rest of your Majesty's Subjects.' The reply of 22 August 1664 was important, although couched in negative terms. The king 'hath been graciously pleased to declare that hee hath not given any particular Order for the molesting or disquieting the Petitioners either in their Persons or Estates, but that they may promise themselves the effects of the same favour as formerly they have had, soe long as they demeane themselves peaceably and quietly with due obedience to his Majesty's Lawes, and without scandall to his Government.' This was the first written document—'a Magna Charta' according to one historian of the community[34]—which, inter alia, was interpreted by the Spanish and Portuguese community in London as requiring its officers to maintain discipline and to suppress disorderly or offensive conduct within their community.[35]

The 1664 letter did not explicitly say that the Jews could practise their religion, but merely that there was no royal order to molest them. It nevertheless permitted them to continue as before, including by implication the right of public worship. Surprisingly in the later controversy between Crown and

Parliament over the king's claim to grant dispensations this particular grant to the Jews was not featured. Nor was it ever challenged in parliament. The nearest approach to a discussion of Jewish matters by the House of Commons was a resolution of 6 February 1671 which set up a committee to 'inquire into the causes of the growth of Popery . . . and also to inquire touching the number of the Jews and their Synagogues, and upon what terms they are permitted to have their residence here.' The committee's report, however, made no reference to Jews.[36]

The royal protection of 1664—which was probably not widely known—was confirmed and improved upon ten years later. The leaders of the synagogue were indicted in 1673 of a riotous assembly, i.e., meeting for prayer. A Grand Jury found a true bill against them. Again the Jews petitioned Charles II asking that they be permitted 'to reap the fruits of your Majesty's accustomed clemency, or to give them a convenient time to withdraw their persons and estates into such parts beyond ye seas where they may live without offence to your Majesty's laws.' An Order in Council dated 11 February 1674 stated that the Attorney General had been ordered to drop all proceedings against the petitioners 'and to provide that they may receive no further Trouble in this behalfe'. In place of the vague offer of protection, the 1674 Order was more positive and gave them dispensation from the laws they were breaking and immunities from their penalties.[37]

No further attacks were made on the Jews in the rest of Charles II's reign, but soon after his successor, James II, ascended the throne, two brothers, Thomas and Carleton Beaumont, took out writs against forty-eight Jews for failure to attend church, contrary to a law of Elizabeth I. Thirty-seven Jews were arrested at the Royal Exchange. A petition to the king received a reply in similar terms as before. The Attorney General was ordered to stop all proceedings, 'His Majesty's Intention being that they should not be troubled upon this account but quietly enjoy the free exercise of their religion whilst they behave themselves dutifully and obediently to his Government.'[38]

Once again, despite the acute conflict between James and parliament over the royal power of dispensation, this particular episode made no public impact. But there was the obvious danger that when parliament reasserted itself after 1688–89 a different approach might be taken. In fact it did not, although there was a chance in 1698 that parliament might adversely affect the free exercise of the Jewish religion. A Bill was introduced in that year 'for the more effectual suppressing of Blasphemy and Profaneness', by writers, teachers and others who were said to be undermining the fundamentals of the Christian religion. In its original formulation it was to apply to those who had 'been educated in or at any time . . . made profession of the Christian religion within this realm', but the Lords proposed these words should be omitted, making all Jews in England liable to the proposed penalties. The Commons refused to accept the amendment on the grounds that because the Jews would be subject to the various penalties, it 'must therefore of necessity ruin them, and drive them out of the

Kingdom; and cannot be thought was the intention of your Lordships, since here they have the means and opportunities to be informed of and rightly instructed in the principles of the true Christian religion.'[39] In this very indirect way 'the practice of Judaism at last received parliamentary sanction in addition to royal protection.'[40]

These matters of religious practice are of prime importance, for without the reiteration of the negative freedom granted by Cromwell there would have been no Jewish community. There were other impediments—to be examined later—to the life of the community, but they were no more than irritations. But it is strange that while the Cromwellian period has attracted so much research by Jewish historians, the subsequent four decades of confirmation have hardly been examined.

Anglo-Jewish historians have produced a few explanations for the favourable royal attitudes after 1660. One is that some Jews performed services for the monarchs, which included assistance to Charles II when he was in exile before 1660, handling the dowry of Catherine of Braganza, Charles's consort, and assisting William when he arrived in 1688–89. Perhaps the strict regime of the Spanish and Portuguese synagogue was seen as reducing a potent source of scandal to Christian piety: they took great pains, for example, to avoid any hint of proselytising among Christians, in addition to controls over their members' economic activities. But it must have been somewhat tenuous at first. In 1662 Augustin Coronel Chacon, recently converted to Christianity, who was acting as agent for the king of Portugal in London, failed financially. This coincided with the failures of 'many other Portuguese Jews . . . for very large sums of money whereby many of his Majesty's natural subjects suffer serious losses.' The London merchants petitioned parliament to prevent 'people of this sort' living in England, and Charles II was reported as having said publicly: 'if the bankrupts do not make full restitution he will have no more Jews in England.'[41] This may be dismissed as the immediate angry response to a situation in which the king was directly involved—he had borrowed from Coronel Chacon. It was obviously a difficult period for the small Jewish group, and the Sephardi authorities' strict control over their members is understandable.

There is little doubt that the explanation for the continuation of formal, legal toleration to the Jews is to be found within the growth of general toleration in the country. On the whole, despite virulent anti-Catholic feeling and the attempt to erect the Church of England as the dominant denomination, one can see signs of greater acceptance of different religious groups in the late seventeenth century. Perhaps the small numbers of Jews—there had been very few immigrants—removed some of the fears; perhaps people did get used to them and thus accepted them. In its pragmatic way the common law from the 1660s accommodated itself to the Jews—they were accepted as competent witnesses in courts, and could swear on the Old Testament. In a case in the 1690s a judge stated: 'A Jew may sue at this day but heretofore he could not; for then they were looked upon as enemies, but now commerce has taught the world humanity.'[42]

We must not exaggerate. If this were a book on the history of antisemitism, it would be easy to provide numerous examples of antagonism towards Jews from the seventeenth century to the present day. Thus, even so minor a reform as the Jews' Naturalisation Act of 1753, whereby foreign-born Jews could become citizens, aroused so furious a public opposition that it had to be repealed the following year.[43] Nevertheless, the community of English Jews in the seventeenth century takes its place along with a few other Sephardi groups in north-west Europe and America which can rightly be described as new centres of freedom. The formal restrictions they faced and the informal hostility they experienced were negligible compared with the majority of Jews in the world. In this sense these Jews were the first to leave the middle ages, as part of the new economy based on the Atlantic.

2

Merchants and Brokers: The Commercial and Financial Revolutions

Religious controversies and antagonisms continued after the restoration of the monarchy in 1660. The Church of England was in law supreme and members of religious groups outside it suffered a number of disabilities. Roman Catholicism was regarded with hostility and extreme distaste: in 1678 Britain was in uproar over a supposed plot to overthrow the Protestant Establishment and assassinate the king. Many Catholics were imprisoned and twenty-four were executed. Yet despite such excesses as this Popish Plot, the general tendency in most western countries was to concentrate on secular affairs. Statesmen and thinkers turned their attention to matters of economic growth, to the encouragement of trade and industry and to the creation of new financial institutions. 'In 1700 there were fewer men searching the Scriptures and bearing arms than there had been fifty years earlier, and more men bent over ledgers and busying themselves with cargoes. There were fewer prophets and more projectors, fewer saints and more political economists'.[1]

These developments, which coincided with the early years of the readmitted Jewish community, set the stage for Britain's emergence as the major economic power. It took over from the Netherlands the role of chief commercial and financial centre, and Britain defeated France, its main rival, after a century of war, at Waterloo in 1815. In the process Britain acquired (and partly lost) an empire with which its trade flourished. At the same time it developed financial institutions and mechanisms whether private (banking, marine insurance, exchange dealing, the Stock Exchange) or public (the National Debt). During the century and a half following Cromwell, it is true, agriculture remained the main economic activity; it developed, as did industry and transport, but it is right to concentrate on the commercial and financial revolutions of the period. If Cromwell, in his positive response to the *conversos*, had at all thought of their possible contribution to Britain's economic progress, the great growth of commerce and the establishment of organised money markets would seem to vindicate such views. One purpose of this chapter is to investigate the role of those middle-class London Jews who were engaged in overseas trade and in finance. The next two chapters discuss the Jews who, in this period, whether in London or the provinces, pursued other activities. Trade and finance were for Anglo-Jewry very much a London phenomenon.

Readmission Jewry

It was, in the first place, a very small community. The great debates of the 1650s on the Jewish question resulted in anticlimax. Neither Jewish hopes nor English fears of England becoming a haven were realised. The Anglo-Jewish community grew at a very slow rate. In the first quarter-century, from 1657 to the early 1680s, the Jewish population trebled, reaching at the very most 450 persons. The only certain figure is derived from a list of the 414 people connected with the Sephardi synagogue in the early 1680s. It includes a few Ashkenazim (who did not have their own synagogue), and if we add other Ashkenazi residents the total of 450 is plausible. During the next decade the number grew more rapidly and in the London Census of 1695 there were at least 751 Jews and possibly another 102 (all identified by name). A few others lived outside the census area in the London suburbs or in the provinces, but not very many. From the 1680s and 1690s Anglo-Jewry grew more rapidly (see Table 1) and began to include more Ashkenazim, who opened their own synagogue in 1690. Moreover, the advent of William of Orange in 1688–89, and the wars which followed, produced major changes in public finance. There is a watershed, therefore, in the 1680s which usefully separates the initial stages of modern Anglo-Jewry from the eighteenth century. We look first at the three decades following the readmission.

In those years the number of London-based Jewish businessmen was small. Some idea of their means is obtained from the size of their contributions to the Sephardi synagogue, whose income came from an *imposta,* a kind of income tax levied on an individual's business turnover (visitors as well as residents paid it). In the period 1663–81 for which the details are published, the maximum number paying this contribution was about forty, and most of the money came from half a dozen individuals. The idea that 'Jewish capitalists and their representatives at once flocked into England' is a gross exaggeration.[2]

This relatively small community concentrated on two main activities, overseas trade and broking, the traders being the wealthier group. Whether refugees from the Inquisition or voluntary migrants from freer environments, they had in common considerable experience in commerce and finance. The *conversos* of the 1650s included, for example, Duarte Enriquez Alvarez (or Daniel Cohen Henriques), who had been chief tax-collector in the Canary Islands. Diego Rodrigues Arias had been a merchant in Mexico. The brothers Domingo and Jorge Francia had been wine merchants in Malaga and came to London in 1655 where they set up as 'Spanish and East (and West) India Merchants and Shipowners'.[3] Duarte (Edward) da Silva handled the dowry which accompanied Catherine of Braganza in 1662.[4] In London such people were able to continue their commercial contacts, and something about their activities can be found in the incomplete London Port Books, in the records of legal suits, and elsewhere. They appear in the early 1660s as customers of Alderman Backwell's bank, and we find them importing and re-exporting a great variety of commodities as well as exporting British goods. The commodities came from and went to many different countries: wine from the Canaries, cloth from northern Europe, sugar from the West Indies, and fish from Newfoundland, for example.[5]

The list of commodities handled is very long, and while many of the cargoes were small, some shipments were large. The Francia brothers in the 1660s imported the entire output of one vineyard-owner in the Canaries, amounting to 800 pipes annually (about 100,000 gallons, worth some £30,000).[6] The da Costas had the virtual monopoly of the import of brazilwood[7] in that decade and in some years Jewish firms imported or exported significant proportions of particular commodities. Gomez Rodriguez and Alvaro da Costa imported in 1688–89 almost one-eighth of the total import through London of white sugar, and ten years later Peter and Piers Henriques shipped almost one-tenth of the total London export of lead.[8] Such people were the substantial merchants, those who often took leading roles in the Sephardi community and of whom much is known from records of the Inquisition. Some idea of their predominance within the Jewish commercial group can be obtained from the London Port Books for the four years Christmas 1675 to Christmas 1679 (unusually, an unbroken series of entries). In that period Jewish merchants imported 800 and exported 500 cargoes; the great majority of them—700 imports and 400 exports—were handled by only seven firms.[9]

The absence of comprehensive information induces caution in making conclusions about this Jewish mercantile activity, but some generalisations are definite enough. The proportion of the total trade of London handled by Jewish merchants was small; there can be no doubt about that. Apart from the diamond trade with India, to be discussed shortly, there is no very clear pattern of specialisation in the trade, either in the goods traded or in the importing or exporting countries. Presumably the immigrant merchants continued with the goods and routes they were familiar with, or took up whatever opportunities arose. There is nothing unexpected in the immigrant Francias, who had been wine-merchants, importing wine into Britain. Perhaps the Jews' lack of knowledge explains their absence from trade with Russia, but it may have been caused by their being debarred from the chartered trading company through their inability to swear the Christian oath required for admittance. That may explain also their non-involvement in the Levant trade. Much more surprising is the relative unimportance of the trade with South America and the British West Indies—although some certainly took place and the evidence is by no means clear.

It has been argued that there was a consistent British trade policy, including the Jews, to transfer the trade between Holland and Spanish South America to England; this, as we have seen, is one of the interpretations of the readmission discussions. Moreover, it is argued, the Jews would also be instrumental in expanding the trade between the West Indies and Britain.[10] The Navigation Acts from 1651 were intended to ensure the carriage of colonial goods in English ships, and Jews settled in both Barbados and Jamaica. The Jews there were aliens but were able to become endenizened so as to enable them to carry colonial goods.[11] Many did so, even before an Act of 1739 permitted naturalisation for all aliens who had been resident in the colonies for seven years. (We can ignore as a temporary aberration a House of Commons resolution of February 1663 that a committee be appointed 'to prepare and bring in Sumptuary Laws, and Laws to prevent Incroachments in Trade by the *Jews* and *French*, or any other Foreigners'.[12] The legislation that emerged did not read in those terms but as extensions to and amendments of the Navigation Acts.)

Whether or not these various actions add up to a coherent policy, they certainly did not result in any massive trade between the West Indies and England carried out by the Jews of those two areas. Such evidence as there is indicates it was on a small scale. Thus Joseph and Menasseh Mendes ('one of the foremost Jewish firms in Barbados') had an average annual turnover in the period 1681–1709 of less than £3,000. 'The foothold which Jewish firms succeeded in maintaining in England's trade with the West Indies was apparently extremely restricted and precarious.'[13]

Amidst this uncertainty about the commercial life of the infant Jewish community one unequivocal field of activity can be identified. From the earliest days of the resettlement, London Jewish merchants were engaged in the diamond trade with India and until the end of the eighteenth century this trade was the most important single commercial activity of the merchant Jews of London.[14] India was the major source of supply of uncut diamonds and Jews in many countries had been involved in handling them, including Portuguese Jews (Goa, the Portuguese possession in India, supplied many diamonds). In the sixteenth century Amsterdam became a major centre for both the diamond trade and the diamond industry, Jews being active in both. During the seventeenth century, diamonds began to be imported into England on a small scale; the East India Company, which had the monopoly of English commerce with India, was not greatly interested in the trade and allowed ship-owners and ships' officers to carry diamonds to England. In the 1660s the Company found that unauthorised people were carrying on the trade and decided it should remain open (under a system of licensing) on the payment of dues to the Company. Traders who were not Company stockholders paid a higher rate; this applied to Jews who were not normally admitted to the Company. It is very likely that the 'unauthorised' importers of the 1660s were London Sephardim. As early as 1662 diamonds were sent from India to London 'for the account of several Portuguese', and a parcel of pearls arrived for Mr. Dormedo (presumably Manuel Martinez Dormido). The earliest known rules of the

London congregation, dating from 1663, fixed a special rate of *imposta* on income received from dealing in precious stones. This was amended two years later to read 'the diamonds, rough or cut, which shall be received here, and despatched elsewhere, or any other kind of gems whatsoever'.[15] The trade consisted of the import of uncut diamonds which were sent on to Amsterdam to be cut and polished (often by Jews) and returned to London for sale. In return, precious metals, coral, and other gems such as emeralds, were sent to India.

Whenever it was that London Jews took up this trade with India it got well under way in the 1660s. In 1666–68 twelve London Jewish merchants were in contact with Sir George Oxenden (who was in charge of the East India Company's factory at Surat), and he acted as their agent for the receipt of silver, precious stones and coral which they sent him, and from whom they received uncut diamonds.[16] Seven of these twelve merchants had the largest banking accounts of the thirty-eight London Jews who were customers of Alderman Backwell's bank in 1663. This trade was sufficiently important for the London merchants to send out Sephardi Jews to India as their agents, and from the 1680s a small settlement existed at Fort St George (Madras). It was there for most of the next century.[17]

There were two further features of this trade with India which were important aspects of the economy of resettlement Jewry. London Jews were engaged in the sale of finished jewellery, several of them—Samuel da Vega, Isaac Israel Alvares Nunes, for example—being described specifically as 'Jewellers'. Retail trade was technically the monopoly of the freemen of the City of London, and admission to that status normally required a Christian oath, but it seems that Jews did not confine themselves to being wholesalers: they are known to have sold retail to customers who included the Court.[18] The second aspect of Indian trade was connected with the import of Indian cloth, which was in fact the major part of the commerce with the sub-continent. Unlike the diamond trade, this was firmly in the hands of the East India Company to which Jews were not admitted. Although they could not take part in the import trade, they were able to attend the public sales in London of these imports, specialising in the purchase of damaged cloth. Their numbers were sufficiently great for the sales to be postponed when they clashed with Jewish holy days.

Despite many gaps in the sources, quite a lot is known about the overseas trading activities of London Jews in the early years of the community, and a certain amount about the offshoots of this trade—the purchase of cloth and the sale of jewellery. Very much less is available on the other main occupation, that of broking. The brokers, who congregated at the Royal Exchange, were wholesalers' agents who dealt in commodities. Admission to the occupation was restricted to freemen of the City, so that Jews were theoretically barred from the trade, but in fact they did become brokers. Solomon Dormido was admitted in 1657 without becoming a freeman, and from 1671 other Jews were admitted.[19] It is unlikely that the City's administration of its powers was efficient and there were always complaints that unauthorised people were acting as brokers: only a handful of Jews were permitted to be brokers, but it will be recalled that in 1685 as many as thirty-seven Jews were arrested at the Royal Exchange (which is not to suggest, of course, that all of them were carrying on broking businesses). Moreover, although primarily handling commodities, London brokers and others began to deal with negotiable instruments such as Exchequer orders and navy bills issued by the government and the stocks and bonds issued by the chartered trading companies.[20] The Stock Exchange began in this *ad hoc* way, but its first main boost came with the expansion of government finance in the 1690s. Before then the brokers were of a low social status and, to judge from the contributions paid by Jewish brokers to the Sephardi congregation, of moderate means.[21]

The Readmitted Community: A Summary

It is strange that so few Jews immigrated to England in the first three decades of the new community. Other aliens were not hesitant to come and the government encouraged them. A proclamation of 1672 proposed that 'the subjects of the United Provinces of the Netherlands . . . transport themselves with their estates and . . . settle in this His Majesty's Kingdom of England'.[22] A similar announcement of 1681 was directed to the Huguenots of France, and perhaps 50,000 to 100,000 of these Protestant refugees arrived.[23] Moreover, while the Jews were mainly engaged in overseas trade, jewellery and broking, not many were wealthy men. Only a few of them had the means to supply the bulk of the income of their congregation. About one-half of the heads of household paid the *imposta* in the 1670s, and another quarter did not choose to pay or were unable to contribute. When the government required funds in 1690 for the prosecution of the war and it was suggested that the Jews, being wealthy, could lend a large sum, the response—that there were only seventeen or eighteen who had considerable means—was probably accurate.[24]

Given such small numbers in the community, it is not altogether surprising that their activities were not wide-ranging. Their concentration in a few fields probably followed only from their past experience and the contacts they brought with them: even the diamond trade was familiar to the Sephardim and Ashkenazim of many countries. It is possible that the formal disabilities they encountered may have assisted their specialisation.[25] Admission to the retail trade and also to the overseas trading companies normally required a Christian oath. Thus, it is often said, Jews could not become retailers or take part in overseas trade.[26] But it is well known that there were constant complaints from the City authorities—from well before the Jews' readmission—that non-citizens of the City were shopkeepers and craftsmen;[27] similarly interlopers, who were not members of the trading companies, could seldom be controlled. In any case only a few trade routes were the monopolies of the companies and it was possible to trade with other parts of the world without hindrance. In practice, these formal restrictions did not mean a great deal and, during the eighteenth century, came to mean virtually nothing.

The Eighteenth Century

From the end of the seventeenth century, accompanying Britain's economic development, the Anglo-Jewish community grew rapidly, at a much faster rate than the country's population. The figures in Table 1—which are no more than guesses—indicate a possible twenty-five-fold increase in the eighteenth century, the rate being faster in the second half. Most of the increase was due to immigration and it seems that the major cause of the movement of Jews into Britain was conditions in other countries. Up to the 1730s, for example, Sephardim came—often direct from Portugal—because of the Inquisition; but as that persecution receded the pressure to migrate was lessened. In fact from early in the eighteenth century the great majority of immigrants were Ashkenazim from Germany and Poland, as both religious persecution and a deterioration in economic conditions impelled Jews to move. Most of them were poor or at least of moderate means and do not come into the discussion in this chapter.

However, Britain's economic development was undoubtedly the motivating attraction for some of the immigrants. It was common for both Jewish and non-Jewish firms to open offices in London and to send a member of the family 'to look after the overseas branch of the business'.[28] This was so in the case of the Pragers, a well-documented family, as will be seen later in this chapter. But the reasons for the immigration of much better-known families—who for two centuries have been leaders of the community—are seldom known. Moses Vita Montefiore came to London from Livorno (Leghorn) to set up as an importer of straw hats, but there is some doubt about the initial occupation of Levi Barent Cohen, the Dutch forebear of another illustrious family. His father in Amersfoort is said to have been a linen-merchant, which occupation Levi may have continued in London.[29] Later he moved into finance, as did his kinsmen, Abraham and Benjamin Goldsmid, the sons of another Dutch immigrant. Virtually nothing is known about other Jews who are vaguely referred to as 'merchant' in some of the literature.

Overseas Trade

The diamond trade continued to be a major preoccupation of eighteenth-century Anglo-Jewry. 'There was hardly a firm in the Jewish-Portuguese community of London which did not, at one time or another, have a stake in the Anglo-Indian diamond trade'.[30] This was so even though the discovery of diamonds in Brazil in the 1720s reduced the importance of those from India. But India remained a major source until the 1780s and London remained the chief market because, although Brazilian diamonds—a monopoly of the Portuguese Crown—were supposed to go to Lisbon and then to Amsterdam, large quantities (perhaps as much as a half) were smuggled, many coming to London. The dominance of the Jews in the Anglo-Indian trade can readily be seen. In the fifty years between 1717 and 1766 the importation of diamonds by Jews was greater than that by non-Jews in all but four years. For the next twenty years the Jewish proportion fell, but recovered for a time in 1785 when the Pragers went into the trade. But the Indian supply was coming to an end and Brazil was to be the major source of the world's diamonds until the South African discoveries. The end of the Indian supply brought to an end the dominant role of the diamond traders within the elite of London Jewry, and in the nineteenth century their place was taken by the financiers.

From early in the eighteenth century a number of Ashkenazim also took part in the trade, notable among them being immigrants from Hamburg such as Abraham Nathan and Marcus Moses. At first they bought only the diamonds that had been brought to London, but they soon became importers as well and some of them went to Madras to join the small Jewish diamond group there. Marcus Moses was the first to go, followed shortly afterwards by London-born Aaron Franks, who was to become the leading London Ashkenazi figure during the first half of the century. Although both Sephardim and Ashkenazim were engaged in the diamond business, there were important differences in their economic methods and roles. One arose from the method of paying for the imports, traditionally using silver as the main export with, as we have seen, some coral (re-exported after having been brought to London from the Mediterranean). During the war of 1702–13 silver was in short supply, and the East India Company would not permit it to be exported. Instead, it threw open the coral trade and from then on Sephardi, but not Ashkenazi, merchants exported coral rather than silver. Coral came from Leghorn, among other places, and its export from London was associated with the settlement within the English Sephardi community of a number of Livornese families who went into the coral-diamond trade. The Montefiores were one—it is not known if they gave up their straw-hat business—but the most eminent were the Francos, whose house became the most important and the greatest among the London diamond community. The re-export of coral became dominated by Jews to a much greater extent than was the import of diamonds. Of the £1,600,000-worth of licences granted between 1750 and 1774 for the export of coral, as much as £1,200,000 (75 per cent) was issued to Jews. The Ashkenazim, on the other hand, having no links with the Jews of Leghorn, tended to export silver—once the restriction was lifted in 1718 on its export—although later its use declined to be replaced by respondentia loans. Ships' captains were lent the money which they used to buy goods for export to be sold in India, the proceeds to be spent in purchasing diamonds.

There was one further distinction between the Sephardim and the Ashkenazim. The importers sold the uncut diamonds to wholesale merchants, who had them cut and polished. The majority of the importers were Sephardim, while the wholesalers were largely Ashkenazim. Among both groups, though, a small number of men predominated: the Francos in particular (who at one stage in the 1740s imported over 50 per cent of the annual value of diamonds), Salvador, Mendes da Costa, for example; and Franks, Moses, Salomons and Goldsmid from the Ashkenazi community. These names appear also in other economic activities.

Compared with the relatively full details of this diamond trade, the information about Jewish commerce of other kinds is patchy, ambiguous and often negative. The only other trading company that, like the East India Company, managed to retain its trading monopoly was the Levant Company, trading to the eastern Mediterranean. It was able to prevent its formal opening until the 1750s. Before then a proposal that the trade should be open did not obtain parliamentary approval. A major feature of the opposition was the fear expressed that English Jewish merchants, if allowed to participate, would monopolise it through an anticipated preference for dealing with Jewish brokers in the Levant. The clear implication is that Jews were not then trading with the eastern Mediterranean.[31]

Of Jewish participation in the other main areas of British trade—with Portugal and the American colonies—the available evidence is insufficient to provide secure conclusions, although in some cases it is fairly unequivocal. Jews do not seem to have been involved in the North American tobacco trade. The large plantations 'maintained direct connections with agents in England,'[32] or sold their products to agents in America who were mainly Scottish. Much tobacco was imported through Glasgow, but there was no Jewish community in that city before the nineteenth century.[33] It is true that Jacob and Joshua de Fonseca Brandon of London were described as the 'greatest Tobacco Brokers in England', according to a statement of 1774. But only one Anglo-Jewish merchant, Abraham Lopez Fernandez, the Brandons' nephew, traded to Virginia and Maryland at that time, as far as we know.[34] Most of the Jews in North America were shopkeepers, and the shippers among them tended to trade with the West Indies: only a few names occur of those who had commercial relations with Britain—Uriah Hendriks, Aaron Lopez, and members of the great London Franks family, who were mainly occupied in the Indian diamond trade, had contacts with the family firm in America. However, the Franks's main business there seems to have been to act as suppliers to the British army. Thus the Jewish role in North American trade was small.[35] This applies to both the London end and to those in the British possessions. As the American historian J. R. Marcus put it, after an exhaustive study of the subject, 'the Jews of colonial North America were hardly in the mainstream of Atlantic commerce or industry'.[36]

The same appears to be the case of the British West Indies. Most Jews in Barbados and Jamaica in the eighteenth century were small men, shopkeepers or servants, and their interest in sugar cultivation was negligible. The sugar trade became increasingly concentrated in the hands of the sugar-planters' agents in London, a restricted and confined circle. Non-planters, including the Jews, did not participate.[37]

During the first half of the eighteenth century, British trade in general grew only slowly, but commerce with Spain and Portugal expanded greatly. Woollen cloth was exported in return for wine and bullion (the latter from South America); the clandestine trade between Spanish South America and the British West Indies was an extension of it. The legal trade was through Lisbon and Cadiz, and British goods received there went to South America in exchange for bullion. The contraband trade consisted of British goods going to Jamaica and South American bullion coming to Britain through the British colony. There is no doubt at all that London Sephardim maintained connections with the Portuguese and Spanish trades; the main problem is to discover its size. It was not easy for the Sephardim to trade openly under their own names for fear that their goods would be confiscated as a result of the Inquisition. *Conversos* in Lisbon would be in even greater hazard if they had trading relations with family members in London. 'The inability to maintain or establish family connections was a serious disadvantage in the Iberian trade which was difficult to handle from afar, and the use of false names in order to get round this difficulty was very common among English Jews of Portuguese extraction'.[38] In addition to adopting aliases, the London Jewish merchants used Christian correspondents in Lisbon, most of them being English (who dominated Portuguese trade).

Such subterfuges necessarily conceal the true extent of the Jewish trade with Portugal. The British ambassador wrote, in 1732, that he thought 'the greatest dealers to Portugal in our woollen goods are the Jews in London',[39] but a recent study of the Anglo-Portuguese trade notes that

> according to the names of signatories of a number of memorials of trade, a majority of the London Portugal merchants had Anglo-Saxon or British names. But merchants of foreign, especially French and Dutch, descent were also well represented, while, although Jewish names appear rarely, part of the trade was carried on by Jews, often Sephardic in origin . . .[40]

There seems also to have been considerable trade with Spain, through Cadiz, and thence with the Spanish American colonies.[41] Since there were no *conversos* in Cadiz, their trading connections were Christian, often English, firms. Among those who are known to have exported and imported a variety of cargoes were familiar names from the Indian diamond trade—Franco, da Fonseca, da Costa, Salvador. Only scattered details are available, but Joseph Salvador, in two pamphlets he wrote at the time of the 1753 controversy over the Jews' Naturalisation Act, argued that the greatest part of the British trade with the Spanish colonies of the West Indies was Jewish.[42] Although the statement cannot be supported by comprehensive statistics, one surviving document of 1756, which refers to the business of Benjamin Mendes da Costa (Salvador's brother-in-law) is instructive. As much as 80 per cent of the £32,000 he had invested in trade was in connection with the Spanish and Spanish-American trade. Only 20 per cent was with the Indian trade.[43] However, it is unlikely that this was a typical example; the London Jewish traders had a much bigger interest in the Indian than in the South American and Spanish trades.

These sundry details indicate that they were active in the trade with Portugal, Spain and Latin America, although to an unknown extent. The evidence about their involvement in the contraband trade between the Spanish colonies and Jamaica is even more sketchy. This was one of the ways in which precious metals reached Europe, and since Jews could live in Jamaica and some London firms had brances there, the likelihood is that they were part of that commerce.[44]

There is no evidence that Jews imported wine in the eighteenth century in return for their exports to Spain and Portugal and the colonies. They probably imported gold and may have transferred from that into importing Brazilian diamonds after the 1730s and 1740s.[45] The caution of such statements is necessary but unfortunate, and it is a pity that this area of Jewish commercial activity should be so little documented.

The last field of trading to be discussed here is the commerce with northern Europe, especially with Amsterdam. Both Sephardim and Ashkenazim in London and Amsterdam were in contact with their respective congregations in the two cities, much of it for financial transactions. Indeed Charles Wilson's study of Anglo-Dutch economic relationships, while insistently identifying individuals by religion, mentions no Jews in commercial dealings between the two countries: all his statements refer to finance. Jews nevertheless were part of the trading connections between the two countries—one such relationship, the re-export of uncut diamonds to Amsterdam for processing and the subsequent import of jewellery, has already been mentioned. London became the chief importing centre for colonial goods, of which much was re-exported to Amsterdam, and Jewish firms were part of that trade. Almost all the information about it is derived from the records of one firm, Prager Brothers, known otherwise as Levin Salomons.[46] It was originally a Dutch firm, the Amsterdam house being run by two brothers Jacob and David; the third partner, their younger brother Yehiel, came to London in 1752. The London part was formally established ten years later, in 1762, where its main business was not importing but almost entirely the purchase in London of colonial imports, especially tobacco and drugs, for re-export to Amsterdam. It traded too in other commodities such as cloth and porcelain, and also entered the ailing Indian diamond trade in the 1780s.

The firm was probably one of the most important London Jewish merchant houses, but it lasted only until the 1790s. It was wound up in that decade after the death of the three brothers and after unsuccessful speculation in commodities. In addition, much of the family's fortune was gambled away by

Yehiel's eldest son. None of the other sons was capable of managing the London house, and the job fell to a non-Jew, George Elliot, who had been a ship's captain on the East Indian route and who married a daughter of Yehiel Prager. But neither his efforts nor those of another son-in-law, the financier Benjamin Goldsmid, proved fruitful. The firm came to an end in 1796.

Apart from the circumstances of its demise, this firm's history was probably typical of others which were engaged in the Anglo-Dutch trade. The emphasis on the export to Holland of colonial goods may well explain why such firms did not settle in the western outports into which growing quantities of colonial goods were received. The main reason was the Amsterdam connection: the outports did not have good shipping routes with Amsterdam and it was therefore necessary for those trading with Holland to work from London. Since the other main Jewish trade, to and from India, was centred on London (which was in addition becoming a great financial centre), Anglo-Jewish merchants concentrated in the capital.[47] They were not normally found in the eighteenth-century provincial Jewish communities.

Associated with overseas trade was the provision of shipping, and during the century 1693 to 1798 thirty-nine Jews were ship-owners (in accordance with the practice of the time usually sharing the ownership of the vessels with others).[48] And there was an overlap with finance, with some Jews providing marine insurance. It is not at all uncommon to come across Jews as insurers and ship-owners, whether plaintiffs or defendants, in court cases.[49]

Two very obvious generalisations can be made from the foregoing discussion. Despite the incompleteness of the evidence and the fact that individual merchants were wealthy, the Jewish involvement in British overseas trade was small; one attempt at quantification puts it at no more than 1 or 2 per cent.[50] Second, what there was was confined to a few major trading activities, and only one of them—the diamond-coral trade—came anywhere near being Jewish-dominated. The explanation for the narrow range is not likely to be found in the existence of formal legal discrimination against them, although personal anti-Jewish feeling was a normal feature of the eighteenth century. The method of organisation of certain trades, such as the major commerce in sugar and tobacco, effectively barred them from participation, but the main reason for specialisation was probably the Jews' conservative adherence to known goods and known routes.[51]

Finance

The second major area of London Jewish business activity was in the burgeoning money markets. One of the sterotypes in cartoons and in literature was the Jewish broker and moneylender: 'to-day we punish a stock-jobbing Jew', went the Prologue in George Granville's play *The Jew of Venice* of 1701.[52] Yet, as in commerce, their range of activities tended to be somewhat restricted and, apart from a few conspicuous individuals, not among the first rank of City financiers. Unlike the custom on the Continent, there were no court Jews in Britain, those financial advisers and administrators of central European courts, who were used when financial institutions were primitive and when local resources were scarce. Britain possessed native expertise as well as that of the Dutch Christians and the Huguenots. Nevertheless, as we shall see, Jews were part of the system whereby the government raised money for its war-time requirements. In what follows, different types of financial activities are examined separately, it being understood that they overlap along with the individuals who are mentioned.

Government Finance and Contracts

From 1689 to 1815 Britain was at war for much of the time, and Jews were associated with the organisation of army supplies and with the raising of loans for the government. In the first of King William's wars (1689–97), the Dutch-Jewish firm of Machado and Pereira supplied bread and bread wagons to the forces of the Crown, their 'factor' being Solomon de Medina.[53] (His mother was a Pereira.) The contracting firm had supplied William's armies from 1672, and later in that decade became 'Providiteurs General of the English forces in the Netherlands'. In the 1690s the firm supplied William's army in Ireland, and Medina in London advanced them money and received payment from the government. In those early days, before the system of public finance had been reformed, a number of *ad hoc* measures were used to raise money, including the Million Act Lottery, of which Medina and Alvarez da Costa were made Commissioners. The irregular flow of funds meant that payment to the contractors was often delayed, and Medina sometimes lent the government money in order to pay the bills of Machado and Pereira that he presented. In 1700 Medina was knighted, the first Jew to be honoured in this way (Augustin Coronel who was knighted some forty years earlier had been baptised first); the next was not to be for over 130 years. Two years later he left Britain and settled in Holland.

When war broke out again in 1702 the British armies were again supplied by Machado until 1706, with Medina associated as before, but Machado died in 1707 and Medina took over the responsibility for bread supplies. This lasted until 1712, when he gave up that occupation in 'straitened circumstances'. The cause of his decline from great wealth was the difficulty in getting payment from the government. He died in 1730 and his story ends with his descendants squabbling about his bequests which they had not received. Indeed the risk of contracting for the government is confirmed by the life of another Jewish army contractor, Joseph Cortissos. His biography has been reconstructed from the petitions and letters to the government asking for the payment of sums due to him. His successors were still petitioning the government in the nineteenth century.[54]

On the Continent, Jews were traditionally engaged in army commissariat services, and in the mid-eighteenth century three other names appear. David Mendes da Costa and Abraham Prado were suppliers during the Seven Years' War; and Moses Franks was one of forty-six men who held contracts to supply troops in North America and the West Indies. He was a member of one of the syndicates, his partners being non-Jews.[55] But this does not amount to a large Jewish involvement, and the reason must lie in the ineligibility of Jews to become Members of Parliament. 'Government contracts were usually held with a seat in the House of Commons'; of fifty merchants in Parliament in 1761, at least thirty-seven had business dealings with government.[56]

The early *ad hoc* methods of financing war—including the establishment in 1694 of the Bank of England (in whose origin no Jews were involved but in which some held stock in the early years)[57]—gave way to more regularised systems. Loan contractors obtained funds from their own group: thus Sephardi money was channelled through a Sephardi contractor. This was not only a domestic, British arrangement. Funds came from Holland, to such an extent that those who deprecated the growth of the money interest referred disparagingly to 'Dutch finance'.

> Under Dutch William and for another century, the savings of Dutch investors, institutions as well as individuals, flowed into the National Debt. The choice of investments, the remittances of dividends, the purchase and sale of scrip was the business of a group of agents of Dutch, Huguenot or Sephardic (Portuguese) Jewish origin . . . Their stamping ground was 'the City'—Jonathan's Coffee House in Change Alley (the later Stock Exchange), the offices of the great joint stock trading companies, the Bank itself. Their social activities centred still round their churches—the Dutch Church at Austin Friars, the French (Huguenot) Church in Threadneedle Street, the Sephardic Synagogue at Bevis Marks.[58]

Alongside these financial agents and brokers were the great loan-contractors, the two London Jews occupying this role being Samson Gideon and Joseph Salvador. Both had made their mark in commerce and both were well-known figures of the period. Gideon (1699–1762)[59] was notorious, not just for being part of the 'moneyed interest'; he had come to public attention because of his unorthodox techniques at the time of the Jacobite rebellion of 1745–46. At a time when government credit was low, he advocated the issuing of government stock on terms which disguised the fact of a higher rate of interest. The hostility towards him on this occasion 'was reinforced by racial prejudice' and he was, ironically, subjected to abuse in the 1753–54 controversy over the Jews' Naturalisation Act, despite his being opposed to the Act. Gideon was a major financial figure but no matter how important or ambitious an individual Jew might be, his path to social acceptance and high social status was restricted because of his religion. He could not enter politics or obtain a peerage— Gideon requested one in recompense for his efforts in government finance but it was refused. He had to be satisfied with one for his son, and the whole family left the Jewish community.

His activities devolved, in the 1750s and 1760s, on Joseph Salvador (1716–86),[60] with some overlap between them. But Salvador was much less successful. As a merchant in the Portuguese trade he suffered losses as a result of the Lisbon earthquake of 1755 and he was adversely affected by the financial crisis of 1763. He was one of the diamond-coral merchants, and had had dealings with Clive of India, but this trade was declining, and he withdrew from it in 1770. By the 1770s he was dropped from the list of loan contractors and in 1784 he went to America, where he died two years later, relatively poor.

Broking

Commodity broking was located at the Royal Exchange, where it had been since before the readmission of 1656. Near by, in Exchange Alley, there developed in the coffee-houses an unofficial market in negotiable paper and in due course these arrangements were regularised in formal institutions. From Jonathan's Coffee House the direct line was to the Stock Exchange, established in the 1770s. In time, rules of behaviour were refined, but from the early days in the late seventeenth century and for much of the eighteenth century, the functions of those who handled stocks and shares were not firmly defined. There was no clear distinction, for example, between the brokers, who acted for principals, and the jobbers who bought and sold stock on their own account. The names were used interchangeably and it was not uncommon to combine broking and jobbing with other activities.[61]

Broking, we we have seen, was one of the few major business activities of the small Anglo-Jewish community during its early years, and it continued to be important in the eighteenth century. Some were commodity brokers: the Brandons in tobacco; the firm of Mocatta and Goldsmid in diamonds as were Abraham de Paiba and Moses Machoro; and Abraham Lara, who obtained South American imports for the Prager firm. But stockbroking was probably the major type although, despite the attempts by parliament to regulate the trade, the numbers engaged in it are unknown.[62] The first effort was in 1697, when parliament legislated that the upper limit to the number of brokers should be one hundred. The City of London, which had the task of administering the Act, decided that of the one hundred, twelve should be Jews and twelve aliens. The first twelve Jewish 'sworn brokers' included ten Sephardim, but the two Ashkenazim were substantial men. Benjamin Levy, the son of a Breslau merchant, was probably the most affluent Ashkenazi at the turn of the century; the other was Abraham Franks, a kinsman of Levy's, and father of the Aaron Franks of the eighteenth-century diamond—and other—trades. A subsequent Act of 1708 removed the upper limit of 100 brokers, but the number of 'Jew brokers' remained until this restriction was removed in 1830 along with other City disabilities, when the requirement of a Christian oath for taking up the freedom was abolished. The limitation to twelve in the number of 'Jew brokers' meant that the licence they obtained became a valuable asset, which in time changed hands for many hundreds of pounds. There were nevertheless many unsworn brokers; and there was no restriction on the number of jobbers—all that can be said is that there were Jews among these various groups.[63]

The stockbrokers and stockjobbers were recruited from a variety of occupations, but most notably from the goldsmith-bankers and from the merchants. The Jews came from the second of these categories because none was a goldsmith-banker. They were a minority of the brokers and jobbers, although quite clearly over-represented in relation to their numbers in London. Insofar as there was any specialisation, the Jews were particularly prominent in the handling of East India Company stock: in his day Samson Gideon was the major East India jobber.[64]

Bullion and the Exchange Business

Jews may or may not have imported bullion—the evidence is uncertain—but they required it for their trade with India during the first part of the century, and dealing in it became a Jewish speciality. Several acted as brokers for the Bank of England and the East India Company and, as well as Isaac Lindo, Joseph Salomons and Abraham I. Keyser, the most important was Abraham Mocatta. It was said that he had been bullion broker for the Bank of England since its foundation; he certainly emerged as the major silver broker for both of them during the early eighteenth century, a position he retained until shortly before his death in 1751. Samson Gideon took over from him for a time but the business reverted to the Mocatta family, Abraham's grandson forming a partnership with A. I. Keyser in 1763. On the latter's death in 1779, the firm of Mocatta and Goldsmid was established, and it remains in the same trade to this day.[65]

The handling of precious metals was certainly one in which Jews were engaged; indeed bullion dealers 'were generally spoken of as "the Jews" '.[66] Gold and silver coins circulated in Britain and the metals were used in international payments, along with bills of exchange.[67] The foreign exchange market was sufficiently developed by the end of the seventeenth century for the rates of exchange in sixteen European centres to be published twice weekly. Generally, bills of exchange were used but, if the exchanges were unsettled, payment would be made in gold or silver, often using the bullion dealers—'the Jews'. Amsterdam had developed the earliest expertise in these matters—bills of exchange on Amsterdam had an international currency—and Jews were especially involved because of the trade between that city and London, and because of the flow of funds from Holland into British stocks, the Jewish part being handled by London Jewish agents. Among the various causes of exchange fluctuations, not the least being periodic wars, was the speculation of the Dutch Jews in British stock. Their activities were said, at the time, to have

led to a financial crisis in 1773. The Bank of England decided to refuse
selectively to discount bills, singling out those bill brokers who had connections with Amsterdam. One unexpected by-product of this policy was the
failure of the Ayr bank, when Alexander Fordyce, one of the partners, was
prevented from discounting a bill on a Dutch Jew.[68] This was by no means the
only occasion when there was difficulty about discounting Jewish bills. It
happened again in 1778 and 1784, and one general reason was the unreliability
of Jewish firms. Because of it, Jews tended to be the last to get credit in times of
scarcity and the discount rate was usually higher for Jews.[69]

There is little doubt that London Jews were active in these international
financial transactions, especially between London and Amsterdam. But the
great names in this field were the Christian firms of Amsterdam—Hope,
Clifford (which failed in 1772) and Neufville. In London, writes Charles
Wilson, most of the Jewish finance houses were 'comparatively small men'.

> In spite of the emphasis laid by eighteenth century writers in England and
> Holland on the part played by the Jews in finance, it is clear that individually
> the Christian firms—the van Necks, the Stapels, the Barings, the van
> Nottens, the Nuilmans, the Bosanquets, the Dorriens—were bigger and
> more important. It is they who move from trade in commodities into
> legitimate banking: on the whole the Dutch Portuguese Jews who came to
> England did not find a permanent place in British finance.[70]

This statement also applies to the Ashkenazim, although some of them, such
as Salomons and Cohen, remained in finance in the nineteenth century. But it is
certainly true that in the succeeding century the Jewish financiers were
immigrants of the post-1800 period and most of them were Ashkenazim.

Conclusion

The history of business Jews of London in the seventeenth and eighteenth
centuries is an important case study in Jewish history. If the nature of Jewish
economic activities in the middle ages is to be explained largely by the
restrictions imposed upon the Jews, then the freer atmosphere of Britain might
have opened up this world and enabled them to enter new and wider ranges of
material life. Such an analysis has to take account of the circumstances of the
time. The numbers of Jews involved were small and the immigrants were
self-selected: it seems that the Jewish business families of the eighteenth
century, whether born abroad or in England, were already people of means at
the outset of their history in Britain. Although there may have been some social
mobility, there is a remarkable absence of evidence of poor Jews becoming
businessmen.

Moreover, the Jews' freedom was limited somewhat by a number of legal
disabilities which effectively barred them from certain positions, as we have

seen. But some of those restrictions were removed during the course of the century, and those that remained were not strictly administered. Generally the professions were barred because either they could not obtain degrees at Oxford and Cambridge universities—the only such institutions in England (although not in Scotland), or the particular profession required a Christian oath. But Jewish doctors did qualify in other countries and practised in Britain, and solicitors were admitted from 1770. And the barriers were religious, not racial. A Jew who was willing to take the oath could enter one or other of the otherwise restricted occupations. In this way Jews obtained commissioned rank in the armed forces, becoming in some cases the progenitors of military dynasties. Those who remained Jews were not too encumbered by limitations, as Moses Cassuto, an Italian Jew, noted when he visited London in 1735:

> Jews may dwell in any part of the City where they wish. They may practise any sort of trade or craft and open a shop in any place outside the City in the suburbs, and even in the City if they have practised the craft seven years under a master, in the same way as a Protestant may, the limits being those fixed for the City.[71]

These comments refer to the retail trade and industry, but their importance lies in the fact that there is no evidence that Jews had to take up certain occupations, such as broking, because they were not allowed to be shopkeepers. In general, formal discrimination was limited in scope and was declining.

There were three further significant features of the eighteenth-century environment. Middle-class Jews would naturally be drawn into the main developments in the capital, into its growing international trade, its financial markets, and its luxury trades (e.g., jewellery). They were the typical activities of people of their class, Jewish or not. Such people would not be engaged in the low-status industrial activities. Second, the dominance of the Indian diamond-coral trade was dangerously transitory. Its decline and demise may have been a factor in the virtual disappearance of the Sephardi elite, although these families often had other interests: the Francos, for example, were also insurance brokers. The point is that, as a case study, eighteenth-century London Jewry was atypical because of the curiosity of this diamond trade. And, third, this small group of businessmen in London was divided into the two main religious sections, Ashkenazim and Sephardim. Their relationships were generally antagonistic to the extent not just of an absence of social intercourse, but even to an abhorrence of marriage between them. Despite some overlap, there is evidence of a degree of different economic pursuits.

But the existence of such separate groups was by no means unusual at that period. It was in accord with the times that 'London Jew dealt with Dutch Jew'[72] and that the loan contractors raised funds from their own community (although not hesitating to go outside it if necessary). Economic institutions were small, economic affairs were risky, and personal knowledge and family connections were crucial. Thus, the 'private provision of credit functioned, as did most of the commercial transactions of the time, upon personal contact; whether arising from membership of the same trade interest, of important racial groups within the City, or from the closer ties of kinship'.[73]

There is much to be said for the view that the London business Jews' relatively restricted economic range is to be explained as, first, the conservative continuation of past experience and contacts, and second, as its continuation because of the nature of eighteenth-century business society. The London Jews were noticeably absent from domestic banking, for example, except as customers. Some of the London banks developed from seventeenth-century goldsmith business, and there were no Jewish goldsmiths then; but this is not a complete explanation. New banks were being established in the eighteenth century and while one would not expect Jews to be West End bankers (who had dealings with the aristocracy), they might have been City bankers who supplied short-term finance to members of the Stock Exchange and discounted bills. None of the seventy London banks was Jewish, mainly because this was very much a Protestant enclave.

3
The Jews of the 'Other' London

One of the first names we come across in the newly-constituted community of the 1650s is that of Deborah Nunez. She appears in the will of the leading Sephardi Antonio Fernandez Carvajal (d. 1659), where she is described as his servant.[1] The Sephardi merchants needed staff to run their businesses and we know of a Jewish bookkeeper at the same period,[2] a relation of a merchant, who presumably got his position through a family connection. Of Deborah Nunez we know nothing apart from her description as, presumably, a domestic servant: it is difficult to imagine she was employed in Carvajal's office. Perhaps she came from a poor family, or one which had fallen on hard times. No doubt people like her were those intended to benefit from Carvajal's other bequest—£30 left to the 'poore of my Nation in London'.[3] We may assume from her name that she was Jewish.

Those who were generally described as 'the poor' were not necessarily paupers. The term comprised many other categories of people; it referred to the lower classes, and in this chapter we shall be looking at those Jews among four main categories of Londoners who were not connected with overseas trade or the financial activities of the City. They constituted the majority of London Jews and properly belong to that large segment of the metropolitan population which has been called 'the "other" London'.[4]

These are the people we shall be concerned with in this chapter starting with those in the fourth, probably the largest, group:

1. master craftsmen and small shopkeepers in the Cities of London and Westminster, and petty tradesmen with stalls in the Boroughs and the markets;
2. skilled journeymen and apprentices;
3. unskilled and semi-skilled—daily labourers, porters, servants, etc.— nominally in regular receipt of wages, and of fixed abode;
4. the 'submerged' and floating population of vagrants and beggars, the destitute, aged, casual workers, 'the poorest of the immigrant Irish and Jews'; equated in 1795 by Patrick Colquhoun the magistrate with the

underworld, and estimated by him at 115,000 people, about one-eighth of the population.

Paupers and Charity

There were poor among the Sephardim from the earliest days. The financial accounts of their synagogue for 1663–81 give details of the heavy expenditures on the relief of their poor, transient and resident. As much as one-third of the income was disbursed for these purposes, paid out from the variously-spelt 'Sedaca'. It has been estimated that about one-quarter of Sephardi households received help in this way.[5] Perhaps to help reduce this burden, as well as to avoid any confrontations with authority, the synagogue tried to discourage the entry of poor immigrants. As early as May 1669, having lodged a complaint with the City authorities about the foreign mendicants besieging the synagogue, the Mahamad (executive officers) ordered 'that all foreigners who were in this city and those who should come for the future in expectation that the Ceddacka would support them, should within five days depart from the country . . . and for their passage the Ceddacka will aid them with what may be possible'.[6] A week later a stronger order was made: they would not admit to the congregation 'any person, of whatsoever quality, unless he should bring an order, arrangement, or business for a lawful livelihood'.[7]

The City authorities also took action. In July 1677 the Court of Aldermen, hearing 'of a number of destitute aliens pretending to be Jews', ordered 'that no Jews without good estate be admitted to reside or lodge in London or the liberties thereof'.[8]

It is taken for granted by some writers that these paupers must have been Ashkenazim who were prevented by the 1677 order from settling in London and therefore went to the provinces to form communities there.[9] Although we really know nothing about these people, often not even their names, there were certainly Sephardim among them. It is not known either if the order was enforced, but it seems most unlikely. There are, as chapter 4 will demonstrate, other explanations for the growth of provincial communities. In any case, along with the rich Jews who followed the arrival of William III, came the poor. His government instituted in 1689 a system of passes for foreigners entering the country, and the published lists, covering the years 1689–96, of the Jews among them include many described as 'poor Jews', most of them Sephardim.[10]

The Sephardi authorities in London wrote to a wealthy Dutch-Jewish merchant in 1692 asking him not to send any more poor people to London. 'His Majesty's Council have just passed a new Order forbidding entry at the ports without a passport which costs £3 10s. 0d., a sum which the congregation cannot possibly afford for all the poor would-be immigrants who are detained thereby on entry'.[11] The financial demands on the synagogue continued, pressed as they were to help Sephardim in other countries which were also receiving refugees from the Inquisition. In 1710, for example, the Mahamad 'having considered the excessive expense which the multitude of poor cause the *Sedaca* that welcomes them, and particularly Italians and Berberiscos, who are of great detriment to the poor of the nation, resolved unanimously that from henceforth anyone who comes to this City to avail himself of *Sedaca* shall have maintenance for three days and 10s. to take themselves away and nothing more.'[12] They had enough to do to look after their own poor without adding the Italians and Moroccans who wanted to come. The published accounts include payments to people moving on.

It was out of the question to discourage refugees, especially those leaving Spain or Portugal, fleeing from the Inquisition. But the numbers were great and the calls on the community's funds were considerable, notably in the 1720s and 1730s when the Portuguese Inquisition became more active. The peak year of expenditure was 1726, when the total of all kinds amounted to £2,786, a very heavy burden on a community which probably did not amount to many more than 1,000 people: men, women and children, rich and poor.[13] One method of resolving the problem was to encourage some of them to re-emigrate to the new world. The best-known example of this was connected with the colonisation of Georgia under a Royal Charter of 1732.[14] It was not a great success, but the community continued to finance emigration. This method of getting rid of the unwanted also applied to the criminals. Around 1740 the synagogue, 'hearing there were many robberies committed by the Jews, sent several of them to Holland.' One of them, Jacob Cordosa, was given two guineas and told not to return for two years on pain of arrest. ''Tis a custom among the Jews,' he said at the trial prior to his execution in 1744, 'if a man goes abroad . . . for two or three years according to the agreement, if he returns within that time he is liable to be arrested.'[15]

Neither of these methods—discouragement and emigration—solved the problem of poverty; the poor were always there, and the community provided a range of services and facilities for them (but not only for them: the Ashkenazim, at least in the early years, received charity from the Sephardi community).[16] In 1664–65 the first charitable institution was established, *Hebra de Bikur Holim e Guemilut Hasadim* (Society for Visiting the Sick and Charitable Deeds). The rules included one for the appointment of a physician who 'shall prescribe what is needful, both in the matter of medicines and the maintenance of the sick person, which when [it is] signed by his hand the Administrator shall be obliged to send him every day.'[17] At the same time a school for boys was started, mainly to teach religious subjects, where the languages of instruction were Spanish and Portuguese, English not being introduced until 1736, along with arithmetic. A girls' school was founded in 1730[18] and an orphanage was established in 1703.

In addition to the legacies left for particular purposes, for example for the relief of widows and for a lying-in hospital opened in 1748,[19] other steps were taken to relieve poverty. An attempt was made in 1739 to raise at least £150 'for the establishment of a society for the employment of those who were capable of useful work', but the scheme was abandoned when only £50 was contributed. Ten years later, however, a similar proposal was realised with the creation of a society under the name *Mahasim Tobim* (Good Deeds) for, among other objects, the apprenticing of boys and girls.[20]

The Ashkenazim also dispensed charity through their synagogues and doubtless individually. They too had some educational provision and other welfare facilities. There was a charitable organisation from 1702,[21] and a Talmud Torah (an orphan charity school) was started in 1732. But there is not much evidence of more than that before the late eighteenth century, when Jewish friendly societies and Ashkenazi charities were founded.[22] The Talmud Torah, for example, was reorganised in 1788 but its efforts could still not have amounted to very much. Among the rules of the new body was the requirement that no boy was to be admitted 'unless he is six years of age and capable of reading the Prayerbook'. As one recent writer comments, 'where did orphans and the poor learn this?'[23] Moreover the attitude to education was narrow. 'Their traditional educational ideal was excellence in talmudical studies only; the homes were Yiddish-speaking. They had little realization of the existence, let alone the importance, of secular culture, and the teachers, themselves immigrants from central or eastern Europe, were incapable of using English as an educational medium even if they had been prepared to consider the possibility'.[24] Towards the end of the century the school did adapt itself in that it tried to prepare boys for employment by obtaining apprenticeships for them when they left school, but the numbers involved were very small.[25]

And the Ashkenazi population was growing; more rapidly it seems from about 1750. Conditions of life worsened in several continental countries and there was a migration westwards. In 1745 the Jews were expelled from Prague, some, not all, being permitted to return in a few years. A little later, those Jews in Prussia who were classified as 'regular-protected' were allowed to transmit their right of residence and occupation only to their eldest son, while those in the category of 'special-protected' could not do even that. Similar restrictions applied in other states of Germany. Many young people had to move on. In Poland the Haidamak massacres took place in the 1760s, and there were continual persecutions by Roman Catholics, which often ended in bloodshed.[26]

Travel from the Continent was easy. Three kinds of passes were available for those wishing to take passage from Holland to Harwich on the British mail-packet: whole, 13s, half, 6s, and 'poor', for nothing.[27] A poor traveller did not need to pay, and the definition of 'poor' was vague and discretionary. Cordosa, the criminal of the 1740s, despite his undertaking not to return from the Netherlands to London for two years, claimed that he travelled to England five or six times a year to buy hardware and pewter for sale in the Netherlands and presumably was not destitute. Yet he travelled free, 'only giving a shilling or two to the clerk for making out a pass'.[28] The Great Synagogue in the late

1760s was quite sure that this free travel was an important contributing factor to the influx of poor Jews, of whom there were too many indeed for their charities to deal with. The synagogue authorities therefore petitioned the government to restrict immigration, and the Secretary of State issued instructions to the Postmaster-General that in future no Jews were to be carried on the packet-boats unless they paid the full fare or were furnished with a passport by a British minister abroad. 'At the same time raids were made on Jewish pedlars throughout the country, and the Lord Mayor publicly offered free passes to any poor Jews who wished to leave England and return to their native lands'.[29] The effectiveness of these measures is not known. Were poor Jews deterred from immigrating? Surprisingly few examples of repatriation have been discovered. The measures were not successful in stemming the tide of Jewish criminality.

Criminals

It has been suggested[30] that 'crime—in the sense of being on the wrong side of the law—was, for vast numbers of undifferentiated working people, normal'. As early as 1677 the Sephardi synagogue paid £18.1s 'for the liberation of Jewish prisoners in this [city]', and in 1698 made a payment to Abraham da Silva 'for help in getting him out of prison'.[31] In the early eighteenth century one of the associates of the notorious Jonathan Wild, a 'thief-taker' and leader of a gang of robbers, was Abraham Mendez.[32] Four Jews were executed in February 1744—Jacob Cordosa, Joseph Isaacs (who changed his name to M'Coy), Samuel Moses and Aaron Seleit.[33] The most publicised case of all was that of the 'Chelsea murders' of 1771 committed by a gang of eight Jews. It aroused considerable interest and some general hostility towards Jews, and has a place in police history for being an early example of the use of publicity to capture the criminals (with the help of one of them who informed on the others). Six were tried and four executed.[34]

The eighteenth century was full of social discontent and rowdiness; the country and London experienced unrest in the late 1760s, and there is no reason why Jews should not have been involved.[35] On the other hand it is of interest that in other countries also there seems to have been an increase in Jewish crime—in France during the revolutionary period one gang was run by a woman, Dinah Jacob;[36] and perhaps one should include the *Betteljuden*, the groups of Polish-Jewish beggars who wandered across Europe.[37] There is certainly a special atmosphere about this period, which is remarkable for the upsurge of Jews as prizefighters. The most famous was Daniel Mendoza, born 1764, but others (perhaps as many as thirty)[38] included Sam Elias ('Dutch Sam') and his son, the Belasco brothers (Aby and Issy) and Barney Aarons. A recent discussion of the prizefighting era notes that 'a significant number of the pugilists came from the immigrant population, and in particular from the Jews, the Irish, and the negroes. Such immigrants found employment more difficult to obtain than the English, and apart from the Irish they did not receive Poor Law benefits'.[39] In fact Jews could get poor relief,[40] and the analysis needs exploring, as does the contemporary discussion of crime, for the light it throws on employment and social conditions at the time.

Contemporary Analysis of the Jewish Poor

Jewish crime was an undoubted fact. A popular print of 1781, 'A Fleet of Transports Under Convoy', shows Jews among the convicts,[41] and they were among the first transported convicts to reach Australia in 1788. By 1852, when this method of punishment ceased, at least 1,000 had been sent.[42] One of them was Ikey Solomons, the 'Prince of Fences', thought at one time to be the model for Charles Dickens's Fagin in *Oliver Twist* written in the 1830s.[43] An engraving of 1777 entitled 'Jews Receiving Stolen Property' illustrates the popular image of Jewish crime.

The standard view was put forward by Patrick Colquhoun, the London magistrate, in *A Treatise on the Police of the Metropolis*, first published anonymously in 1795. It went into several editions and was translated into French. In his references to the Jews, he drew a distinction between the Sephardim and the Ashkenazim. The former community, wealthier and more closely knit, contained not 'a single beggar or itinerant'. Among the Ashkenazim, a community which he estimated as between 12,000 and 15,000, the proportion of pedlars and beggars was very high. He put this down to the community's absence of roots and lack of education, and to the fact that very few were trained for employment. According to him they contributed many of the receivers of stolen property, coiners and utterers of false money.[44]

Colquhoun's strictures were a small part of his large work, but he was answered specifically on his Jewish discussion by a doctor and publicist, Joshua van Oven. He agreed with Colquhoun's views, but went into detail on the reasons for the Jews' position. It was almost impossible, he wrote, for a Jewish parent 'to put his son forward in life in some honest industrial employment. The restraints and observances of the Jewish ritual are such an insuperable difficulty to the initiation of the Jewish lad into any craft or trade, as makes it impossible for him to be bound to a master who is not of the same persuasion.'[45] Poor, untrained Jews therefore went into petty trading, notably peddling and dealing in old clothes—the latter naturally being closely connected with receiving. The centre for the second-hand clothes trade was Rosemary Lane, later Royal Mint Street. A 1770 description stated that it

> has been long noted for the sale of old clothes, and all sorts of wearing apparel. It is commonly called Rag Fair; and it is amazing to see the great number of Jews who resort to it every afternoon with such things as they have purchased during their morning walk through London.[46]

An American visitor to London in 1805 similarly referred to the fact that old clothes were collected 'principally by Jews who go about with bags on their shoulders crying, with a peculiarly harsh guttural sound "Clothes, clothes, old clothes". You will meet them in every street and alley in London, and, at evening, they repair to Wapping, where a grand display is made of every species of apparel, in every stage of decay'.[47] Cartoonists often displayed Jews as old-clothes dealers, and it is relevant that a synagogue was founded in 1748 in Rosemary Lane. Another synagogue, of Polish Jews, was started about 1790 in Cutler Street, another centre of the second-hand clothes trade.[48]

The rest of this chapter is devoted to an examination of the occupations of the Jews of the 'other' London in order to test this analysis, and one or two general problems about it are worth mentioning. No statistics are available to obtain some idea of the numbers involved. There are no censuses, comparable to those taken in many countries, from which we could establish the occupational distribution of the Jewish population. We are therefore left with a variety of sources, many of uncertain reliability, which may provide only statements of names and occupations—much Anglo-Jewish historical research consists in trying to establish whether names in a list are Jewish or not. We also have only minimal information about occupations. A person might be an employer, self-employed, or an employee. He might be a producer and a seller—such as a man making the products which he sells as a street-trader. Even if accuracy is not attainable, it is worth setting out what is known. Apart from the old-clothes dealers and street-sellers, what did the others do?

Occupations of London Jews

Not much is available on the seventeenth century. Four Ashkenazi workmen were paid for some work in connection with the rebuilding of the Sephardi synagogue in 1674–75; presumably they were unskilled. The accounts normally identify various craftsmen—stonemason, carpenter, etc., all paid respectable sums—but the Ashkenazim (described in the accounts as 'Tudescos') between them got less than £2. Two of them were paid 'for moving the things of the Synagogue', the others 'for help whilst the synagogue was being built'. Two Sephardim were also paid for certain painting work.[49] The 1684 list of members of the synagogue includes descriptions of three doctors and three synagogue officials: the editor of the published list identifies one as a diamond-cutter.[50] The London Census of 1695 lists a few occupations: two Jewish jewellers, Samuel Helbert and David Nunes, were men of substance, but there were also eight domestic servants, both Sephardi and Ashkenazi.[51]

Domestic servants crop up much more in the eighteenth century. The historian of the Sephardi community argues that service in Sephardi households was about the only occupation available to Ashkenazi immigrants.[52] The few wealthy Ashkenazi families also employed Jewish servants, and there were some Sephardi servants, according to the 1695 Census. We find servants mentioned in the surviving accounts of the Great Synagogue, the first of the Ashkenazi houses of prayer, established about 1690: Isaac, servant of Franks; Isaac, brother of Berl, the servant; Ber, the servant; Samuel Levy of Epsom, servant of the Rodrigues, and also Leizer Epsom, cook. Perhaps Abraham Cook was a servant, and also Zalman ben (son of) Nathan, footman. This last name appears in a list of members of the synagogue, and it is important, as an indication of the existence and possible extent of these occupations, that the Great Synagogue excluded 'servants from full membership and liturgical honours and flatly forbade them to attend service wearing their livery'.[53] It is possible that the employment of Jewish domestic servants by rich Jewish families declined during the eighteenth century. Moses Cassuto, the Italian Jew who visited London in the 1730s, noted that wealthy London Jews employed Christians, [54] and it has been argued that this was one reason for poverty among London Jews—that they could not get employment as servants.[55] This may be so, but one certainly comes across later references to Jewish domestic servants, Sephardi and Ashkenazi. We may assume that Mrs Filer Foa, who died in 1781 aged 110, and who had been in the service of the d'Almeida family for almost eighty years, was Jewish.[56] In 1803 there was a Dutchwoman, 'Rachel, wife of Joshua Palache, servant to Mrs Deborah Machovro (Machorro)'.[57] In any case the obvious question is: what else could Jewish girls of this class do? Certainly little, except domestic service—although those who happen to be mentioned in eighteenth-century documents are often described as necklace-makers.[58] The fragmentary records of the Great Synagogue provide more general information about the Ashkenazim. The names of 310 members survive, including various officials of the synagogue (to whom can be added, from an entry in the accounts, Mordecai the grave-digger). Apart from men in high-status occupations, including a few doctors and physicians, we come across those who must have been craftsmen and small traders, e.g. typically: watch-maker, necklace-maker, seal-engraver, painter, pen-cutter, pencil-maker, sugar-baker, gold-embroiderer (goldstucker), diamond-polisher (diamantschlaffer), printer, tinman (kratzwascher, presumably tinsmith) and several tailors (schneiders). There were perfumers (some so described, others as 'pulvermacher'), butchers, barbers, hatters, a 'fishman', a poulterer, a lemon-man (itinerant fruit-seller?). These occupations are all taken directly from their names, and Cecil Roth mentions another two known to have been a silversmith and a gem-dealer.[59]

There is no reason to be surprised that this list contains only two names and descriptions of men in the old-clothes trade. 'R. Joseph Schraga, or Ragfair' must presumably have been associated with the Rosemary Lane market; perhaps his son, 'Leib ben Joseph Schraga, or Ragfair', was in the same business (but the 'Ragfair' may refer to his father). This ambiguity in the material is the reason why it is not possible to give exact numbers of those with stated occupations. Perhaps the old-clothes dealers belonged to the minor synagogues; we should not expect them to have been members of the Westminster Synagogue founded in the 1760s for the benefit of those who had left the City and East End for the pleasanter atmosphere and to take advantage of 'the opportunities for trade and commerce presented by an affluent population already resident in Westminster', the seat of the court and government. Thus, 'luxury trades such as high-class tailoring, jewellery, gold-embroidering for military and court uniforms; callings such as portrait-painting, engraving, antique-dealing and the like—all these are found among the early Jewish settlement'.[60] This generalisation by Arthur Barnett, the historian of the synagogue, is supported in part by the evidence he provides. Of forty members in the 1770s, five occupations are listed: three gold-embroiderers, one seal-maker and a painter.[61] Those who signed a lease for new premises in 1797 included a jeweller, a button-dealer, a mercer, an auctioneer, two salesmen, a sealing-wax-maker and an embroiderer. One of the subscribers to the building fund was a fishmonger, and some of the painting work was done by one Meir ben Abraham.[62] These occupations do not seem very different from those of the Great Synagogue and some of those mentioned might have been street-sellers. Possibly the synagogue had an old-clothes dealer or two; it is most interesting that one of the residents of the area in the 1760s (thought by Barnett to have been Jewish) was 'Skinner Myers' of Pall Mall: 'hare and rabbit-skinning was not an uncommon occupation of the Jews of this period', he writes.[63] This pursuit was also associated with old-clothes dealing.[64]

If the Ashkenazi synagogue records are silent on the subject of these dealers in old clothes, those of the Sephardim are not. The Aliens List of 1803 gives details of 138 Sephardim and 78 occupations (the remainder are pensioners, widows, wives, or have no occupation stated). Of these, twenty-two are dealers or vendors of one sort or another: six are described purely as dealers, chapmen or pedlars; the others are dealers in hardware, spices, glass and china, clothes and slippers, and horses. Three are given as clothes (or old clothes) dealers, and three as rhubarb-sellers.[65] This last occupation was a speciality of Eastern Jews.

This list of Sephardim usefully extends our range of jobs. Apart from a few merchants and brokers it includes four clerks in Jewish merchant houses, five teachers, a manufacturer, three labourers, a jeweller and silversmith, a leather-maker, a slipper-maker, a garter-maker, a carpenter, a watch string-maker, and two silk-workers. Presumably the confectioners and tobacconist were shopkeepers, or perhaps street-sellers. A pattern of trades begins to emerge. Among the handful mentioned by Dorothy George were three pencil-makers, a diamond-cutter, two glass-engravers (master and apprentice). She also mentions that in T. Mortimer's *Universal Dictionary* of 1763 two of the six principal embroiderers were Jews. The snuff-maker (one of those executed in 1744) was a representative of the widespread Continental Jewish interest in tobacco. More generally, Mrs George says: 'Jewish working jewellers and watchmakers seem to have been not uncommon, though Jews were often dealers in jewellery and watches'.[66] In eighteenth-century London there were several watch- and clock-makers: e.g., Aaron Hart, Westminster, 1790; Levy Isaacs, 57 Mansell Street, 1769–83; Joshua Israels, 1775; Judah Jacobs, 1769–71; Moses Levin, 7 Cook's Court, Carey Street, 1790–94; Hyam Levy, 121 Whitechapel High Street, 1775–85.[67]

A few more details will demonstrate the range of jobs undertaken by Jews: innkeepers and proprietors of coffee-shops;[68] the Sephardi lying-in hospital employed Jews as matron, dispenser and apothecary;[69] Jewish sailors in the Royal Navy.[70] The titles of these occupations are ambiguous, but some were skilled.

Apprentices

Jewish youths were apprenticed to a number of craft occupations in the eighteenth century. A. P. Arnold has extracted 'Jewish' names from the books which recorded the payment of Apprentice Tax for the period 1710 to 1773,[71] although possibly not all the people he lists were Jews. We find the familiar occupations: jeweller, diamond-cutter, pencil-maker, diamond-polisher, engraver, silversmith, goldsmith (at least two in each of these categories); attorney, notary public, barber, capuchine-maker, tallow-chandler, glass-cutter, lace-joiner, lapidary, milliner, musician, perukier, stationer, stocking-weaver and toy manufacturer.

Several of the masters were apparently Jewish: Raphael Galindo, diamond-polisher; Henry Levi or Levy, lapidary; John da Costa, notary public; Isaac Henriques, jeweller, also described as diamond-cutter; Moses Noah, engraver; Abraham Abrahams, watch-maker; Solomon Mordechai, diamond-cutter; Samuel Levy, barber; Sam Levy, perukier; Isaac Hayman, diamond-cutter; Abraham Levy, diamond-cutter; Moses Levy, engraver (of the firm of Moses Levy and Charles Newton); Mordecai Levy, glass-cutter; Henry Judah, toy-maker; Solomon Joseph, diamond-polisher; Henry Lazarus, pencil-maker; Isaac Isaacs, watch-maker; Mordecai Levy, engraver; Samuel Noah, engraver; Benjamin Mordecai, silversmith.

Despite the inevitable danger of identification by name, the trades which are mentioned, together with the addresses—Whitechapel, Houndsditch, Duke's Place, Goodman's Fields—provide pretty conclusive evidence that they were Jews. This list is interesting moreover because some of the masters were not Jewish: there was plainly no absolute barrier to Jews being apprenticed to Christian masters. Moreover Ashkenazim, it is apparent, figure as apprentices and masters.

This list goes only to 1773, but one comes across other details from elsewhere, for example: Jacob Rey, an inmate of the Sephardi orphanage, apprenticed in 1771 to a City house as a clerk;[72] Daniel Mendoza, the future prizefighter, apprenticed at the age of thirteen to a glass-cutter.[73]

Entertainment

As early as 1667 Samuel Pepys referred in his diary to Mrs Manuel, 'the Jew's wife formerly a player', who sang for him, but the first authentic actress was Hannah Norsa who played Polly Peachum in John Gay's *Beggar's Opera* in 1732. Other famous singers included John Braham (1774–1856) and Michael Leoni (d. 1797); Breslaw (1726–1803) was a conjuror. It has been suggested that the role of the Jew as popular entertainer can be traced to certain social features of weddings and festivals. 'On the Continent the seven-day feast in celebration of a wedding was accompanied by continuous musical performances as well as the presentation of Hebrew plays specially written for the occasion and a *marshalik*, or jester, was invariably present'.[74] Some of the singers were cantors in synagogues, and it seems that in London the East End theatres were training grounds for Jewish entertainers:

> The local theatres, such as the Royalty in Goodman's Fields, the East London in Wellclose Square, and the Garrick in Leman Street, were well-known Thespian centres. Both Garrick and Braham made their first appearances at the Royalty, and the boards of the local theatres were training grounds for a host of distinguished actors and actresses, among them Leoni, Mrs. Bland, I. Isaacs, J. de Castro, H. Phillips, the Slomans, Mrs. Wallack sen., Miss Poole, Delpini, and Henry Russell.[75]

An Alternative Classification

Although we have no statistics of these various people, it is clear that the Jews of the eighteenth-century 'other' London were to be found in all the four categories mentioned at the beginning of this chapter. This was an occupational classification: shopkeepers supplying the needs of the wealthy; skilled men, such as watch-makers; Jewish domestic servants among the unskilled and semi-skilled; and the pedlars and old-clothes dealers among the mass bordering on criminality.

One writer has suggested that the London trades could be categorised in a different way:

(a) Trades which were dependent on the fact that London was the country's main port and the centre of the inland distribution trade. These included those producing for the home and export markets together with the warehouse and entrepot trade;
(b) the production of high class goods, clocks, watches, jewellery, etc.;
(c) trades supplying the wants of a large luxury-loving population, including coffee-houses, peruke-makers, barbers, tailors, milliners, etc.[76]

Generally speaking Jews in industry—which is what this classification refers to—were mostly in groups b and c. It is very possible that most Jews, however, were in some form of distribution, as pedlars or as old-clothes dealers. The trouble is that we have no notion of numbers. The impression given by many writers, both contemporary and modern, is that in the late eighteenth century the majority of London Jews were people of the street, peddling or collecting old clothes, and they follow the line of thought of Colquhoun and van Oven. It was certainly a powerful set of ideas, so much so that it greatly influenced attitudes and policies in the first half of the nineteenth century, as we shall see. But enough has been said to cast a little doubt on it: for example, the suggestion that the Sephardim were able to solve their social problems internally, within the community, does not seem to be borne out by the facts. If the Ashkenazim attracted more attention it was because there were more of them. Moreover, despite the range of Sephardi institutions, including the possibility of apprenticing their youths, it is interesting that as many as one in five of Sephardi bridegrooms from 1837, when the information begins, until 1850 were 'general dealers' (including hawkers).[77] When Henry Mayhew wrote his essays on London life in the early 1850s he devoted whole sections to Jewish street-sellers. He said their proportion was declining, but it is important that the Sephardi congregation's Mahamad made grants to their members between 1842 and 1864 for the purchase of hawkers' licences. And in 1859 a Hawkers' Licence Aid Society was formed for the same purpose.[78]

The conclusions to be drawn from this are not definite. Obviously there is substance in the old accounts of Jewish street-sellers in the eighteenth century. This is what new immigrants were likely to become if they came with little money and less knowledge of the language—the contemporary descriptions imply that they were foreigners—and if they came from those parts of the Continent where restrictions on Jewish economic life often made peddling a major activity for Jews. There seems to me rather more doubt about the occupations of the children, as evidence exists that they were not completely debarred from apprenticeships and other kinds of jobs. Is it not likely that contemporaries would draw attention to the Jews who were visible: those in the streets and those collecting old clothes with their characteristic sacks and with several hats perched on their heads? They could be captured in drawings and cartoons, and were the stereotype image. Colquhoun, as a magistrate, would be intimately knowledgeable of those who came in front of him. The others—the craftsmen, the apprentices, the shopkeepers—would be rather less in the public eye. They were not picturesque or a social problem, so no one wrote about them.[79]

4
The Provinces, before the Railway Age

During the whole period of Jewish residence in Britain, London has been the major settlement. In the early years the prototype immigrant, having disembarked, made his way to the neighbourhood of the Sephardi synagogue at Bevis Marks in the City, or the Ashkenazi Great Synagogue near by. As the eighteenth century progressed, there was a widening of the area of settlement. Some wealthy Jews moved eastwards to Goodman's Fields, a district laid out about 1700 when 'it was regarded as a most desirable place of residence'.[1] Less wealthy Jews went to Houndsditch, and a synagogue was established at Westminster in the 1750s. A small number of well-to-do Jews resided in the outer suburbs, in Highgate, Islington, Hampstead and Hackney in the north, and Richmond, Tooting, Wimbledon in the south.[2] Their lives and work focused on London, yet even before 1700 a few were to be found elsewhere. Isaac Abendana was in Oxford in 1662, in Cambridge from 1663 to 1676, and then back in Oxford, where he taught Hebrew to members of the university and sold Hebrew manuscripts. Some went to such distant places as Dublin and Edinburgh, and—nearer London—to Ewell in Surrey and to Worcester.[3] During the eighteenth century the number of places in the provinces where Jews lived grew rapidly, at least twenty of them supporting an organised religious community by 1800.[4] An even greater number of towns and villages became familiar to Jews in their role as pedlars and hawkers.

It is no great surprise to find Jews so widely scattered. London certainly exercised a magnetic attraction, but the great bulk of the British population lived outside it; moreover the seaports, where there was some tendency for Jews to congregate, rose in importance with the expansion of trade and with the needs of war: the large navy when in port was a ready market for local traders. All in all there were perhaps 700 market towns and seaports in England and Wales: 'every week many thousands of people flocked into their markets and shops from the surrounding countryside, as well as from the backstreets of the towns themselves, and the total volume of urban trade in England must have been very great indeed.'[5]

It was the Ashkenazim in their characteristically unorganised way who were responsible for this Jewish dispersal. The process was spontaneous. Unlike in the later nineteenth century, there was no plan for a reduction of the congested London population; none emerged from within the community and none from the public authorities. Some individual Sephardim lived in the provinces, including Dublin, but only a handful. Most remained in London, no doubt because their London synagogue retained a tight control. Their Ascama (rule) no. 1, adopted in 1663, stated that: 'for His greater service we in unanimity and harmony forbid that there be any other Congregation in this city of London, its districts and environs.' While this was not a bar on residence elsewhere but only a prohibition on the creation of new Sephardi congregations, it undoubtedly hindered provincial Sephardi settlement, for the rule continued that if 'in future times to come through circumstances that may happen it may be needful to divide ourselves as may be found fitting', then the 'disposition remains reserved for the Mahamad' (the executive officers).[6] No other Sephardi congregation was established during this early period. For their part the Ashkenazim were not so disciplined. Their fissiparous tendency was manifested in London even when their numbers were comparatively small. Within less than two decades of the establishment of the first Ashkenazi synagogue in 1690, moves were made to form a separate congregation. In general, a religiously conforming Ashkenazi would have no inhibitions in creating a new community wherever he happened to be. He had to ask no one for permission to do so. Thus from comparatively soon after the mid-seventeenth-century resettlement, Jews were to be found in numerous places, even where no organised community was subsequently established.

A record exists of four living in Edinburgh between 1691 and 1717. The Town Council possessed the power of controlling entry to retail trading, and on 4 September 1691 it granted permission to one David Brown, a Jew, to trade in the town; Moses Mosias was granted a licence to trade in 1698 (and unlike the other three he was also enrolled as a burgess); he was followed by Theodore Marine in 1700 and Isaac Queen (Cohen?) in 1717. Queen must have had some resources. The minute referring to him, dated 27 November 1717, stated: 'for the benefit of the toune he paying a hundred pound he might be endowed dureing his life with the priviledge of useing and exercising any trade, merchandise or employment within the city and libertys thereof and he being present and payd the said hundred pound the motion was approven of and that priviledge granted accordingly'.[7] We know they were Jews because the Town Council minutes mention this, including, in the case of David Brown, a long Council discussion about the principle of allowing Jews these rights.

During the eighteenth century the number of places of Ashkenazi settlement rapidly increased. In the list of members of the Great Synagogue we find nicknames such as 'Greenwich', 'Margate', 'Lincoln', 'Bristol'. Among the Jews who emigrated to America in the period up to about 1840 were a number who came from Britain, many from the provinces: Simon Nathan, born 1746 in

Frome (Somerset); Solomon Hyams, born Dublin; Joseph Sampson, born Bury St Edmunds, and others born in Hull, Glasgow, Liverpool, Bristol, Canterbury, Plymouth and Portsmouth.[8] Equally unimpeachable as sources of information are the circumcision registers, the records of names upon whom the operation was performed. The published register of Reb Judah Leib of Portsmouth shows that from 1762 to 1807 he carried out over 100 circumcisions. Most were carried out in Portsmouth, no doubt on local children, but the register sometimes states that the child lived elsewhere. The places mentioned include: Winchester, Southampton and Gosport in Hampshire; Cowes (Isle of Wight); Arundel and Brighton in Sussex; Poole in Dorset; Bath; Rochford in Essex.[9] Other, unpublished registers record circumcisions at Bushey, Folkestone, King's Lynn, Chesham in Buckinghamshire, Coventry, Southminster in Essex, Watford, Spalding in Lincolnshire, and many other places.[10] To these one can add such newspaper reports as one of 1769 which refers to two Jews in Wakefield. The item is headed 'Jews Bankrupts' and refers to Samuel Joseph and Jonas Israel 'Merchants and Partners' (together with Isaac Joseph of London).[11] It is not at all unusual to come across 'Jewish' names in eighteenth-century towns where no other such references are found for many decades following and certainly well before any organised religious community was established. The Newcastle-upon-Tyne community came into existence about 1830, but a century earlier a Solomon Phillips had lived there, who may have been Jewish, and perhaps David Henriques, who died in 1775, was. There is a curious reference from the middle of the century to 'a party of Jews' establishing near Newcastle 'a Prussian Blue manufactory'. The first *Directory* of the town included the name of I. Levi, glass-grinder and flowerer.[12] Examples like this can be found in many towns and although it is not known if these individuals were Jews—especially if a name is the only evidence—since they are known to have lived throughout the country, there is nothing implausible in the suggestion that they may have been Jewish.

The Pedlars

The Jews of the provinces were mainly of two kinds: the pedlars and hawkers; and the shopkeepers, whether pure traders or craftsmen. Aside from such isolated and unequivocal examples as the shopkeepers of Edinburgh, most of the evidence for the first half of the eighteenth century refers to pedlars. After that we hear more about settled residents, usually shopkeepers, but the pedlars continued long into the next century. The following are a few illustrative examples, intended to show how widespread they were and how early they began.

One of the first was Moses Emanuel, who 'was familiar in the Leicestershire countryside, and used to discuss theological questions with Samuel Carte, Vicar of Hinckley from 1720 to 1735'.[13] There is a legend about Jacob Harris, a Jewish pedlar who committed murder in 1734 at the Royal Oak, Ditchling, near Brighton; he was hanged 'at Horsham, and his corpse suspended for many years from a gibbet outside the Royal Oak, where there was a post for many years known as Jacob's Post'.[14] Pedlars carrying cash and goods were more likely themselves to be the object of violence in isolated places. Isaac Soloman, licensed hawker, was attacked in March 1740 in Lancashire.[15] In 1754 Jonas Levi was murdered near Crickhowell (Wales) and the body of 'Little Isaac', a travelling Jew, was discovered in Devon in 1760.[16] In 1744 Jewish chapmen (pedlars) were reported in Morpeth, Northumberland.[17] Two of the four men who signed the lease for the Portsmouth cemetery in 1749 were chapmen.[18] In 1735 a meeting was held in Cambridge 'of the Heads and Tutors to consider how to remedy the mischief arising from peddling Jews dealing with scholars'.[19] We read of Hyam Barnett, a silversmith of Gloucester, who on his death in 1815 was reported to have been 'well known during near forty years for the extent of his dealings throughout this county, Hereford, Monmouth and South Wales'.[20] There was Solomon Meyer, a travelling salesman in the north who settled in Hull as a pawnbroker and became President of the synagogue.[21] A travelling jeweller of Lincoln named Samuel Samuel died in Louth in 1804. Barnet Levy of Guernsey, who died in 1784, 'travelled the Channel Islands for over twenty years'.[22]

The survival of these names is a matter of chance, and there is no way of knowing how many pedlars there were. Those mentioned here—and the others in the literature who are identifiable by name only and may therefore not be Jews—hardly amount to a small crowd, but there is some general evidence that their numbers were not insubstantial. It is of great interest that from the 1770s booklets in Yiddish and Hebrew were published, presumably for the pedlars. They contained coaching information—frequency of coaches, times and fares; details of markets and fairs; holidays; inns and hotels.[23] Israel Solomon of Falmouth wrote that up to about 1830 the inns on all the main roads catered for Jewish dietary needs, providing a locked cupboard for cooking-utensils used solely by a Jewish traveller who after use would write on them in chalk in Hebrew his name, the (Jewish) date and the portion of the Law read on the Sabbath. In populated areas the pedlars would congregate on a Friday evening for the Sabbath. They would form a club and one of their members (licensed by a rabbi to slaughter animals) would get to the inn early on a Friday to kill an animal, or to purchase fish, and cook or supervise the cooking. The club would recompense him for his loss of trade on the Friday.[24] There is support for this from other evidence. A Moroccan Jew who arrived in Britain in 1811 became a pedlar: 'I lodge once at Taunton, at a house where a woman keeps a lodging-house for de Jewish people wat go about wid de gold tings, de jewellery.'[25]

One particular group of itinerant salesmen require a separate note. These were 'cheap-johns' (or 'cheap-jacks'), the elite of the licensed hawkers, who travelled by horse and cart to the major fairs and markets, selling slightly superior goods, in larger quantities. In the first half of the nineteenth century there were probably fewer than 1,000 of them in any one year; some of them were Jews. We know something about them from Charles Hindley's fascinating *The Life and Adventures of a Cheap Jack: By One of the Fraternity*, which deals mainly with the 1830s and 1840s just before they began to decline. There we meet Aaron and Henry Jessell,[26] Mo Jacobs, Ned Abrahams, Jacob Jewell, Moses Jacobs (or Ugly Mo) and one Hyams. (Two others are mentioned, Samuel Levy or Sammy Schnoodle, and Isaac Hart alias Shicer. They were not cheap-johns but ordinary pedlars who accompanied the others in their travels.) It seems they mainly worked from London, although Aaron Jessell came from Ramsgate and Samuel Levy from Chatham (where his brother is described as one of the largest contractors of turnpikes—presumably Lewis Levy; and another brother, Jonas, bought government stock at the Tower, presumably an old-clothes dealer). It is clear from this book that while the Jewish cheap-johns followed their religious practices ('when we got to Manchester Aaron [Jessell] said he was going to lie up for three weeks, it being Passover time'), there is no mention of special dietary arrangements or of contacts with the Jews in the provincial towns they visited. In general they were in the provinces but not of it.

Finally, we should note that the pedlar was captured 'in innumerable contemporary sketches, cartoons, engravings, silhouettes, even terra-cotta groups and porcelain'.[27] Presumably artists knew what they were portraying: at any rate the popular view was that 'Jew' equalled 'pedlar'. When Lord George Gordon embraced Judaism in the 1780s, the caricaturists portrayed him as a pedlar.

It is easy to exaggerate the role of Jews in peddling. While there is no doubt that many Jews were rural pedlars, just as Jews were street-sellers in London, and they must have formed a sizeable proportion of the Anglo-Jewish community, within the British economy they were a minority. The first great expansion of 'wayfaring traders and merchants'[28] occurred during the period 1570–1604, well before the resettlement. In the eighteenth century there were numerous middlemen and travellers, including such non-Jewish groups as the 'Scotch drapers' or 'Scotch hawkers', the 'English merchants' of Glasgow and the 'Flashmen' of Staffordshire.[29] Jews were not among the manufacturers' agents who sold goods to retailers: their function was to sell direct to consumers. There was plenty of opportunity for this. Traditionally the very large agricultural population made its purchases 'after Michaelmas, when money earned in the harvest fields was being transferred to shopkeepers and pedlars'.[30] But although Jewish pedlars were to be found throughout the country, many towns hardly knew them. Oxford, for example, an obvious magnet for such traders, seems to have been ignored by Jewish pedlars. A recently compiled index for the local newspaper covering the period 1753–80 mentions only two or three Jewish names of traders, and among the twenty-four listed dealers and chapmen not one is Jewish. Neither are the solitary pawnbroker and the single dealer in second-hand clothes. For the 1790s Roth found two Jewish names among the inhabitants of a large tenement. Since they had no families, he suggests they were pedlars, and the place may have been where pedlars congregated. It is pretty thin evidence.[31]

Nevertheless there were many Jewish pedlars in the provinces. An alien immigrant of a different culture and language could become one with no difficulty. No apprenticeship was needed, very little capital, and even the hawkers' licence of £4 was avoidable. Petty trading of this kind was a common occupation of European Jews, and in the eighteenth century there was a growing consumer demand at a time before fixed shops were the accepted suppliers: travelling salesmen sold from door to door and markets and fairs were the great occasions for retail sales. But did Jews become pedlars in the provinces because they were unable to take up more stable jobs, such as shopkeeping? It was normal for boroughs to regulate trade within their boundaries—the City of London and Edinburgh have already been mentioned—and it was often necessary to be a burgess (or of some similar status) in order to be a shopkeeper or craftsman. In 1757 the Bristol Council ordered Moses Cone (Cohen) 'who keeps a shop with glass windows before same and therein sells gold and silver without being a free burgess be prosecuted for same'.[32] If this were at all widespread, then Jews would have been reduced to becoming pedlars. But there is no evidence that Jews were generally restricted in this way and the most likely explanation for the existence of Jewish pedlars is poverty. The experiences of a nineteenth-century immigrant may not be typical, but they illustrate the point. He was born in 1814, the son of a corn-merchant, and worked as a clerk for his guardian after his father died. He came to London in 1835 to try to obtain a legacy from the estate of a wealthy uncle. Nothing came of it: he received only £2, and having lent some money to a school-friend whom he had met on the journey, was without funds. He stayed at a boarding-house in London kept by a Polish Jew, which was frequented by many foreigners, one of whom advised him to get some goods for sale. He started to sell pencils, pens and other writing materials in the London streets, and then went into the countryside.

He travelled for about two years (managing to save £15 during the first eighteen months), before deciding to settle down. He chose Bedford. 'Several attempts which I made there to sell goods proved successful; I seemed to like the persons with whom I came in contact, and I was kindly received by all; and having likewise heard that there were some Jews living in the town I determined to make this town, as it were, my central settlement, and to limit my travels to its immediate neighbourhood.' He married in 1839 a Jewish girl from Bedford, and having fallen ill looked for a different job. He became a teacher of German, supplementing his income by selling jewellery.[33] By that time, and for many years previously, borough restrictions had been in abeyance, and it was not those that caused him to become a pedlar. His economic downgrading was a consequence of poverty.

Pedlars and Shopkeepers

Many obvious questions arise about the peddling economy. Where, for example, did they get their supplies of trinkets, cheap jewellery, pencils, and the like? If they travelled the countryside, did they have a base of some kind? Since it seems that many rural pedlars remained in the provinces and had no connection with London, they must have got their goods locally. This was the case in Falmouth, Cornwall, according to Israel J. Solomon, who was born there in 1803, the third generation of his family to live there. His *Records of My Family* was published in New York in 1887 and he describes how the community began with Alexander Moses, known as Zender Falmouth, a silversmith who settled there about 1740. He entered into a compact with a number of Jewish pedlars in the district whereby he paid for their licences, and 'advanced, on credit, a stock of small cutlery, buckles, jewellery and watches which they hawked round the country. They, for their part, undertook to return to Falmouth every Friday in time to act as one of the *Minyan;* on Sunday they settled their accounts and received fresh stock before resuming their travels of the following week.'[34]

Two of these pedlars were his grandfathers. His mother's father was Barnet Levy, who came from Alsace in the middle of the eighteenth century and at first went to London. His trade was that of soap-boiler, but, unable to make a living, he 'reluctantly took to peddling, his travels bringing him to Falmouth'. Three other pedlars also descended from an immigrant from Alsace, one Joseph Joseph. When he died, his two eldest sons became pedlars based on Canterbury, then moved to Cornwall and thus into contact with Zender. They persuaded their step-brother to join them. Eventually they all set up shop in Falmouth or in near-by towns and villages—Redruth, Truro, Penryn, Camborne and St Austell—their wives working as milliners and dress-makers. They would return to Falmouth on Sabbaths and festivals, and the clear impression is that the whole exercise had for Zender less of a financial than a religious motive—to create a community, a sufficient number of Jews to enable services and other religious functions to be performed, and to provide the comfort of a common culture. Or it may be regarded as the building of a large family. When Zender died in 1791 there was perhaps ten or twelve families in Falmouth, five of the spouses being his own children, and other relations lived elsewhere in Cornwall. It is this that makes Solomon's story so convincing. He was born it is true after some of the events he described; he never knew three of his grandparents, and the one alive in his time was nearly eighty when he was born. However, the descendants of the half-dozen or so pedlars, all living in the area and in close contact with each other, must have possessed among them a collective memory of these happenings which was largely accurate. (One must perhaps allow for some embroidering in the telling, and some misremembering by Solomon when he wrote in his eighties.)

It is possible that this kind of arrangement—settled shopkeepers associated with rural pedlars—may have existed elsewhere. Certainly the small community at Liverpool—one of the handful of provincial Jewish communities which were established at mid-century—could call on pedlars at near-by places, 'Chester, Newton, Parkgate, etc., where there existed Jewish lodging houses—to invite the struggling Hebrew in his capacity of hawker, to attend divine worship'.[35] However, although it is said[36] that Benjamin Yates of Liverpool, a seal-engraver, and Moses Aaron of Birmingham, a pencil-maker, acted as did Zender Falmouth in his roles of economic and religious head of the community, no other evidence exists of such arrangements elsewhere.

Peddling was a precarious way of life in terms of both personal safety and economic gain. As in London, the provincial pedlars often lived on the margin of crime, including fraud and theft. In 1776, five years after the Chelsea murders, six men—three of them Jews—were arrested and tried at Chester Assizes for robbery: two of the Jews were seal-engravers, who made the tools for forcing locks and bolts. One of the Jews turned King's evidence and the other two, along with two of the gang, were executed.[37]

Shopkeepers

For many, peddling was a preliminary to a more settled way of life and the typical career was from peddling into shopkeeping. There are plenty of examples of this happening to particular individuals, yet very often the first known Jewish inhabitant in a town is a shopkeeper who may or may not have graduated from peddling: often there is no information about his earlier life. The second major Jewish provincial activity, after peddling, was shopkeeping. In his pioneering compilation about provincial Jewry, Cecil Roth wrote, after referring to Abraham Ralph (a silversmith who died in 1805 after forty years' residence in Barnstaple), that this 'provides us with another instance, in addition to those already given in the previous pages, of the Jewish silversmith and watch-maker in the English country-town in the middle of the eighteenth century. It is becoming apparent that the pioneers of these early Anglo-Jewish communities followed more dignified callings than was formerly imagined'.[38] Whether or not 'silversmith' or 'watch-maker' are dignified is a matter of opinion and definition. In his brief but excellent study of Jews in Devon, Bernard Susser lists eighteen Jewish occupations and trades in Plymouth in 1812. Two were umbrella-maker and straw-hat-maker. The other sixteen were classified under nine headings such as jeweller, silversmith, dealer in naval stores, merchant, broker. All these descriptions, says Susser, 'really mean the same thing, a general dealer's shop with perhaps an emphasis on silverware or naval stores'.[39] His note of warning is valid. The titles of occupations are usually taken from trade directories compiled at the time with greater or lesser degrees of meticulousness. Does 'silversmith' really mean pawnbroker? Or might 'jeweller' mean 'moneylender'? The names, moreover, indicate a degree of specialisation which did not exist. Among the earliest members of the Hull community were Israel Jacobs, jeweller, goldsmith and dealer in clocks and watches, and Joseph Lyon, silversmith and pawnbroker. But some of them were certainly craftsmen, as we shall see.

Whatever its ambiguities, the Plymouth list of 1812 was typical of the provincial communities of the period. Throughout all the literature one reads again and again: jeweller, silversmith, goldsmith, watch-maker, dealer (often slop-seller), navy agent. A man such as Zender Falmouth, a silversmith, is the earliest known Jewish inhabitant in a town. In 1732 at Cambridge there was Israel Lyons, silversmith and Hebrew teacher; in 1743 at Ipswich, Salamon Levi, silversmith; at Sunderland, Abraham Samuel, jeweller and silversmith; at Yarmouth, Simon Hart, silversmith. The first known Jew in Hull was a watch-maker. These are just a few examples. All in all perhaps one-half of all the occupations mentioned by Roth in *The Rise of Provincial Jewry* are jewellers, silversmiths and goldsmiths.[40]

While some of them may well have been general dealers, there is no doubt that there were craftsmen among them who made as well as sold their products. Some of the goldsmiths had their marks registered at the assay offices of Exeter, Chester, Birmingham, Cork and Waterford. Emanuel Cohen and Moses Jacob of Redruth are known to have made clocks. Several carried on the traditional Jewish craft of engraving. The man who may have been the founder of the Portsmouth community in the 1740s, Benjamin Levy (d. 1784), was an engraver, and his two sons Isaac and Elias continued the trade. One of the first Jews in Liverpool was Benjamin Goetz (later Yates), an engraver who settled there in 1762. He was also a working jeweller and occupied a number of religious roles within the community (the Liverpool *Directory* of 1790 describes him as 'High Priest'). His son Samuel (1757–1825), having been a pedlar in Dorset, took over the trade in 1798, presumably on his father's death, and it continued later as the firm of Yates and Hess (Israel Hess being his son-in-law). Another engraver in the mid-eighteenth century, Moses Mordecai, was also a goldsmith whose mark was registered at Exeter. Another goldsmith at Exeter, Ezekiel Abraham Ezekiel, was an engraver and watch-maker, having also been apprenticed as a jeweller. His trade card describes him as 'Engraver in General. Optician. Goldsmith and Printseller'. Two brothers, Abraham and Joseph Daniel, combined the crafts of miniature painting with jewellery and engraving. Another brother, Phineas, was a watch-maker, silversmith and engraver. Abraham Daniel's apprentice in 1779 was a Jew named Samuel Hart. They worked in the west country at Plymouth, Bath and Bristol.[41]

In addition to these familiar occupations other Jews are described as '———-maker', and as with the watch-makers may or may not have made things. Lazarus Cohen of Exeter was a shoe-and patten-maker (1790); Lemuel Lyon of Bedford was a lace-maker (1825);[42] the Plymouth Aliens List of 1803 includes a box-maker, a pen-cutter, an umbrella-maker, spectacle-makers and cap-makers.[43]

Whether pure sellers or craftsmen as well, the Jewish shopkeepers in the provinces were able to take advantage of the growing economic opportunities afforded by an expanding and wealthier population. This provided the market for them and the handful of quasi-professionals such as opticians as well as 'quack' doctors. But they seem to have operated for the general population and the middle class rather than the very wealthy. Unlike in London, one does not come across wig-makers and perfumers, few were tailors, but there were some in the clothing trades. As Israel Solomon noted, the shopkeepers' wives in Cornwall were often dress-makers and there were also straw-bonnet-makers, milliners and a feather-maker.[44]

The Seaports

Although the first provincial communities were in the ports, many of the Jews there operated for the land-based population: their occupations of silversmith and watch-maker as well as possible connections with the rural pedlars in the hinterland tell us that. But they were also associated with the life of the ports, and Jews acted as ships' chandlers, sailors' outfitters and as navy agents. A report of the 1840s on seamen's conditions noted that 'the outfitting business is in the hands of low Jew slop sellers'.[45]

They exchanged foreign money for crews returning from service abroad. For this purpose and to relieve sailors of some of their accumulated wages by the sale of trinkets, it was common for port-based dealers to go out to the ships in small boats. At Falmouth the boats owned by local Jews were called 'tailors' cutters'; one was given the name *The Synagogue*.[46] There are several references to this activity. One tragic incident occurred in 1758 when eleven Jews from Portsmouth died when their boat capsized.[47] Here in particular was a major naval establishment which must have provided a great deal of fruitful trade. The minutes of the Portsmouth congregation refer to members being fined for desecrating the Sabbath by trading on board on that day.[48] It was not only traders who boarded the ships. A slight incident recorded in 'Lord' George Sanger's *Seventy Years a Showman* tells of two conjurors, Israel and Benjamin Hart, who during the Napoleonic Wars boarded a ship at Deal to entertain the sailors, were pressed into service and served for the rest of the war.[49] This Jewish trading relationship is taken for granted by Michael Lewis in his *Social History of the Navy*. In a reference to the incidence of smallpox among sailors, he states that the infection was usually taken aboard when ships were in port 'by the Jews, the bumboat women and others allowed to enter the ship'.[50]

The growth of naval activity during the wars of the eighteenth century culminated in the vast expansion during the Napoleonic Wars, with correspondingly increased opportunities at the ports. The Plymouth Aliens List records a number of Jews going to the port at that period. Many were appointed as navy agents, authorised to trade with crews.[51] Some Jews served in the navy, and they shared the likelihood, common to seaport populations, of being pressed into service. One was Barnet Asher Simmons, who lost a finger at Trafalgar, settled in Penzance, married a grand-daughter of Zender Falmouth, and served as Minister to the Penzance synagogue.[52]

One community, that of Sheerness, was vitually a creation of the war. It came into existence in 1790 and declined rapidly when peace returned. More generally, many of these smaller port communities declined and even disappeared during the nineteenth century. Those towns which more or less ceased to be ports—Boston in Lincolnshire, for example—lost their communities. At Falmouth after the packet service was withdrawn in 1850, there was a rapid exodus to other towns and abroad. This would suggest that it was the port rather than the rural hinterland that had provided the main economic incentive. But a narrow economic interpretation is hardly sufficient. No doubt there were other reasons for the decline of these communities. One was outmarriage. Another, perhaps, was the desire of younger generations to widen their horizons.[53]

Not much remains of these early seaport communities: one or two, like Portsmouth, have a continuous history; others, such as Hull, Sunderland and Liverpool, were reinforced by later immigrations and by the growth of economic activity in those areas. But the name of one Penzance Jew, related by marriage to the Israel J. Solomon of Falmouth, has a continuing place in British life. Lemon Hart (presumably originally Lemmle Hart) was a purveyor of rum to the Royal Navy. 'Lemon Hart' is the name of a rum still sold in this country, a not unpleasing reminder of this comparatively brief association of one section of Anglo-Jewry with the sea. Another was Henry Russell (1812–1900), born at Sheerness, 'a man of intense patriotism who wrote songs of the sea which the British people took to their hearts. Among these, the popularity has survived to this day of at least three; they are "Cheer, Boys, Cheer", "I'm Afloat", and also "A Life on the Ocean Wave"—this latter has become today the regimental march of the Corps of Royal Marines.'[54]

Miscellaneous Activities

The provincial communities and even the isolated Jewish residents were mainly in the south of England, where they were engaged in trading with consumers, sometimes associated with small-scale manufacturing for that market. Inevitably a few eccentric occupations were taken up. Isaac Alexander of Colchester ran coaches between that town and London and also between London and Brighton until the railways killed that trade.[55] Levy Emanuel Cohen founded the *Brighton Guardian* in 1827 and ran it until his death in 1860. Provincial Jewry included—to judge from their names—a few glass-cutters and glass-flowerers (engravers), but two Jewish firms of glass-makers came into existence at Bristol and Birmingham.[56] Lazarus and Isaac Jacobs of Bristol was one of the major English glass-making businesses, specialising in blue glass, and became glass-makers to King George III. Lazarus arrived in Bristol from Frankfurt-on-Main probably about 1760 and started off in a modest way (in 1771 he is described as a glass-cutter at whose premises, during the fair, were sold 'superfine best seconds, and livery, broadcloth'). But the firm soon became known for its glass and it flourished under Isaac, who took over in 1796 on his father's death. The Bristol glass trade was in difficulty, however, and by 1820 the firm had to borrow large sums and the business collapsed. The Birmingham glass firm of Mayer Oppenheim, who was born in Bratislava about 1720, was even less successful. He received a patent in 1755 (when he was described as 'of the City of London, Merchant') for making red glass, but by 1762 he was in Birmingham advertising in the local paper that he wished to buy children's buckles and offering his glass premises for sale. But he continued in the business and in 1770 his patent was extended, but by 1777 he was declared bankrupt and while he was in the debtors' prison a relative, Nathan Oppenheim, took over; but nothing more is heard of the firm and Mayer Oppenheim went to France, where his business also ran into trouble.

Birmingham is unusual in this story because, although inland and increasingly industrial, it may have had a Jewish community in the mid-eighteenth century when all the others were seaports. The Birmingham rate books contain seven 'Jewish' names in the 1750s and a local commercial directory of 1777 has seventeen. About half were in characteristic Jewish trades—watch-maker, spectacle-maker, glass-grinder, pencil-maker, sleeve-button-maker. Others 'had entered some of the more characteristic trades of the town and we find a watch-chain-maker and even a firm of Jewish jobbing smiths'.[57] But there is little evidence of Jewish participation in Britain's industrial revolution, at any rate before 1800—apart from Nathan Mayer Rothschild, who arrived in Manchester in 1799 and set up as a cotton-merchant. In the next chapter this matter is examined further, and it is shown that following Rothschild a number of German-Jewish immigrants entered the Lancashire cotton trade and industry. But these developments, and others such as the growing Jewish involvement in the clothing trade—although taking place before the railway age—properly belong to the development of the industrial communities.

Two final, negative, points about the provincial communities need to be made. Unlike in London, they produced no working class. It is possible that some of the dress-makers and those in similar jobs may have been employed, but more likely they were self-employed, making clothes in their own homes. Apart from the apprentices, who intended to become masters in due course, only one 'errand boy' appears, in 1851, with an undoubted employee's title; but even he may have been working in the family shop.[58] The proletarian clothing-workers of Manchester make no appearance before about the 1840s.

The second field in which Jews of the provinces are notably uninvolved was country banking, which expanded greatly towards the end of the century. A few names have surfaced. Samuel Levi, who was German-born, probably about 1730, settled in Haverfordwest with his brother Moses and were befriended by a Phillips, whose name they took. Samuel Levi Phillips, who was also a jeweller, was a founder of banks in Haverfordwest and Milford Haven in Wales. Both brothers were baptised and merged with the general community, one of Samuel's descendants being Hugh Price Hughes, the famous Welsh nonconformist preacher. Israel Barned of Liverpool, who was active in the Jewish community in the mid-nineteenth century, was another, and perhaps also the Andrade of the Lancaster banking firm of Andrade and Worswick.[59] There may have been others, but whatever credit facilities provincial Jews such as pawnbrokers may have provided, they did not become country bankers because they were not engaged in the activities from which country banking developed. One group of bankers were industrial entrepreneurs, 'whose approach to banking was strongly influenced by the need to provide a local means of payment'. Jews in the provinces were not engaged in this kind of industrial activity, which involved the problems of financing fixed capital investment and of finding cash to pay employees. A second group were the money scriveners, or more generally the legal profession. 'Rural investment was peculiarly dependent on the money scrivener, for he was a specialist in land conveyancing and mortgages'. This again was not a Jewish activity; Roth discovered only one money scrivener with a Jewish name.[60] A third group of activities—remittance—included in the origins of country banking is more relevant to Jews since both retail and wholesale traders participated. Yet retail trade 'was not an outstanding source of regular bankers', although there are some examples. The wholesale traders whom L. S. Pressnell mentions as being engaged in banking seem on the whole to have been more substantial men than the majority of provincial Jews, or were engaged in such pursuits as overseas trade or ship-owning, which few provincial Jews followed. (Another type of remittance was revenue-collecting; but since Jews could not perform public office, this was outside their competence.)

Conclusion

The Jews who lived in the provinces chose to live there for any number of reasons and were enabled to peddle or open shops by the growth of demand and by the decay of local regulating restrictions. They were generally of a lower social status than the business Jews of London, although a few of them prospered. Jacob Nathan of Plymouth certainly did: he was a goldsmith and also an owner of houses (as were his two brothers and a sister). He was the largest benefactor to the congregation. One man, Lyon Joseph of Falmouth, was a ship-owner who 'made a fortune shipping goods to the ports of the Peninsula unoccupied by Napoleon'. But when he continued this after the British evacuation, his goods were confiscated, one of his ships was misappropriated by its captain, and a Jewish importer at Cadiz stole a shipment. 'He lost his fortune and retired to Bath a broken man'.[61]

In the new industrial age of the nineteenth century many of these provincial communities disappeared, and rather than living in these seaports and southern market towns, provincial Jews became concentrated in the great industrial cities of the north.

5

The Middle Class: Industry, 1800–80

During the period when Britain became the world's major economic power the number of Jews in the country was small. The commonly-quoted estimates and guesses of the Anglo-Jewish population suggest that the 25,000 of 1800 grew to 35,000 in 1851 and 60,000 in 1880. The growth-rate may have been even less than appears from those figures: detailed investigations of the Jewish populations in 1851 of Manchester and Birmingham give lower numbers than those in Table 3.[1] These findings confirm the very small expansion in the first half of the nineteenth century, a consequence of the slow rate of immigration. But from about the 1840s more newcomers arrived and Anglo-Jewry's numbers grew more rapidly in the next thirty years. By the end of the period the influx was becoming even greater, building up to a dramatic transformation of the social and economic structure of the community.

For much of the time Anglo-Jewry consisted therefore of a growing proportion of anglicised and native-born people. They could take advantage of Britain's economic growth and also of the removal of the last remnants of formal discrimination.[2] The requirement of a Christian oath was abolished piecemeal and Jews could take public office, become Members of Parliament, obtain degrees at Oxford and Cambridge universities, and enter more professions. Moreover, the new universities which were established did not administer religious tests.[3] The number entering the professions was small, but the anglicised and native-born element was becoming increasingly middle class through the opportunity presented by economic growth. In addition some of the immigrants went straight into middle-class occupations, in shopkeeping, trade or industry.

This was not the whole story, as chapter 5 will show, for there also developed a Jewish working class in the main cities. Newly-arrived immigrants formed its main constituent except for London, where the native-born and anglicised also contributed to this section. In the provinces there were three main types of economic and social structure. Some of the older, eighteenth-century communities declined, and did not attract immigrants. These small decaying settlements were largely middle class. The new immigrants who settled in the provinces went to towns and cities in the industrial areas to form the second type of settlement. The great majority of new Jewish communities which were established in the first seven or eight decades of the century were located in the coalfield areas: Cardiff, Merthyr Tydfil, South Shields, Newcastle, Bradford, Leicester, Hanley and Glasgow, for example. Only a handful of the new ones—at Aldershot, Grimsby and Stroud—did not fit that pattern.[4] These new, small communities were probably composed mainly of shopkeepers and pedlars. The third type of provincial growth was in older settlements in industrial areas, of which Manchester was the supreme example. The immigrants who arrived there included a sizeable working-class element.

It is to be expected that the expanding industrial towns would attract them, but London continued to house the majority of Jews in Britain. Although by-passed by technological innovation it was a great port, the seat of government and of the court, and the world's chief money market. It was also a major manufacturing centre, its vast industrial population working in workshops rather than in factories, not using steam-power or modern machinery to any great extent.[5] Since the working-class immigrants—those who started as tailors or cap-makers or pedlars or glaziers—could do these jobs anywhere, there was no special reason to seek out one town rather than another. Some of the middle-class immigrants, on the other hand, did have particular economic interests, and went to the town or city where their expertise could be used.

However, those middle-class immigrants who came from Germany were greatly influenced by the consequences of emancipation in that country: The Jews there, freed from many discriminatory restrictions, had moved out of their previously confined economic range. But they were not completely free and some of those who wanted to enter certain occupations adopted the option of conversion to Christianity in order to do so. Moreover, emancipation had broadened the Jews' horizons and many began to question old religious ideas and associations. Thus the German-Jewish immigrants to Britain included, in addition to those who were members of Jewish congregations, those who were not, including some who formally embraced Christianity and others who became Unitarians.[6]

Features of the Middle Class

Despite the ambiguity of the term, 'middle class' can be used for those Jews who were not in paid employment. They can be further sub-divided into lower middle class—the shopkeepers and small-scale manufacturers—and the upper middle class, which included the financiers and the professionals. Among the latter were those to whom the title of gentry can properly be applied, for whom 'breeding rather than wealth was the admission to their tiny, closed circle',[7] or who acquired the culture of the leisured classes. When Samuel Marcus Gollancz applied in the 1850s for a post in the Hambro' Synagogue in the City (the second oldest Ashkenazi synagogue in London), he discovered 'that there is very little done during the summer months, as most people are in the country. Therefore it was impossible to receive a reply to my application, as the Wardens and the greater part of the congregation were away from home'.[8]

An approximate idea of the development of the more affluent part of the middle class is obtained from two indices: the type of education their children received, and the district of residence. Some children had private tutors but others were sent to private schools, including Jewish boarding-schools. The best known, attended by the subjects of many biographies and obituaries, was founded by Hyman Hurwitz around 1800 in Highgate, north London, was taken over by Leopold Neumegen in the 1820s, moved to Kew in south London in the 1840s and closed in the 1870s.[9] Day schools too were founded. One was attached to the newly-founded Jews' College—'for the sons of our middle ranks' as the Chief Rabbi put it—which lasted from 1855 to 1879; another in central London, the 'Jewish Middle Class School', also closed before the end of the century.[10] Similarly the Manchester Classical and Commercial Schools came into existence consciously to cater for the needs of middle-class children. The *Jewish Chronicle* commented that it had arisen 'to provide a special Jewish education for the rising generation among the more fortunate Israelites'.[11]

Others went to those non-Jewish day schools which were not restricted by their charters to the admission of Christians. From the earliest years of the century a few went to the Manchester Grammar School.[12] In the early 1830s about twenty boys a year were attending the new University College School (in whose foundation I. L. Goldsmid had played a part and which eschewed religious tests). The City of London School, founded in 1837, also admitted Jewish boys: in 1851 out of a roll of 600, 17 were Jews, one of them being school captain.[13]

These were for boys. The education of Victorian girls was notoriously neglected; in the middle of the century the large demand for Jewish governesses could not be met 'owing to the paucity of educated Jewish girls'.[14] But there was a private Jewish girls' school for a few years in the 1850s in Manchester,[15] and towards the end of the period, in 1873, the first institution of the Girls' Public Day School Company (later Trust) included one Jewish pupil.[16]

Although some parents consciously chose to send their children to day schools so that they should not be separated from their family and Jewish environment,[17] others went to non-Jewish boarding-schools. At some, Jewish Houses were established later in the century and it became possible for a few to combine a conventional upper-class English education with the maintenance of a Jewish upbringing. One was Polack's House at Clifton starting in 1878, or, as a less integral part of Harrow School, the private dwelling of the Reverend Joseph Chotzner which accommodated Jewish boys between 1880 and 1892. Up to 1880 the school limited the number of Jewish boys to six, thereafter it was twelve. In the dozen years of Chotzner's residence forty to fifty entered the school.[18] There is a splendid summary of the consequences of these various

changes in the posthumous biography of Robert Henriques. He was born, we
read, in 1905, 'into one of the oldest Jewish families in England. Like many of
his ancestors for the preceding four or five generations, he entered the Regular
Army at the conclusion of his education at Rugby School and New College,
Oxford'.[19] But there were not many like that.

A second indication of middle-class status was growing numbers living in
better-off districts. The opening of Saul Myers's Dining Rooms at Cornhill in
1843 testified 'to the development in London of a commuter class of Jewish
businessmen who had settled in the suburbs but travelled daily into the City to
work and insisted on observance of the dietary laws'.[20] No doubt Sophia
Leon's restaurant at Blackfriars in Manchester performed the same function.[21]
The move to the inner suburbs began mainly in the 1830s and 1840s, made
possible by the setting out of new housing estates and by the development of
public transport, especially the horse bus. The outward movement can be
readily traced. In London, at first, the preferred districts were Bloomsbury to the
west and Canonbury and Islington to the north. Later, in the 1860s and 1870s
they were Bayswater to the west and Highbury and Hackney to the north.[22] In
Manchester they went to Cheetham Hill and then to Chorlton-on-Medlock.[23]
In Glasgow the well-off lived in Garnethill.[24]

As we shall see in chapter 7, these suburbs were not exclusively for the
well-off: they contained the poor as well. This is important if we wish to gain
some idea of the size of the middle class. Table 4 summarises the findings of
Joseph Jacobs, who tried to establish the social and economic structure of the
Jews of London at about 1880. He was well aware of the errors and uncertainties in his work but thought that those in the upper groups (A and B)
approximated to the membership of synagogues in the wealthy districts. He
probably over-estimated the numbers. As they stand, his figures suggest that
one-half of London Jewry was middle class. More reliable are the statistics for
Manchester, which was rapidly becoming the main provincial settlement; they
are based on the occupations of people identified by their names as Jews in the
Population Census. The 1871 Census gives 1,170 Jews who were in gainful
employment (193 of them being women). At least 300 were in middle-class
occupations: the number is uncertain because the Census did not always
distinguish between employer and employed.[25] There may have been perhaps
between a quarter and a third of Manchester Jews who can reasonably be called
middle class.

Anglo-Jewry contained a larger proportion of middle-class people than did
the general population, although they formed only a minor part of the total
middle class. In this and the next chapter we examine their occupations to see if
any discernible patterns can be established. This 'functional' analysis suffers
from an absence of clear lines of demarcation between different types of
activity. The Population Census recognised this by not always distinguishing
between employer and employed in a number of economic pursuits. Sometimes
the same entrepreneur would be engaged in both manufacture and selling. But

these matters do not detract from the usefulness of the approach, and when overlap occurs it can be identified.

The Staple Industries

Britain's nineteenth-century pre-eminence was based on coal, steam-power (including railways), engineering, textiles, iron and steel, and shipbuilding. In these industries' formative years in the eighteenth century the Jews played no part, and Jewish industry was confined to the output of craftsmen-shopkeepers. The Jews responded only in part as the Dissenters had done; like the Jews they had been unable to participate fully in society and they used their energies 'towards labouring in their vocations of industry and trade. Non-conformist iron-masters, bankers, brewers and mill-owners repaid their exclusion from university, local government, army and navy, parliament and Cabinet by practical education and economic exertion'.[26] The Jews' 'economic exertion' had been in the City and in trade rather than in industry. Perhaps their neglect of early industrial development was a consequence of the way industry developed. The early industrialists seem to have entered the new industries through some economic connections. The exploitation of coal, for example, depended on the legal fact that land-owners owned the minerals under the soil. It was not at all uncommon for them to be involved directly in working their coal seams, but more usually they leased the right to do so. The lessees came from many backgrounds but especially from agriculture, the iron industry, and later from within the coal industry, mining engineers and colliery managers.[27]

Jews were not land-owners, neither were they among the early iron-masters, many of whom came into iron manufacture from their previous interests as users of iron, as craftsmen or as iron merchants.[28] Textile manufacturers tended to have been craftsmen in that industry of merchant-manufacturers, the capitalists of the domestic system.[29] Again, Jews had not been part of the putting-out system: they had not been settled in the provinces long enough to have become part of it.

Yet once industrialisation got rapidly under way in the nineteenth century, some Jews became entrepreneurs in the staple industries. David Jonassohn (1794–1859), a merchant in the north-east from the 1820s, sank Usworth Colliery in County Durham along, it seems, with a Jewish mining engineer. Later Saul Isaac (1823–1902)—the first Jewish Conservative M.P.—took a lease of Clifton Colliery in Nottinghamshire soon after it was opened in 1870 during a great colliery boom, and Colonel Joseph Joel Ellis (1807–85) was the owner (i.e., lessee) of a colliery and also chairman of the Ellistown Brick and Pipe Company in Leicestershire.[30] The first Rothschild to settle in England, Nathan Mayer (1777–1836) was a leading promoter of two companies, formed in the boom of 1824–25, for working mines and slate quarries in North Wales.[31] One of the very few Sephardim engaged in industry was J. D. Samuda

(1813–85), an engineer and naval architect, involved also in a short-lived attempt to build railways on the 'atmospheric' principle. His main activity was as a Thames shipbuilder, at one time in the 1860s employing several thousand men.[32]

Other industrialists were of Jewish origin and are worth mentioning even though they are on the peripheries of our story. A major shipbuilder was Gustave Edward Wolff, born in 1834 in Hamburg, both of whose parents were baptised. Part of his education was at Liverpool where his uncle, G. C. Schwabe, a merchant, lived. He served an apprenticeship with the famous engineering firm of Joseph Whitworth, after working as a draughtsman. Wolff became a partner of E. J. Harland in 1858 to form the Belfast shipbuilding firm of Harland and Wolff. The arrangement was effected by his uncle, who agreed to lend Harland £5,000 provided his nephew was taken into partnership. It has been suggested that Schwabe, a considerable merchant in Liverpool, was instrumental in getting orders for the shipbuilding company. Wolff had nothing to do with the Jewish community, and in the 1890s withdrew from industry to concentrate on his public work as a Member of Parliament.[33]

Sir Alfred Yarrow had a yard on the Thames which was transferred to the Clyde in 1906 (Samuda's had closed on the death of its owner). Martin Samuelson's of Hull built at least sixty-six ships between 1853 and 1866, when it was sold to the Humber Iron Works Co. Ltd. His brother, Sir Bernhard (1820–1905), was much better known. He was a major steel manufacturer in the north-east and had colliery interests there. Yarrow's father was not Jewish and his parents were married in church; the Samuelsons' father became a Christian early in the nineteenth century; none had any connection with the Jewish community.[34]

In the development of British railways the Jews played a small part, unlike on the Continent where for example the Péreire brothers and the Rothschilds were major contenders in political and financial battles.[35] In Britain the great financial institutions were not needed for the raising of capital and—as with industry generally—there was no comparable intermingling of banking and industry. Some individual Jews were shareholders in railway companies and a handful were directors. The financiers Benjamin, Abraham and Asher Goldsmid were among the proprietors of the first (horse-drawn) public railway of 1801. In the abortive railway promotion boom of 1824–25 four Jews were associated with unsuccessful railway companies: Isaac Lyon Goldsmid and Moses Montefiore were directors of two companies and Edward Goldsmid was an auditor. In connection with his North Wales mineral proposals, Nathan Mayer Rothschild was associated with a projected railway-line in the district. But all came to nothing and there is no evidence that the Rothschilds were engaged later in railway promotion in Britain, a major contrast with the European members of the banking family.

Later, in the 1830s and during the great railway boom of the 1840s, a few more Jewish shareholders appear, as well as a transitory phenomenon of the speculative boom, the 'share-hunters', who applied to companies for letters of allotment which were then sold to prospective shareholders. Among those who promised to take shares or become directors were Isaac Lyon Goldsmid and Moses Asher Goldsmid; Moses Montefiore; David Salomons (one of the very few Jews in joint-stock banking); Zadok Aaron Jessel; and one or two of Jewish origin—John Lewis Ricardo and Leo Schuster. Francis Henry Goldsmid, the first Jew admitted to the Bar, was counsel to one company, and David Mocatta, an architect, designed railway stations. These people were primarily London financiers, but one provincial, Lewin Mozley of Liverpool, was a company director, and Schuster had been a Manchester textile merchant.[36]

Cotton Textiles

The various textile industries were the one part of the basic British industries which did attract Jews both as merchants and manufacturers. Most of them were immigrants and many had been connected with these industries through international trade: often they had been importers of British goods. They began to arrive from about 1800, mainly from Germany, but later on Sephardim came from Mediterranean countries. They were to be found in Manchester and Liverpool (cotton), Bradford (worsted), Dundee and Belfast (linen), and Nottingham (lace). Not all of them remained in the Jewish community and it is not always possible to distinguish them from the numerous non-Jewish immigrants who also came to Britain to engage in the textile trades (one of the better-known being the socialist Friedrich Engels).

Cotton was the major textile industry, growing rapidly in the later eighteenth century, some of the importers in Germany being Jews. Although it was not uncommon for merchant houses to send representatives abroad, the interruption of trade during the Napoleonic Wars provided an important stimulus to the arrival of Continentals in Britain. The one of whom most is known—although many gaps in knowledge remain—is Nathan Mayer Rothschild of Frankfurt.[37] The family traded in English textiles but the father was also the financial agent to the Elector of Hesse-Cassel, the supplier of mercenary troops to Britain. His son came to London in 1798 to gain commercial experience with Levi Barent Cohen (1740–1808), and also with Levi Salomons. In 1799 he moved to Manchester and his textile business remained in existence until 1811, although he opened a permanent London office in 1808, two years after he married Hannah Cohen, the daughter of Levi Barent Cohen. This London move reflected his growing interest in finance and increasing concentration on government loan contracting. It was in these activities that he and his four brothers who settled in important Continental centres made their name and fortune, but his textile episode was a significant preliminary. He was not a manufacturer, but obtained cloth, for which he paid cash, from a variety of small spinners, going as far afield as Nottingham, Leeds and Glasgow. He sent the cloth out for printing and sold it direct to Continental buyers, thus by-passing the traditional fairs. He sold at three months' credit and some of the necessary funds to finance this were obtained from London Jews who discounted his bills, and from Continental connections. This supply of capital was an essential feature of his method of low-cost buying, high turnover and low profit margins.

At the time Rothschild was leaving the textile trade, other Germans were arriving as a consequence of the French occupation of Hamburg and Frankfurt and of the French blockade.[38] When their imported English goods were confiscated during the Hamburg occupation, part of the Schuster family came to Britain,[39] and so did a number of Germans, many of them non-Jewish who, like Rothschild, eventually moved into finance. Among those who remained in the Jewish community was Solomon Levi Behrens who settled in Manchester in 1814 (he was one of the five German merchants who settled in the city between the collapse of the blockade in 1812 and 1814, of whom three were of Jewish descent).[40]

As Manchester became the 'international emporium for cotton goods', hundreds of warehouses came into existence and the town attracted manufacturers from the provinces, warehousemen from London and merchants from overseas. Among the 'German, Dutch, Swiss, French and Italian merchants' who came to Manchester after the Napoleonic Wars followed by 'Greeks, Spaniards, Portugese, Russians' and others were a number of Jews.[41] For example, in the boom years of 1834 to 1837, "the number of foreign export firms' in Manchester rose from 78 to 101, of which 75 were German. Other firms came from London. As many as thirteen of the newcomers were Jews, five coming from London and eight from Germany.[42]

The general attractiveness of Manchester as the centre of the world-wide market in cotton goods is one explanation for the concentration there of foreign merchants. In the middle years of the century there was a further one, with the development of more distant and therefore riskier markets. The trade expanded slowly because British exporters were not keen to handle it. 'Credit crises, the difficulties of distant trades, the quest for security in a more unstable commercial and financial climate persuaded small men to abandon the more remote foreign markets'. With a few exceptions, 'the characteristic pattern for the thirties, forties and fifties was for trade, still very largely in cotton manufactures, to be absorbed by other nationalities'. Among these distant markets—which included Latin America and China—were those areas of the Ottoman Empire, where 'trade in British cotton manufactures was handled almost exclusively by Levantines—by Greek, Armenian, or Jewish houses, acting often through their own nationality in Manchester'.[43] Thus there was in the Lancashire city a group of Sephardi Jews 'from North Africa, Turkey, and the Levant', who formed a permanent congregation in 1872 after a decade of using rented rooms for services.[44]

The Jews in the cotton industry were mainly, but not entirely, export merchants, and some went into manufacturing. One of the first to do so was

Aaron Jacobs, in 1808, as a manufacturer of fustians, by 1811 owning a factory. He had been a slop-seller, retailing cheap ready-made clothing.[45] Philip Lucas and Henry Micholls, who set up in partnership in 1834, were cotton-spinners as well as merchants. (Micholls was the son of a Yarmouth watch-maker and had come from a family which had passed 'through the classic stages of country hawking and provincial shopkeeping'.)[46] Solomon Levi Behrens, the 1814 immigrant, bought a spinning and weaving mill at Catteral near Garstang in 1841. By that time he had expanded into merchant banking in Bradford, Leeds and Glasgow.[47] At the time of the 1851 Census nine Jews were engaged in some form of textile manufacture, but only two in 1861 and four in 1871. (These figures do not include those of Jewish origin who were no longer part of the community.)[48]

Liverpool too had its Jews in various aspects of the cotton trade although not as cotton brokers, perhaps because of the way these were recruited. They had been men who, in most cases, had been cotton manufacturers. 'The market required (inter alia) . . . an understanding of the specific technical requirements of the industrial hinterland. It is, therefore, scarcely surprising that most of the early cotton brokers of any importance migrated to Liverpool from Manchester and from the manufacturing districts'. In 1800 five of the nine firms in existence had been founded by men previously engaged in cotton manufacture; four decades later eighty of the ninety extant firms could trace their descent 'through successive generations of apprenticeship' from the original nine.[49] Only one Jewish firm, Bahr, Behrend, shipbrokers, seems to have been of any importance in this aspect of the trade of Liverpool.[50]

Other Textiles

The immigrant Jews in other textile industries came to Britain for similar reasons. Some had been importers on the Continent and came to Britain in order to export, overseas trade having become specialised in the hands of intermediary merchants (the home trade was often supplied directly by the manufacturers). The move to England provided the benefits of both quality control and knowledge of price determination. As with cotton, some of them became manufacturers. Jacob Behrens, nephew of S. L. Behrens of Manchester, was the eldest son of Nathan Behrens, a Hamburg importer of woollen and cotton goods, and established a factory and warehouse in Leeds in the 1830s, in 1838 transferring to Bradford. (His firm also exported cotton cloth from Manchester, this trade being conducted by his brother Louis.)

Jacob Behrens's move to England has been explained in these terms:

> The commission merchant on the spot in England, buying for foreign customers, with expert knowledge and at market prices, had obvious advantages over the stock-holding merchant on the continent who . . . far from knowlege and control of his source of supply, bought from one or two manufacturers at whatever rates they chose to fix.[51]

The concentration of the worsted industry in Bradford especially from 1830 onwards resulted in a rapid expansion of production and many merchants were drawn to the town. By 1861 out of 157 merchants 65 (more than 40 per cent) had foreign names. Many were German and they settled in an area which, E. M. Sigsworth recorded in 1958, 'today forms a police beat known officially as "Germany" '.[52] Among them were Jews who formed their own (Reform) congregation, and included such families as the Rothensteins whose assimilated descendants became better known in the world of art.[53]

Similarly we find a small concentration of Jews in the Nottingham lace industry. From about 1830 a stream of immigrants, 'mostly German-Jewish', began to arrive 'like so many salmon pursuing a river to its source'.[54] Some of them represented houses such as R. D. Warburg, which were already established in London and other towns in Britain. Others came from Hamburg, Frankfurt and elsewhere as agents of German firms. They included Lewis Heymann (1802–69), who founded the firm of Heymann and Alexander, lace manufacturers—pioneers in the making of lace curtains—and lace-merchants. Edward Goldschmidt (1827–1903), unlike the others, began as a wholesale stationer in the 1850s soon after his arrival in the town. Later he became an importer of silk and a silk-throwster. These westernised, middle-class Germans tended very quickly to become active in local affairs. Goldschmidt, for example, was a member of the local council from the 1870s, and chairman of its finance committee for twelve years. He was instrumental in piloting the University of Nottingham settlement through the local council. He was also chairman of the Nottingham Brewing Company.[55]

There is a comparable background to the emergence of German Jews in the linen industry in Dundee and Northern Ireland. From early in the nineteenth century a number of German firms, some of them Jewish, mainly from Hamburg, sent their representatives to Dundee, where they developed into independent merchants. The best known was Daniel Joseph Jaffé, who transferred his linen business from Hamburg to Dundee in 1845, but there were perhaps a dozen Jewish firms in Dundee. Jaffé's head office moved to Belfast in 1851 and the two brothers Daniel Joseph and Isaac founded Jaffé Brothers there. They engaged in the manufacture of many types of linen goods.[56]

Chemicals

German immigrants settling in the north-west in the 1860s and 1870s were also the main Jewish contributors to the chemical industry. Ludwig Mond (1839–1909) arrived in England from Cassel in 1862 and with John T. Brunner established a works at Winnington, Cheshire, for the production of soda using a process patented by Mond, a chemist. Brunner, Mond and Co., was one of the constituent firms of Imperial Chemical Industries, formed in 1926.[57] Ivan Levinstein (1845–1916) established a plant at Blackley in 1865 for the production of sulphuric acid and naphthalene. Dr Charles Dreyfus, from Alsace, arrived in England in 1869 at the age of twenty-one. A chemist, like Mond, he founded the Clayton Aniline Dye Company.[58] Another chemist engaged in the development of dyes was British-born Raphael Meldola (1849–1915), the grandson of a Sephardi rabbi. He discovered several new dyes, was a Fellow of the Royal Society, and Professor of Chemistry at Finsbury Technical College.[59]

Two contrasting interpretations can be made of this information about Jewish entrepreneurs in the basic industries. Not many, it could be said, were engaged in production as distinct from marketing the output, and one line of approach would be to inquire why so few were producers. But, equally, such an inquiry could be regarded as pointless: the relatively small number of Jews who owned collieries or textile factories still amounted to a more than proportionate group, for the Jews were a very tiny section of the total population. If there had been none at all, their absence would bear investigation, as would a very large number of them, but neither is the case. Even so, most Jewish masters were in the consumer goods industries, the majority of them on a very small scale, making umbrellas, sticks, pens and the like. But two industries of importance can be identified: tobacco manufacture was perhaps the single most important Jewish trade in London before 1880; the various clothing industries (including footwear and hats) developed rather more slowly as Jewish manufacturing activities.

Tobacco

The Jewish tobacco manufacturers tended to concentrate on the making of cigars and were located mostly in east London, although a few were found elsewhere. 'The Peninsular War brought in the cigar',[60] and in the 1820s duties on imported tobacco were reduced. As early as that decade Jewish boys were being apprenticed to the industry, and reference to Jews, both as employers and employed, become more frequent from the 1840s. The firm of Godfrey Phillips began in the 1840s, as did the immigrant family business of Salmon & Gluckstein who opened a factory in Soho and moved to Whitechapel in the following decade.[61] A. and H. Isaacs was established first in Commercial Street, Shoreditch, before moving to the City Road and were instrumental in popularising British-made cigars, introducing two well-known brands, 'M.P.' and 'Victoria Reina'.[62] By the late 1880s it was reported of cigar-making that 'this trade, as far as the masters in East London are concerned, is entirely in the hands of the Jewish community'.[63] However, there was no comparable concentration in the other main centres of the tobacco industry, at the seaports of Liverpool, Glasgow and Bristol. In total the Jewish manufacturers of east London were a small section of the total number of 570 licensed manufacturers throughout the country.[64] It seems it was a not very profitable industry. Capital requirements were low and entry was easy, with the resultant competition reducing profit margins. It was for this reason that the great Bristol firm of

Wills did not take up cigar manufacture until later on, and that Jews were beginning to enter the cigarette industry.[65]

Footwear and Clothing

The industries which have been described so far, although not necessarily requiring large amounts of capital, were often factory-organised. In other industries a great variety of organisation existed often side by side: small workshops where goods were made for retailers or wholesalers; outworking, where goods were made in the worker's home; goods made on the premises of retail shops, or in factories. In some industries the long-term trend was from small-scale to large-scale units, but this was not the case with clothing, where the introduction of machinery enabled outworking to spread. In the production and sale of some consumer goods there was much overlap, one enterprise performing both functions; for convenience they will be separated here, manufacturing being examined here, distribution in the next chapter.

The footwear industry exhibited various kinds of organisation, not least the shopkeeper-craftsmen who produced goods for the wealthier market. One such was a shoe-maker in the West End who advertised in the *Jewish Chronicle*:

E. A. Solomon, Ladies', Gentlemen's and Children's BOOT and SHOE MANUFACTURER, 50 Mortimer-street, Regent-street, respectfully solicits the patronage of the Jewish Public. All boots and shoes made by E. A. S. are warranted of superior quality, at extraordinarily low prices. Families waited upon.[66]

It is very likely that some of those provincial Jews who are described as tailors, cap-makers and boot- and shoe-makers (for example) were producing in the same sector.[67]

In the 1860s a shoe-maker explained to a parliamentary commission that having begun work with a journeyman when he was twelve, 'afterwards I was at a Polish Jew's: I was seventeen then, he had three men besides his own family'.[68] Presumably this was a workshop supplying a retailer or a wholesaler. It was a much smaller enterprise than the retail business of David Lewis of Liverpool, who opened a shop in 1856 to sell goods produced in his own workshop, later to extend to the making of boots and shoes.[69] And it was at the other end of the scale from the specifically shoe-manufacturing concern of Philip Haldinstein (1820–1901) at Norwich, a footwear centre. He was born in Prussia and settled in Norwich, eventually becoming a partner in the old-established Jewish firm of shoe-makers, Soman and Son; he married the owner's daughter in 1846. The partnership was dissolved in 1853 and his own firm, Philip Haldinstein and Sons, shoe-manufacturers and leather-merchants, later opened a London branch.[70]

Abraham Flatau (born 1807) and his brother Woolf were partners in a shoe-making firm which probably started in the 1820s, at a time when shoes were made by outworkers. They opened a factory later on at Ropemaker Street, Finsbury, and claimed to have installed the first machine in the industry—the Blake sole sewer—in 1859. It expanded sufficiently for the company to be a large exporter, producing three-quarters of the women's shoes imported into Australia.[71]

The other main consumer-goods industry with which Jews were connected was clothing. The significant developments in the early nineteenth century were changes in method and organisation introduced to meet the demand for cheap clothing from the working and lower middle classes. Moreover, cheap clothing was demanded by the government for its employees and for convicts. The production of large quantities of cheap clothes meant the sub-division of work. Skilled cutters were required, but sewing could be done by unskilled workers in their own homes or in workshops.[72] Mass sales, low profit margins, and advertising often in doggerel verse were some of the main features. The pressure to keep costs down was exacerbated by the actions of the Poor Law authorities who, being responsible for providing work for the able-bodied poor, accepted contracts for making clothing at extremely low prices. In the great outcry about sweating in the 1840s which led for example to Thomas Hood's poem 'The Song of the Shirt', *The Times* argued that it was 'the New Poor Law, and that alone, has brought this state of things to pass' and reported the case of a girl inmate of a workhouse who made a shirt for one farthing. It was the Poor Law authorities in Stepney and Portsmouth, it said, which were 'first exposed as admitting of this ruinous and wicked practice and as paying wages for the Jew slopsellers out of the pockets of the ratepayers'.[73] Henry Mayhew, writing at the end of the decade, noted that

> small as are the earnings of those who depend for their living upon the manufacture of ready-made clothes for the wholesale warehouses of the Minories and the adjoining places, still the incomings of those who manufacture the clothes of our soldiers and sailors, Government, railway-police, and custom-house officers, are even less calculated to support life.[74]

One consequence, for labour, was the opposition of the journeymen tailors, for although this was an expanding market they could not avoid experiencing the downward pressure on wages and the clear downgrading of their skill. The union in London, although not very successful in the eighteenth century, had been at its peak in the early nineteenth, but while as yet unorganised tailors in Manchester won a battle in 1833, both there and in London in 1834—in the year of high general union activity followed by the disaster symbolised by the Tolpuddle Martyrs' episode—the tailors lost in bitter disputes. Employers thereafter did not have to bother much with labour problems, the unskilled women outworkers being notoriously unorganisable.[75]

Low pay was one feature of the industry, for costs were kept low to maintain low prices. Another was the fact that the main skills required by the entre-preneurs were buying the cloth, organising the distribution and collection of the clothes, and selling, rather than the skill of tailoring or supervising labour (the work was largely outwork). Many who entered the trade came from slop-selling rather than from master-tailoring. And selling involved the attraction of customers by advertising and by the opening of 'show shops'. Mayhew described 'the flashing palace of the grasping tradesman. Every article in the window is ticketed—the prices cut down *to the quick*—books of crude, bald, verses are thrust in your hands, or thrown into your carriage window—the panels of every omnibus are plastered with showy placards, telling you how Messrs. . . . defy competition'.[76]

These were the most significant changes in the clothing industry in the early part of the nineteenth century, the mass production of cheap clothing pre-dating the introduction of the sewing-machine, probably beginning in the 1820s. Many individuals were engaged in it, the great majority being non-Jewish: none of the sixty-two masters who joined together in Manchester in 1834 to fight the tailors' union was Jewish;[77] and in 1843 only three were Jewish among some forty London firms, including shirt manufacturers.[78] Heny Mayhew's special targets for attack included the non-Jewish firm of H. J. & D. Nicoll in the West End, but when he referred to the Jews among the clothing firms, 'his rhetoric became xenophobic and anti-semitic'.[79] In the 1830s and 1840s the two best-known clothing companies were Jewish and were singled out for special obloquy. They were E. Moses & Son, which began in London, and Hyam Brothers, of an Ipswich family.[80] Coincidentally both set up in 1832: Moses as a slop-seller at 137 Ratcliff Highway, near the docks, later moving to 154–7 Minories and 83–6 Aldgate in the City. Benjamin Hyam, aged twenty-two, arrived in Manchester in the same year. Both probably began new methods some time in the first half of the 1830s, and others also moved from slop-selling into tailoring. In 1832 no Jews were listed among the 124 tailors and drapers in Manchester, but there were 15 Jews among the 37 clothes dealers (slop-sellers). By 1836 seven of these had become tailors (as well as three others living near by: one in Warrington, one in Preston and one in Stockport).[81]

The chronology of events is unclear. Moses claimed in an 1860 pamphlet, *The Growth of an Important Branch of British Industry*, that 'ours was the first House in London, or we may say in the world, that established the system of New Clothing Ready-Made'. But it is pointless to try to establish which individual may have been the first to produce either bespoke or ready-made clothing on a mass scale. Even Hyam may not have been the first Jew in Manchester to have been in the trade: during the strike of 1833 several Jewish employers were attacked—and presumably they were producing cheap clothing—but Hyam is not mentioned as a producer until 1836. While many firms, Jewish and non-Jewish, were involved, there is no doubt that within a few years Moses and Hyam had expanded and were probably the biggest firms in the new industry. Hyam, it is said, 'created modern mass tailoring in Manchester';[82] by 1841 he was able to move his premises in Manchester, the new one being entitled the Pantechnethica which had four branches at Birmingham, Bristol, Colchester and Bury St Edmunds; in 1851 there were thirteen, three in the West End of London. The firm was by then moving into a higher class of trade.[83]

Both Moses and Hyam came into the public eye in the 1840s. In 1843 the newspapers reported the case of a poor needlewoman, reduced to pawning the articles she had been given to make at home. *The Times* wrote angrily of 'the white slaves of England' who worked long hours and seldom earned as much as six shillings a week. (The lawsuit was brought by a woman who had stood surety for the sum of £2: it was the practice for the employer to demand some form of security.) An editorial expressed the opinion that 'in treating with Jews accurate calculations are advisable' and 'the very Jews are revenging on the poor of a professedly Christian country the wrongs which their forefathers sustained at the hands of ours'.[84] Henry Moses replied, making two points. He asserted that his firm's payments for work were higher than in many other houses and that the firm's profits were only 5 to 7 per cent.[85] Hyam was somewhat less castigated but the Chartist paper, the *Northern Star*, reported in 1844 a meeting to organise tailors in Colchester 'who eke out a miserable subsistence at slop work for the "respectable" Messrs Hyam & Co.', then the largest firm in the town and with depots elsewhere in the country. The firm had 1,500 workers on its books, two-thirds of them being women.[86] Plainly in this early part of the history Jewish firms employed non-Jewish labour (although Moses employed Jews as managers). Apparent too is the fact that the Jewish employers were natives, unlike later in the century when new immigrants were regarded as the sweaters. By then the old image had gone from Moses and Hyam. They had moved away from the cheap trade, and changed their names from Moses to Marsden and from Hyam to Halford.

Before then they had become very well known indeed, and they featured, for example, in a descriptive account of the British economy, published in the late 1850s:

> What stranger has passed through any part of Great Britain that has not been introduced to the firm of Moses and Son? Or who has not scanned the seemingly Cabalistic Pantechnethica on the blank walls of our town. The three brothers Hyam, and the father and son Moses, have long been identified with the ready-made clothes business of the Kingdom. Whether this comparatively modern trade has been of real service to the community or not; we cannot say. One thing is certain, the public has enabled them to obtain important social positions. A good deal is said about the low standard of wages this class of men pay for their labour; but if the public will have cheap garments, we hold that they are equally as much to blame in the matter as the manufacturers.[87]

The close, continuing association between Jews and the clothing industry got under way with the mass immigration of east European Jews, later in the century. But it began with the small-scale immigration of the 1840s and 1850s, and since production was often carried out in small workshops the immigrants provided their own masters. This was the case of the cap-makers of Manchester for example at mid-century and also the Manchester waterproof clothing industry. Jewish immigrants such as Philip Frankenstein entered this industry in the 1850s, a generation after Charles MacIntosh had started it there, in the 1820s.[88] And Leeds, which was to become the centre of the wholesale clothing industry, had little to show before the 1870s. In the 1850s the non-Jewish firm of John Barran had sub-contracted some work to Herman Friend, and David Lubelski and Jacob Woolfe became important wholesale clothiers. But many of the firms there in the 1870s, a number of which had migrated there from other British cities, were not Jewish. In general the distinction between the English and Jewish sections of the Leeds industry—the one in large factories the other in workshops—was present before the mass immigration emphasised and confirmed it.[89]

6

Trade, Finance and the Professions, 1800–80

Retail Distribution

The Jews who were engaged in retail trade were occupied in all the four categories that existed: shopkeepers who were pure sellers, obtaining their products from manufacturers, growers or wholesalers; those who sold goods made on their own premises; those who sold from stalls at the market halls especially in the growing industrial towns; and the pedlars and hawkers. The first two—those operating from fixed shops—catered for the needs of the well-off, whereas the markets and street-sellers continued to supply the working class.[1] But it was a changing pattern: more shops were being opened and patronised by the working class, for example in the purchase of clothes, as we have seen, resulting in a decline in the number of Jewish old-clothesmen. More goods were being made in factories and workshops and less frequently at retail premises. And while the typical unit was the single small shop operated by the owner, some chain stores and department stores were coming into existence.

The characteristic Jewish shopkeeping trades were, as before, in watch-making, jewellery and associated goods and, as the clothing industry became transformed, in that business too. As many as fifty of the men married at Hull between 1838 and 1870 were jewellers and twenty-one were tailors, and the outstanding lay leaders were a silversmith and a jeweller.[2] The outstanding Jew in Southampton—successively senior bailiff, returning officer and sheriff—was Abraham Abraham, a jeweller and silversmith.[3] From the Liverpool watch-making firm of Moses and Lewis Samuel, founded in the 1820s, is descended the watch and jewellery concern of H. Samuel.[4] The small and declining Jewish community of Cheltenham contained two jewellers, a watch-maker and, in the clothing trades, a boot- and shoe-maker and a furrier.[5] In Manchester, as early as 1841, one-half of the Jewish shopkeepers (forty-four out of eighty-eight) were sellers of clothing of one kind or another; twenty-six sold jewellery and hardware, and another nine sold stationery. These eighty-eight shopkeepers formed about one-third of all the Manchester Jews who were in gainful employment.[6]

In London the picture was similar, but there was one important difference. In the provinces the selling of food by Jews was not an important activity. Towards the end of the period, in 1871, Manchester it is true mustered twenty-four Jewish shops selling foodstuffs of various kinds (inclusive of seven boarding-houses) as well as twelve tobacconists.[7] But elsewhere in the provinces they were few. In Brighton the occupations of spouses and their parents during the period 1838 to 1901 were, as against thirty-three jewellers and silversmiths, fourteen clothiers and outfitters (and ten tailors and tailoresses who may have been employees, self-employed or retailers), only three in the food trade—a baker, a fish-merchant and a fruiterer (together with two tobacconists).[8] Similarly of the estimated 750 Jews in Birmingham in 1851 only 4 sold food (a wine-merchant, a confectioner, a provision dealer and a fishmonger), and 3 were in the tobacco trade.[9]

In view of Jewish dietary requirements the lack of Jewish food shops—especially butchers—is surprising, but their absence may have reflected the smallness of many provincial communities. Manchester had a kosher restaurant and lodging-house as early as 1819 but, it seems, no kosher butcher shop until the 1850s.[10] London, with its large Jewish population, possessed food shops for the community's religious needs, but a major speciality—dating from the previous century and continuing to the present day—was the sale of fruit. Earlier there had been the 'lemon-men' and in the early years of the nineteenth century itinerant Moroccan rhubarb-sellers were familiar to the public. So was the street-selling of cherries and oranges. It was reported in the 1830s that Kentish cherries were brought to London on Sunday mornings and were purchased that day by Jews who hawked them round the streets. They did not sell peas and potatoes, for these were carried to London on Saturdays and for religious reasons the Jews could not buy them for re-sale on that day.[11] Similarly oranges were sold by Jews: 'orange-boys' figure among the Jewish convicts who were transported to Australia.[12] Henry Mayhew, writing at mid-century, described the Jewish fruit-sellers and argued that the Irish were taking over the street sale of oranges by being able to undercut the Jews, their standard of living being even lower.[13] But the continuing connection between young Jews and the fruit trade was remarked on in a parliamentary inquiry of 1847 into Sunday trading, in the course of evidence given by Henry F. Isaac. With his brother, he was proprietor of Phils Buildings, Houndsditch, a general market used by stall-holders for the sale of many types of goods.[14] He described the self-help societies,

formed principally by Jewish youths, who go round among the subscribers, and some subscribe 1*d.* a week, some 2*d.*, some 3*d.*, and some 1*s.*, according to their own feelings; and those are institutions originating with youths, and they then give persons recommended to them a certain sum of money in goods as stock to commence business with.

He was asked, 'You do in fact, or the youths of your persuasion, rather than they should be idle, give them a stock in trade of fruit?' Isaac agreed that 'they have no occasion to be idle; there is no difficulty in a Jew boy getting a stock in trade; 18s. is enough to start him in trade'.[15]

Duke's Place, the site of the Great Synagogue in London, was a street of Jewish householders which, in Mayhew's time, had an orange, lemon and nut market. His description of the street provides a useful glimpse into certain aspects of Jewish business life at that period. 'Almost every shop', he wrote, 'has a Scripture name over it, and even the public houses are of the Hebrew faith'. He explained that these had a specialised clientele, 'appealing to the followers of those trades which most abound with Jews'. There was the 'Jewellers' Arms', used by jewellers on Sunday mornings 'to exchange trinkets and barter among themselves'; the 'Fishmongers' Arms' was 'the resort of vendors of fried soles', and concerts were held in the evenings whose performers and audience were Jews. A third meeting-place was 'Benjamin's Coffee House', used by old-clothesmen. (The proprietors of these three places were also licensed to make cigars.)[16] Once again we see jewellery, food and clothes as Jewish trades.

Thirty years later, around 1880, they were still the major types of Jewish retail trade in London, according to Joseph Jacobs, who tried to calculate the total number of trades. He provided two different figures, one of them, of 2,500, given in Table 4, being little more than a guess. The other he obtained from *Kelly's Post Office Directory* of 1883 by the identification of 'Jewish' names: he was aware of the dangers of this method but tried to allow for them. Using this approach he obtained 1,161 'tradesmen' with Jewish names.[17] The true number was probably more than that, even if he included some non-Jews in his list. He omitted any names 'which are at all doubtful, preferring to err on the side of omission'. Perhaps there were 1,500 of them. His 1,161 tradesmen operated in 115 different trades, but the three broad groups were still dominant. There were 369 in food (including tobacco), 270 in clothing and 111 watch-makers, jewellers and silversmiths. Although tailors provided the biggest single category, they formed only 6 per cent of the total number of tailors in the *Directory*, while the fruiterers comprised as many as 9 per cent. (Pawnbroking, so often considered a specifically Jewish trade, provided only sixteen Jewish names, less than 2 per cent of the total. But doubtless some at least of the watch-makers and jewellers were in the money-lending business.)

Jacobs separately recorded the wholesalers, finding forty-four in footwear and thirty in the fur trade, and perhaps the sixty furniture-brokers were in this line of business. It may be, of course, that some of the tradesmen mentioned earlier were wholesalers; it was not unusual for some shops to sell both to the general public and to other shops. The most important Jewish name in wholesaling was that of Faudel-Phillips and Sons; the family provided two Lord Mayors of London.[18]

Three final points need to be made. The first concerns the process by which this trading group was created, and in particular whether it was recruited from the street-traders. It is easy enough to find examples of pedlars and street-traders who took up retailing from a fixed shop, some of them founding long-lasting firms. Moses Moses, an old-clothesman, leased two small shops in Covent Garden, at first dealing in the same articles and in misfits. Eventually—much later—it changed to making clothes and went into the clothes-hire business under the name of Moss Brothers.[19] However, most of the pedlars are unknown: of the forty-six who appear in the Manchester Census of 1841, only six eventually became shopkeepers in the town.[20] A move from hawking might imply a decline in the numbers of Jews engaged in the street trades. Mayhew certainly thought this was happening, but this simple transfer into retailing accompanied by a fall in the itinerant trades did not necessarily occur. The sons of some pedlars went into paid employment, as we shall see; more important was the fact that new immigrants often took up hawking and peddling, including, the east European trade of glazing. Thus in Manchester, for which detailed figures are available, the number of itinerant traders increased at every Census from 1841 to 1871. In the former year 46 were counted, 3 of them being women; thirty years later the number was 197, 4 being women. Over half (107) were itinerant glaziers.[21]

The second point relates to the numbers of Jews in distribution. The approximate estimates given here indicate that they probably formed a higher proportion of the total retailing population than their percentage of the British population, although occupying only a small part of the field. If there were as many as 1,500 in the early 1880s in London, and if we assume there were 86 shops for every 10,000 people, i.e., 37,000 retail outlets, then the Jewish shops amounted to about 4 per cent.[22] Other evidence supports the conclusion that Jews were in a small minority. In the long-continued controversy and agitation about shop-workers' hours little mention is made of Jewish shopkeepers: on the contrary those advocating improvement often castigated the Christian owners for their un-Christian behaviour towards their employees. Jews were of course more involved in the controversy about the Sunday opening of shops, for many of them shut on Saturdays and traded instead on Sundays (or sometimes kept open on both days). But this was a minor part of the discussion.[23]

Third, to what extent were Jews innovators in retail trade? The show shops have been mentioned, and the Jews among them introduced fixed, ticketed prices and sold cheap clothing. But apart from Moses' and Hyam's multiple shops only Lewis in clothing and Salmon & Gluckstein in tobacco opened chains (other Jews had one or two shops). The major food multiples, such as Lipton's, were non-Jewish. Similarly the great names in the department-store business—Debenham, Swan & Edgar, Whiteley, and Kendal, Milne (Manchester)—were not Jewish.[24]

Commerce

In view of Britain's pre-eminence in international trade in the nineteenth century it is not surprising, as we have seen, that Jews were among the merchants attracted to Britain to engage in commerce. In Liverpool, the second port to London, the Jewish community was augmented from about the middle of the century by Jews from London, Germany, France, Holland and America, who were active in the cotton exchange, the Stock Exchange, the wheat and metal markets, and had maritime and shipping interests.[25] The longest-established, Bahr, Behrend, was mainly engaged in shipbroking, but the firm did not specialise on any particular function. It was a steamship agent, it imported tobacco and accepted bills of exchange.[26] Other provincial Jews associated with overseas trade were the Alexanders of Bristol who had a shipping and maritime insurance company, and Joseph Abrahams of the same city, a wine importer. Birmingham was the home of Moore, Phillips and Co., of which Jacob Phillips was the principal, exporting guns and other local products and importing goods from China.[27]

Joseph Jacobs identified in *Kelly's Directory* over 600 London merchants with Jewish names, some with specific titles. As well as general merchants there were specialists by country, e.g., Australian merchants, but more usually by product: Birmingham merchants, cane importers, coconut merchants, sponge importers, sponge merchants.[28] They were probably in a small way of business. The histories of nineteenth-century overseas trade seldom include the names of Jewish firms; but one has received some attention.

It was founded by Marcus Samuel (1798–1870), who imported shells for the decoration of boxes and other ornaments; the trade grew notably with the opening up the Far East. After the founder's death his sons, Marcus and Samuel, concentrated on the trade with Japan, exporting machinery, tools and textiles and importing Japanese silk, chinaware and other goods. The biographer of Marcus Samuel junior (born 1853) notes that 'most accounts of the rise of Japan and of the Meiji era put Samuel and Co. as one of the original British firms which made remarkable contributions to the country's industrial development'. It was from this firm that the Shell Transport and Trading Company originated, its entry into the oil business beginning about 1890.[29]

Finance

Britain's industrial pre-eminence was the foundation of her nineteenth-century economic primacy, providing the basis for her dominance of world trade in manufactured goods. Alongside industry and overseas trade, an elaborate financial system developed which, not without alarms and setbacks, evolved into a smooth-running mechanism to make the City of London the financial centre of the world. The system involved the Bank of England as the central bank, the domestic banks and the discount houses, linked through the bank rate and the handling of short-term financial instruments. The bill of exchange on London became the main means of effecting payments in international trade, and the whole was orchestrated by the Bank of England. In the long-term capital market London was the chief centre, supplying through its institutions funds for foreign governments or for investment in overseas countries.

In this field the Jews played a conspicuous part, but almost entirely in one section of it. Only one Jew—a Rothschild—was ever a member of the Board of Directors of the Bank of England; they were not known in the discount houses, and few were connected with the joint-stock banks or with the declining country banks. Only two were involved in joint-stock banks before 1880: Sir Moses Montefiore, of the Provincial Bank of Ireland, and Sir David Salomons of the London and Westminster. (A third was Sir Felix Schuster [1854–1936], but he became a director of the Union Bank when it took over his family bank in the 1880s.) Apart from the Stock Exchange, where, according to Joseph Jacobs, Jews numbered 138 in the early 1880s, about 5 per cent of the total, they were primarily merchant bankers, which in Britain was the title given to those engaged in international financial matters: dealing with overseas loans and share issues, and with bills of exchange.

During the eighteenth century Amsterdam had been the world's major money market and the 'giants in investment banking' were Barings of London, Hopes of Amsterdam and Gebrüder Bethmann of Frankfurt, none of them Jewish. The turning point was the Napoleonic Wars, which 'gave rise to financial transactions on a scale never before imagined. New bankers appeared in all the money markets of Europe, and old bankers learned new tricks'. It was their task to handle the vast expansion of government remittances and loan business which the wars required. 'To name only a few of those houses which were to grow in importance during the decades to come': in France, the Hottinguers of Switzerland and the Foulds of Germany; in Vienna, the Sinas of Greece; in Germany, the Oppenheims, the Mendelssohns, the Heines and the Rothschilds. Some were Jews, especially among the German contingent.[30]

For Britain the wars meant the raising of funds for government expenditure, the transmission of money to meet the costs of her armies abroad, the sending of loans and subsidies to her allies. 'Every year from 1793 to 1815 at least one government loan was issued, and an average of £20m. of stock was laid on the market in each of the war years'.[31] The London money market was as yet not properly developed and could not easily absorb such large quantities of stock; each issue was disposed of *en bloc* to contractors who already had the customers to take it. Very often these loan contractors operated as a consortium consisting of both Jews and non-Jews. The latter included Henry Thornton; Smith, Payne and Smith; Harman, Hoare & Co.; Barings; Boyd, Benfield & Co. The only major Jewish firm at first was that of Abraham and Benjamin Goldsmid, which started these operations in 1795 but—as others did—over-reached themselves and went under, the brothers committing suicide, in turn, in 1808 and 1810.[32]

As we have seen, many foreign firms came to Britain during the Napoleonic Wars, usually having been engaged in importing British goods. They subsequently moved into finance: alongside Jews like Rothschild were non-Jews such as Schroeder (arrived 1802), E. H. Brandt (1805), Frederick Huth (1809), and Frühling and Goschen (1814).[33]

The original mercantile connections were important in effecting the transition to finance. Nathan Mayer Rothschild had built up connections with other financiers who had supplied funds for his textile transactions, and these associations were useful when he went into the government loan business. And his trading expertise—especially the reputation which his bills of exchange in Manchester were accorded—led directly to the development of his firm as an acceptance house, handling international bills of exchange. This side of the business is not well known for the early years of the century, being eclipsed by the better documented governmental financial dealings. Rothschild made his name for the part he played in providing specie for paying the British armies in Spain. He seems to have come into this in 1813, in association with John Herries, the Commissary-in-Chief. Between 1811 and 1815 Herries paid out £42,500,000, of which at least half was handled by Rothschild. The gold was transmitted across France by his younger brother James.[34]

The end of the war, during which financiers had so much to do, brought them even more work. Indemnities had to be paid, funds were needed for reconstruction and international borrowing expanded. 'In the decade from the fall of Napoleon to the panic of 1825, more securities were floated on the markets of the world, above all in London, than had previously been floated in the entire preceding century'.[35] Many firms took part, with Barings leading the way (now joined to the Hopes by marriage); it was they who were responsible for handling the loan in 1818 to finance French reparations. If one date can be given to the emergence of the Rothschilds to world fame it was 1822 when the family, at the behest of Metternich, raised loans for the Holy Alliance, Russia, Prussia and Austria. In gratitude the Austrian Empire conferred baronies on the brothers.[36] While others in London raised loans in the 1820s for revolutionary governments in South America and elsewhere, the Rothschilds' reputation as the financiers of legitimate government grew. Nathan Mayer Rothschild took the place of Alexander Baring in London as leading spokesman on financial matters; the latter also lost to Rothschild his position as the major issuer of European securities, and began to concentrate on the American market.[37] Thus of the twenty-six principal foreign government loans which were contracted in London during the years 1818 to 1832, N. M. Rothschild was responsible for seven, as well as another jointly with a non-Jewish firm. The seven loans were to a nominal value of £21 million, about 38 per cent of the total value of the loans. Another Jewish firm, B. A. Goldschmidt, accounted for about 17 per cent.[38]

The five sons of Mayer Amschel Rothschild settled in Frankfurt, London, Paris, Vienna and Naples, maintaining close contact by means of a remarkably efficient courier service. The service included cross-Channel shipping; an account of the London Rothschild bank, by a man who took up employment in it in 1925, noted that its couriers during the 1920s and 1930s were 'recruited for the most part in the Folkestone area; many of them were descendants of the mariners who manned the cutters used by the firm in its early days to convey agents and despatches across the Channel'.[39]

The consolidated capital of the House of Rothschild for the years 1815 to 1875 is shown in Table 5. These very approximate figures were first published in the 1960s, but contemporaries did not need them to know of the Rothschilds' extraordinary progress. A whole body of unreliable literature was published purporting to explain their success; the family disdained to answer the numerous pamphlets, books and newspaper reports. Perhaps the best-known early story concerned Rothschild and the Battle of Waterloo, and his being the first in England to know of the victory (one version had him observing the battle and rushing to London ahead of the despatches). In London, it was said, he depressed the market with his gloomy appearance, bought stock at low prices and made a large profit when they rose. The story still appears—as recently as a book published in 1973—although Lucien Wolf demonstrated before 1914 that it was false.[40] Stories about his share speculations which appeared in newspapers (and are used by historians)[41] are not easy to check: even today the number of bargains only is published, not the names of the participants.[42] Most information centres on the issuing of long-term loans, but the firm was engaged in other activities.

Given the background of merchant bankers like the Rothschilds, we should expect them to handle specie, and from at least 1823 Nathan Mayer was obtaining gold from the Bank of England 'for his international transactions'; thirty years later the firm set up its own refinery.[43] It is possible that Rothschild continued with activities familiar to someone used to international trade. Barings, for example, as late as the 1830s were performing all manner of services for their clients: buying and selling securities, bullion and bills of exchange; the firm accepted bills of exchange, received remittances, made collections and effected payments. It negotiated insurance and even assembled passengers and freight on behalf of packet lines and other ship-owners.[44] On the other hand Rothschild may not have pursued these other activities, as he had given up his textile interests in 1811. In 1834 he advised: 'Stick to one business. . . . Be a brewer, and a banker, and a merchant, and a manufacturer, and you will soon be in the Gazette'.[45] Nevertheless he did have interests in a few outside activities: the North Wales slate industry, the Alliance Assurance Co. and the Grand Surrey Docks and Canal Co. (Surprisingly too he was interested in the ideas of Robert Owen, the pioneer socialist and co-operator, providing him in 1818 with letters of introduction for his visit to Frankfurt.)[46]

The merchant bankers of London, notably those of foreign origin, were, and still are, acceptance houses, guaranteeing the bills of exchange used in international trade. The Rothschilds were among those who performed this function: a surviving statistic for one discount house shows that the 6,332 bills it handled in 1874 contained as many as 848 names of acceptors.[47] Many, though, operated on a small scale and in Walter Bagehot's pioneering exposition of the London money market, written in the 1870s, he noted that 'the foreign exchange trade is carried on by a small body of foreign bill brokers, of whom Messrs. Rothschild are the greatest'.[48]

The issue of foreign securities was the best documented field of their work: proposed issues were advertised, commented upon in the press and sometimes subject to political discussion. From early in the nineteenth century London became the world's main centre for the raising of funds, and all manner of people took part, native and foreign, Jews and non-Jews. Among the native Jews were the Waggs, resident since the early eighteenth century, the firm of Helbert Wagg and Co. being formed about 1800; R. Raphael had been a gold and silver refiner in London since 1787; Isaac Lyon Goldsmid came from the family which earlier had produced the loan-contracting firm of Abraham and Benjamin Goldsmid; in the 1850s Samuel Montagu (originally Montagu Samuel), a member of a family established in Liverpool since the end of the eighteenth century, opened a bank in London. Among the Jewish immigrants in the first half of the century were Hambro's bank, established 1839—having been initially set up as a branch of the Danish family bank; David and Hermann Stern (1844); and Henry Bischoffsheim (1846).[49] But the great expansion in the market came after 1850.

A 'table of foreign government loan issues in London, 1860 to 1876, inclusive', published in Jenks's *Migration of British Capital* shows that over fifty houses were concerned in the issue of over £700 million of stock.[50] As well as the familiar names of Rothschilds and Baring it includes a number of British banks, e.g., Manchester and County Bank, and Glyn, Mills; several 'Anglo-foreign' banks, such as the Anglo-Italian Bank; foreign firms which arrived earlier in the century, Frühling and Goschen, for example; and newcomers like Erlanger (arrived 1859). Probably ten of the fifty were Jewish family firms, and Jews were associated with some of the other institutions such as Hermann Stern, a director of the Anglo-Austrian Bank. Some of them appear only once in the list: Louis Cohen and Co., the London stockbroking firm is listed as issuing a loan to Turkey in 1869 in association with the Comptoir d'Escompte. (Cohen refused to negotiate a loan for Romania in 1872 'on the express ground of the ill-treatment received by Jews in that country'.[51]) But it is more important to know the relative proportions of the various participants. As expected, Rothschilds and Barings were still predominant. Of the total of over £700 million issued, 'Rothschilds were sole agents for loans of nearly £110 million (nominal) and shared the agency (with Barings, J. S. Morgan and Co.

and Seligmans) for a further £130 million. Barings handled only £10 million entirely on their own but shared the agency for a further £135 million'. The joint Baring-Rothschild issue totalled £65 million, so that these two firms had a hand in about £320 million.[52]

The great financial activity in London naturally attracted to it people with the appropriate expertise, especially in the 1850s and 1860s. Branches of foreign firms were set up as were new types of bank—the 'Anglo-foreign' and chartered banks. New kinds of financial organisation were established in the 1860s with the extension of limited liability to financial organisations; financial associations, few with a long life, mushroomed in the 1860s to help finance railway-building and many other activities. Some Jews were involved in these: David Salomons, Bischoffsheim and Goldschmidt, and Hermann Stern. The most notorious was Albert Grant, born Abraham Gotheimer in Dublin in 1831. The son of a poor pedlar, he rose from clerk to company promoter and Member of Parliament, remembered now for his creation of Leicester Square as a public open space. Among other things he was general manager of two of these companies, the Crédit Foncier and the Crédit Mobilier, which fused to become Crédit Foncier and Mobilier of London. He promoted a number of fraudulent companies and the charlatan Augustus Melmotte in Anthony Trollope's novel, *The Way We Live Now*, 1875, is thought to be based on him. He died a pauper in 1899.[53]

Jewish firms were among the newcomers: the Sassoons from Bombay (1858); F. E. Erlanger from Frankfurt, via Paris (1859); Speyer Bros. from Frankfurt via America (1861); Seligman Bros. from America, originally Bavarian (1864); and, later, Lazard Bros. from Paris (1877).[54]

David Landes has argued that international financiers, in all countries, were often immigrants or members of minority groups. He notes that their operations, in a period of poor communications and incomplete information, depended on confidence and trust, on having someone—perhaps from the same family—in another country, who could be relied upon. Sometimes the close relationship was based on common national origin or religion. 'A shared faith was more than a bond. In a profession that was of its nature international and depended on the closest mutual confidence, the dispersion of certain persecuted or disfavoured groups with common values and ways of life to cement them from within, and common pressures and prejudices imposing unity from without, was a positive advantage'. The Jews, he says, were one such group; but so were the Calvinists, and so were the Greeks. Landes is aware of important qualifications to his statement—one being that some of the Jewish bankers (such as the Oppenheims, the subject of his detailed study) moved out of the Jewish community very quickly.[55]

But it is not clear whether these kinship connections were crucial. English banks such as Glyn, Mills, and H. H. Gibbs took part in international financial operations without them; and a study of American banking is critical of the notion that Jewish bankers had significantly different characteristics from other bankers.

> Whatever in-group characteristics contributed to the success of the German-Jewish banking elite [sc. of New York], such as strong family ties and foreign attachments, these had their counterpart within the Yankee banking community. Moreover the Jews hardly possessed a prerogative on either cosmopolitanism or European financial know-how; a similar claim can justly be made for the New Englanders who early in their careers had looked to England as the world's workshop and banker.[56]

It is probably fruitless to try to explain the success of some of these enterprises. The Rothschilds became very wealthy, but not everything they touched came to fruition. Their handling of an Austrian loan in 1859 'failed miserably',[57] for example, and in the same year James de Rothschild of Paris was virtually dismissed by the Pope as his financial agent because of his support for Cavour and Victor Emmanuel; he was replaced by Catholic bankers.[58] Earlier, in the 1840s, Lionel de Rothschild of London asked Lord Palmerston 'to present a memorial through the Washington legation on behalf of the State bondholders'—there had been defaults; but the application was refused.[59] Nevertheless this family above all others was important and influential, even if it took thirty years of agitation before Lionel was allowed to take his seat in the Commons of 1858 as the first Jewish Member of Parliament.

Apparently he never said anything in the House, but both he and his son Nathaniel (1840–1915) were sufficiently important to be the confidants and intimates of Disraeli and to some extent of Gladstone. Disraeli for example got foreign intelligence through the Rothschild connection, and the Rothschilds were among his regular dinner guests. In 1875 the house of Rothschild supplied the funds, at short notice, for the purchase by the British government of the Suez Canal shares.[60]

But, as always, it is difficult to establish the exact nature of their influence. Did the editor of *The Times* in 1863 (when the Russians put down the Polish insurrection) and in 1872 (when Russia was advancing into central Asia) come out in opposition to intervention against Russia because Lionel de Rothschild advised non-interference?[61] The verdict of Bertrand Gille, the historian who has produced the most detailed study of the family, is that its members were basically pacifist, preferring peace to war; and their actions, wherever they lived, were in accord with their own government's foreign policy.[62] They were in close contact with statesmen, but the tone of their relationship is seen, perhaps, in the discussions in 1884 about the renewal of a Rothschild loan to Egypt. The British government were trying to settle Egyptian financial questions and Nathaniel Rothschild, now the head of the English family, delayed any decision on the renewal to avoid embarrassing the government. Lord

Granville, with whom Rothschild was in touch, reported to Gladstone, the Prime Minister, that 'he asked me what the Gov't. wished him to do'.[63]

The Professions

The first professing Jew to be admitted to the Bar was Francis Henry Goldsmid, in 1833. A few Jews had been solicitors from the late eighteenth century and there had been the occasional architect and doctor; but most Jewish doctors had been unqualified quacks. During the nineteenth century it became possible for Jews to enter the professions when the admitting bodies dropped the requirement of a Christian oath. Similarly it was possible to obtain degrees. Right at the end of the period even women came into the picture. One of the earliest women students at Girton College, Cambridge, was Sarah Marks (Hertha Ayrton), surprisingly a scientist.[64]

While the lay leadership was heavily concentrated among City men, it began to include a sprinkling of professionals, especially lawyers. Among the first to be connected with the Jewish Board of Guardians in London, from its foundation in 1859, were a dentist, a solicitor and a barrister (who was also Professor of Political Economy at University College London)[65] Indeed the first generation of lawyers, mainly from wealthy families, rose rapidly into high positions in the profession, Sir George Jessel becoming Master of the Rolls.[66]

Joseph Jacobs's count of 'Jewish' names in a London directory of 1883 gave the following professionals: 12 architects; 27 barristers and 47 solicitors; 19 dentists and 12 surgeons; and 11 'private schools'.[67] His last category grossly under-rates the number of Jews in the teaching profession. At the time of the 1871 Census, the largest professional group in Manchester consisted of twenty male and nine female teachers (some of the latter being governesses).[68] Two of the grooms married at Swansea between 1840 and 1901 were teachers, of languages and of navigation. In the same period two were married at Brighton (one being a 'Professor of Music'). Birmingham in 1851 had two 'Professors of Languages', a Hebrew teacher and a 'Professor of Music'.[69] The Jews' Free School in London trained teachers of both sexes, several of whom became heads of Jewish schools in London and the provinces.[70] Others taught in state schools. The *Jewish Chronicle* reported in 1874 the appointment of A. Levy as headmaster of an East End school, presumably the first such appointment.[71]

The high proportion of lawyers, reported by Jacobs, was not repeated in the provinces. There was no Jewish lawyer in Birmingham at the 1851 Census; Manchester in 1871 had four solicitors, compared with four dentists, two doctors, four accountants and two architects.[72] Dublin produced a number of doctors, who often went into the Indian Medical Service, and the small Swansea community did not have a Jewish solicitor until the late 1880s.[73]

Some of these professions required more training and were more costly to enter than others. The barristers usually came from wealthy families, for example, and the first generation were often scions of City dynasties. Others, however, included two brothers, John and Lionel Hart (solicitor and barrister respectively), who were the grandsons of John Isaacs, a singer and actor who played in opera at the turn of the century.[74] In any case some funds were necessary and it is not normal to find the sons of the working class or shopkeepers trying to become lawyers or doctors or architects. They were most likely to become schoolteachers, who were normally recruited from the lower classes.[75] One, for example, was Israel Zangwill who made his name as a novelist, but was originally a teacher. He was the son of a pedlar. Engineering and science enjoyed a low status in Britain, and the sons of wealthy families seldom entered those professions. Upper-class Jews, accommodating to British practice, similarly neglected them. And not many obtained commissions in the armed forces, partly because Queen's Regulations did not officially recognise the Jewish religion until the 1880s. Several, however, were officers in the militia.

7
The Working Population, 1800–80

The activities of the Jewish elite and the business classes were well publicised, so much so as to mislead. It is curious to read the remarkable lapse by Arthur Ruppin, the pioneer of the sociological study of the Jews. Towards the end of a lifetime of research he wrote: 'The Jews who settled in France, Belgium and England before 1880 were almost exclusively occupied in banking, wholesale trade or the independent professions, and belonged to the upper social strata'.[1] On the contrary: many of the immigrants went into manual work, as did the native-born. Whether newcomers or old settlers, this development was associated with the creation of new jobs for Jews in workshops and to some extent in factories and offices. Less and less is heard of such traditional Jewish trades as umbrella-making or pencil-making and more of cabinet-making, tailoring and tobacco manufacture.

It was for these people that there came into existence such bodies as the Sunday Evening Jewish Working Men's Lecture Committee and the Sussex Hall adult education scheme as early as the 1840s. There was also the Jewish Mechanics' Sabbath Observance Association, established in March 1874, whose purpose was described in an advertisement:

> To afford to Masters and Hands the opportunity of effecting their mutual arrangements about employment, &c., without the necessity of doing so in the public streets on Sabbaths or other sacred days.[2]

The discussion in this chapter begins with the poor, for the analysis of the problem of Jewish poverty—immigrant and native—which was made by the Jewish authorities is an important part of the story. Their efforts to deal with it went beyond relief into the creation of a respectable body of people. Their work—of apprenticing for example—may have touched a small minority only, but it is a useful preliminary to this examination of the pre-1880 working class (which produced, *inter alia*, some of the leaders of the Jewish trade unions later on: they did not all come from eastern Europe).

The Poor

Jews seldom figured in the great parliamentary inquiries into health, housing and poverty. The much larger numbers of Irish immigrants attracted attention and dismay. But the Jewish community was very conscious of its poor, especially from the 1840s when Jewish newspapers began to be published regularly: the *Jewish Chronicle* began its continuous publication in 1841. A news item in that paper in 1845, for example, solicited funds for a slipper-maker with a wife and six children, the wife dying of consumption.[3] The diaries of Sir Moses Montefiore disclose that in 1829 the Sephardim—so often regarded as a very wealthy group—were giving assistance to 1,200 of their own 2,500 congregation. And in the following year Sir Moses recorded his impressions of a visit to the Petticoat Lane district of east London. He and his wife spent seven hours visiting the rooms of just over 100 people. 'We witnessed there many distressing scenes'—the large families 'with little or no fire or food, and scarcely a rag to cover them; without bed or blanket but merely a sack or rag for the night. . . . In fact the distress and suffering appeared so great we could not refrain from giving away all the money we had in our pockets'.[4] In 1848, another year of economic depression, a Manchester synagogue proposed unsuccessfully that the Board of Deputies of British Jews should collect various statistics on 'mendicants, relief, crime, etc.' In the synagogue's opinion, 'there was, among the Jewish population, a larger amount of ignorance, want of employment, poverty, and misery than among other denominations'.[5]

Jewish poverty was not confined to London. Almost all the provincial congregations who responded in 1845 to a questionnaire sent by the Chief Rabbi reported that they had charitable endeavours of some kind. Brighton, for example, had no special organisation but relieved the casual poor from the congregational funds. Canterbury similarly gave allowances to four old people and to casual strangers. Birmingham, Bristol (two societies: one for relief to poor residents, another for assistance to poor 'lying-in' women and for educating poor girls), Dover, Exeter (for the itinerant poor), Edinburgh (the Hebrew Philanthropic Society was a contributory scheme providing sick benefits; a branch gave casual relief to members and 'strangers'), Falmouth, Glasgow, Hull (contributory scheme for sickness and financial benefits), Liverpool (for the relief of resident poor during the winter months), Manchester, Portsmouth, Sheffield and Swansea.[6] A Hebrew Philanthropic Society of Ireland was formed in 1846, the year of the famine; six years later, the community of perhaps 200 people dealt with 150 cases.[7] The Liverpool Hebrew Philanthropic Society, founded in 1811, distributed relief to twenty-two families during the winter of 1857.[8] In the small Bristol community, 'a sum of money was distributed by the family among the poorer members of the congregation' after the funeral in 1867 of J. Abrahams (who had been mayor the year before).[9] It is not part of our task to examine the history of Jewish charitable effort, but its existence is significant. Even apart from the abortive schemes—such as the 1802 proposal, vetoed by the Sephardim, to establish a charitable organisation for the whole of London Jewry; or Nathan Mayer Rothschild's suggestion of the 1820s for the 'establishment of a fund for advancing sums of money to the industrious poor, to be repaid in small instalments'[10]—there were plenty that did come into being augmenting the assistance available from individual synagogues, from private persons and from the national Poor Law.[11]

This upsurge in organisations did not imply necessarily that poverty was growing. 'The early and mid-Victorian rush to establish institutions to alleviate or prevent destitution and suffering may have meant, not that there was more suffering and destitution to alleviate, but that society was becoming more worried or compassionate about it'.[12] Early nineteenth-century middle-class comment on the poor reflected the fear of revolution and of riot. Contemporary descriptions of the Jewish poor used terms wholly familiar to social historians of the period; they were 'degraded', 'almost bordering on barbarism' and exhibited 'moral and social degradation'.[13] The answer was to be found in education, through which the unpredictable and dangerous mob would be civilised and improved. The Sephardi authorities, in an appeal for funds in 1829, stated that one of the purposes of the instruction of the poor was to teach them 'to respect the rights of property and station'.[14] One sees the same kind of approach in a short-lived newspaper, the *Hebrew Observer,* in a column praising the Jewish adult education institution, Sussex Hall: 'There cannot be a more efficient antidote to the poisonous doctrines of socialism, communism, chartism and other utopian solutions lauded by designing demagogues or short-sighted philanthropists than this frequent intercourse between the higher and humbler classes on the common ground afforded by the platform of the . . . Institution'.[15]

This is not to deny that other motives besides social control and the prevention of revolution led to the creation of these various organisations: a desire to improve the image of the Jew in Gentile society; a need for religious education to prevent conversion to Christianity and for its own sake; a traditional religious obligation to give charity; and no doubt an honest compassion at the sight of economic distress. The proposed solutions went further, based as they were on a generally accepted diagnosis which closely followed the late eighteenth-century analysis. Jewish youths, it was said, were unable to receive apprenticeships for one reason or another and they turned to blind-alley jobs, such as street-selling. If they were trained in a craft, their economic and moral position would improve. By mid-century sixteen Jewish schools were in operation in Britain, catering for 2,000 pupils, mainly in London but also in the provinces (not necessarily catering only for the poor).[16] Emphasis was placed on the need for subsequent apprenticeships. In addition, emigration to the colonies was encouraged.

Not that contemporaries defined what they meant by 'poor' or had any notion of the numbers involved. At a London meeting, called to discuss the 'prevailing distress' in 1859, one speaker asked: 'Why should there be ten per cent of the Jewish population sunk in abject poverty (a voice, "Is this the case". Cries, "Yes, Yes") when the general position of the Jews was improving'. Another said that 'hundreds of most deserving co-religionists were allowed to pine away in wretchedness and starvation'.[17] The (London) Jewish Board of Guardians, established in 1859, collected statistics which, including the separate welfare activities of the Sephardim and some individual synagogues, suggest that in the 1860s and 1870s 'of the London Jewish population . . . some 25 to 30 per cent were in receipt of at least occasional relief'.[18]

The Jewish poor were a greater proportion than this, if we use a broader definition. 'Poverty', wrote Patrick Colquhoun in 1806, 'is that state and condition in Society where the individual has no surplus labour in store, and, consequently, no property but what is derived from the constant exercise of industry in the various occupations of life; or in other words, it is the state of every one who must labour for subsistence'.[19] The Jewish poor, or as contemporaries might have said, the 'labouring poor' or 'the working population' were therefore more numerous than those who received relief. Two statements made in the 1850s are instructive. John Mills wrote in *The British Jews* that of 25,000 London Jews 12,000 were in the 'lower class', of whom 'many are in daily want of the necessities of life and a still larger number scarely able to obtain sufficient to support existence'. The *St James Medley* in 1855 thought that seven-twelfths were in the 'lower orders barely making a living'.[20] These figures included, from the 1840s, an increasing number of immigrants, after a small influx in the earlier years of the century. More references begin to be made to the arrival of poor Jews. There were Ashkenazim from Amsterdam, at that period containing perhaps the largest Jewish community in western Europe, many of them working class.[21] They usually settled in London, but the east European immigrants who generally arrived at Hull often stayed in the provinces (or went on to America).[22] The small London Sephardi community reluctantly received poor immigrants. In 1862, three years after the outbreak of hostilities between Spain and Tangier had produced a Jewish refugee problem,[23] the Mahamad of the Sephardi congregation stated in their annual report (in reference to both Dutch and Moroccan Jews):

For some years past they [indigent Sephardim] have been emigrating to this country in considerable numbers, and are still constantly arriving with large families, encouraged to come over by their relatives who hold out to them the advantages of immediate admission for their children into our schools and to sharing equally with our native poor in all the charities of the Congregation. The facilities of marrying is [sic] another inducement of which they fail not to avail themselves and thereby pauperism is augmented.[24]

Apprenticeship

It might be argued that these new arrivals, often requiring relief and entering the traditional low-status job of hawking, somewhat reversed the earlier efforts—mainly directed at the young British-born Jews—in education and apprenticeship. The 1840 Report on Handloom Weavers had fulsomely praised

> the greatest efforts which were being made by the more opulent to afford their poor brethren the means of education, both civil and religious, and to teach the boys industrious trades, by which they may be withdrawn from buying and selling about the streets, and may become more useful members of society. . . . Buying and selling cheap, useful articles in the streets is an employment, which naturally falls to the weak and destitute; and a body of men like the Jews, in possession of fine physical condition, do not beneficially employ themselves in such an occupation.[25]

And Henry Mayhew, it will be recalled, in his descriptions of street-selling a decade later, while noting that may Jews were engaged in it, suggested that their numbers were falling.[26] The apprenticeships arranged by the Jewish institutions, it has been said, 'were largely responsible for raising the condition of the Jewish poor in the first half of the nineteenth century'.[27] The minutes of the Ashkenazi Talmud Torah (the precursor of the Jews' Free School)—extant for the period 1791 to 1818—'abound with references to apprenticeships', the most popular trade being tailoring. 'Mention is also made of pencil-making, watch-making, and glass-cutting'.[28] The Jews' Hospital, a residential institution, contained a mahogany-chair shop, and shoe-making and basket-making shops. By mid-century boys were being apprenticed to a variety of trades, including 'tailors, carvers, gilders, ladies' shoemakers, clickers (i.e., cutters out of boot and shoe "uppers"), men's bootmakers, upholsterers, broom and brushmakers, cigar-makers, hat-makers, manufacturing jewellers, cabinet-makers, chair-makers, turners and carvers, ivory and bone brush-makers, dressing-case and fancy cabinet makers and watch finishers'.[29] The girls were taught housework, needlework, cooking and the like. When girls reached the age of fifteen, 'they were apprenticed either as servants—as the rules have it—in a respectable family, or to some reputable tradesman'.[30]

From 1817 the largest Jewish educational institution was the Jews' Free School, which quickly expanded from 100 pupils in 1817 to over 1,000 in 1851. We know unfortunately very little about the subsequent occupations of the children, apart from a general statement that the girls usually went into domestic service (the largest single paid occupation for women in Britain at the time), and that some boys and girls were trained as pupil-teachers.[31]

More specific information is available for the fifty-three Sephardi boys apprenticed through the *Mahasim Tobim* charity between 1823 and 1839.[32]

Tailors	12	Carver	2
Shoe-makers	10	Glass-cutter	2
Cigar-makers	3 ⎫ 8	Watch-maker	2
Tobacco	5 ⎭	Picture-framer	1
Penmaker	1 ⎫	Painter	1
Pen and quill	3 ⎬ 5	Chemist	1
Pencil-maker	1 ⎭	Pin-cutter	1
Printer	2 ⎫ 3	Furrier	1
Lithographer	1 ⎭	Tinman	1
Cabinet-maker	3		

The scrappiness of this information induces caution: How many in total were formally apprenticed? How many received training during their apprenticeship? How many remained in these trades? At the time it was argued that the institutional training at the Jews' Hospital was poor and those trained did not take up jobs in their appropriate trades.[33] Nevertheless some general statements can be made. The first is that these occupations, except possibly pencil-making, were not specifically Jewish or immigrant. Clothing and footwear were among the largest employers of labour in London, and Jews whether employers or workers were a tiny minority. Yet there is no reference to apprenticeships in engineering and only one (a painter) in building. Some, such as carver, glass-cutter, printer, were highly skilled, but presumably the concentration of Jewish apprentices into particular trades (clothing, footwear, furniture, tobacco, pencil- and pen-making) was a result of the inertia of the apprenticing bodies. Or perhaps the masters most likely to take these boys were Jewish and engaged only in this limited range of occupations.

Does it all add up to an improvement in the condition of the Jewish poor? Such useful indices as earnings and hours of work are not available for the Jewish workers in these various occupations, but, while some boys who might otherwise have been pedlars were now tailors and cabinet-makers, the change may not have been altogether beneficial. The clothing, footwear and furniture industries were undergoing changes which reduced craftsmanship. Demand for cheap goods was growing, but with no changes in technology the greater output could be met only by increasing the numbers employed. As the product was of low quality, skilled craftsmanship was not required: reductions in costs fell on wages or on the quality of the product.[34] In these circumstances, apprenticeship was of little importance. Cheap labour was required, and in this period of rapid population growth children and women were abundant.

All of this was associated with changes in the organisation of production, by 'the displacement of small masters (employing a few journeymen and apprentices) by large "manufactories" and middlemen (employing domestic workers or sub-contracting)'.[35] Between the 1840s and the 1860s such innovations as the sewing-machine and the bandsaw had the effect of underlining the vertical disintegration in those industries. The capital equipment was cheap and portable, able to be used in workers' homes or small workshops. The material being processed was of no great value, and direct supervision was unnecessary. Factories did not develop in London, and it is no surprise to read one estimate that in the 1860s four-fifths of all male London tailors worked in their own rooms.[36]

We need not labour the point. For a number of reasons the conditions in some of the major industries into which Jews were going were deteriorating during the nineteenth century. The Jewish boys apprenticed to tailoring, to boot- and shoe-making and the furniture trades were thus being directed into occupations which were becoming notorious for sweating, for low wages and for seasonal work. It is, therefore, surprising at first sight that the Jewish Board of Guardians should have encouraged the movement into tailoring. A gift in 1861 from Charlotte, Baroness Lionel de Rothschild, enabled the Board to acquire ten sewing-machines. These were hired out to individuals who by paying small weekly sums could acquire them. The money so obtained was used to buy further machines and the process continued. By 1874, 412 had been issued, and the method was discontinued in the late 1870s only when the manufacturers began to issue them on the same terms as the Board. The Board also provided hire-purchase facilities for glaziers, carpenters, cabinet-makers, shoe-makers, printers and bookbinders, enabling them to obtain tools. It may be that the provision of sewing-machines eased the transition from hand-sewing and thus was beneficial to the Jewish tailors. Few jobs were open to girls and the Board established a workroom in 1867 for training girls in the needle trades: dressmaking, shirt- and collar-making, and embroidery; all poorly paid occupations. Six years later the Board consciously tried to apprentice young boys to trades other than tailoring and cigar-making. This new apprenticing function of the Board led by 1879 to nine apprentices in printing and kindred trades and five in instrument-making (but there were thirty-seven in furniture and fourteen in boots and shoes). To this we can add the interest in training Jewish children for clerical work: in 1877 Jewish schools began to teach shorthand.[37]

These small efforts towards the end of our period to move away from apprenticing to a narrow range of trades do not, it seems to me, invalidate the general point that Jewish workers were often in some of the most undesirable trades.

Tobacco-workers

One of the trades to which entry was being discouraged by the Board of Guardians in the 1870s was the manufacture of tobacco products. The industry was a major employer of Jewish workers perhaps because the East End contained many establishments and many Jewish employers. In the middle years of the century it was the single most important occupation for Sephardi men: between 1841 and 1880 just over 20 per cent of all men married at the Sephardi synagogue were makers of cigars.[38] The 1,105 known occupations of members of the Jewish Working Men's Club in 1875 included 184 cigar-makers (about 17 per cent); and 10 per cent of the Jewish Lads' Institute in the early 1880s were makers of cigars and cigarettes.[39] A similar proportion (146 out of 1,588) of applicants to the Board of Guardians in 1882 were in the tobacco industry.[40]

In his description of 'itinerant cigar-vending' which was 'principally in the hands of the Jews', Henry Mayhew observed: 'The manufacture of the cigars sold at the lowest rates, is now almost entirely in the hands of the Jews, and I am informed by a distinguished member of that ancient faith, that when I treat of the Hebrew children, employed in *making* cigars, there will be much to be detailed of which the public have little cognisance and little suspicion'.[41] It was by no means an attractive industry for boys: the Children's Employment Commission of the 1840s exposed the long hours and low earnings of boys in the tobacco industry, conclusions which were repeated twenty years later in the massive inquiry into chidren's employment. The report of the 1860s noted that in Glasgow—where Jews were not engaged in the industry—'"tobacco boy" and "street ragamuffin" were synonymous terms'; a view echoed by an Inspector of Factories in 1876. He commented that: 'In many parts of the kingdom they are a wretched class of boys who work in the tobacco manufacture'. The 1860s Commission included details of what appears to have been a Jewish firm, Messrs Schiff and Brothers, 16 Great Alie Street, Goodman's Field, (in the Jewish area). The evidence of three children is given. Jacob Moxley went to the Jews' Free School and started work at the age of ten, four years before the date of his evidence. He earned four shillings a week and worked from 8 A.M. to 6 P.M. Morris Garrod, aged sixteen, began seven years before as a 'call boy' at two shillings but was now earning twelve to thirteen shillings a week. The third was Abraham Myers, aged nearly fourteen, who had come from Austria two years earlier.[42]

The most illustrious product of the industry's employees was Samuel Gompers, the future American trade-union leader, born in London in 1850. The family emigrated to America in 1863 because the father, a cigar-maker, could not earn enough for his growing family. He was a member of the cigar-makers' trade union, 'whose members were frequently unemployed and suffering', and which established an emigration fund—as did other unions of the period—'that is', as the young Gompers wrote in his autobiography, 'instead of paying the members unemployment benefits, a sum of money was granted to help passage from England to the United States.'[43] Gompers's statement gives us a clue about one feature of the cigar-makers which is well worth emphasising—his father's membership of the union. The Jewish cigar-workers of London were probably one of the earliest groups of Jewish workers to attempt by collective action to influence their conditions of work. They took part in the first industrial dispute between Jewish workers and Jewish employers, rather earlier than is usually stated, and it took place in London rather than in Russia, to which priority is normally given. Information about it is very sparse: we do not know the numbers of people involved, nor are all the facts about its course and consequence readily available.[44] The first reference is in a letter to the *Jewish Chronicle* of 8 January 1858 in which the writer speaks of 'there being so many poor Jews in the trade willing to work, but intimidated by those on the strike, and consequently in great distress', and advises them that 'they may successfully appeal for protection to the magistrate'. The following week, 'An Oppressed Cigar Maker' gives his interpretation in a letter to the paper about 'the injustice and the growing evil the Jewish masters are inflicting on the London congregations'. The evil, he says, is the sweating system. 'The masters being unable to procure English workmen (whose wages do not average 20s. per week) to submit to the lowering of wages, resort to the practice of travelling to Holland and other parts of the continent, and, exaggerating the state of the cigar trade in England, fill the poor Dutchmen's minds with buoyant hopes of *high* wages. Arriving in a strange land with their wives and families they too soon discover that not only have they been duped but are as badly off as they were in their own country'. The men have not struck, he says; it is the Jewish masters, who, 'taking advantage of the depressed condition of trade, have entered into an agreement to employ no workmen but those who will agree to work for half the present low prices'. The men were resisting this demand, which would reduce them to beggary and degradation, and they were receiving some help from more fortunate fellow-workmen and a few of the public. 'Trusting', he ends, 'you will insert this letter both as a means of vindicating the position of the Jewish cigar-makers and greatly reducing Jewish pauperism'.

He got little support from the paper. An editorial comment on the letter was a brief lecture on the law of supply and demand and the inevitability of reducing wages when trade was slack. It makes the point also that 'cigar-making is a trade which is easily acquired, requires little skill either manual or mental, and no considerable body exertion'. When a trade is brisk, workers flock into it, and thus wages become depressed when the supply of labour is abundant. In the following week a further letter, in the form of an advertisement, appeared from Samuel G. Solomon, the Honorary Secretary of the Cigar Manufacturers' Association. He argued that the masters were not trying to reduce wages. 'The Jewish masters are only endeavouring to resist an unnatural rise on the part of the workmen. When, some time ago, the cigar trade was exceedingly brisk, the men took advantage of it, and compelled the manufacturers to pay a rise; since when trade has become quite depressed, and the masters were compelled to determine to resist the rise, and to employ only such workmen as are satisfied with the wages of 1856'. He offered to open their wages book for inspection by 'the leading men of the Jewish charities' whose benevolence 'has been diverted from deserving objects by rendering assistance to the undeserving'.

The inadequacy of the details does not obscure the fact that Jewish workers were on strike, and this attempt to affect employers' decision-making was probably not isolated although there was no further strike action in our period. The evidence for other kinds of action comes from the late 1860s and early 1870s. In 1867 the legislation dealing with certain factory conditions was extended to deal with workshops, i.e., those enterprises employing fewer than fifty people. The Board of Deputies pressed for amendments to the two Bills (Factory Acts Extension Bill and the Workshop Regulation Bill) and succeeded in getting some of their demands met. Clauses were inserted in both permitting Jews who closed their premises on the Jewish Sabbath, i.e., from sunset on the Friday to sunset on the Saturday, to re-open at the Saturday sunset and employ young persons and women until 9 P.M. on the Saturday. This concession was to meet the prohibition by the 1867 legislation on the employment of women and young persons on Sundays; the Saturday evening opening was to compensate for the loss of production on the Saturday, if the factory or workshop was closed.

There were two consequences. One was that some employers opened their premises for work on Sundays, and several were prosecuted. This led to the law being amended in 1871, at the instigation of Sir David Salomons, M.P., who introduced a Bill to enable Jewish owners to open on Sundays and to employ Jewish workers on that day, provided the premises were closed on the Jewish Sabbath. The Act was confined to workshops and to tobacco factories. Parliament was amenable to this—despite some opposition by the strong Sabbatarian lobby—after the Factory and Workshop Acts Commission had passed a resolution that the law required amendment. No doubt they were influenced by a report of an Inspector of Factories in 1868, the year after the various changes in factory legislation. He made a special reference to the cigar and tobacco industry which he said employed many women and young persons (the special interest of the Factory Acts). Before the 1867 legislation, he wrote, it was common practice in the East End of London, where 'the manufacture of cigars is largely prosecuted by persons professing the Jewish religion', to employ women and young persons on a Sunday for a few hours. Now this was forbidden, but the legal right to open late on Saturdays was, he said, useless. The workers would not come back to work at that time. The cigar factories were therefore really open for only four and a half days a week. By not working from Friday afternoon to Monday morning these girls and young persons would lose some of their manipulative skill during the weekend, and they would produce inferior products. The point is that once again the cigar-workers were resisting their employers by not working on Saturday evenings.[45]

Statistics of London Jewish Workers

During the mid-Victorian years, well before the immigration of large numbers of poor Jews from eastern Europe, a Jewish working class was growing in

London. Its number is unknown, but some clues are available. The first report of the Jewish Working Men's Club (1875) reported a membership of 1,459 (of whom 352 were women). The 1,105 with known jobs were spread among thirty-one occupations, but with concentrations in a handful: tailoring 305 (or 384 if all branches of clothing and the making of hats are included); 197 general dealers; 184 cigar-makers. Among them were seventy-seven travellers, twenty-seven clerks, fifteen furniture brokers and twelve teachers. Several were printers, bookbinders and had other skilled jobs.[46] It is instructive also to read of the 1,815 members of the 'London Taylors Jewish Benefit Society' in the 1870s (but they may not all have been employees), and of 'very large meetings held by the operatives' after the prosecutions in the late 1860s for infringements of the Factory and Workshops Act.[47] Another statement refers to 3,000 to 4,000 Jewish tailors and tobacco-workers in London in that period.[48]

Joseph Jacobs also published the known occupations of 323 members of the Jewish Lads' Institute, established in 1883 ('which may serve to indicate the occupations of the coming generation in the lower social grade'). He was impressed by the diversity 'which bids fair for the future and points to the final disappearance of Jewish restriction in occupations'. Some unusual trades were certainly among them: leather-dresser, harness-maker, lace-maker, dyer, two gas-fitters, a dentist, a turner, an engineer, a decorator, for example. But the great majority were still in the four main categories: tailoring and other clothing; tobacco; furniture; footwear. Jacobs noted that while tailoring was the largest single occupation this was true of the older lads. 'In the last three or four years a general disinclination for that occupation has been shown by Jewish parents of the lower classes'.[49]

Jews were to be found in a number of 'unusual' occupations before this. The convicts transported to Australia included chimney-sweeps, unskilled labourers, a stable-lad, a woman mantua-maker, a coachman and groom, a soldier, and prostitutes. Occasional news items refer to a cab-driver in the 1850s and of a former pupil of Joe Grimaldi the clown who eventually became an officer of a magistrate's court.[50] More comprehensive information comes from the small Sephardi congregation on the occupations of those married in its synagogue, beginning in 1837. The grooms were less frequently in the 'traditional' trades of footwear and tailoring, but their numbers increased during the period. As well as the cigar-makers and general dealers were a cabman, a stonemason, a waterman, a dock labourer, several clerks, printers, a seaman, a leather-dresser and a sign-writer. Only about sixty brides entered an occupation in the marriage registers; of these well over half were dress-makers and tailoresses. Seven were servants.[51]

The Sephardi marriage records are useful for another purpose, in understanding what happened to the street-sellers of London. The fact that over 20 per cent of the grooms in the 1840s were general dealers and hawkers would suggest that the 'improvement' of the London Jews had not gone very far. But after 1850 the proportion falls steadily to just under 9 per cent in the 1870s. In that decade 17 of the 196 grooms with known occupations were general dealers, compared with as many as 41 of the 180 grooms' fathers whose jobs are known. The sons of the forty-one general dealers were in paid employment: fifteen cigar-makers, four boot-makers, a cabinet-maker, three tailors' cutters, a diamond-polisher, a musician, an artist. A few had moved into some other form of trading: tool-dealer, fruiterer, for example. As many as eight were general dealers. This clearly indicates no widespread move by Sephardim from peddling to shopkeeping. In addition to the eight grooms of the 1870s whose fathers were also general dealers, the fathers of the others were tailor, two travellers, a butcher and a clothier (four occupations are not given).

The Provinces

The London Jewish working class began to develop early in the nineteenth century and grew more quickly when greater numbers of east European Jews arrived in the generation or so before 1880. One plausible generalisation about the provinces, on the other hand, is that the working class was largely composed of the east Europeans. At the time, this provincial working class was not very well known. M. S. Oppenheim, the spokesman for the Board of Deputies to the Factory and Workshop Acts Commission of 1875, stated: 'there are very few Jewish operatives employed by Jewish employers, from the simple fact that there are not many such operatives in the provinces'. He gave his evidence in June 1875; the Report of the Factory Inspectors for the half-year ending 31 October 1875 specifically referred to two cases in Birmingham of Jewish tailoresses said to have been working long hours in contravention of the Factory and Workshops Acts.[52] Similarly the boot and shoe workers' union was complaining of the influx of pauper Jews to Manchester and Leeds (in addition to London), where they were working in the footwear industry.[53]

The characteristic trades can be seen from the detailed figures for Manchester, derived from the Population Census: they do not distinguish however between employer and employee in all cases.[54] The first important group to emerge were the cap-makers, who numbered in 1851 thirty-six men and eleven women. A decade later the tailors and dress-makers, together with the waterproofers, had become the largest segment, totalling eighty-nine men and seventeen women. Ten years later in 1871 there were 316 men and 95 women in these trades. Another noticeable feature was the growing number of servants: in 1871 nine men and twenty-eight women were employed as cooks, domestic servants, nursemaids, and the like.

Such people were clearly employees but other occupations are not so definite. The growing numbers of tailors may have included employers, and some of the following trades of Jews in Birmingham in 1851 may be the same, but some certainly were employees: watch-maker's apprentice, frame-maker, cigar-makers, pencil-case-maker, slipper-maker, cordwainer, bookbinder, gilder and carver, shoe-maker's assistant, gas-fitter, and clerks. In Brighton between 1839 and 1901 the occupations of spouses and parents included: baker, builder, carver and gilder, clerk, dress-maker, gold-wire-worker, laceman, librarian, servant, storekeeper, tailors and tailoresses, and a turner.[55] The Dublin community of the 1850s included 'bog-oak ornamentalists, makers of mathematical instruments, pencils, umbrellas and parasols, of brushes and picture frames'.[56] In Sheffield one comes across a journeyman watch-maker,[57] and possibly there were some Jewish employees of Weinberg's lace-making establishment in Nottingham.[58]

Finally there were the white-collar workers, the clerks who have already been mentioned. When N. M. Rothschild came to Manchester he employed an English clerk, Joseph Barber, but later Manchester merchants often employed Jews, both immigrant and native-born.[59] In 1841 there were twenty of them, forming almost 10 per cent of the employed Jewish males in the city. Their numbers fluctuated: ten in 1851, thirteen in 1861 and thirty in 1871, a reflection no doubt of those who returned to Germany and of those who moved on to set up in business on their own.

As ever, we know most about those who succeeded, and they may not have been representative. Isidor Gerstenberg, from Russian Poland, worked for the Manchester merchant and banker Abraham Bauer—himself an immigrant of the 1830s. Gerstenberg married a daughter of Bauer and he was set up in business as an exchange broker and banker. Two brothers, Benjamin and Ellis Abraham Franklin, the sons of an English-born shopkeeper, also began as clerks: the former for his uncle and the second for Bauer.[60] These all ended up in business, but a fourth man who began as a bank clerk in Dublin did not. He was Moses Angel and he was at the bank for only a short period in the 1830s.[61] In the next decade he was editor of the newly-established *Jewish Chronicle*, and then moved on to become headmaster of the Jews' Free School. He held this position for most of the second half of the century. Perhaps he had obtained his temporary banking job through Sir Moses Montefiore, a director of the bank, patronage being a normal feature of recruitment in such occupations.

It is unlikely that many, if any, obtained employment on the railways, a major source of clerical employment, but they may have done in the civil service once entry began to be based on competitive examination. In total the number of Jewish clerks was probably not very great before the end of the century. Thus of 759 Sephardi marriages in London between 1838 and 1880 only about a dozen grooms described themselves as clerks. Similarly in 1875 the Jewish Working Men's Club membership (of whom the occupations of 1,105 are known) included 27 clerks. There is no evidence that any women had clerical employment.[62] There was not much more for them apart from the clothing industry, textiles or domestic service, and Jewish girls do not seem to have worked in the textile trade.

The ambiguity of some of this information in no way seriously modifies the point that there was a growing Jewish working class in Britain, in a variety of occupations, but increasingly concentrated in what were to become the major jobs for the next few decades. The clothing trades, footwear, cabinet-making—these were to be the typical Jewish jobs, taken by the immigrants who came in great numbers from eastern Europe from the 1870s and 1880s. In this way Anglo-Jewish economic life was to be transformed, to be given the features which remained dominant until World War II.

8

The Transformation of Anglo-Jewry, 1880–1914

About 60,000 Jews lived in the British Isles in 1880; by 1914 the number had grown to perhaps 300,000. The existing community, containing a high proportion of people born in Britain, many of whose ancestors had arrived in the seventeenth and eighteenth centuries, was now overwhelmed numerically by foreigners. The anglicised community, working- or middle-class, was accustomed to freedom; the newcomers came from countries which were economically under-developed and politically authoritarian; where the Jews lived on sufferance, often separated socially, geographically and economically from the non-Jewish population. Numerous problems can be expected when any group is augmented so rapidly in such a relatively short period; the distinctive qualities of the newcomers ensured that they would be severe. During much of this period alien immigration and the associated problems of overcrowding and sweated industries were live issues in British politics. After some two decades of argument the Aliens Act was passed in 1905, placing restrictions on immigration, one of the first manifestations of a move away from traditional nineteenth-century notions of liberal economic policy in which a cornerstone was the right of people freely to enter or leave Britain.

The immigrants came overwhelmingly from eastern Europe, mostly from Russia and that part of Poland which was under Russian jurisdiction. Others came from German Poland (Posen), Austrian Poland (Galicia), and from Romania. Jews from these countries were not a novelty to Britain: from the seventeenth century east European Jews had been moving westwards across Europe, some finding their way to the British Isles. In the first half of the nineteenth century more arrived, often landing at Hull, where a few stayed to join the local community; some went to other towns in Britain to settle in Leeds, Manchester or Birmingham, for example, but most of them probably went on to America.[1] Soon they were replacing the immigration of Jews from northern and central Europe. As late as 1861 the (London) Jewish Board of Guardians noted that 'Holland continues to supply most of the foreign poor'. By the end of that decade the Board's statistics (first available in 1869) show that the 'no. of cases arrived in current year' were mainly of Russians and Poles: not many were Dutch, German, or Austrian.[2] But the total numbers staying in Britain were as yet not very great; the first year in which more than

130

100 Jews arrived at Hull was 1851. Thereafter the rate rose. In Leeds, whose Jewish population was largely east European, the average annual number of weddings was 2.5 in the 1860s. In 1869 it jumped to 14, the average for the seven years 1869–75 being 20.[3] But the major influx to Britain really started in the early 1880s and continued for some thirty years, before coming to an end with World War I.

These Jewish immigrants in Britain were part of a massive wave of migration from eastern Europe. Millions of people, Jews and non-Jews, were on the move westwards, most reaching their target—America. Others went elsewhere, to South America, Canada or South Africa, while some travelled only to countries in north-west Europe. Britain was one of these destinations, but she had the particular role as a staging area astride one of the main migrant routes. Immigrants for America commonly disembarked at a British port to take another ship across the Atlantic. Most arrivals in Britain landed in London, with Hull on the east coast next in importance. Grimsby too received many immigrants and smaller numbers arrived at other ports. Some, not many, stayed at the east coast ports; others, on their way across northern England, alighted from their train at some convenient place—Leeds, Sheffield or Manchester—instead of continuing to Liverpool, the port of exit. As many as 40 per cent of the Jews of Leeds were said to be in transit in 1889 and not expected to settle.[4]

Some of those who finally got to America had stayed in Britain for lengthy periods.

> [Perhaps as many as] 400,000 to 500,000 Jews . . . crossed the Atlantic as English natives or as East Europeans having passed two or more years in the British Isles. Probably they knew a bit of English and had experience of urban life in which their lives would be spent. Their children were attending school and had quickly made the linguistic transition. . . . A substantial Toronto congregation is named Hebrew Men of England. Local lore explains that its founders early in this century were immigrant Russian and Polish Jews of the customary type, but proudly considered themselves 'men of England' for having spent a few years there en route to Canada. Tens of thousands of Jewish immigrants to the United States and Canada had some exposure to Anglo-American society and culture in England, and made their first painful adaptation to the modes of making a living in an advanced industrial country.[5]

It would be quite wrong to conclude, however, that the permanent settlement in Britain of a small segment of this mass migration was purely residual, its members composed of those who were stranded through lack of money or from want of initiative. Folk-stories are common of the migrants who landed in England thinking they had made the complete journey to America. However, the Yiddish press in eastern Europe, one (often inaccurate) source of information for intending emigrants, contained reports of conditions in Britain;[6] some migrants certainly intended to join friends and relatives who were already living here, travelling hopefully with their bundles and an address.

The majority of the immigrants went to live in the areas of existing Jewish settlement. The East End of London filled to overflowing; the Manchester community expanded to become the biggest provincial community, followed by Leeds, Glasgow, Dublin, Liverpool—the cities attracted them most. They eschewed the old-established communities in the south—Cheltenham and Falmouth for example—which were declining; nor did they settle in any great numbers in such industrial cities as Leicester. While it is true that new communities were formed in the provinces, for example, Cork and Limerick in Ireland, Aberdeen in Scotland, Blackburn in Lancashire, in the mining areas of South Wales and north-east England, the total number of people involved was not great. The majority settled in the major cities. to a large extent for social and religious reasons: because other Jews were there.

Immigrants to any country normally live near each other: the east European Jews' gregariousness followed from their religious needs, their different culture and their fear of the non-Jewish world. Within the cities, they concentrated in particular districts. The East End of London had been the main Jewish area since the seventeenth century, and was within walking distance of the docks; those who arrived at Liverpool by train took up residence close to the railway station, at Brownlow Hill. The main area in Manchester was Strangeways, not far from Victoria Station. At Leeds the incoming railway passengers were assisted in their residential concentration by the efforts of local non-Jews:

> The immigrants were led to the Leylands by Gentile guides who gathered round the railway stations looking for them. The guides grabbed their bundles and pushed both bundles and greeners on to flat handcarts. Thus they were taken in state to the Leylands. When the immigrants had no address slips, the guides knew enough Yiddish to ask them where they had come from. As soon as they heard 'Lodz, Riga, Lokever, Vilna, Marienpol . . .' off they moved to the homes of people who once had come from those places; the guides knew them all. In this way, landsmen kept together.[7]

No one knows exactly how many stayed in Britain temporarily or permanently. The British authorities did not keep detailed records of the kind that provide elaborate information about those arriving in the USA: numbers, country of origin, religion, occupation. Neither contemporary inquiries (e.g., by the Royal Commission on Alien Immigration, 1902–3) nor recent researches succeeded in establishing how many Jews came to live in Britain. But some guidance is provided by the 1911 decennial Population Censuses, taken near the end of the immigration period. On the assumption that most of those recorded as Russians, Russian Poles and Romanians were Jews, there must have been about 120,000 to 150,000 east European Jews in the United

Kingdom by 1914.[8] This figure includes those brought over as children—the migration included a high proportion of families, the men sometimes coming in advance to prepare the way for their wives and children—but naturally excludes those who were born in Britain. Even so the total is remarkably small, the immigrant Jews forming a very minor part of the increase of ten million in the population of Great Britain between the Censuses of 1881 and 1911.

The Jewish immigrants in Britain were a small section of those millions of Europeans who decided to leave their place of birth for, it is usually argued, economic reasons. During the nineteenth century the population of the Old World grew fast to surpass its economic capacity, and the surplus population migrated, much of it to America.

> The evolution of the Atlantic community could be described in terms of two frontiers—the ever-widening frontier of surplus population in the Old World and the moving frontier, of economic opportunity in the New. The 'Malthusian Devil' crossed the European continent from Ireland to Germany, then to Scandinavia and finally to Southern and Eastern countries where his sway was to be greatest of all. Each crisis of overpopulation was a milestone in the process of building up the industrial strength of America.[9]

The Jews of eastern Europe shared in this rapid population growth and its adverse consequences for living standards. In many respects they were in a worse and even more deteriorating position than the bulk of the population. Such industrial development as there was in Russia before World War I (which ameliorated some of the economic distress) hardly touched the mass of the Jews, as much of the new industry was sited away from the main area of Jewish residence. From the late eighteenth century, under a series of decrees, the Jews of Russia, including Russian Poland, had been largely confined to a specified part of the country, the Pale of Settlement in the west. Its area was large, perhaps 400 miles wide and 600 miles long, stretching from the Baltic in the north to the Black Sea in the south: but it was overpopulated in the sense that few economic innovations occurred there and the increasing numbers of Jews (with perhaps a higher birth-rate than the Gentiles) had to compete for a limited number of jobs. Traditionally these were petty trading, and certain craft employments such as tailoring, shoe-making, metal-working. In the south there were Jewish agriculturists, encouraged along with Serbs, Bulgarians and Greeks to colonise the area—the most famous Jew to come from that background was Leon Trotsky, the revolutionary leader.[10] Some Jews worked in textile and tobacco factories but typically the Jews of the Pale were pedlars, carters and especially workers in small workshops where they suffered the obvious consequences of severe competition for jobs: poor working conditions, low wages and the production of inferior goods with poor tools, in industries whose output was subject to severe seasonal fluctuations.[11] The typical picture of Jewish life, as given for example in the Hebrew novels of the

1870s and 1880s, 'is one of crushing and ever-increasing poverty. Time and again the novelists describe the wretched struggle to wrest the meagrest of livelihoods from a hostile environment'.[12] Many such contemporary impressions include one by Richard Cobden the free-trading M.P. On a visit which took him to Latvia in August 1847 he noted:

> The villages through which we passed on the high road . . . were generally peopled with Jews, a dirty, idle-looking people, the men wearing long robes with a girdle, and the women often with turbans, the men also wearing the long beard. These wretched beings creep about their wretched villages, or glance suspiciously out of their doors, as if they had a suspicion of some danger at every step. They never work with their hands in the fields or on the roads excepting to avert actual starvation.[13]

Apart from a few businessmen and intellectuals, such was the life of well over half the world's Jewish population, the six million or so who lived in the Pale, in those areas of Poland under German and Austrian jurisdiction, and in Romania, where very similar conditions prevailed. In the three decades before 1914 two million left Russia, about one-third of that country's Jews. A quarter of the Jews of Austria-Hungary emigrated and more than half of those of Romania. They totalled two and three-quarter million migrants (see Table 6).

In Jewish history and folklore one date, 1881, is identified as the onset of this mass migration. In that year pogroms against Jews in a number of Russian towns followed the assassination of the Tsar: one of the assassins was a Jewess. Subsequent peaks of emigration succeeded similar hostility towards the Jews. One was the expulsion of Jews from Moscow to the Pale in 1891: another the Kishineff outrage of 1903, when Jews were attacked and murdered. There is little reason to doubt that while the basic causes of migration may have been economic, its incidence and intensity were related to persecution.[14] For while the mass migration of both Jews and non-Jews from Russia coincided with a period of repression of many religious and political groups, the Jews were singled out for special treatment.

The notorious 'Temporary Laws' of May 1882 affecting the Jews—they lasted until 1917—were in line with the traditional policy towards them. They included the prohibition of business activity on Sundays or on Christian holidays, restrictions on mobility and rights of residence, and the prevention of Jews working the land or living in rural areas. This was only the beginning.

> Within the next decades, repression and discriminatory laws fell thick and fast on the hapless Jews—for example, the quota system in schools and universities, exclusion from employment with public authorities, the loss of franchise rights in zemstvo and municipality. The process reached its climax in 1891 and 1892 when, without warning and in bitter winter, the Government evicted many thousands of Jewish artisans from Moscow and cleared

the Jews from a wide belt of territory on the western frontiers. The Jews were forcibly 'resettled' in the ghettoes of the interior.[15]

In the final analysis, emigration is often a personal decision: a compound of emotions, calculations and individual circumstances. Two autobiographies illustrate the variety of reasons told to the children of emigrants to Britain. The authors, both born in southern Russia in 1888, were brought to London in the 1890s and published their accounts in their old age. One came from a culturally-assimilated family of some substance. According to his daughter, Vladimir Isserlis did not return, one day in 1890, from his pre-breakfast swim. 'His body was found in the Dnieper three days later, lower down in the river. What caused his death we were never to know. My mother was left a widow at thirty-two. No longer protected by her husband's position in Czarist Russia, that seethed with discontent, where pogroms were frequent and anyone expressing liberal views liable to be sent to Siberia, my mother decided to emigrate to England'. More succinctly the second author, Selig Brodetsky, wrote: 'We had left Russia largely because of the anti-Jewish discrimination in education'.[16]

Brodetsky's family was the more characteristic in being poor and religious. Typically the emigrants came from the shtetls, small towns and villages, and had lived separate lives from the surrounding population. Their language was Yiddish and the emphasis of their lives was on the Torah. However some, including students at *Yeshivot* (religious seminaries), were influenced by radical and revolutionary movements in Russia: others, in examing their position, concluded that the solution to their problems was a return to Palestine. The immigrants brought with them these various cultural baggages but they were not necessarily a representative sample of the Jews of eastern Europe. It is most unlikely that the very poor were among them, for the lot of the destitute is apathy and resignation. Emigration cannot have been in the minds, for example, of the 40 per cent of the Jews of Vilna who were in receipt of relief.[17] Even though steamship fares were low, passports had to be obtained, costing £1.10s per person. While many crossed the borders illegally, the cost of emigration was not thereby necessarily reduced—local guides had to be paid and officials bribed.[18] The fact that perhaps only 10 per cent of the emigrants obtained financial help for travel from Jewish communal organisations clearly indicates that the vast majority were not poverty-stricken.[19]

Does this mean that those who left eastern Europe were the most enterprising? During the period 1899–1914 two-thirds of the Jewish immigrants to the USA described themselves as skilled workers, compared with only one-fifth of the Gentile immigrants. This could be interpreted to mean that the Jewish emigrants were those who 'were no longer resigned to a pitiful existence' and who 'began to rebel against their sordid existence and to dream of a new life'. Their expectations were high but were frustrated in Russia: 'it is therefore a gross error to see Jewish emigrants of that period as "shlimazels" who were thrown out of economic existence, with no option for survival but to gather their belongings and wander in search of refuge'.[20]

To have suggested in the Britain of the late nineteenth century that the Jewish immigrants were in some sense the 'best' of the Jewish community of eastern Europe would have evoked incredulous laughter. The language used to describe alien immigrants—by which phrase was usually meant Jewish immigrants—gives the opposite impression. Take the 1909 publication, *The Case Against Radicalism*, published by the National Union of Conservative and Constitutional Associations, a handbook for candidates in the 1910 general election. The five pages on 'Alien Immigration' recount the efforts by the Unionist government of 1895–1905 to pass the Aliens Act of 1905, and complain of the gentle way the Liberal government subsequently administered it. The handbook talks of Britain being 'an asylum for criminals and paupers from all parts of the world'; and 'the criminal and vagrant pauper—the scum of every foreign slum, the refuse of Europe'. The Aliens Act of 1905 came at the culmination of nearly two decades of political debate in which such language was commonplace.

Those who took the contrary line and opposed limitations on immigration based their argument on principle, on the undesirability of reversing liberal free trade doctrines. Few sentiments were expressed out of regard for the immigrants: one does not come across millenarianism, for example. But favourable voices were not completely unknown, usually expressions of the aliens as, somewhat surprisingly, non-producers of social problems. A report to the Manchester corporation in 1903 dealt with 'the community of poorer Jews who mostly dwell "on the lower part of the space between the Irk and the Irwell" '. They 'showed little sign of deterioration, in spite of their squalid surroundings. They were no cleaner than other slum dwellers, and they were so poor that most houses were overcrowded with lodgers. Nevertheless, the children were well cared for, the community was almost free from drunkenness, it produced few prostitutes, and had remarkably few deaths from phthisis.'[21] Similarly a survey of women's work in Birmingham published in 1906 mentioned the intelligence and alertness of the Jewish tailoresses there.[22] More generally, and in the more widely known work of Leo Chiozza Money, comparable sentiments are to be found. In his book *Riches and Proverty* he advocated severe restrictions on the employment of married women. He supported his argument by lauding the 'Jewish community amongst us, the very aliens who are despised by the race they are supplanting in the East End of London. . . . The Jewish children are much healthier and stronger than their Gentile neighbours because they are better mothered. Jewish women find their true avocation at home. The Jew, however poor, does not live on his wife's earnings, and it would be counted shame for a Jewess to work during pregnancy or after childbirth.'[23] The children were reported on favourably for their ambition and hard work in school,[24] and the immigrants were not regarded as a police problem. 'The coming of the Jews in greater numbers than ever before to Whitechapel had the result of transforming streets which had previously composed one of the most persistent and most famous of London's criminal areas into places of low criminality, despite poverty'. One reason perhaps was that they were accustomed in Russia to complying with officials and policemen, and did not wish to make trouble.[25] This does not imply complete docility and acceptance of the *status quo*. Jewish radical movements came into existence, of various shades of anarchism and marxism, but they were mostly peaceful in intention. The Sidney Street Siege of 1911, when two members of a gang of shopbreakers were besieged in an East End house by troops called in by the Home Secretary, Winston Churchill, certainly led to anti-alien feeling: the gang were immigrants (not necessarily Jews), they may have been anarchists, and three policemen had been killed during the robbery.[26]

But this was a very special circumstance and the Jewish area was remarkably peaceful. Its notoriety rested on appalling conditions of housing and work, especially in the early part of the period. At one of the first elections held for the London County Council (formed in 1888), G. G. Coulton, better known as a medieval historian, canvassed for the Progressives, the party of Radicals and Socialists.

> Being one of the few who could speak German, I had the Jewish refugees assigned to me. . . . They were mostly Poles or Russians, but they generally had a little barbarous German. Their housing conditions, of course, were such as to make one wonder how any of them could take any interest in anything whatever. One typical case is clear in my memory. Five or six cobblers were working in a room perhaps fifteen feet square; more likely, smaller.[27]

Descriptions of overcrowding in insanitary accommodation and of the long hours of work abound in the inquiries of the time—by parliamentary committees and royal commissions as well as such privately-sponsored investigations as Charles Booth's meticulous study of London whose first results were published in the late eighties. From time to time the provincial communities were in the news: in 1903 and 1904 reports of attacks on Jewish workers at the Dowlais (South Wales) steel works and on Jewish miners in the same town; a so-called 'pogrom' in Limerick (Ireland) and a boycott of Jewish shops there; attacks on Jews in Monmouthshire during the first national railway strike in August 1911.[28] Each of these incidents had its own special characteristics—the Welsh outbreaks of 1911 cannot be divorced, for example, from the extraordinarily rapid growth of the South Wales coal industry and its accompanying frictions, the violence that characterised industrial disputes in that region, and the general upsurge of militancy in that period of British history. But in general 'provincial anti-semitism . . . was conspicuous by its absence',[29] and the great political debate about immigration, beginning in the late eighties, centred on conditions in London. Whatever the difficulties, whatever the social and economic problems of the provinces, the great controversy rested on the East End of London.

'In 1914, no city other than New York and Chicago contained more East European immigrants that London',[30] perhaps half of all those in Britain, the great majority in the East End. The traditional Jewish settlement there was not far from where eight immigrant ships per week landed, and in the East End newcomers could find the Poor Jews' Temporary Shelter (established 1885) providing temporary accommodation and advice, and many other communal institutions. But they arrived at a time when the inner areas of London were already over-full. 'By the 1880s overcrowding had reached a crisis point in central London. Figures of population per house had mounted steadily since the 1840s',[31] not least because many houses had been demolished for railway construction, street improvements and the extension of warehouses. The actual number of houses had fallen, but as yet not many people had been able to move out to suburban areas: the cost of travelling was too high, and many people needed to be within walking distance of their work. The population was meantime increasing rapidly. From the late 1880s, it is true, some progress was made as cheap transport became more available and people moved outwards, but up to about 1900 the arrival of the Jews in the East End could only add to the difficulties. The 'traditional' area of Jewish settlement, just east of the City, was soon thickly populated, whole streets becoming Jewish. Then they moved outwards, along the Mile End road and just to the north and south of it. Generally they did not live in the areas immediately adjacent to the docks—the close-knit dock-working communities opposing, sometimes physically, their attempts to live there. Neither did many move northwards at first into Bethnal Green, where similar local pride and solidarity barred their way.[32]

It is to be expected that the arrival of largish numbers of people of alien culture in a comparatively small part of London would cause problems. There would obviously be friction between the locals and the newcomers over housing, jobs, and differences of culture and religion. Yet the great outcry that their immigration occasioned rested on deeper foundations than these. The settlement of the Jews took place just at the time, in the 1880s and 1890s, when 'London's role in national politics [became] dramatic'.[33] For much of the nineteenth century public attention had been directed to the new industrial towns. The condition of housing, of public health and the state of the factory population—all these were the subject of numerous enquiries. In the late nineteenth century the spectacle of the capital's discontents urged the need for thought and action.

During the 1880s the unemployed of London increased both in numbers and militancy. A crowd of 120,000 people had gathered in Hyde Park in 1884 to offer support to the government when its reform proposals were being approved in the House of Lords. This was described as 'the greatest Reform demonstration ever held'. More novel and more ominous, to Conservatives and Liberals alike, were the Socialist demonstrations of the late 1880s. The riots in Trafalgar Square in 1886 and 1887 were riots of London's unemployed, and the animosities which they aroused were animosities against the propertied and privileged people in London.[34]

The dock strike of 1889 symbolised the ability of seemingly unorganisable casual workers to take collective industrial action, and to succeed. No wonder that the multi-volume survey of London life by Charles Booth made such an impact. Its meticulous demonstration that some 30 per cent of the population of London were in poverty confirmed the foundation of discontent. The political implications of the existence of mass poverty were clear. Here was a great, destitute segment of society, liable to sudden outbursts, possessed of the vote, and likely to be suborned by the dogmas of the new socialist organisations of the eighties. 'In the second half of the nineteenth century', writes Gareth Stedman Jones in his splendid study:

Victorian civilisation felt itself increasingly threatened by 'Outcast London'. Stripped of the mythology which surrounded this phrase, 'Outcast London' symbolised the problems of the existence and persistence of certain endemic forms of poverty, associated together under the generic term, casual labour. London represented the problem of casual labour in its most acute form, and the fears engendered by the presence of a casual labouring class were naturally at their greatest in a city which was both the centre and the symbol of national and imperial power. Such fears permeated conservative, liberal and socialist thought alike.

There were special reasons for the great concentration of the casual poor in London at the end of the nineteenth century, not least the absence of large-scale industry. But within Britain as a whole the anxieties about popular unrest were part of a more anguished examination of Britain's situation. Other countries were now beginning to catch up and overtake her in economic matters; progress could not be regarded as automatic, and another ideology was needed to replace that belief. At the same time the major political parties were adjusting to the reality of the widened franchise, to the need to respond to working-class needs in order to maintain political power. The wide-ranging debate included, for example, the discussion of national efficiency: 'an attempt to discredit the habits, beliefs and institutions that put the British at a handicap in their competition with foreigners and to commend instead a social organisation that more closely followed the *German* model'.[36] In the more general arguments, which included the importance of the empire, social reform and secure employment through imperial preference—these taking the sting out of socialism by remedying the main problem of poverty—all were clearly linked to the objective of a stronger Britain.[37]

Jewish immigration coincided with these anxious reappraisals of British economic and social affairs. Allegations and rumours about the supposed adverse consequences of unrestricted entry were sufficiently insistent for the House of Lords in 1888 to set up a select committee on sweated industries, followed a year later by a Commons committee on immigration. Soon after, at the general election of 1895, restriction on immigration was part of the programme of the Conservative Party, although it was ten years before legislation was effected and not before a full-scale inquiry by the Royal Commission on Alien Immigration (1902–3). The politics of the matter were two-fold. First, regulation of entry to Britain was consistent with the policies of those demanding positive state action to remedy the deficiencies of existing society. It was a very short step from the advocacy of keeping out foreign goods, in order to protect home employment, to keeping out foreign labour. Joseph Chamberlain, a leading spokesman for protection, spelled out the connection clearly to a working-class audience in Limehouse, in the East End, at the height of the agitation leading up to the Aliens Act of 1905.

> You are suffering from the unrestricted imports of cheaper goods. You are suffering also from the unrestricted immigration of the people who make these goods. . . . I refer to it now as an illustration of my general argument—an illustration of Free Trade fanaticism. . . . I am now in favour of giving the Executive Government the strongest power of control over this alien immigration.[38]

For political parties the argument meant, second, a means of attracting the working-class vote. The demand for restrictions on entry was common among trade unionists and socialists, and the Trades Union Congress passed resolutions to that effect. The trade unions were traditionally associated with the Liberal Party which insistently favoured free trade, and one method of weaning them away was for the Conservatives to recommend restrictions.[39] In this way although Jewish immigration was a small and localised matter, it became incorporated into national politics. But its role must not be exaggerated. In two studies of regional politics at this period the topic is hardly mentioned.[40] The Conservatives, whose Aliens Act received the Royal Assent in August 1905, were defeated overwhelmingly by the Liberals at the subsequent general election. The political issues of the day were numerous and complex, including free trade, temperance and social reform. The problem of the aliens was a symptom of the general discussion, not in any way a central theme.

The impact on the Jewish community was more far-reaching. The older Anglo-Jewry had, by the 1870s and 1880s, worked its passage into British society. The Jews were formally emancipated and anglicised. They had adopted British traditions in their institutions whose very titles reflected the local environment. The Board of Deputies (established 1760) took its name from the association of nonconformist deputies set up earlier in the eighteenth century.

The Boards of Guardians borrowed the title from the Poor Law organisations set up by the Poor Law Amendment Act of 1834. In addition, the United Synagogue formed in 1870 had succeeded in uniting into one organisation many of the London synagogues. It was all orderly and respectable: the synagogues were ministered by 'Reverends' who wore clerical collars; the Chief Rabbi sported episcopal gaiters.

But now there arrived this large group of foreigners, overnight transported from a restrictive and fearful environment to one which was almost limitlessly free. They preferred their own insanitary houses of prayer, of which many were established; often they insisted that their particular ritual and tradition were superior to the arrangements in other synagogues, and they wished to maintain their own autonomous institutions. They were not amenable to English notions of order and discipline. The gap between the two communities was wide and hard to bridge, and not just in matters of religion and organisation. It was very difficult for the established community to put across to the newcomers that the marriage laws of England were different and had to be obeyed; in particular on the permitted degrees of consanguinity.

In histories of the period the older-established group who had positions of authority in the community and in society are portrayed as the villains of the piece. The appeals of lay and synagogue leaders to the emigrants not to come to Britain, and their efforts to get them to return to eastern Europe; the advocacy, by some Jewish M.P.s and candidates at elections, of restrictions on immigration seem despicable and unworthy.[41] Yet, in a wider perspective, these aberrations fall into place. In his brief but perceptive study of Jewish migration, Tartakower notes that in the process of facing and adjusting to 'economic psychological and moral problems. . . . Jewish migrants . . . have usually been more fortunate than those of other peoples in their local co-religionists: for the latter have been eager to help them and to smooth the path of adjustment to new conditions'.[42] And it is a nice irony that in comparative studies of race relations in Britain the notion of Jews as sponsors is held up as a useful example in the discussion of how immigrants can be assisted to become accepted by society.[43]

9
The Immigrant Trades, 1880–1914[1]

The prototypical Jewish immigrant from eastern Europe reproduced his familiar environment in the ghetto areas of British cities, spatially distinct and socially distant from other groups of people. The experience of persecution induced a fear of the non-Jewish world; the immigrants' strict religious upbringing imposed an insurmountable barrier between them and the Christians, and to prevent the crime of intermarriage, social intercourse was frowned on and, where possible, prohibited. They were separated too from the older-established Jewish residents, the poor as well as the rich, the Ashkenazim from central Europe in addition to the Sephardim. The working-class Jews of Dutch and German origin were looked down on and referred to disdainfully as 'Dotchkes' or 'Choots'; to Russian and Polish Jews they seemed to be people who had been suborned by the English environment. They were the kind of people, for example, who joined the army, in sufficient numbers for commanding officers at Aldershot in 1882 to be instructed, in divisional orders, 'to facilitate the attendance of men of this persuasion' at Saturday and holy day services at the local, civilian synagogue. Arrangements were made generally in 1883 and 1885 for Jewish soldiers to have leave on Jewish holy days; in 1900, during the Boer War, the Admiralty gave orders that Jews 'should be given facilities for the practice of their religion'.[2] One serving soldier was Joseph Miller, 'who came to Sunderland from Latvia when quite young, enlisted in the army during the South African War, where he "earned" the D.C.M.', and remained in the peace-time army in a commissioned rank.[3] But he was unusual among the east European immigrants. For Jews, service in the Russian army in the nineteenth century was a story of horror: of ill-treatment, degradation, very long service, conversion to Christianity and often death (not necessarily in battle).[4] The Jews who left Russia included some escaping from conscription and deserters from the army. In any case the moral imperative was to remain within the Jewish group and to avoid contact with the outside, Christian world: many occupations were just not considered suitable, and the immigrants fixed their gaze on a limited range of jobs and activities.

The characteristic pattern was to take up an independent occupation, such as peddling, to work for another Jew, or to set up as an employer. Almost all the immigrants stayed at first in areas where a few Jews already lived and it was possible to get work with them. In Leeds there were the clothing firms of Lubelski and others; in Manchester the raincoat manufacturers Frankenstein and Mandelberg; in London numerous owners of small workshops. In some cases, admittedly, the immigrants probably worked in non-Jewish enterprises: in the 1870s, when there were few Jewish footwear firms in Leeds, the Jewish workers were probably scattered among the city's industry. However, during the 1880s and 1890s, the Leeds slipper industry became increasingly Jewish, in ownership and workforce.[5] Presumably too the Jewish tinplate-workers of the East End of London, making articles of metalware, were at first employed within non-Jewish firms until Jewish enterprises were established.[6] And it is not impossible to find examples of individual immigrants taking up 'unusual' jobs; one was Samuel Goldwyn (1882–1974) who, en route to America to become a film magnate, temporarily worked as a blacksmith's assistant in Manchester.[7] Some girls became prostitutes.[8] In the late 1890s there is said to have been a Jewish House Painters' and Decorators' trade union.[9] Yet so surprising is it to read of Jews outside a narrow range of jobs that a recent writer dismisses a report of 1903 which referred to physical attacks on Jewish miners in Dowlais, South Wales: 'it is possible that the attack was really against foreign workers, to whom the term Jew was applied merely by way of abuse'.[10] In fact a number of Jews were working as labourers at the Dowlais steel works and, after conflicts with the local workers, were assisted to move on to Canada by the Jewish Board of Guardians. In some contemporary accounts they are described as miners.[11]

The problem is that it is not always possible to correlate the different sections of the Jewish community with the various economic activities or residential patterns. Although the *Jewish Chronicle* reported, in 1873, that 'in the new towns of the north, the congregations are almost entirely composed of foreigners. In some (West Hartlepool for example) the proportion they bear to Englishmen is at least 9 to 1',[12] it is possible that some of the other, new, small provincial communities such as Blackburn were made up of second-generation British Jews. To counter 'the assertion . . . that I object to the employment of Jewish labour', a non-Jewish candidate for Alderman to a City of London ward took up one and a half pages of the *Jewish Chronicle* in 1891 with a list of the Jews working for him.[13] It cannot be known if they were recent immigrants (or their children), east Europeans or central Europeans. The same doubts surround the young Jews and Jewesses (aged fourteen to twenty) who are recorded as having entered Jewish Friendly Societies in 1913, and whose occupations are shown as clerks, shop assistants and typists.[14] Sometimes the particular section of the community is known. The Sephardim, for example, can usually be identified by their names; and the occupations of bridegrooms in the period up to 1901 have been published.[15] From the last source we know that the number of cigar-workers was declining and tailors and boot- and

shoe-workers increasing. A few were in 'unusual' trades—gasfitter, bus conductor and the like. Moreover among the Ashkenazim it seems that the
jewellery-workers in Hatton Garden were usually of central European origin,[16] as were some of the sugar-workers of the East End. This was an industry
in which few native workers had much experience, and 'German and Polish
Jews, skilled workers, were brought over'.[17] (An alternative view is that the
working conditions were so dreadful that no locals would tolerate them.[18])
Perhaps too the fur-workers, who were brought over in the busy season by the
German-Jewish employers in London—they received perhaps 8s. or 10s. per
week, food and beds (the forms and tables in the workshops where they
worked)—were German Jews.[19]

    Yet, despite these sundry problems, there is no doubt at all about the main
immigrant occupations. The most important was clothing, for women (i.e.,
young, unmarried girls) as well as for men. The men were usually tailors, and
the girls tended to work as milliners and dress-makers. The furniture trade was
mainly for men, but both men and women worked in the tobacco industry.
Another important group were pedlars; and others were glaziers, and those
who supplied the needs of the community—bakers, butchers and various
religious functionaries. The Census of Population gives *inter alia* figures of the
occupations of people born abroad; from them some idea can be obtained of
the jobs of Russians, Russian Poles and Romanians, most of whom were Jews.
Thus in 1911 in England and Wales about 50 per cent of the men were in the
clothing trades (including headwear and footwear), and 10 per cent in furniture. Even allowing for the incompleteness of the returns, for the lack of
knowledge about those born in Britain, for the fact that people moved
temporarily from job to job (as we shall see), and that the non-Jewish Russians,
etc., are included in them, the general picture is clear enough. 'Son of an
immigrant tailor' is a commonplace phrase in obituaries and biographies of
Jews born in Britain after about 1880. The clothing industries were particularly
important immigrant occupations in the three main areas of settlement, London, Manchester and Leeds, but tailors were among the immigrants almost
everywhere they settled. Sheffield, the steel town, boasted a Jewish Tailors'
Sabbath Observance and Benefit Society, and in Newcastle there existed for a
time a Jewish branch of the Amalgamated Society of Tailors.

    The reasons for this concentration are plain enough. In the first place they
reflected the characteristic occupations of the Jews of eastern Europe. Out of
9,047 newly-arrived 'cases' who attended the Poor Jews' Temporary Shelter in
London in various years between 1895 and 1908, 2,599 (29 per cent) were
makers of garments; 2,054 (23 per cent) were in trade and commerce; 977 (11
per cent) were boot- and shoe-makers; and 719 (8 per cent) were carpenters: a
total of 6,349 or 71 per cent. The next sizeable group were 205 agriculturists (2
per cent of the total). 'The remaining 2,493 immigrants were spread thinly
among a wide variety of trades, including butchers, bakers, printers, coopers,
barbers, furriers, jewellers, coachmen, locksmiths, bricklayers, cigar-makers,

painters, and descending numerically to one acrobat'.[20] It is not surprising that some trades, such as engineering, were absent from this labour force. The immigrants came from countries which were either rural or just beginning to industrialise, and few Jews there had any experience of modern machinery.

This is not to say that the immigrants necessarily went into their familiar jobs, or did not try for others. Some who settled in Leeds attempted to get employment in breweries, mines and on the railways, but were refused.[21] Others went into tailoring and hawking, despite having been in different occupations in eastern Europe. The second reason for their concentration into a narrow range of occupations was an amalgam of discrimination by non-Jewish employers, the immigrants' fear of the outside world, and the availability of Jewish employers who would be prepared to employ them, who spoke the same language and would understand their special religious requirements such as not working on Saturdays.

The third explanation follows from their gregariousness, from preferring to settle within a familiar, Jewish environment. They were attracted to the East End, it has been said, 'not by jobs and high wages but by the presence of other Jews',[22] and that would apply to Leeds, Manchester and elsewhere. The choice of one town rather than another might depend on luck—where an immigrant's money ran out, for example; or he might have immigrated purposely to join a friend or relative; or the name of a town might have been his only information on emigration. In one or two cases conscious efforts were made to direct immigrants to particular jobs and towns. The Jewish Dispersion Committee encouraged Jewish tailors to move to Leicester to get work in a Jewish clothing firm.[23] And 160 Jews were taken from London to Glasgow to work in the cigarette industry.[24] Although few went to Leicester, at least both these towns had Jewish communities. The absence of an existing Jewish community in Colchester must explain why immigrants did not go there, even though it was a major centre of the clothing industry.

One of the communal organisations which dealt with immigrants, the Russo-Jewish Committee, succinctly summarised their economy in its *Report* for 1894:

> The so-called Jewish trades naturally take a large proportion [of immigrants], (1) because they were the only trades in which the newly-arrived immigrants could understand the language of their employers and fellow workers; (2) because these were frequently the original trades of the applicants; (3) because in certain cases of adults who had never had any handicraft occupation, these trades were found to be the most readily learnt.[25]

The Jews, according to the Booth survey, 'work and meet their fate almost independent of the great stream of London life surging round them'.[26] The 'immigrant trades' were Jewish-owned, with a Jewish labour force and often separate Jewish trade unions. Sometimes they specialised in a particular part of the industry and thus did not compete with the non-Jewish section. London

Jews were not among the makers of silk hats, who had a strong trade union and systematic apprenticeship. The demand for those products was falling and Jews worked in the expanding cap-making section: the silk-hat-makers were old, the cap-makers were young. 'Caps, whether for bicycling, golf or travelling, are chiefly made in the Jewish workshops of East London, although these feel keenly the competition of Manchester, where the factory system is more developed than in the East End. Even caps bearing the names of well-known hatters are made in Whitechapel'.[27] There is moreover some evidence that the 'immigrant trades' specialised by introducing new products, such as velvet and velveteen hats, coming into competition with the old-established headwear industry located in the Luton area only when the latter took up the making of velvet hats.[28] Another innovation by immigrants was the making of ladies' jackets and mantles which had previously been imported from Germany.[29] The Leeds Jewish tailoring workshops formed a distinct part of the local clothing industry.[30] The English section was mainly organised in factories, each employing up to 2,000 workers—a high proportion being female, especially in the machining section (men were employed as cutters). The work was highly specialised with separate departments for each process and with extensive division of labour: this was not a speciality of the Jewish section. Generally all processes were carried out on the premises, but in the busy season English female homeworkers would be employed on certain finishing processes such as buttonholing and button-sewing. Another section comprised the small-scale bespoke (made-to-measure) craft tailors who made the whole of a garment and used no outworkers.

In the Jewish branch a handful of wholesale manufacturers, pre-1880 immigrants, employed up to 150 workers each and were similar to the large English wholesale firms in the employment of female labour, both in the factory and as homeworkers in the busy seasons. The most important task was to receive cloth, already cut in the factory, to be completed as garments. The workshop, in a sense, was a small-scale replica of the factory in which all the processes, except machine-cutting, were performed. It was ancillary to the factory, an important function, but it is evident that the development of the Leeds clothing industry depended essentially on the availability of female labour for the English wholesale manufacturers. Of the 23,542 tailors in Leeds in 1911, just over two-thirds (15,917) were women; in the forty years from 1871 the number of male tailors had increased five-fold (1,523 to 7,625); but the female labour force had increased thirty times, from 483 to 15,917.[31]

However, from about the 1890s the Leeds factories began to change from the production of ready-made clothes to bespoke (made-to-measure) and the Jewish workshops suffered, only the larger ones continuing to supply the warehouses as before. The Jewish tailors also moved on to bespoke tailoring, in very small workshops or in their own homes, coming into competition with the old craft tailors.

Leeds had earlier experienced competition between Jewish and non-Jewish workers, in one part of the footwear industry, the making of slippers. There had been a few Jewish slipper-makers before 1880, but the Jewish workers monopolised it by the 1890s. It was argued at the time that they had undercut the native workers, producing goods at half the price by working extraordinarily long hours, from 7 A.M. to midnight.[32]

Examples such as this, even though probably a small proportion of the total Jewish immigrant economy, were sufficient grounds for the Trades Union Congress to pass a resolution in the early 1890s opposing the influx of alien labour. The cry that immigrants were taking jobs away from Englishmen was associated also with the intensive contemporary discussions about sweated industries. The immigrants' misfortune 'was to arrive shortly before various social inquiries focussed attention upon East End problems. Jews were prominent in the most distressed districts and sectors of the press, the public, and the trade union world too readily diagnosed immigration as the crux of the problem'.[33]

The charge that the immigrants were responsible for sweating was denied by those who examined it at the time, a denial confirmed by historical research since. Beatrice Webb, for example, who investigated East End conditions for the Booth Survey in the late 1880s and gave evidence to the House of Lords Select Committee on Sweating (1888), concluded that sweating was widespread in Britain. She argued that it was found in all those industries which were not within the regulations of the Factories Act and which were not organised by trade unions.[34] One of the most notorious sweated trades was the making of chains at Cradley Heath, Staffordshire, an industry with which Jews were completely unconnected, as employers or workers. The fact remains that the immigrants were concentrated in trades which were sweated.

Long hours of work, low wages and very poor working conditions were the most publicised features of sweating. Some of the descriptions recall Henry Mayhew's accounts of London working life of the late 1840s and early 1850s. A workshop could well be an attic, a cellar or even one of the rooms within a house—a bedroom for example. My paternal grandfather's cabinet-making place of work was a cellar below the family residence. Conditions would inevitably be foul, tailors in particular suffering from the heat and steam of the pressing process, as well as damaging their eyes from the continuous sewing in poor light. Some statistics from Leeds dramatically illustrate these matters. Systematic studies of Jewish children before World War I demonstrated unequivocally that their physique was superior to that of comparable non-Jewish children. They were heavier and taller on average and fewer suffered from rickets. But one in five of Leeds Jewish recruits for the armed forces in World War I was placed in Category IV, three times the average for non-Jews. The main reasons for rejection were myopia and lung disease, the industrial diseases of tailoring. Similarly tailors suffered from tuberculosis: by 1910, 20 per cent of the cases in Leeds were Jews.[35]

Conditions of work were further exacerbated by intermittent employment.

The immigrant trades shared with many others extensive fluctuations in the demand for the products they made. In the various branches of clothing manufacture employment was high in the spring and early summer, from about March to June. For the next two or three months the number of workers required was perhaps one-third of those working in the busy period. A lower peak of activity in September and October was followed by a depressed winter. In such industries workers could expect to be unemployed or under-employed for half the year: that was bad enough, explaining no doubt the large numbers of such people applying to the Board of Guardians for assistance (Table 7). In the busy season, employees worked very long hours and extra workers were called in, the system depending on an elastic supply of labour, a pool ready to be called upon. London possessed many industries with this pattern of production, and it contained a plentiful supply of labour which could be brought in for the periods of high output. 'Thus the excess of work at seasonal peaks of production tended to retain, within these industries, surplus workers who might otherwise be driven into other forms of permanent employment'.[36] A familiar feature of the East End of London was the congregation of tailors in the Mile End Road, waiting for work: these assemblies lasted until well after World War II.

With an abundant supply of labour ready to be used for sudden increases in production, employers had little incentive either to stock up during the slack season or to invest in capital equipment. Small-scale workshops were flexible and did not require investment, and were therefore able to maintain their existence. Moreover since it was not at all difficult to set up as a master in industries of this kind—the tools and machinery required were not expensive and any building however small would serve—it was not uncommon for workers to set up as small masters. Given also that in some of these industries the level of output might vary from week to week and even day to day, it is clear that 'a substantial proportion of the work-force remained in a casualised limbo, filling in time between short periods of employment by invading an already overfilled general unskilled labour market'.[37]

The foregoing discussion is based on Stedman Jones's analysis of late-nineteenth-century London, but was not uncharacteristic of the provinces. The Leeds Jewish slipper industry, for example, experienced six months of low activity each year during which workers went into hawking, peddling, tailoring or baking—the last of these being considered the last possible resort, apart from idleness. Its unsavoury reputation meant that it was manned by the old or by men unable to work in their regular occupations.[38] The difference between Jews and non-Jews who worked in such seasonal trades is that the Jews were probably unlikely to take work in the 'general unskilled labour market', but would remain within the traditional Jewish trades.

Two obvious conclusions follow from these points. One, of course, is the difficulty of establishing the exact size of the labour force in each industry where the workers were likely to be unoccupied for considerable periods of the year. More important, the lack of continuous employment together with the fragmented nature of many of these industries mean that neither wage rates nor earnings were uniform. Statistics collected by the Board of Trade in the early years of immigration about earnings in Jewish clothing workshops (which included non-Jewish girls) bear this out. As expected, the different skills would get different rewards; a male presser or machinist might get as much as 9s. or 10s. a day, and a feller perhaps 6s. Women generally got less: a machinist 6s. and a feller 5s. However even within these particular grades the variations were enormous: from 2s.6d. to 9s. a day for male pressers, and 1s.8d. to 6s. for female machinists, for example.[39] It is almost impossible to know the average number of days they were likely to work, but Beatrice Webb suggested that the most skilled men might have employment for as much as four to four and a half days a week, and the least skilled perhaps two days or less. Thus men in the clothing industry would probably earn between 15s. and 45s. per week, the average being 20s. to 25s. Women probably got around 13s. or 14s. This put the tailors—apart from the highly skilled—approximately on the poverty line, as defined in the Booth survey.

These figures relate to London. The capital's rates of pay were usually higher than in the provinces, and clothing-workers in Leeds and Manchester earned rather less than in London. But a fuller examination of earnings, undertaken in 1906 by the Board of Trade—which did not separate the Jewish from the non-Jewish section of the trade—showed that while male clothing-workers in London earned more than their counterparts in the provinces, women in Leeds and Manchester received higher pay than in the capital. The explanation for the latter was that the textile industries of the north competed for women's labour; and in London, especially in the East End, the female labour force was augmented by large numbers of married women—notably the wives of dockers—who worked to supplement their husbands' low earnings. Thus the initial effects of the Trade Boards Act of 1909, which through its machinery fixed minimum wages in ready-made and wholesale bespoke tailoring, were hardly to affect women's wages in Leeds because the minimum rate was lower than the amount they had already been receiving.[40]

No firm conclusions can be drawn from this very sketchy information about the standard of living of the immigrant clothing-workers. They, at least, were working in an expanding industry, but other Jews, e.g., in the boot and shoe industry, and the hand-made cigar and cigarette industry, were less fortunate: both employment and earnings probably fell. Inevitably very different conclusions can be drawn from this incomplete evidence. A non-Jewish writer, recently recalling his boyhood in Salford before World War I, described some of the Jews living there 'in a poverty so appalling that it shocked even us'.[41] Yet, the number of 'cases' applying to the Jewish Board of Guardians, after having risen during the early immigration period, fell in the early years of the twentieth century (Table 7).

Beatrice Potter (later Webb), who examined the East End Jewish community in the late 1880s for the Booth survey, suggested that for the east European immigrants manual work was the bottom rung of a ladder, which they ascended as quickly as they could into the world of trade and finance.[42] One part of the upward route was through petty trading which many entered during the slack season of their normal trade. In this way an immigrant would become 'a tiny capitalist—a maker of profit as well as the earner of a wage'. In this way he was able to move to better accommodation, and to buy jewels and furs for his wife. His family ate poultry on Sundays. She noted that her analysis did not apply to all the immigrants: the 'Jewish passion for gambling' was an outlet for the feckless to employ their enforced leisure in the unemployed periods.[43] Such people were not likely to spend their time making money or aiming to become workshop sweaters.

It may be that, as she said, the east European immigrants were often more ambitious than the population among whom they lived in the East End; she characterised the latter as apathetic, degraded and resigned. But there are some difficulties about her analysis. Between 1880 and 1914 about one-fifth of the applicants to the Jewish Board of Guardians in London were hawkers and general dealers, which suggests that it was not a particularly rewarding occupation. Further, while it is true that the immigrants generally worked in small-scale enterprises and it was easy to become an employer, Beatrice Webb also made the point, in a different context, that the sweaters were generally no better off than the people they employed.[44] And in general the great majority of immigrants remained employees.

A few, nevertheless, managed to do well during the immigration period. One was Ephraim Sieff, the son of a villager miller in Lithuania, who arrived at Hull, thinking he was in America, and was stranded there: he had been swindled into thinking he had bought a ticket for the whole journey.[45] He was advised to take up peddling but, after being insulted by a woman at the first house where he tried to sell imitation jewellery, decided to go to a large community for 'the physical and psychological security which he knew he was in need of'. He took the train to Manchester, where by chance he met a man he had known in his Lithuanian village, who took him to the master tailor for whom he worked. In the basement he saw scraps of cloth which he sorted and carted to Beaumont and Co. Eight years later he bought out the English company. This might be seen as an example of a young immigrant who was initially socially and economically downgraded in his occupation on arrival in Britain, and took up a job rather similar to the old-clothesmen of an earlier period. He did not progress from employed manual work to independence and business.

His son became a business partner of Simon Marks, whose father, Michael Marks, had founded Marks & Spencer.[46] The father was born in 1863 in a village in Russian Poland, and came to Britain in 1882 to which his older brother had already emigrated. The brother had in fact gone on to America, and Michael Marks after a short period in London went to Leeds, where he knew there was a clothing firm called Barran's which gave work to Jewish refugees. By a chance meeting in Leeds he became a pedlar instead of a tailor, and after hawking from house to house, set up as a market trader in the markets of northern towns. He made his reputation as 'M. Marks: the original Penny Bazaar'—selling a whole variety of goods at one penny each. He expanded, and in 1894 opened a shop in Manchester; he began to buy direct from the manufacturers instead of through wholesalers, and went into partnership with a non-Jew, Tom Spencer. By 1900 the firm had thirty-six establishments, and three years later it became a limited company.

This was an uncharacteristic history, and very few of the immigrants were able to advance themselves in this way. It is relevant that in Paul Emden's *Jews of Britain: A Series of Biographies,* published during World War II, the great majority of the élite names he discusses are Sephardim or Ashkenazim from central Europe. Few of the east European immigrants, or their children, had become successful even as late as the period of Emden's book: apart from Marks & Spencer, he mentions Montague Burton, who had begun as a retail trader and moved into the manufacture of clothes for sale in his shops. But the typical immigrant in the years between 1880 and 1914, if he did attempt to move out of a sweated job or street-selling, might become a workshop sweater, or a shopkeeper. The Jewish middle class at that period was composed mainly of the older-established Anglo-Jewry. The children of the immigrants had little option but to go into the traditional trades.

10

Jewish Trade Unionism, 1870–1914

Much has been written about the Jewish garment workers in the United States, but what of those across the Atlantic? They produced no counterparts to the David Dubinskys or Sidney Hillmans who became dominant voices in their country's labor movement. In the U.S., Jewish garment workers built powerful trade unions and played a decisive role in converting a stronghold of the sweatshop into an orderly, respectable industry, renowned for its peaceful labor-management relations. In Britain, however, there has been little comparable achievement.[1]

This valid statement can be extended beyond the clothing industry. In addition to such nationally-known trade union leaders in America the chief position, president of the American Federation of Labor, was occupied by Samuel Gompers. Britain has never produced Jewish trade union leaders of comparable status and the Jewish unions in Britain have seldom rated more than a reference to their ephemeral existence.[2]

A comparison between Britain and America is useful, if unfair. The massive Jewish immigrant population of New York dominated the clothing trades, whereas even in Manchester and Leeds they were a minority. And during the immigration period labour organisations in America were weaker than the British and it was possible for newly-formed unions to occupy leading positions. On the other hand, in Britain in the 1860s and 1870s national unions had been formed in the three main industries into which the Jews mainly went: the Alliance Cabinet Makers' Association (1865); the Amalgamated Society of Tailors (1866); and the National Union of Boot and Shoe Rivetters and Finishers (1874)—the name being subsequently changed to the National Union of Boot and Shoe Operatives. These unions were not particularly strong and were experiencing many problems, for example the effects of technical change and the greater division of labour which reduced skill. But at least they existed and Jewish workers could have joined them. Some did become members of English unions, but separate Jewish unions were also formed. Since trade union history is about the long-term trend towards large, amalgamated organisations, these Jewish unions appear almost unhistorical, a blemish on the standard pattern.

Moreover, most writers who have at all considered them—beginning with Halpern's study of 1903—have tended to write them off as short-lived, small, unimportant and very much a passing phase. Much of the discussion was directed to explaining the reasons for their insignificance. These included the nature of their industries which, being on a small scale, were poor sources of union material. The Jews were aliens unused to British institutions and ignored instructions from union officers, often striking without authority. Their unions were riven by political disputes between different types of anarchists and socialists, all of them opposed by the religiously orthodox workmen. And they did not join unions anyway because they were ambitious to become masters. The analysis was based largely on London experience, but these general explanations have none the less persisted even though the same writers have generally mentioned in passing that these characteristics did not apply to the Jewish clothing-workers of Leeds: and, plainly, sweeping statements about the supposed Jewish reluctance to be trade unionists were not sustainable in view of the success of the American unions.[3]

The emphasis in this chapter will be Jewish trade unionism in the main 'Jewish' industries, whether there were separate unions or Jews joined British unions. It is not possible to look at their membership in other unions beyond noting that an occasional name appears: Moses Sclare, as we shall see, was an official of the Amalgamated Society of Engineers in Glasgow and Emanuel Shinwell was an official of the National Union of Seamen. (A letter-sorter in the Post Office named Jacobs who gets a brief mention in the union's history may or may not have been Jewish.[4])

Early Skirmishes

The history of Jewish unionism is mainly an account of the Yiddish-speaking eastern European immigrants, but, it will be recalled, it was the Dutch Jews in the cigar trade who were the first off the mark, to the extent of striking briefly in 1858. Jews continued to be among the union's members throughout the period and while it was a relatively peaceful union it was sufficiently radical to send delegates to the First International.[5]

Jewish trade union activity really begins, in the immigrant trades, in the 1880s, but there was a passing interest in the previous decade when small, short-lived unions were set up in London and Leeds. A great deal is known about the London body through the chance survival of its records, which show that it was an offshoot of a body founded by Aaron Lieberman (1849?–80): *Agudat HaSozialistim HaIvriim* (Hebrew Socialist Union).[6] It consisted of forty working immigrants and was primarily a political society, preoccupied with theoretical discussion about socialism, but is particularly important in the history of the Jewish labour movement as being the first Jewish socialist body and for its discussions about the role of Jews. Should they contribute to the overthrow of capitalism by remaining a separate Jewish body or by becoming part of the general labour movement? Such controversies were of much greater significance in eastern Europe, but they also had a part to play in Britain.[7] The Hebrew Socialist Union was critical of religious orthodoxy, so that despite its small size the organisation was taken seriously by the Anglo-Jewish establishment. It was attacked by the *Jewish Chronicle,* which suggested that the 'puerile tracts' being issued originated with 'the enemies of the Jews, and were put into circulation to injure them'.[8] It went further in a later issue and stated explicitly that the socialists were really Christian conversionists.[9] The accusation went home: plenty of Christian missionaries were active among the immigrants. A trade union for tailors was formed, with which Lieberman had little to do, and which eschewed socialist propaganda; some 300 members are said to have joined, but it collapsed after three months; the treasurer absconded with the £80 it had collected—a not uncommon occurrence in that period of union history.

Lieberman's organisation was set up in 1876, but the Leeds Jewish Working Tailors' Trade Society was registered as a trade union earlier in the year, in February. It is surprising that it got to that stage since there could have been no more than a few hundred Jewish tailors in Leeds at the time. Nothing is heard of it, but a few years later, in 1884, three separate Leeds unions were in existence, for tailors, machiners and pressers. The local Jewish employers tried to crush them by means of a blacklist and during a strike in 1884 imported Jewish blackleg labour from Liverpool. Yet the one-week strike for union recognition was successful: the unions were recognised. But it was one thing to get an agreement and another to ensure its enforcement. The agreement was a dead letter and this pattern of quick strikes, some of them successful, followed by disillusion as the agreement was ignored, was to be repeated for much of the period. Thus a two-week strike in May 1885 for a shorter working day was successful, the masters agreeing because the busy season was on them. Once that was over, to be followed by the depression of 1885–56, the blacklist came back and the leadership emigrated. Yet the unions survived and claimed a number of victories, with officers being able to settle disputes in the workshops.[10]

The much larger Jewish clothing workforce in London had even less to show. A Jewish Tailors' Union was formed in 1883[11] but nothing is known about it, and in the following year, as a result of adverse publicity about sweating, the *Jewish Chronicle* went so far as to urge the Jewish Board of Guardians to unionise the tailors. Samuel Montagu, the wealthy M.P. for Whitechapel, founded the Jewish Tailors' Machinists' Society in 1886, but this came to nothing.[12] In the same year the London Tailors' and Machinists' Society was formed with London-born Lewis Lyons, aged twenty-four, as its secretary. Its purpose, according to its rules, was to recruit 'any man following any divisional part of the Tailoring Trade (those employing hands excluded)', for a fee of 2d. a week. The objectives were very limited: to reduce hours of work; to maintain a normal day's work 'namely 8 to 8 (subject to alteration), with an interval of one hour for dinner and half hour for tea'; and to obtain healthy workshops. The rules say nothing about a wage policy, presumably because the union hoped to recruit all grades of worker and the industry anyway was characterised by individual piece-work bargaining: there were no standard rates. The only benefit to be paid by the union was dispute pay.[13] Probably more successful, at any rate in recruitment, was the Hebrew Cabinet Makers' Union, formed in 1887, which impressed the Booth survey by quickly having some 200 members out of an estimated 700 Jewish cabinet-makers in the East End of London.[14] Its rules show it to have been a typical skilled union. It was open to journeymen cabinet-makers and carvers; its fee was 4d. per week; those who wished to receive sick benefit could pay higher contributions; a death benefit was payable; the union fixed the rate for the job and members could be fined for working at a lower rate of pay.[15] The East Manchester branch of the Alliance Cabinet Makers (the British union) contained, in 1888, 380 members, of whom 140 were Jews.[16]

The increasing activity of the 1880s reflected a number of disparate features. Continuing immigration provided potential recruits at a time when the British trade union movement was awakening in the years which led up to the great explosion of 1889, symbolised by the dock strike. Public attention was being drawn to the sweating system and a House of Lords Committee was examining it. And socialist ideas and institutions were making an impact. Coinciding with the general trade union ferment, the years 1888–90 witnessed an impressive Jewish trade union effort, in London, Leeds and Manchester. Yet it began with a resounding defeat, in Leeds, where a 'general strike' of tailors in 1888 was called for union recognition, reduction of hours to 58 per week, and extra payment for overtime. At the same time it was hoped to influence the Lords Committee on Sweating by drawing attention to the conditions of Leeds Jewish tailors. The strike lasted from 12 May to 2 June and as many as 1,400 men and 1,700 women, apprentices and other young people took part.[17] It was led by Morris Kentner, assisted by Tom Maguire, the West Riding of Yorkshire socialist, who wrote 'The Song of the Sweater's Victim' for the strikers:

> . . . every worker in every trade,
> in Britain and everywhere,
> Whether he labour by needle or spade,
> Shall gather in his rightful share.[18]

But the funds ran out, the Leeds Trades Council gave only moral support, work was taken to other towns, and the strikers trickled back to work. The strike fizzled out; it was the last 'general strike' of Leeds Jewish tailors until 1911.

However, during the great upsurge in union militancy in 1889 and 1890,

Jewish workers—whether separately or with non-Jews—were more successful in their strikes. These included Manchester cigarette-makers in February 1889; East End tailors in the autumn of that year; London stick-makers in February 1890; London footwear-workers in March; Manchester tailors in April; London tailors in May (to reaffirm the terms of the settlement of the autumn 1889 dispute); Manchester cabinet-makers in May; Manchester waterproofers and footwear-workers in the autumn of 1890. It is possible to suggest a number of reasons for this activity, not least the general labour ferment of the period and the public interest in the sweated trades, as well as the 'alien question'. From the mid-1880s the immigrants had their own Yiddish socialist paper, the *Arbeiter Freint* (Workers' Friend), which provided a sympathetic, if strident, commentary on events more attuned to their ears than the anglicised, establishment *Jewish Chronicle*.[19] A more detailed examination of these disputes of 1889–90 extends the discussion and throws important light on these early years.

The Manchester cigarette strike, the first involving Jews in that city, arose from a proposal by an employer to reduce the piece-rate. This action was opposed by the Jewish workers who, with the assistance of the local trades council, formed a branch of the Cigarette Workers' and Tobacco Cutters' Union, with a Jewish secretary. A few days later a strike was called with only the Jews taking part, and was soon settled in the workers' favour. It was a very small affair—some twenty or so workers were affected—but it was important in the local context because it publicised the existence of sweating in Manchester, just as the Leeds strike of 1888 had exposed it there. It led to Jewish union activity in other trades, and Jews generally joined unions which were not specifically Jewish. Indeed in Manchester only one Jewish union was formed—this was the Jewish Machinists', Tailors' and Pressers' Trade Union, formed at the end of 1889. In the locally important waterproof industry the Waterproof Garment Workers Union was formed by Jewish workers and had a Jewish secretary, Isidore Sugar, but it recruited non-Jews too (in that industry the male workers were Jews and the females were Christian). Cabinet-makers and boot- and shoe-workers joined the appropriate English unions.[20]

In London the centre of activity was the Berner Street Club (officially the International Workers' Educational Club), which took over control of the *Arbeiter Freint*. It was a centre for meetings, and political and union activities. It was, for example, the address of the Cigarette Workers' and Tobacco Cutters' Union. Founded in 1888, this was open to men and women above the age of sixteen, who were engaged in any part of the cigarette-making or tobacco-cutting trade, at a fee of 3d. per week. It was a strike body, the only benefit obtainable being dispute benefit. A supplement to its rules emphasised its political origin: 'The Union has been started first of all to bring a brotherhood among toiling persons, young or old, male or female, so that it [sic] should henceforth be brothers and sisters'.[21]

The Berner Street Club was the starting-point for a 'synagogue parade' organised for Saturday 16 March 1889 by the Jewish Unemployed Committee, one of whose secretaries was Lewis Lyons: the other was Philip Krantz, the editor of the *Arbeiter Freint*.

The background to this event was hostility against the Delegate Chief Rabbi, Hermann Adler, for his lukewarm attitude towards sweating. He had delivered a sermon in May 1888 exposing sweating, but a more recent one, early in 1889, advised the workers against socialism and of the impossibility of remedial action by the state. A leaflet advertising the 'synagogue parade' announced that it would proceed 'with music' to the Great Synagogue, where the Chief Rabbi would deliver a sermon to the unemployed and the victims of sweating. The march took place, attracting 300 to 400 (*Jewish Chronicle*) or 2,000 (*Arbeiter Freint*), but police prevented the marchers from entering the synagogue. The men dispersed after passing resolutions condemning the Chief Rabbi and sweaters, and calling for an end to the capitalist system.[22] Five months later a great strike of East End tailors ended in a victory for the strikers.

The synagogue parade may have been a contributory factor in the strike, but probably of more importance were a number of local trade union events: the match girls' success in 1888; the rapid obtaining of a reduction of hours in August 1889 by the newly-formed Gas Workers' and General Labourers' Union; and the start of the dock strike in the same month. During the summer there were other, sporadic strikes in the East End and a public meeting on 26 August called for a 'general strike' of tailors to start two days later. The chairman of the meeting was Lewis Lyons. The strikers demanded shorter hours—a maximum of twelve per day with an hour and a half off for meals; government contractors to pay the union rate of wages; and no work to be given out to be done at home after working hours. The tailors followed the pattern of the dockers' strike of holding processions and meetings addressed by leaders of the new unions, John Burns, Ben Tillett and Tom Mann. The Jewish strikers contributed to the dockers' strike fund and the dockers reciprocated when their strike ended, supplying £100 out of a total of just under £400. Money for the tailors' strike fund also came from other unions: the Amalgamated Society of Tailors (from the Executive Council and the West London District); two societies of cigar-makers; the London Society of Compositors; and the Amalgamated Society of Boot and Shoe Makers. Small amounts came from individuals, including £10 from 'City Clothing Manufacturer'; Samuel Montagu sent £30.10s, and Lord Rothschild supplied £75. The money was used mainly for relief; coupons were issued which could be exchanged for goods in certain shops.[23] As in Leeds, the strikers were provided with a song, printed in English and Yiddish by the *Arbeiter Freint*.

> Up in the morn at break of day,
> To the Sweater's Den we go;
> We sweat our health and strength away,
> And pale and sickly grow.
> That the sweater may dwell in Mansions Fair

And wear the costliest clothes
While our children starve in hovels bare
Where the sunlight seldom goes.
So we strike for our babes,
We strike for our wives,
Together we stand or fall,
Determined to win true manly lives
For the workers one and all.[24]

The strike ended on 6 October, following mediation by Samuel Montagu, with victory for the strikers.

This was the Jewish East End's main contribution to the peak of union activity in the late 1880s. In the euphoria during the aftermath of the tailors' strike, a public meeting was held on 28 December under the auspices of eight Jewish unions (two of tailors, two of shoe-makers, one each of cabinet-makers, furriers, cap-makers, and stick-dressers). The meeting, said to have been attended by 4,000 Jewish workers, resolved to combine into a Federation of East London Labour Unions. Some of these unions were new, and one of them, the International Society of Stick Makers, successfully struck in February 1890.[25] Jewish boot- and shoe-makers joined in a large strike of London footwear-workers in March 1890 for the abolition of outwork.[26] The victory here was as short-lived as that of the tailors the previous October; the unions could not enforce the agreement and the employers ignored it, as they did after a second strike of tailors in May 1890 succeeded in getting the October terms re-affirmed.

The May 1888 strike had been a resounding defeat for the Leeds tailors, and the employers took their revenge by blacklisting and by lengthening hours of work. But although the unions were virtually destroyed, by February 1890 there was a new departure. In that month the recently successful gas-workers (they had obtained their demand for an eight-hour shift) opened their doors to the Leeds Jewish tailors. As a result of this alliance the Leeds tailors quickly won a demand in August for a reduction in hours. As in London, though, the victory was short-lived and despite the assistance of the gas-workers in, for example, attacking non-union shops, within a few months the old conditions had returned. The alliance between the tailors and the gas-workers ended in mutual recrimination.[27]

During this early period, in the 1880s, the emphasis was on recruitment, recognition and the improvement of the worst conditions, especially on attempts to reduce hours of work and resistance to wage-cutting. At that period these objectives had normally to be pursued by strikes, given the hostility of employers to the unions and the absence of agreed procedures to handle industrial differences. These are common aspects of the early history of all unions in all countries, as are successes and failures. More interesting in the

Jewish context are two facts: that whether in separate unions or not, there was a high degree of association with non-Jews. For example, the secretary of the three Leeds tailors' unions was J. H. Sweeney, even though he, along with Tom Maguire who had helped in the 1888 strike, was opposed to Jewish immigration. The relationship was a fluctuating one, and comradely feelings were liable to change to expressions of exasperation when Jewish unionism was weak, as we shall see when the 1889–90 peak had passed. The second feature was that many of the Jewish union leaders of the time were not new immigrants but had been settled in the country for several years. At least one of them—Lewis Lyons—was born in Britain. They had, in other words, several years of experience of British conditions and were able therefore to associate with British unionists.

The 1890s

As we have seen, victories in these strikes were usually short-lived. It was all very well, in a seasonal trade, to gain something in the busy period, but the slack season inevitably produced a reaction as employers took their revenge and workers scrambled for jobs. The unions were often little more than strike bodies with primitive organisation, and as early as June 1890 the *People's Press*, John Burns's paper, was complaining that 'these self-assertive and individualistic' people had 'but the faintest idea of the principles of trade unionism'. Their unions were impermanent, had no clear purpose, were undisciplined, prone to internal strife and aloofness, and had poor leaders.[28]

Similarly the secretary of the Leeds branch of the Alliance Cabinet Makers' Association told the Royal Commission on Labour in 1892 about the problems of recruiting Jews. There were, he said, about 350 to 400 cabinet-makers in Leeds, of whom 100 were in his union and perhaps 70 in another. Perhaps eighty Jewish cabinet-makers worked in the city, but no more than ten were unionists. 'Are they reluctant to join you?', he was asked. 'They say they cannot understand our terms. Only if there is going to be a strike then they can understand our terms. If we are agitating for an advance they can understand English then. They can understand the terms so as to join us and receive 18s. a week if we should come out on strike. But still when we ask them to join the Union they say they do not understand English'.[29]

These complaints had some validity; Jewish unions in the 1890s were often weak and unstable. The Jewish Vest Makers' Union began life in 1896 and recruited ninety-six members in its first year, but disappeared the following year. The United Hebrew Compositors' Union was formed in 1895 with twelve members, rose to eighteen, and was dissolved in 1898. The London unions were often led by socialists, and to counteract their influence the Jewish National Tailors', Machinists' and Pressers' Union was formed in 1899 to organise orthodox workers. It lasted only two years.[30] The experiences of the

Workers' Union later on were very similar. The union was founded in 1898 by Tom Mann and organised workers in a wide range of industries, including Jewish tailors.

> The difficulties were immense: the workers were mainly occupied in seasonal trades such as tailoring, conducted by numerous small employers. Language differences created problems of communication (for one meeting the Whitechapel branch advertised 'speakers in Russian, English, Yiddish, Polish, German, etc.'). The union was also handicapped by a growing mood of racialism, and by occasional police violence. Even so, several branches were opened, and recruitment was subsequently extended to Jewish tailors in the Soho area. But while a membership of some two hundred was maintained for a year or so, this too collapsed entirely.[31]

Very often little more is known than the name of the various Jewish unions, but one of the transient organisations is worth special mention. The International Boot and Shoe Workers' Union was founded in 1900 and quickly recruited 978 members in London. On 1 January 1901, after two workers in a firm were discharged, the other employees struck in sympathy. The London employers responded by forming an association which locked out the men, demanding they sign the 'document', i.e., that they would renounce the union. The men countered by demanding higher pay and 1,340 men were locked out by twenty-six Jewish firms. After two weeks an independent arbitration found in favour of the men, and they won their right to join a union and to receive higher pay.[32] At the end of March the regular column, 'Jewish Labour News', in the *Jewish Chronicle* commented: 'The rising tide of Trade Unionism among the Jewish workers, originating with the formation of the Boot and Shoe Workers' Union, and manifesting its strength in the success of the now historical lock-out, seems destined to encircle many branches of industry before finally spending its force'. Existing unions, it said, were actively recruiting, and moribund ones were reviving.[33] But it was a passing phase and not much more is heard of these temporarily enthusiastic groups—such as the Cardiff International Tailors', Machinists', and Pressers' Trade Union—and the boot and shoe union quickly disappeared.[34]

Yet this is only one part of the story. During the 1890s all unions in Britain were on the defensive in view of trade depression and the antagonism of employers. Those formed in the late 1880s were especially vulnerable and collapsed even more spectacularly than did the Jewish unions. Of six 'new unions' which in 1890 claimed a membership of over 40,000 each, two were dissolved in 1894, and the remaining four had lost large numbers of members.[35] The recent verdict on this period of a labour historian is instructive:

> Trade unionists in the newly organised trades like dockers and gasworkers were rarely more than a minority of the labour force, and to achieve their main objectives of higher wages, shorter hours, and union recognition, with

or without a strike, brought them right up against the prejudice, ignorance and apathy of important groups in their own class who were not prepared to accept the need for, or the decisions of, the unions.[36]

For the Jews there was the special circumstance of a renewal of persecution in Russia in the early 1890s, which produced more immigrants who swelled the labour market. A number of leading Jewish activists left for America and in the prevailing dismay there was much internecine conflict between competing factions. For example, Lewis Lyons, secretary of the International Tailors', Machinists' and Pressers' Union, was accused of mismanagement by the *Arbeiter Freint* and condemned at a meeting chaired by John Burns.[37]

While these political and personal arguments were real enough, they do not tell the whole story, nor was it always the case, even in London, that unions typically were formed during boom periods and disappeared soon afterwards. Table 8 lists the main Jewish unions of the 1890s which—despite legitimate suspicion about the membership figures—suggests some degree of continuity. The London unions were certainly separate from each other, but those in Manchester and Leeds were not. In both cities the Jewish tailors were able to form single unions (the Manchester-based waterproofers' union is not included here because although dominated by Jews it was not confined to them). The Manchester union had a continuous existence until 1906, when it became a branch of the Amalgamated Society of Tailors. The Leeds union was formed in October 1893, soon after the Jewish tailors withdrew from the gas-workers' union. The union, which lasted until 1915, was open to Jewish tailors of all grades (unlike the 1880s unions which organised the various main clothing occupations separately). More important, the union, although including members with all manner of political views, was able to overcome these differences and to concentrate on building an organisation geared to industrial matters. It had a full-time secretary: Sam Freedman from 1895 to 1906 and Moses Sclare thereafter. It paid friendly benefits and even had an education committee from 1896. It set up a Jewish Tailoresses' Union with 200 members in February 1896 at a time when the total number of organised women in the industry was no more than 500. Having learned its lesson from the 1888 strike, the union pursued its policies by striking against individual employers, and paid strike benefit from funds raised through levies. This strategy earned them a local reputation for obdurate militancy.[38]

1900–1915

Union activity fluctuated with economic conditions. During the sittings of the Royal Commission on Alien Immigration, 1902–3, Jewish witnesses enthused about union progress. Lewis Lyons said that among the tailors the immigrants were more highly unionised than the native born: 2,000 Jewish tailors were members of unions in London, whereas out of the much larger number of natives only 1,600 were organised. His view was consistent with that of David Policoff, the secretary of the Manchester Jewish Tailors, Machinists' and Pressers' Union, who claimed that his 900 members comprised three-quarters of the total number of Jewish tailors in the city. More generally Isidore Solomons, secretary of the United Capmakers' Union (120 members) told the Royal Commission on Alien Immigration: 'I find they do take readily to Trades Unions; and, in fact, no sooner do they get into work than the first thing they inquire after is the Trades Union'.[39]

The trade depression of 1903–6 however saw leaner years, and even the Leeds union lost members, but a revival began in 1905–6 and new unions were formed. One of them, the United Cigarette-makers, Cutters, Packers and Shippers, founded in December 1905, was enterprising enough to produce its own journal printed in English and Yiddish.[40]

During 1906 several groups of Jewish workers were on strike: 'hardly a week passes without a fresh strike breaking out in one or other of the trades', wrote the labour correspondent of the *Jewish Chronicle* in February. They included the stick-makers, whose union had been moribund for years, cabinet-makers in London and Liverpool, cap-makers and journeymen butchers.[41] The greatest event was a mass strike of tailors in east London. Some 5,000 workers were on strike for eleven days, the Amalgamated Society of Tailors took over the leadership and an agreement was reached for a reduction of the working day from thirteen to twelve hours, the substitution of day-wages for piece-work, and the establishment of a conciliation board. One consequence was an influx of many Jewish workers into the Amalgamated Society, but with the rapid return of depression, and competition for work, the membership fell.[42]

The last stages of this history came in 1911 with a 'general strike' of Jewish tailors in Leeds, followed in 1912 by a similar-sized dispute in London. The Leeds union had begun to revive during the 1906–7 period, when Moses Sclare of Glasgow, formerly a branch secretary of the Amalgamated Society of Engineers, became the full-time secretary of the Leeds tailors' union. Under his guidance the provincial Jewish tailors formed a federation which included all the Jewish tailors' unions in the North and the Midlands. A lock-out in February and March 1911 in Leeds was successfully fought, among the gains being a reduction of hours of work and an end to sub-contracting.[43]

A comparable victory was won in London in the summer of 1912. A dispute began on 1 May, when tailors and tailoresses struck in west London, and the East End tailors came out in sympathy on the 12th. According to Rudolf Rocker, the non-Jewish leader of the Jewish anarchists, this sympathetic strike was called because 'strike-breaking work was being done in the small East End tailoring workshops'. The various Jewish tailoring unions decided to call a general strike to prevent this happening. Their funds were low, but the Jewish Bakers' Union provided bread and the cigarette-makers supplied tobacco. Joint meetings were held with the dockers, who were also on strike. The West End strike was settled, but the East End dispute lasted for thirty-six days. It resulted in the reduction of daily working hours to twelve, together with increases in pay.[44]

These events took place during the great upsurge of union activity in Britain just before World War I, when membership rose and strikes were frequent. Amalgamation of unions was in the air and in 1915 the first important merger of clothing unions took place, by which some Jewish unions joined the first industry-wide union. Some of the Jewish unions had already come together, perhaps as a response to the anti-alien sentiment exemplified by the Aliens Act, and several Jewish unions now had large memberships: the biggest was the Leeds union, with 4,465 members in 1913; another was the Jewish Tailors' and Tailoresses' Trade Union of Great Britain and Ireland which had 1,981. One major clothing union, the United Ladies' Tailors and Mantle Makers, remained separate until World War II; and the last separate Jewish union lingered on until the 1960s. Textbooks on trade unionism used to refer to this tiny London Jewish Bakers' Union as an extreme example of the size variations of British unions. Essentially, the separate Jewish unions, and the separate Jewish sections of British unions belong to the immigration period.[45]

Conclusion

It is necessary to rescue these organisations from the patronising footnotes where so often they have been fated to appear. In the broader context of British labour history they do not appear unusual or eccentric. Before the great wave of amalgamations during and soon after World War I, and before the vast expansion of union membership during the war-time period, most unions in Britain were small. In 1900, a not untypical year, as many as 1,252 unions catered for a membership of 1.9 million, an average of about 1,500. One hundred large unions organised a total of over one million and the average of the remaining 1,152 was 650 each. Many had fewer than a hundred.[46] Nor was it unusual for groups of workers to secede from existing unions and form their own new ones; or for entirely new ones to be established even if an industry or occupation already possessed workers' organisations. Jews were no more individualistic in this respect than British workers, and their alien culture and, to some extent, distinct economic sector, encouraged the formation of their own unions. In describing the Jewish branch in Manchester of the Alliance Cabinet Makers' Association, a witness told the Royal Commission on Alien Immigration, 'we separate them on account of the language. We have our rules printed in Yiddish'.[47] The International branch of the Transport and General Workers' Union, catering for foreign hotel workers in the 1970s, provides a modern example.

Compared with the provinces, the London Jewish unions were weak and recruited proportionately smaller numbers, but this was a reflection of the state of union organisation in the capital. For all the excitement of the late 1880s at the time of the dock strike, London was notoriously poorly organised until

World War I.[48] Similarly the clothing industry was then, and has remained, an industry whose unions have had to struggle to recruit members and to make any impact on their wages and conditions. Even today its membership is not particularly high. Indeed, given the extraordinary difficulties of organising Jewish workers in the period of immigration—their lack of knowledge of modern industrial society, the small size of their workplaces, fluctuations in employment, anti-alien and antisemitic sentiments—it is surprising they did anything at all. That they seem to have joined unions in certain industries in greater proportions than did non-Jewish workers is all the more remarkable. It is that, rather than their avoidance of unions, which needs to be explained.

Finally, what is to be said of the flurries of activity, the rapid enthusiasm, in periods of busy trade, sometimes resulting in successes of one kind or another, to be followed by a return to the previous conditions when the industry was in depression? There is of course nothing surprising in unions vehemently pressing claims in boom periods and finding themselves on the defensive during slumps. This applies to organisations with a continuing existence, whose members will remain with them during bad times; but even the short-lived unions which came into existence to press a claim and whose members then drifted away have a role in union history. Many labour historians have reacted against the older attitude of the Webbs, who concentrated on unions with a continuous history; they now give credit to groups of workers who in adverse circumstances tried to make some impact, even temporarily, on their conditions of life. In this perspective 'seasonal' unionism—taking action when employers are more likely to concede demands—was tactically sensible, and it had the positive function of providing preliminary experience for more permanent organisation.[49]

11

Business and the Professions in the Era of Immigration

'If 1881 to 1914 is the period *par excellence* of the immigrant quarter, it is equally the period of the rise of Jewish suburbia'.[1] As the east Europeans crowded into the central districts of the main cities, there was a counterbalancing efflux into more salubrious areas. Even before 1914, while immigration was still continuing, the effect was to halt the rise in house rents in London's East End, where overcrowding in the later nineteenth century had forced them up. Such Jewish settlement was part of the rapid urban spread of the period, especially in London with its expanding transport facilities. Jews moved out to augment congregations in earlier districts of suburban residence, in the Hackney area, for example, but such new places as Hampstead and Hammersmith also began to support local synagogues. On the eve of World War I small numbers of Jews were living as far north as Golders Green, once that stretch of the underground railway had been opened.[2]

Although some of these new Jewish residential districts—such as Tottenham, and East and West Ham—were not middle-class places, many of the new and expanded suburbs were. In the provinces too there was a clear difference between the immigrant areas and those of higher status. Middle-class Jews in Manchester lived in Victoria Park; in Glasgow their district was Garnethill.[3] Israel Sieff of Manchester described in his autobiography how, as his immigrant father's business prospered, the family's economic and social progress was marked by a series of residential moves. 'The social ascent could almost be equated topographically—almost by yards north-west up the Bury New Road'.[4]

As would be expected, it was the middle-class areas which supplied the Jews who obtained commissioned rank during World War I. The addresses are known of those who were killed in action, and it may be assumed that they were representative of all Jewish officers. About one-third had lived in north-west London, and the deceased Manchester officers had lived at Didsbury and in the Kersal and Victoria Park districts. Conversely, although about one-third of all Britain's Jews lived in the East End of London, only 1 per cent of the dead officers had lived there, and the largely immigrant, working-class population of Leeds suffered only one officer death. Of the 1,229 former pupils of the Jews' Free School who served in uniform, only 19 received commissions as did only 3 of the 163 who had attended the Borough Jewish Schools in south-east London.

These World War I figures indicate another important feature of this middle-class segment. It consisted to a large extent of the more anglicised, long-resident section of Anglo-Jewry. Before conscription was introduced in January 1916, some 10,000 Jews volunteered for service, most of whom, it is safe to assume, came from families who had originally come to Britain a generation or more before. The east Europeans, on the other hand, did not readily volunteer. The horrors of conscript life in the Russian army—for many an important reason for emigrating—combined in any case with an objection to fighting on the same side as the country which all the emigrants had thankfully left. An indication of the social structure of the longer-resident immigrants is provided by the fact that as many as 1,140 of the 10,000 volunteers in the early part of the war were officers, a much higher proportion than for the general population of the country. When the east Europeans joined the forces in great numbers, the proportion of officers to men slumped to below that of the general population: not many east Europeans obtained commissions, for, although large numbers had been born and brought up in Britain, very few had achieved the social status which the rank of officer required.[5]

This chapter deals with the Jews who, in the immigration period, were business and professional people. It will encompass more than the anglicised, long-established, suburbanites referred to so far, and there are modifications to be made to the equation between place of residence, anglicisation and economic function. Not all the suburbs were middle class, for example, and such places as Soho, Notting Hill, Edmonton and New Cross contained working-class Jews. A description of Jewish life in Tottenham on the eve of World War I reads exactly like contemporary accounts of the poor immigrant areas.[6] Some of the new arrivals were middle class when they came. William Ruttenau came to Manchester from Alsace in the 1870s, starting as a commission agent and manufacturer of hat leathers (leather bands inside bowler hats). He soon acquired the Good Hope Mill at Ashton-under-Lyne and on his marriage in 1879 bought a house in Victoria Park on which he spent over £1,000 to make it 'suitable for bourgeois habitation'.[7]

On the other hand, not all business and professional Jews lived in the suburbs. At one extreme were the country gentlemen, like the Rothschilds; at the other were the shopkeepers and workshop entrepreneurs who lived in the immigrant districts. Some of the latter, it is true, were quickly able to move into the upper middle class in the suburbs. The Sieffs of Manchester, for example, began with the buying and sorting of discarded cloth cuttings. Few of the immigrants achieved that progress and the entrepreneurs among them were often little different, economically and socially, from their employees: they were part of the immigrant community, sharply distinguishable from the 'West End' Jews. The turnover among such people was high, and in time of boom there would be an expansion in the number of workshops, to be succeeded by closures when trade became slack, the erstwhile entrepreneurs reverting to employee status or to peddling and hawking. Retail trading was often a promotion from manual work or from street-selling, but some who entered it did so as 'a refuge from disaster'. One who opened a grocer's shop was a Mrs Levy whose husband's 'speculative building and surveying ventures' went bankrupt after his death. They had lived comfortably at Sedgley Park, Manchester, where she was accustomed to domestic help, the family having long country holidays, and three of the sons were at boarding-school. She sold the house and with financial help from relations opened a shop. It failed twice, and two of the sons were sent to the Jewish orphanage, the rest of the family went to live in a 'bug-ridden hovel', and Mrs Levy 'was forced to earn her living in a cap works and let lodgings'.[8]

The Financiers

One of the great ironies of Jewish history is that alongside the persistent themes of persecution, discrimination and humiliation are to be found the names of those who achieved wealth and influence, who advised governments and received honours. They can be likened to the court Jews who performed similar functions in the early modern period and who regarded themselves as leaders and protectors of their religious community. However much they might be recognised for their importance, they were used and tolerated rather than accepted—in late nineteenth-century Germany for example the great German-Jewish banker and confidant of Bismarck, Gerson Bleichröder, was very much the inferior outsider.[9] Britain's social system was looser and freer and it was possible for Jews who had made their mark to mix more readily with the upper classes, even with royalty. In the 1860s the Prince of Wales formed a friendship with Nathaniel Rothschild when both were at Trinity College, Cambridge, and remained close enough to the family to attend the wedding in 1881 of Nathaniel's brother Leopold and sign the register.[10]

For all their association with finance, the Rothschilds, three generations away from the Frankfurt ghetto, were now country gentlemen in Buckinghamshire, just as the Salomons had settled in Kent. They were art connoisseurs and familiars in the horse-racing world, and they moved freely in the world of politics and in society. Numerous memoirs of the period record these connections, when week-ends at the Rothschilds were the 'perfect' resort for 'tired statesmen and men of business'.[11] This personal acceptance was formalised in 1885 when Nathaniel Rothschild was elevated to the peerage, the first Jew to be so honoured. Admittedly, it had taken many years to overcome the opposition of the Queen, who had objected to the grant of a peerage to a Jew. It is true too that the simultaneous elevation of the non-Jewish Baring (as Lord Revelstoke) clearly indicated that it was the City's importance that was being recognised. This was the period when overseas investment increased enormously to reach a proportion of the country's resources greater than ever before and never to be surpassed since.

Most conspicuous in this field were the Jewish houses, often linked by marriage. Rothschilds married Rothschilds—there were plenty of them, descended from the ten children of Mayer Amschel, the founder. Even before the Rothschilds had emerged from the Frankfurt ghetto, one of them had married a Stern and another had married a Worms (two of the latter's sons worked for Nathan Mayer in London when they arrived in 1814). Sterns and Bischoffsheims later became related by marriage, and a Bischoffsheim married a de Hirsch. Frankfurt had been their place of origin, so that the three Jewish peers of the 1890s (Sydney James Stern became Lord Wandsworth and Henry de Worms became Lord Pirbright in 1895: the third was Rothschild) were all from Frankfurt banking families.[12]

By no means were even the most illustrious Jewish bankers and financiers all connected in this way. Hannah Rothschild married the fifth Earl of Rosebery—despite both families' objections—who became prime minister after her early death.[13] Sir Ernest Cassel, who was not a banker but made his money reconstructing and rescuing companies—and countries—which were in financial difficulties, became a Roman Catholic in the 1890s and his grand-daughter married Louis Mountbatten.[14]

As in the early part of the century, the merchant bankers among them were mainly concerned with the handling of foreign loans: only one of the Frankfurt bankers was eminent in domestic joint-stock banking. This was (Sir) Felix Schuster, whose family bank in London was taken over in 1887 by the Union Bank of which he was Governor from 1895 to 1918. But their activities sometimes went beyond merely raising money for governments and companies abroad. Rothschild was involved in the creation in the 1880s of the diamond syndicate in South Africa headed by Cecil Rhodes and associated with a number of Jews such as Barney Barnato and Sir Alfred Beit. Cassel helped to finance the Central London Railway and Edgar Speyer became chairman of the Underground Electric Railways Company, both in London.[15]

Many of the financiers prospered, but not all: Barnato, the son of an East End shopkeeper, jumped overboard from a ship travelling to England and was lost. But whatever their origins, functions and fates, they all attracted hostility and obloquy, especially from the political left. There was a long history to the equation between capitalism and finance, but it deepened in the late nineteenth century when international finance was associated with imperialism. Nowhere did the connection appear more naked than in South Africa, and the Boer War seemed to be fought on behalf of the financiers. More than that, the pioneering study of imperialism by J. A. Hobson, which was subsequently adopted and expanded by Lenin, consciously showed an intimate connection between the

European acquisition of territory and overseas investment. Hobson specifically identified within the development of imperialism the financiers who formed, as he put it, 'the central ganglion of international capitalism'.

> United by the strongest bonds of organisation, always in closest and quickest touch with one another, situated in the very heart of the business capital of every State, controlled, so far as Europe is concerned, chiefly by men of a single and peculiar race, who have behind them centuries of financial experience, they are in a unique position to manipulate the policy of nations. No great quick direction of capital is possible save by their consent or through their agency. Does anyone seriously propose that a great war could be undertaken by any European State, or a great State loan subscribed, if the House of Rothschild and its connexions set their face against it?[16]

Although in a different context, the 'Marconi scandal' of 1912 added to the hostility. David Lloyd George, Chancellor of the Exchequer, and the Master of Elibank, Liberal Chief Whip, bought shares in the American Marconi Company at the time the British government was about to place contracts with the English Marconi Company. Its chairman was Godfrey Isaacs, brother of Rufus Isaacs, the Attorney-General. The ensuing scandal and parliamentary inquiry did not adversely affect their political careers—Rufus Isaacs, for example, became Lord Chief Justice and then Viceroy of India—but the whiff of corruption was enough for influential writers such as Rudyard Kipling and G. K. Chesterton to lampoon the Jews involved and to attack Jewish financial activities.[17]

There is no doubt at all that in the thirty years or so before World War I Jewish houses were conspicuously active in the major financial centres. Along with the non-Jewish firms their work inevitably took them into politics, especially in those countries such as France and Germany where foreign policy and overseas investment were expected to support each other.[18] Despite their competition with each other they could work together financially and politically. During the negotiations which proceded the Treaty of Berlin, 1878, the Jewish bankers in particular mounted a campaign to insist that Romania should be forced, by the Treaty, to remove anti-Jewish discrimination in that country. Similarly, when Russia wished to raise loans, the Jewish bankers in many countries refused to handle them unless the Tsarist government modified its anti-Jewish measures. In 1878 the bankers won and an appropriate clause was included in the Treaty, but in practice nothing changed and the Romanian government continued as before. They were completely unsuccessful in their anti-Tsarist efforts: the Russian government got its money and the antisemitism in that country continued. The much-vaunted power of the Rothschilds did not prevent Britain forming an alliance with Russia.[19]

The ear of the king and intimacy with political leaders did not necessarily bring power. It was normal for ministers to consult such leading City figures as the Rothschilds on economic and financial matters, but the political history of the period does not accord the financiers the central role that, say, Gerson Bleichröder occupied in Germany, without whom the story of the rise of Bismarck would be incomplete. The so-called 'court Jews of Edwardian England' were much less than the title implies—although Cassel did put the financial affairs of the Prince of Wales on a sound footing. One wonders whether the week-ends at the Rothschilds were anything more than social occasions tinged with political gossip and talk of horse-racing.

Overseas Trade

Despite the progress of such countries as Germany and the United States in the pre-war period, Britain remained in 1914 the world's major trading nation. Opportunities were available for exporters, such as the textile merchants of Manchester, and for others engaged in commerce. Generally they were less wealthy and less renowned than the great financiers, but some made their mark. One of these was Philip Goldschmidt, who was born in Oldenburg in 1812, came to Bradford in the 1840s and settled in Manchester as a trader with the West Indies and South America. He took an active part in local affairs as chairman of the relief committee during the cotton famine of the 1860s and as a city councillor from 1869. As Lord Mayor in the 1880s he was the first foreign-born person to hold that office in Manchester. No doubt one reason why Ludwig Mond, the chemist, came to England and to Manchester in particular was that he was a kinsman of Goldschmidt.[20]

A new departure was the entry in the 1890s of the London trading firm of Marcus Samuel and Co. into the oil business.[21] By that decade, the oil industry, some forty years old, was monopolised by Standard Oil (Rockefeller), the Nobels of Sweden and the Paris Rothschilds. They had eliminated competition among themselves, but there remained open the oil of the Far East for which the Samuels went, it being a part of the world with which they were familiar. The Samuels were introduced to the trade by Fred Lane, a partner in Lane and Macandrew, the London broking firm through which the Samuels chartered their vessels; he was also the London agent for the Paris Rothschilds' oil interests. The Samuels were able to succeed in the Far East against Standard Oil—which always tried to undercut competitors—by being able to sell their oil cheaply in many markets. They could do this because of their experience of widely dispersed trading throughout the area; they had the necessary contacts and the knowledge of Far East trading conditions. The crucial development came in 1892 through the use of special tankers designed to pass through the Suez Canal. The first ship went through in August 1892, carrying oil from the Black Sea to the Far East. By this means the Samuels, together with their British associates (Jardine, Matheson and Wallace), assisted by the Paris Rothschilds, obtained a sizeable portion of the Far Eastern market.

During the 1890s the various British oil interests worked together as the Tank Syndicate, conducting the trade on a joint account in order to prevent

Standard Oil picking off individual firms. But supplies of oil from Russia could not be relied upon and the British firms trading in oil took steps to safeguard themselves. In 1897 they established the Shell Trading and Transport Company: the name intentionally recalled the commodities in which the Samuel firm had originally traded half a century before. Ten years later it joined with the Royal Dutch Company to form Royal Dutch Shell, the ownership being 60 per cent Dutch and 40 per cent British, and the leading light thenceforth was the Dutchman, Henri Deterding.

Marcus Samuel was elected Lord Mayor of London in 1902. It was in character that he should route his inaugural procession so as to take in that part of the East End where he was born and to show himself to the newly-arrived eastern European immigrants. It was characteristic, too, that he should refuse to invite the ambassador of Romania to the Lord Mayor's banquet because of the persecution of the Jews in that country. He was now in the higher realms of Anglo-Jewry, having 'worked his passage' by means of his wealth and public service. His peerage, as Viscount Bearsted, finally put the seal on his ambitions.

Main Jewish Industrial Activities

As in Britain generally, most Jewish industrial enterprises were on a small scale. The great majority operated in a narrow range of industries, emphasised by the numerical dominance of the immigrants from eastern Europe, but there were changes in the products which were made. One hears less of such older Jewish pursuits as pencil-making (and, more important, cigar-making) and much more of clothing. At the same time several entrepreneurs emerged in the newer industries of the late nineteenth century—the London underground railways have already been mentioned—and most of these were immigrants too, but usually from central rather than eastern Europe, and usually with a middle-class background.

The Jewish East End cigar-making trade declined in the face of its being taken up by the large tobacco companies such as Wills of Bristol and as cigarette-making began to surge ahead. By 1914 only a handful of them remained, notably Godfrey Phillips, which was still a relatively small family concern. The largest tobacco firm, Salmon & Gluckstein, which had produced a variety of tobacco products and had also opened a chain of 140 tobacconists' shops, left the industry in 1902. This was a result of the reaction by the British tobacco industry to a threatened incursion by American firms, and thirteen British firms formed the Imperial Tobacco Company in 1902 to prevent this happening. None of the thirteen was Jewish, and the Company was dominated by Wills, which accounted for nearly £7 million of the £12 million capital. The tobacconists' shops, although owned by Imperial Tobacco, continued to operate under the name of Salmon & Gluckstein until World War II.[22]

The British tobacco industry was thus dominated by the major firms, but newcomers were able to enter it: Rothman, Redstone (Balkan Sobranie), Wix

(Kensitas) and Ardath, among others. These and other Jewish firms were on a small scale, often producing cigarettes by hand, and some of those in the above list did not greatly expand until the inter-war years. One of the newcomers was Bernhard Baron, born in Brest-Litovsk in 1850, who arrived in America in 1866 and at first worked in a cigar factory with Samuel Gompers, the future American labour leader. In the 1890s he invented a cigarette-making machine and formed the Baron Cigarette Machine Company in London in 1896 to market it throughout the world. When the old-established London firm of José Joaquin Carreras was for sale in 1903, Carreras Ltd was formed to take it over, with Baron as its managing director, later becoming chairman.[23]

To judge by the reports in that short-lived union journal, the *Cigarette-Maker,* it was not unusual for hand-made cigarettes to be made in conditions more typically ascribed to the more familiar sweated trades. But like boot and shoe production that method was declining in the face of large-scale mechanisation. Factory production was also growing in the main immigrant industry, clothing, but the normal unit was still the workshop and this industry provided more Jewish entrepreneurs than did any other. There were others, such as in the making of boxes,[24] but clothing was a very large industry and dispersed throughout the country. In virtually every Jewish settlement there were Jewish workshops; not just in the large cities with major Jewish communities. While some of the very smallest settlements, as in the Durham and South Wales coalfields, seem to have consisted largely of pedlars and shopkeepers, there were clothing workshops in Slough, Bristol, Newcastle, Wigan, Sheffield and elsewhere. By the time of the mass immigration, from the 1870s and 1880s onwards, a number of entrepreneurs already existed, including some of the waterproof firms in Manchester and the Leeds wholesale clothiers, and it is likely that some of those who became masters in their own right began in these older firms. Later immigrants might begin in the workshop of a friend or relation, but whatever the details of their initial years, the immigrants invariably spent some time as employees before setting up for themselves. A few examples of firms which have had a long history will illustrate the point.

One Polish immigrant of 1867 started on his own account ten years later; another who arrived in the late 1870s worked at first for a man called Birnbaum and founded his own business about 1885.[25] Similarly Charles Green, the son of a Polish tailor, who came to Britain in the 1890s at the age of twelve, began the manufacture of women's clothes with two friends a few years later, and Alexander Steinberg started up in 1902, four years after he arrived at the age of thirteen.[26]

A fuller account is available of the career of Samuel Goldstein, born 1889 in a small town near Warsaw. He was the youngest of eight children whose father, a dealer in timber, horses and cattle, had died in debt. Six of the children emigrated to England, the other two remaining behind with their invalid mother. Samuel's brothers in England advised him to become apprenticed to a tailor and come to England to work in that trade. He arrived in London in 1905 to work for his brother Solomon, who had a small workshop making up garments as a sub-contractor for wholesale mantle (women's dresses) manufacturers in the City of London. He worked for fifteen hours a day, six days a week, for eight months of the year but was not paid during the remaining slack periods. After a short interval in America as a machine operator he returned and resumed working for his brother at a regular wage of thirty shillings a week 'which was quite good at the time'. In 1910, his brother's health having deteriorated, the elder brother decided to give up the workshop and open a retail fashion store and offered the workshop to Samuel. He 'wanted £100 for his interest and having discussed the matter with the late Mr. W. J. Ellis who was employed as a stock cutter, we managed to scrape together the purchase money'.[27]

Such accounts of poverty-stricken beginnings followed by translation into employer are commonplace: in Beatrice Webb's report for the Booth survey they begin with the 'greener' working for no wage, his reward being 'a shake-down, a cup of black coffee, and a hunch of brown bread'. But while it is true that those immigrant firms which prospered and in post–World War II years have become large enterprises, whether in manufacturing or in retail trade, began in this way, there was another side to the story. Parallel to the Greens and the Steinbergs in the dress-making industry, the Sussmans (shirts),[28] the Offenbachs (women's and children's clothes),[29] Gliksten (cabinet-making and timber),[30] there were those who did not attempt to become employers and those who did but failed. (The failure is a familiar character in Jewish folklore.) In boom periods workshops would mushroom, to collapse in slack times.

The small sub-contracting workshops made clothes for a wholesale house, usually, but an important feature of the clothing industry was the growing integration between manufacture and retail trade.[31] First, specialist shops appeared for the sale of men's or women's clothes, often supplied by their own workshop or small factory supplemented by supplies of ready-made clothes bought from outside. In the 1870s and 1880s such firms opened branches and externally-made, ready-to-wear goods became an increasing proportion of their sales. Most of these multiple organisations were non-Jewish, but at least two of them were: the Grand Clothing Hall, run by the clothing manufacturers of Leicester, Hart & Levy, and the Cash Clothing Company (Levy Brothers of Leeds). The largest men's clothing firm was Joseph Hepworth of Leeds, and the largest in the women's trade was Fleming, Reid & Co. of Greenock, neither of them Jewish.

A further stage in the men's trade was the establishment in the first decade of the twentieth century of companies controlling a chain of shops selling bespoke (made-to-measure) men's clothing. Montague Burton of Leeds was the best-known Jewish name among the twenty or so which were in existence in 1914, but the leading firms were non-Jewish, the largest company being Stewarts the Kings Tailors of Middlesbrough.

Other Industries

In general the industries mentioned so far were—in the Jewish context—an immigrant interest and small scale. Those not in one or other of these categories were unusual: Sir Israel Hart of Leicester, for example, came from an established family in Canterbury; A. & W. Flatau, the footwear manufacturers, had started in the 1820s and moved to Tottenham in the early years of the twentieth century to larger premises at about the same time as did the furniture-makers, Harris Lebus.[32] The first multiple-shop jewellers was H. Samuel of Manchester, which originated with Moses and Lewis Samuel, Liverpool clock-makers early in the century. It had fifty branches in 1914 and the firm was both a retailer and manufacturer.[33]

The Jews who operated in industries other than these characteristic 'Jewish' ones were not normally recent immigrants from eastern Europe. Some were the anglicised descendants of earlier, usually central European, arrivals; more were newcomers from that area, usually from a middle-class background. Some of the latter can be described only as Jewish in origin, and like middle-class immigrants from Germany earlier in the nineteenth century, are somewhat marginal to this story.

The 'home' entrepreneurs in the metal industries included two who originated earlier in the century. In Sheffield, the steel centre, there were no Jews in the steel-making industry, which required extensive capital, but it was easier to enter the small-scale metal-using industries. Even so Horatio Bright (1829–1906) built up a large business making dies for the minting of coins. His family had come to the city in the 1780s and set up as watch-makers (others of the family in the same trade were at Leamington and Doncaster). Horatio, who married Mary Alice Turton who was not Jewish, set up in business as Turton, Bright & Co., Steel Manufacturers. His brother Augustus, who died in 1880, headed the firm of A. Bright & Co., Cutlery Manufacturers and Hardware Merchants.[34] Since the typical Sheffield cutlery firm was very small, it was not difficult to become a small master ('small mester' in the local dialect), and it is probable that some Jews entered it, although only one of the early firms—Viner's—has had a long history.[35]

The second, older, firm was that of George Cohen, which began in 1834 in Aldgate, east London, handling scrap iron. In the 1870s it began to deal in machinery and moved to 600 Commercial Road, near by, hence its trademark '600'. Its main trade was in scrap (on a large scale: it took the Great Western Railway's rails when that company relaid its line from the broad to the standard gauge) and in machinery supplying, but it also moved into engineering.[36]

A third anglicised entrepreneur was Meyer Hart Goldstone, the grandson of Michael Goldstone of Warsaw, who arrived in the 1820s as a hawker of quills, for a time dependent on the Liverpool synagogue's charity. In the 1840s he began manufacturing steel pens in Salford and then became a watch-maker and a jeweller. In 1892 the grandson was a founder of the Salford electrical engineering firm of Ward & Goldstone.[37] Two others in the electrical and engineering industries were newcomers. Siegfried Bettman (1863–1951) was born in Nuremberg, the son of a Bavarian land-owner's agent. He came to London in the 1880s, exporting bicycles on which he stamped his own trade name, Triumph. He moved to Coventry to join the bicycle boom and began to manufacture in 1890 (with another German, Mauritz Johann Schulte). By 1914 the company was also making motor-bicycles and Bettman was chairman of the Standard Motor Company, which began operations in 1903. In that year he was Mayor of the city.[38] Those industries were highly competitive, but another new one in which Hugo Hirsch (later Hirst, 1863–1943) was engaged was notoriously monopolistic. He was born in Bavaria, where his family ran a distillery, and came to Britain in 1880 because he objected to the attempts being made to Prussianise Bavaria. An uncle in London, a doctor, had encouraged him to come, and he worked at first in a variety of jobs, mostly in the new electrical industry. He was virtually in control of the newly-formed General Electric Company from 1889, although not made managing director until 1906. The company made a variety of products, but its most profitable line was electric light bulbs. It entered the field in 1893 when the patents of Edison and Swan ran out, and within the next twenty years was one of the partners in a cartel. GEC had established in 1909 the Osram lamp works jointly with Auergesellschaft of Germany, and the cartel was formalised three years later when GEC and the other two British lamp-producers (Siemens and British Thomson-Houston) established the Tungsten Lamp Association which pooled patents, fixed prices and licensed competitors.[39]

It goes without saying that there were specialist food manufacturers for the Jewish community—notably the makers of bread and cakes—which were to be found in most towns and cities which had a sizeable Jewish population. Among those supplying the general market was Streimer's Nougat Ltd, which was set up in the 1890s at Stratford, east London, by Morris Streimer (1857–1935), an immigrant from Austria.[40] Associated with the teashops of J. Lyons & Co. (which will be discussed below) was the sale of food products such as bread and cakes. A third firm originated in New Zealand with Joseph Edward Nathan (1835–1912), who was born in England. The New Zealand firm handled a variety of merchandise but at the end of the nineteenth century began to concentrate on the manufacture and export of dairy products, especially dried milk. For this purpose the firm of Glaxo was registered in Britain in 1906, producing dried baby milk.[41] The last food company did not enter production in Britain until World War I, but it is convenient to mention it here. The van den Berghs of Holland, exporters of Dutch butter, sent two members of the family to London in the 1860s to open a London office. The company subsequently went into the factory manufacture of margarine in a number of countries: the war-time factory in Britain was for that purpose.[42]

The remaining 'unusual' industries comprise a miscellaneous list in a variety of activities. They were all long-lasting and for that reason are known, but while it us unlikely that they were unique—others may have come and gone— evidence about them is scarce. Future research will no doubt uncover Jewish firms in other industries, but their discovery will not alter the generalisation that most Jewish industry was narrowly confined. Samuel Joseph founded the building firm of Bovis in 1909,[43] in an industry that attracted very few Jewish entrepreneurs. One firm was certainly unique: the enterprise of David Gestetner, who was one of the pioneers in the development of office duplicating equipment. He is described as a penniless immigrant from Hungary who, in 1881, when working as a stationer's assistant at Fairholme & Co. in Holborn, London, invented a cyclostyle wheelpen for writing on a stencil. The cost of the patent was defrayed by Fairholme, to whom he made over his patent, the company taking his output for re-sale in Britain. Gestetner started production with one girl assistant and gradually expanded, moving his premises several times. In 1906 he moved his enterprise to Tottenham, the third Jewish firm to move to that area.[44]

It is convenient to conclude this section with a reference to publishing—at most a handful of names. Two older firms were the fine art publishers, Raphael Tuck & Sons, and Shapiro, Vallentine, which specialised in the production of Jewish books: it was not unusual, though, for Jewish religious works to be imported from the Continent or, as in the case of the standard *Singer's Prayer Book,* to be published by non-Jewish firms. Within the immigrant community were the printer and publisher Narodiczky, producing Yiddish works, and Mazin. These were all small, as was the music-publishing firm of Elkin & Co., incorporated in 1903.[45] There was only one major Jewish publisher, George Routledge, originally founded in 1834 and 'Jewish' after its reorganisation in 1902. As a result the chairman was Arthur E. Franklin, senior partner in the banking firm of Keyser & Co., and one of the two managing directors was Laurie Magnus, a relation of the chairman. (The other was William Swan Stallybrass, formerly Sonnenschein. His father was a refugee from Hungary after the 1848 revolution who married the daughter of the Reverend Edward Stallybrass. William established a publishing house under his original name of Sonnenschein.[46])

Apart from the specifically Jewish newspapers such as the *Jewish Chronicle* and the various Yiddish papers, two newspapers in general circulation were Jewish-owned. One was the *Daily Telegraph,* which began in 1855, when the newspaper tax was reduced, printed by Joseph Moses Levy. The first owner rapidly became insolvent and Levy, with others, took it over. In the meantime he was proprietor of *The Sunday Times* for about a year. The new *Daily Telegraph* appeared in September 1855 at the very low price of one penny, the first London paper at that price. The editor was his son Edward (1833–1916), who assumed the surname Lawson (thus Levy-Lawson), married a Christian lady and was raised to the peerage as Lord Burnham.[47] One other Jewish interest in newspaper production was the ownership of *The Sunday Times* between 1893 and 1904 by Rachel Beer (née Sassoon).[48] The so-called 'newspaper revolution' of the 1890s—the cheap, popular dailies—was not a Jewish innovation.

Distributive Trades

There are two ways of analysing the Jewish role in retail and wholesale trade. One is to separate the older settlers from the new; another is by function, ranging from peddling to chain stores and multiples. A useful first approximation is to link these two, to associate the anglicised Jews with a higher social and economic status, their shops being of a superior kind. They compare with the immigrants, who might be pedlars or shopkeepers in the immigrant areas. A not atypical example of the former group was Alexander Gollancz, one of the children of Rabbi Samuel Marcus Gollancz, who came to Britain in the 1850s to officiate at one of the wealthier London synagogues. Of his nine children two, Hermann and Israel, became university teachers, eventually occupied chairs and received knighthoods. A daughter, Emma, was educated at Queen's College and at Newnham College, Cambridge. Alexander, another brother, went into business in what his son described as a 'small' way, 'midway between a jeweller with a shop and a petty wholesaler, whose income from a twelve-hour day varied from five or six hundred a year to an occasional thousand'. They lived in Elgin Avenue, West London, and despite the smallness and pettiness of the business were of sufficient standing to own a brougham and to employ a coachman. Alexander's son Victor went to St Paul's School and then to Oxford University.[49]

Some of the older-established Jews were among the relatively small numbers of traders who had a number of stores. Lewis's of the North was one such firm, selling mainly clothes and footwear. Salmon & Gluckstein had extended from tobacco manufacturing into tobacco retailing to become the largest tobacconists in the country before they sold out in 1902. The firm moved instead into the food trade, beginning in 1887 when the brothers Montague and Isidore Gluckstein, their cousin Alfred Salmon and Joseph Lyons obtained the catering contract for the Newcastle Exhibition of that year. After a few other contracts the firm of J. Lyons & Co. was incorporated in 1894 and their first teashop was opened: by 1914 there were 200 of them, designed for clerks and lady-shoppers, providing cheap food. In 1896 the company opened the Trocadero in Piccadilly for the needs of the wealthy and the Throgmorton in the City for the same clientele. Its first 'Corner House' was opened in 1909. Among the several chains of teashops which were opened to provide for the growing body of clerks and shoppers, Lyons was the fastest-growing and the most successful.[50] The teashops had come in partly to replace the old chop-houses and were in some instances features of the temperance movement. But one other Jewish firm went into the public-house business, to grow into Levy & Frank's firm with the well-known trademark 'Chef & Brewer'. The founder was Isaac Levy, a travelling salesman who became a bookmaker, but turned into a publican when, it is said, he 'noticed that so many punters who backed horses and had money to spare were in fact publicans. He decided to join them', buying the Pitts Head public house in Old Street in the City of London, followed two years later by the Bell in Shoreditch. His son Dick and son-in-law Harry Franks formed a partnership in 1892, which became a private company in 1911. Their idea was to alter the image of public houses from being gin palaces to places where food was available, notably to City workers at lunchtime; this concept, of providing food, was copied by all other public-house operators.[51]

These various examples from the anglicised group are in sharp contrast to the more usual immigrant traders. At the one extreme were, as ever, the pedlars, some operating in towns, others in the rural areas. The Irish Census of 1901, for example—the only part of the United Kingdom where religion was thus recorded—listed among the Dublin Jews of foreign birth as many as 223 pedlars and hawkers, 88 commercial travellers and, in a related occupation, 64 general dealers. This was when Dublin's total Jewish population, including those of longer residence, was only 2,048. The other main groups, apart from 200 schoolchildren and students, were 261 drapers, 72 tailors (employment status unknown) and 66 domestic servants. The immigrant Jews of Dublin were by no means typical of those in the United Kingdom, but peddling was certainly a characteristic trade. 'Knowing no trade but peddling, most of them began by hawking bundles or trays of goods through the streets of Dublin and the outlying districts, usually allowing their customers to pay by weekly instalments. Soon the enterprising ones learned the sources of their wares and supplied the next contingent of settlers with stock-in-trade, and in the course of time many became wholesale merchants and manufacturers'. As in the eighteenth century, Jewish pedlars operated in the rural areas so that, in Ireland, congregations were founded in Cork, Limerick, Waterford, Londonderry, Dundalk and Lurgan.[52] In Great Britain pedlars were to be found in the more isolated industrial and colliery villages, for example in Durham. In the north-east generally, which for many immigrants was the first experience of England, 'credit-drapers, travellers, and retail shopkeepers were prominent among the occupations of . . . first generation immigrants'.[53] They operated among the the colliery villages, for a time even settling in those places, e.g., at Tudhoe Colliery and at near-by Spennymoor.[54] In South Wales and Scotland there was a similar pattern of pedlars and petty shopkeepers, the travelling salesmen—whose accents were a mixture of Yiddish-English and Scottish—being recorded well into the twentieth century.

The two main elements in Anglo-Jewry, according to length of residence in Britain, were not so clearly distinguished as this. The immigrant group included a few who prospered and whose sons went to public schools and university. Two of the best-known have already been referred to: Michael Marks who, with a non-Jewish partner, established a chain of bazaar stores—

over 100 by 1914—and Montague Burton's tailoring shops. One activity which attracted some Jews was the furniture trade, which, unlike the clothing industry, exhibited no signs of integration between manufacture and the retail trade. A number of firms came into existence at the turn of the century which sold furniture on credit, a new departure for those days: many of them claim to have originated it. They included the company started in 1894 by John Jacobs for himself and his eight sons, each of whom was provided with a shop with a different name which eventually came together as the Times Furnishing Company.[55] A second firm was founded by Joseph Cohen of Dublin, a partner in a wholesale firm selling a variety of goods. They sold up and went to Newcastle with a capital of £1,200, acquired the business of James Woodhouse and by 1914 had about twelve shops, selling furniture on credit. Unusually, the firm also opened a store abroad, in Canada, in 1911.[56] A third firm of a similar kind was founded in 1908 by Benjamin Drage (Cohen), whose mother had sold shoes on credit in Whitechapel.[57]

It is relatively easy to identify those Jewish retail firms which had a number of shops and which were long-lasting. The overwhelming majority, however, are anonymous and they included a fluctuating population with easy entry and frequent demises. Yet a few generalisations can be legitimately made. An obvious one is the tendency to concentrate on particular types of goods: grocery and other food-shops; jewellery, including watch-making and extending into pawnbroking; clothing, including hat- and footwear; and furniture. One seldom comes across chemists (the great name here being that of Jesse Boot of Nottingham), nor are hardware stores often referred to. A second feature is that, apart from the shops supplying a wealthier clientele, they tended to go for the cheaper market which involved large turnovers with small margins, and this applied equally to J. Lyons's teashops and to the credit furniture stores.

Professions

By the 1880s entry to the professions was open to Jews, the last religious barriers having been abolished. At the same time high-status white-collar jobs were increasing in number: entrance to the civil service was by competitive examination, and the institution in the 1850s of 'Local' examinations by the Universities of Oxford and Cambridge assisted the development of a professional elite.[58]

There are several general indications of a growing Jewish entry into these occupations. One was the attention paid by the Board of Deputies of British Jews when proposed examinations were to be held on days which clashed with Jewish holy days. As early as 1859 the Board successfully protested that if the Local examinations were extended over a Saturday, this would debar professing Jews.[59] From the 1880s similar representations were made to many bodies, and the Oxford and Cambridge Local examining bodies agreed to a procedure to be adopted in future, whereby special papers could be set.[60] The same interest was shown by the Board of Deputies in examinations set by national bodies such as the Science and Art Department; and others of more local interest, e.g., the Glasgow bursaries. It made representations when scholarships and foundations were apparently unavailable to Jews or to sons of immigrants.[61]

These examples presumably refer to examinations and grants for children and teenagers—as when twenty-seven candidates were enabled to sit the examinations of the Intermediate Education Board of Ireland, which had coincided with a Jewish festival.[62] Others were for examinations held by the National Shorthand Association and by the City and Guilds of London Institutes. Representations were made to a number of universities and teacher-training institutions: the Queen's College, Cork; the Royal University of Ireland; the Queen's College, Belfast; Trinity and St John's Colleges, Cambridge; the London hospitals; Yorkshire Training College, and the Society of French Teachers. In addition the Board intervened about examinations for entry into the civil service and Sandhurst Military Academy.[63]

These anonymous details clearly indicate that a number of religious Jews were taking examinations in preparation for white-collar jobs, including the professions, and that some were already in such occupations. To them can be added those whose examinations did not fall on awkward dates, and the non-religious, who did not bother about these matters.

In those countries where statistics identify the population by religion, there was a noticeable movement of Jews into the liberal professions and government, including the armed forces. This happened in Italy, Germany, Austria, even in Russia. Some occasional figures for Britain illustrate the same trend.[64] A handful of Jews served as commissioned officers in the army and the militia even before Queen's Regulations in 1886 formally recognised the Jewish religion for serving men. When the Reverend F. L. Cohen became Jewish Officiating Chaplain in 1892 he knew of sixteen Jewish officers; in 1903 there were forty-one in the Regular Army and many in the militia and the Volunteers (but others, he wrote, disguised the fact that they were Jewish).[65] We may assume that most of the 128 Jewish officers of the Royal Army Medical Corps during World War I were doctors, along with the five of surgeon rank in the Royal Navy (that service did not readily accept anyone of foreign descent). Other Jews were medical officers in the Royal Air Force and its predecessor, the Royal Flying Corps.[66]

Otherwise one is left with vague allusions or with references to particular individuals. The Maccabaeans, a society of professional men, was formed in 1893, of whom eighty served in World War I. One wonders how many people Isidore Harris was addressing in a letter to the *Jewish Chronicle* at the time of the 1905 general election when he suggested that those graduates of the University of London 'who may desire to return to Parliament Sir Philip

Magnus, the Unionist candidate' should take the necessary procedural steps.[67] Some individuals are known and can be listed—they appear in memoirs, obituaries or in collections of 'notable' Jews—but such details are not reliable or comprehensive.[68] It is interesting to record that David Schloss was an official of the Board of Trade who wrote official reports on immigrant conditions in the 1880s, or that Sir Lionel Abrahams was Assistant Under-Secretary for India at the time of World War I. There were half a dozen architects[69] and—to extend the definition—a couple of musicians,[70] a few novelists and some artists.[71] Inevitably records of this kind seldom refer to schoolteaching or nursing which, for women at any rate, were the two main professional occupations.

There is no doubt, however, that some generalisations about Jewish professionals can be made. The most popular occupations were medicine and the law, and most of the 'higher' professionals were men (several of the high-status professions—religious organisations, the armed forces, engineering, science, the law—were not open to women or admitted very few). In general not many Jews took up scientific pursuits: the well-known ones include Elim d'Avigdor (1841–95) and Cyril Q. Henriques (1881–1976), civil engineers, the latter in the Indian Civil Service; Sir Robert Waley-Cohen (1877–1952), one of the first scientists in the oil industry; Arthur Blok (1882–1975), an electrical engineer employed in the Patent Office, probably the only Jew in that government department;[72] Leopold Kessler (1866–1944), a Zionist leader who was a mining engineer. One might include the second Lord Rothschild, Lionel Walter (1868–1937), a zoologist, and another member of an old Anglo-Jewish family, Sir David Lionel Salomons (1851–1925), (an electrician, an engineer, an expert on motor mechanics when few Englishmen knew what a motor car was, a photographer of note . . . one of the first to devise a system of automatic signalling on the railways'.[73] The solitary woman among them was Sarah Marks (1854–1923), the first woman member of the Institute of Electrical Engineers.[74]

In general, the chemists in the Manchester area excepted, these were from old-established families: even Helen Bentwich, one of the first social workers with an academic qualification (in social hygiene) came from the long-resident Franklin family.[75] But the immigrants also produced some professionals, notably doctors, teachers and nurses, as well as the Yiddish journalists, writers and actors. A few from a poor immigrant background became university teachers (Morris Ginsberg, 1889–1970, in sociology, and Selig Brodetsky, 1888–1960, in mathematics).[76] And one or two others from eastern Europe were already trained before they arrived, their background being middle class: Chaim Weizmann, the chemist, obtained a university post at Manchester in 1904 and his wife Vera, with a Swiss medical degree, who obtained the necessary English qualification in 1913 and took up employment in the local authority medical service.[77] They were very much from the Yiddish environment of eastern Europe in contrast with Lewis Bernstein Namier, subsequently holder of a chair in history, whose culture was Polish.[78] (But in total not many Jews had university posts before 1914.[79])

Conclusion

The numerical preponderance of the immigrants completely altered the social and economic structure of Anglo-Jewry. It did not, however, halt the process, which had been under way earlier in the century, of upward social mobility. The older-established community certainly continued the trend towards white-collar, business and to some extent professional careers; they were augmented by some of the newer immigrants who were to be found almost entirely in the immigrant trades and in shopkeeping. The typical unit, as in British industry generally, was small, but some of the firms were important and significant: the merchant bankers, obviously, and industrialists such as Marcus Samuel and Edgar Speyer.

12

The Working Class in the Inter-war Years

World War I marked a turning-point in British economic history. Up to 1914 Britain retained its prime position despite the growing strength of other industrial nations: the war put an end to that superiority. Traditional economic relationships were interrupted; London lost its financial dominance, and the country's staple export industries—coal, textiles and others—experienced severe depression and long-term decline. But the inter-war years had another, brighter side. Prices fell in the 1920s and early 1930s and greater real incomes encouraged the growth of new, mainly consumer, industries.

Moreover the severe unemployment—averaging 14 per cent, never less than 10 per cent and, at the height of the world depression, affecting almost one in four of the working population—was to a large extent concentrated in the old industrial areas. The image of out-of-work miners and shipbuilders is a real part of social history, just as are the marches of the unemployed to London to try (unsuccessfully) to get something done. Yet elsewhere in Britain, in the south-east and in the Midlands, there was relative prosperity: factories were busy producing cars and radios, and a housing boom produced vast suburbs.

Britain shared with the world many of the economic difficulties of the period—persistent unemployment, the stagnation of international trade, the unprecedentedly deep depression of the late 1920s and early 1930s. Yet in Jewish history these economic problems take second place to events which more disastrously affected the community. The twelve years between the coming to power of the German National Socialists in 1933 and the end of World War II marked the worst period ever in Jewish history, culminating in the Nazi massacre of six million Jews during the war of 1939–45. This very enormity has inevitably overshadowed the serious but smaller-scale attacks on Jews in other parts of Europe in the 1920s and 1930s. In the Ukraine they were massacred after the 1917 revolution. In the new Poland which emerged after 1918 the two million and more Jews were caught in a depressed economy and a virulent antisemitic nationalism. Antisemitism and fascism went hand in hand in many other countries, not excluding Britain; few would doubt that economic depression was a major cause of the dissemination and popular attractiveness of these doctrines.

For Anglo-Jewry the inter-war years marked the end of mass working-class immigration from eastern Europe. Not that immigration stopped completely: despite the generally less liberal attitude throughout the world towards migration, Jews came to Britain from eastern European countries, in the 1930s from the countries under Nazi control—Germany, Austria, Czechoslovakia—and some Sephardim arrived from Persia, Salonika and Bokhara. Many went on to America, Australia and elsewhere, but perhaps some 50,000 to 60,000 Jews in total settled in Britain. Two significant features of that immigration stand out. First, without it, the community's numbers would probably have remained static, a marked contrast to the rapid expansion between 1880 and 1914. As with the British population generally, the Jewish birth-rate and average family size fell. With the extra numbers from immigration and natural increase the Jewish population rose, it is estimated, from 300,000 in 1914 to 385,000 in 1939.[1] Second, the immigrants—notably those from central Europe—included a high proportion of middle-class people who did not settle in the old immigrant districts, the 'East Ends' of cities. Some were able to set up in business or continue their professional careers. Many, especially those who arrived in 1938 and 1939 immediately prior to the war, were virtually penniless and had to take up what jobs they could get.[2]

Their eschewing of ghetto districts meant that the old settlement cycle was now broken. In the past as Jews had moved out new immigrants had taken their place. But now the outward movement received no such compensation and those districts experienced long-term decline. Along with the general population, Jews moved from central city areas to near-by districts or to more distant commuter suburbs. The great expansion of suburban London in this period was facilitated by the development of transport, both private and public. The Northern underground line to Golders Green was opened in 1907; by 1930 its synagogue had over 500 male seat-holders and ten years later over 600.[3] Near-by Finchley, further north, with only three Jewish families in 1912, developed later and more slowly, awaiting the arrival of the motor-car in the 1930s. Its synagogue was opened in 1926 with 20 members, reaching 67 in 1930 and over 300 ten years later.[4] Table 9 confirms that the outward movement in London had not gone very far by 1930: much took place in the following years.

The outward movement is best documented for London, but it was happening elsewhere. In Manchester the Jews left Strangeways for near-by Cheetham, with some going further out to places liked Crumpsall.[5] In Leeds they were leaving the Leylands for Camp Road and Chapeltown. At the end of World War I there were nine synagogues in the Leylands, two in Camp Road and one in Chapeltown. By the late 1930s only two remained in the Leylands, but there were eight in Camp Road and six in Chapeltown.[6]

Unemployment

Although the commuter suburbs, notably in the London area, were growing—denoting a degree of personal economic improvement—very large numbers of Jews remained either in the old East End[7] or its neighbouring extensions in working-class and lower-middle-class districts. The same was true in the provinces. For while many benefited from the more prosperous 1930s, numerous others shared the common experience of poverty and unemployment. This was despite the fact that most Jews lived in the less depressed south and did not work in the main slump-ridden staple industries. They could not avoid, however, the effects of the general deficiency of demand, especially at the depths of the depression in the late 1920s and early 1930s, which hit the south as well as the north. *The New Survey of London Life and Labour* estimated that in 1929, 13.7 per cent of east London Jews were in poverty, higher than the local average of 12.1 per cent; and this was before the depression was at its deepest.[8] It was 1933 when the (London) Jewish Board of Guardians was faced with its inter-war peak number of cases, totalling 3,954. And that was not the full number of Jews receiving relief because of the extension of statutory services. Unemployment insurance had been widened to cover almost all employees, and Public Assistance was available. The number of Jews obtaining help from these public sources is unknown, but it certainly inflated the figure of Jewish recipients of relief.[9]

Published reminiscences of the period bring these statistics to life. The future novelist and poet Emanuel Litvinoff left school in 1929, at the minimum age, and was accepted by the Cordwainers' Technical College for further education. The letter offering him a place 'seemed a reprieve. Otherwise, at fourteen, like any other unsuccessful boy, I'd be dressed up like a man of forty sawn off at the knees and pitched into a turbulent labour market. The choices were few and gruesome. I could boil a glue-pot and sweep up wood shavings, carry a tailor's sack from workshop to retailer, learn to baste a hem, press out a seam, nail a fur, lather a chin, weigh sugar into one-pound bags, or diss a stick of lead type with average competence.' He left the College after a few weeks and worked at a variety of unskilled jobs in the fur trade and as a Smithfield meat porter.[10]

One man, Maurice Levinson, born 1911, had to enter the Jewish Orphanage in 1917 when his father died, one of the 400 children there. 'The secretary of the After-Care Committee seemed to think that the poor can only succeed in life if they are tailors, barbers or cabinet-makers. Those were the three elite occupations in the East End. I was made a cabinet-maker because I was good at painting and composition'. He worked at first in a sweatshop for 8 shillings (40p) a week, working ten hours a day, then moved on to a mass production factory employing 1,000 men where it was possible to earn £4 a week. Levinson took part in a strike, being sacked after its collapse. After a period of unemployment during which he obtained Public Assistance he and his two brothers became taxi-drivers and 'was never unemployed again'. 'Nearly every man,' he wrote, 'who wanted to be a taxi-driver before the war did so because he was desperately in need of a job'.[11]

Another cabinet-maker was Max Cohen, who became unemployed in 1931, and after being in and out of work for a few years ended up as a carpenter in the building industry. He recalled that 'it was only natural, in fact it was inevitable, that men should do their utmost to escape from the . . . cabinet-making trade. . . . The trade could only offer different degrees of insecurity. None except the most favoured knew from one day to another when they would be out of work. Jobs could last such a short time that it was hardly worth while to drag a box of tools to and from the factory.'[12]

A further indication of the times is provided by a parallel to the late eighteenth-century upsurge of Jews as professional boxers. Some twentieth-century Jewish boxers learnt their fighting trade, and earned a living, in three-round contests at the Wonderland in Whitechapel; others came up through amateur boxing before becoming professionals. One of the earliest was Ted 'Kid' Lewis (born Gershon Mendeloff: 1893–1970), who won the British featherweight title in 1913 and the world welterweight championship in 1915. One or two—notably Al Phillips—fought even after World War II. In the years between, Jack 'Kid' Berg (born Judah Bergman in 1909) won the British lightweight championship in 1934 by defeating Harry Mizler, another Jewish boxer, formerly an amateur champion. Johnny Brown (born Phillip Eckman, 1903–75) learned his boxing at the (Jewish) Oxford and St George's Club, becoming an Association for Jewish Youth champion. As a professional he became British and European bantamweight champion in 1923, retaining it for five years. Other well-known boxers were Benny Caplan and Lew Lazar. Less familiar were Moe Moss (1912–73), 'Kid Bones' (Alfred Burnett) who, *inter alia*, sold newspapers and worked in a tailor's workshop, and Bert Cannons (Reuben Segal), who became a taxi-driver on his retirement from boxing.

Although this evidence is ambiguous—some may have taken up boxing because they enjoyed it as a sport—others did so 'because they were un-employed, and, in the traditional parlance "hungry" '.[13]

Traditional Jewish Occupations

This handful of boxers provides an interesting episode, a marginal corrective to the historical image of the timid, cowering Jew. But they have as little general significance as the Jewish road-sweepers and lavatory attendants of Stepney[14] or the few coal-miners and coke-oven-workers in South Wales.[15] A 1928 study of the clothing industry and its workers, on the other hand, refers to Jews on almost every page. 'The considerable Jewish population in Manchester', wrote the author, 'is . . . principally engaged in some kind of tailoring'. He guessed there were 5,000 Jewish tailors in Leeds.[16] *The New Survey of London Life and Labour* soon afterwards concluded, from a study based on the identification of

'Jewish' names, that in East London 29 per cent of the men were makers of clothing and even more—50 per cent—of the employed women.[17] It suggested that the estimated 20,000 Jewish men in the London clothing trade in 1932 comprised about a quarter of the total number of gainfully occupied male Jews in the capital.[18] Similarly with cabinet-making, *The New Survey* gave a figure of 6,000 to 8,000 Jews in the east London furniture industry, where they formed about half the local labour force.[19] And characteristically about half the parents of children at the Liverpool Jewish School in the late 1930s were either tailors or cabinet-makers.[20]

It is noticeable too that the outward movement from the immigrant areas did not greatly reduce the association with the old trades. Cheetham in Manchester and Chapeltown in Leeds housed many Jewish clothing-workers; Hackney's old houses contained large rooms which were suitable for use as furniture workshops;[21] and Jewish boot- and shoe-workers are said to have accompanied the move to Hackney and Tottenham of London footwear factories.[22] (But, as will be seen later, their numbers were probably small.) These impressions and figures are seldom more than guesses; nor do they always distinguish between employers and employed. Nevertheless, they clearly indicate the persistence of the old occupations of the immigration era.

This is not to ignore sundry changes in those industries, some particularly affecting Jews, others being general. In the tailoring section of the clothing industry in Britain as a whole, the number of male employees had remained fairly static since the turn of the century while the number of tailoresses continued to rise. At the Population Census of 1911 for the first time there were more women than men in the trade, and thereafter their numbers increased. There were several reasons for the lack of male recruits, among them the poor reputation of the industry, despite improvements since the days of the pre-1914 anti-sweating campaigns. Wages were now fixed by Trade Boards and compared well with the national average, hours were shorter, and—while still seasonal—the industry, producing for the home market, did not suffer the severe unemployment of the exporting industries. Yet 'working tailors are only too anxious to see their children and their friends' children escape from an occupation the accompanying evils of which they appreciate from bitter personal experience.'[23] This verdict referred mainly but not entirely to conditions in the workshops, an important segment of the industry, for despite the growth of factory production the majority of enterprises, employing most workers, were still small. The forty-five clothing factories in London in 1930, each employing 100 or more workers, accounted for only 15,000 out of some 85,000 clothing workers in the capital.[24] Between that date and the outbreak of World War II the number of small plants in the London women's outerwear industry is estimated to have trebled, from 250 to 750.[25] The furniture industry's 76,000 employees in 1938 were employed in 4,000 firms, of which about 3,000 each employed less than ten people. Only thirty-seven factories had more than 300 workers.[26]

The environment of the workshops had hardly changed from the conditions described in pre-1914 investigations. The 1928 study of the clothing industry described the life of workers 'cramped in a small room, with poor ventilation, an atmosphere made damp by pressing which is frequently performed in the same room as the sewing and machining, and where government inspection is unknown'.[27] In Manchester there were numerous small workshops: 'a couple of dark rooms in a old house, a machine or two and perhaps with machiners who along with the boss did everything else besides'.[28]

It is understandable that people should have tried to avoid that kind of work, and to have preferred others, if they had the choice. In Leeds where the Jewish workshops had traditionally supplemented the wholesale bespoke factories (whereas elsewhere workshops supplied the retail trade), Jewish workers left 'the relatively squalid conditions of the small workshops and [entered] the modern factory where they earned more regular wages under far more congenial conditions.'[29] The long-term trend, though, for both Jewish and non-Jewish men was to avoid the industry. In the case of the Jews the decline of immigration meant that there was no longer a supply of people willing to work in almost any conditions, and some of those who had worked in clothing contrived not to send their sons into it.

This is borne out by the figures in Table 10, which show the occupations of teenage east London entrants to Jewish Friendly Societies in 1913 compared with the entrants of 1930. In the earlier year some 70 per cent of both girls and boys worked in the clothing or furniture industries, especially as tailors and tailoresses. By 1930 only about half the boys and just over half the girls were occupied in those industries, tailoring showing marked falls, and the earlier, small proportion of male hat- and footwear-workers had virtually disappeared along with the female underwear-makers and shoe-makers. Hardly any boys or girls worked in the tobacco industry. But there was an increase in the percentage of boys working as furriers and in furniture, and a large increase in the percentage of female dress-makers.

It is necessary to be cautious, and to avoid reading too much into these figures. We do not have the absolute numbers involved, only percentages, and those joining the Friendly Societies may not have been representative of young Jews in east London—or of the major provincial communities like Manchester and Leeds. Those cities had a less diverse employment structure than the capital and were located in the more depressed parts of the country: the possibility of alternative employment was correspondingly much less. In Cheetham, I was told by a Manchester informant, 'you either became a tailor or a market man. There was nothing else.'[30]

Signs of Change

The obvious question to ask is: what was happening to those who were not entering the immigrant jobs, or were leaving them? Some became employers, but those who remained employees were tending increasingly to enter white-collar work. Table 10 shows this quite clearly. In 1930 about 30 per cent of the boys and 40 per cent of the girls were employed as office-workers (as many as one in four of the girls was a clerk or typist), or as shop assistants and travellers. The service industries were expanding; young Jews could obtain work in family shops; they were native-born and anglicised; and more had received their education at grammar schools (from which office-workers were largely recruited). More children were able to attend grammar schools when fees were reduced or abolished, and in the 'Jewish' areas of east London, Jews attended them in large numbers. Half of the pupils at Clapton County School were Jews, as were 40 per cent at Hackney Downs School.[31] But despite an expansion in their numbers, the grammar-school Jews remained in a minority. As late as 1950 about one-quarter of Manchester Jewish children received a grammar-school education. This was higher, certainly, than for the general population,[32] but the figures mean that three out of four Jews there did not get the kind of education which would normally lead to white-collar work.

Presumably the clerical workers obtained jobs in the larger, more bureaucratic organisations—the civil service and local government—as well as in private industry such as the four main-line railway companies and in large commercial and manufacturing enterprises.[33]

More generally, the evidence suggests, in addition to an expansion of white-collar work, an extension into a wider range of employment. The dance-band era provided employment for Jewish musicians, for example, and also for Jewish dance-band leaders.[34] The Jewish Board of Guardians in London continued with its task of arranging apprenticeships, although on a small scale (in the 1930s the maximum number in any one year was 188, in 1934). However, it tried to 'widen the range of trades; placement in the motor and film trades was suggested by a Sub-Committee of Inquiry':

> As a result the number of different trades to which boys were apprenticed rose from 64 in 1934 to 87 in 1936, though there was a decline in the number of boys being apprenticed.[35]

Some other statistics, of parental occupations of children at the Liverpool Jewish School in 1910 and 1939 (Table 11), do not quite support the London evidence. This may be because the school was located in the city centre and, although children travelled to it from other districts, the figures probably represent those Jewish families which remained in the old locality. Thus the decline in the proportion of 'manufacturers' and of those in the distributive trades, as well as the absence of clerical workers, may reflect the movement of more ambitious Jews away from the city centre. In that case we should expect a continuing importance, even if less than before, of tailoring and cabinet-making. Yet the slight increase in 'craftsmen' and 'manual workers' suggests a move away from the traditional trades. The largest increase was of men described as seafarers, presumably men who worked in the kosher kitchens or as ships' musicians during that era of ocean travel.

The evidence presented here suggests that alongside the not inconsiderable vestiges of a definable Jewish labour market (characteristically, Jews working for other Jews in a small number of industries), the second and third generation were moving into the wider world of employment. It was not plain sailing: this was the era of organised antisemitism and Jews were not necessarily accepted by employers or by non-Jewish workpeople. This applied not only to religiously orthodox employees who would have required sympathetic attention to their religious needs, such as time off for holy days. One of the tasks of the Trades Advisory Council, established in 1938 by the Board of Deputies of British Jews to combat antisemitism—including the encouragement of 'ethical' practices by Jewish businessmen such as accepting trade unions in their enterprises—was also to take up cases where Jews complained of discrimination at work. It is not known what were the effects of antisemitism: did it prevent Jews taking up certain kinds of employment?

Jewish Trade Unionism

The heyday of separate Jewish trade unions was in the immigration period. From World War I onwards they amalgamated with the appropriate British unions, although sometimes they continued as identifiable sections of those unions. The Independent Jewish Cabinet Makers' Union, for example, became part of the National Amalgamated Furniture Trades Association to form its East London United Branch No. 15. The secretary from 1919 to 1947 was Sidney Fineman.[36] Yet a few separate unions remained and others were established during the period, so that it was possible for a conference of Jewish trade unions in 1922 to support strikers in the meat markets, and to call on the Chief Rabbi to order the withdrawal of the *shochetim* (ritual slaughterers) for this purpose.[37] In 1934 a Jewish Labour Council was set up, with A. R. Rollin (London organiser of the National Union of Tailors and Garment Workers) as chairman: its purpose was to oppose fascism. In 1937 a United Committee of Jewish Workers was formed (secretary S. Lever of the London Jewish Bakers' Union) to protest at anti-Jewish excesses in Poland and Romania.[38]

These were primarily political activities. In the strictly industrial sphere trade unions in Britain had expanded rapidly during World War I and in the boom immediately after it. Groups which previously had been poorly organised (especially women workers) joined in great numbers, wages rose and better conditions of work—such as shorter hours—were obtained between 1914 and 1920. With the onset of the slump in 1921 the unions entered a period of weakness. Membership fell and wages were cut, but it was not all dismal, and the bright patches included areas of Jewish interest. The London Jewish Bakers' Union was 'small but powerful in the sense that nearly every Jewish baker belongs to it. Every master baker employing men from the union is compelled to attach to every loaf a label guaranteeing that the bread has been baked . . . under trade-union conditions'. Moreover, the men organised a method of helping the unemployed members. Work-sharing (called 'jobbing') was a system whereby each member stayed off work one day a month, his place being taken by an unemployed member.[39]

Baking was on a small scale and localised, and easier to organise than the more diffuse furniture and clothing industries, the two main fields of Jewish employment. In them much effort had to be put into recruiting and into getting employers to accept them. Sometimes, in some plants and areas, the union was successful in the sense of recruiting at a high level. Sidney Fineman described an incident in the 1930s at an East End furniture factory where all the workers were members of the union. It was discovered that two men were working overtime without union permission, 'which was very bad at a time of mass unemployment'. The men were fined by the union, but refused to pay, and a strike was called which lasted 'three or four months'. Fineman made the point that the unemployed, 'far from strike-breaking', turned out to assist the strikers.[40]

The furniture industry probably had a greater density of union membership than did the larger, more diverse and more widespread clothing industry. The weakness of the unions in that industry because of low membership was compounded by divisions within the labour force: separate unions (although the number was reduced by amalgamation); hostility between the main union, centred on Leeds, and the membership in other areas, especially London; and the existence of factions, often militant and left-wing. 'It is not surprising', wrote a commentator in 1928, 'that there has been continual strife, sometimes open, sometimes subterranean'.[41]

One of the constituent unions at the amalgamation of 1915 had been the Leeds Jewish union, but the waterproof-workers, many of them Jewish, who had at first taken part, soon withdrew and continued as a separate organisation. And one part of the industry in which many Jewish workers were to be found, the making of women's garments, tended to operate on a small scale, thus making unionisation more difficult. However one important union did exist, the United Ladies' Tailors and Mantle Makers' Union, which absorbed a number of smaller unions. Like many unions it prospered during World War I, and reached a high point when it struck in 1918 for the eight-hour day (funds were provided by the General Federation of Trade Unions). It built its own headquarters in 1921 and remained a separate union with about 3,000 members until 1938, using Yiddish for its union business until well into the 1920s.[42]

The long-term trend towards amalgamation was interrupted by the changed policy of the Communist Party in the late 1920s. Instead of working within existing unions it began to form its own, in opposition. One of the few that were established was the United Clothing Workers' Union, with mainly Jewish officials and members. It did not last long and came to an end having been defeated by the (national) Tailors' and Garment Workers' Union, the breakaway union's general secretary, Sam Elsbury, being expelled by the Communist Party.[43] But there were many other disputes during the 1930s when clothing-workers went on strike against the advice of the union which complained of communist influence: a period of internal bitterness and hostility.[44]

One reason for the antagonism was that the national union after 1920 centralised its funds in Leeds. Most branch money went to head office, which appointed and paid all full-time officials, down to branch level. To workers who had been used, in their own, small unions, to running their own affairs this was hard to take, especially as the union was in a distant provincial city, and there was resentment among Jewish workers at the union being controlled by 'a quite alien religious and ethnic group'[45]—the leadership included many who were Roman Catholic and of Irish origin.

In Leeds itself things were different. For one thing, its clothing industry suffered less than did London during the depression, and the Jewish union had had a long history of unity and stability. They formed the No. 2 branch of the amalgamated union under a Jewish secretary.[46] 'Most of the Jewish operatives', it was reported in the 1920s, 'women as well as men, have been drawn into the union. Among the Gentiles this was not the case, the women being rather poorly organised, and in sections other than the men's tailoring trade hardly so at all'.[47] This changed in the 1930s when the total Leeds membership of the union expanded to reach 30,000, the Jews forming only a small proportion.

Different again was the Waterproof Garment Workers' Trade Union, a small union, highly localised in the Manchester area. It lost membership in the depression of the early 1930s and 'there were several industry-wide strikes, mostly the result of proposals by employers to decrease piece-rate prices. The yearly agreement with the employers was then signed in October, a time of the year noted for slackening in the trade. In the current cut-throat conditions employers inevitably asked for decreases',[48] and strikes or lock-outs would often follow. This small union also had its own unofficial pressure group, to some extent communist-inspired, which also had little success. It supported a union member Ted Ainley (Theodore Herzl Abrahamson) in his unsuccessful bid to be the general secretary.

As against these examples of Jewish trade union activity must be seen the fact that the increasing number obtaining white-collar jobs on entering some of the newer industries were joining poorly organised sectors. Apart from the civil service, the railways (and teaching), white-collar unionism was very weak, and the new industries were often run by anti-union employers.

Conclusion

Generalisations about the inter-war Jewish working class have to be qualified in two ways: experiences varied according to geographical location, and men's employment was different from that of women. A distinction needs to be drawn between London and the provincial communities in the industrial areas:

the latter had higher unemployment rates and fewer alternative jobs in new industries. The main trend, though, is clear: there was a proportionate fall in the main type of male Jewish employment, the clothing industry. Most Jewish tailors lived in London, but in the 1930s the capital's greater prosperity enabled many to move out of it, or if they stayed their sons did not join them. It remained the main single source of employment for male Jews in Britain but because of its predominance, the fall in the number of Jewish male workers necessarily meant that the total Jewish male manual working class fell. This conclusion is not seriously disturbed by the fact that some Jews took up other kinds of manual work; or by the buoyancy of employment in the furniture and fur industries; or by the refugees from Nazism who took up all manner of jobs. For the fall in Jewish male manual work in tailoring was augmented by similar declines in the footwear, tobacco, slipper and cap trades. However, Jewish boys were taking up white-collar work.

On the other hand girls were becoming employed in greater numbers, partly replacing men in some sections of the clothing trade, and also in white-collar jobs, as office workers and sales assistants. Although they were usually a temporary feature of the labour market, leaving it on marriage, it is possible that the total, male and female, Jewish employed labour force did not decline during the 1920s and 1930s.

13
Business and the Professions in the Interwar Years

From the beginning of World War I, every year the number of anglicised Jews increased. The old died, the proportion who were native born increased, and there was no large-scale immigration of working-class east European Jews. A repetition of the nineteenth-century experience could be expected, as those brought up in British society came to form the majority of the community. In economic terms this could have meant a greater degree of integration, expressed in a broader range of activities.

A writer in the *Jewish Year Book*, surveying the development of Anglo-Jewry during the reign of the late king, George V, 1910–36, thought this was happening. 'The close of the reign', he wrote, 'found the basis of Anglo-Jewry much wider, both economically and geographically, than it had been at the beginning'.[1] As we have seen, there was a move from the ghetto areas; the working class was declining or taking up new kinds of jobs. The *Jewish Year Book* had two groups in mind, noting first the changes among the elite, lay leadership from a domination by merchant bankers to those engaged in industry. 'The heyday of the private banks, which had been represented in England by the Rothschilds, the Montagus and the Sterns, was waning. The age of rationalization and of multiple stores, of chemicals and of oil had dawned'.[2] The author referred particularly to Sir Marcus Samuel of Shell Oil (raised to the peerage as Viscount Bearsted in 1925, two years before he died) and Sir Alfred Mond, a government minister from 1916 to 1922, whose chemical firm, Brunner, Mond, amalgamated with other companies to form Imperial Chemical Industries, which became one of the largest companies in the country. He had also been instrumental in creating one of the colliery combines, Amalgamated Anthracite Collieries in South Wales. He too was raised to the peerage, in 1928, and died in 1930.[3] The author could have added the names of other great industrialists, whose firms had originated before 1914. The General Electric Company expanded in response to the growing use of electricity, producing all manner of items from heavy electrical equipment to radios and lamps (the company being part of the electric-lamp cartel).[4] The giant firm of Unilever was created out of, among others, the van den Bergh margarine and food company,[5] and J. Lyons & Co. rapidly became one of the major suppliers of food products alongside its increasing number of teashops and restaurants.[6]

The other people to whom the *Jewish Year Book* was referring were the more recent east European immigrant group. They had been enabled to move to the suburbs, it asserted, through economic improvement directly attributable to World War I. Their industries had prospered because of the great demand for, among other products, millions of uniforms. The long-term adaptation had been hastened fortuitously by the war.

There was some truth in these observations. The great merchant bankers were less important as a result of the stagnation of international trade and the decline of London's role in overseas lending.[7] And there were changes in personnel. For example, Sir Edgar Speyer left Britain in 1922 following attacks on him during the war because of his German origins, culminating in 1921 in the revocation of his Certificate of Naturalisation and his being struck off the list of Privy Councillors. Speyer Brothers' bank in London was wound up and Speyer returned to the USA, his country of birth.[8] Of Stern Brothers it is said the bank became 'little more than an office for the payment of coupons on the loans they . . . issued in the past',[9] and a description of the inter-war life at Rothschild's gives a clear impression of an easy-going, routine, lackadaisical existence.[10] It is true that in the 1930s three Jews, Lords Melchett and Bearsted and Sir Albert Stern, were members of the boards of joint stock banks, that the merchant banks became involved in domestic share issues, and other Jews were engaged on the Stock Exchange and other City institutions.[11] But the great nineteenth-century financial days were gone.

At the same time, while there was an undoubted move by the other group, the east European immigrants and their children, into business and the professions, two important features can be identified. Their economic activity tended to remain concentrated in a fairly narrow range and they tended to operate on a small and medium scale. Very few were successful enough in the inter-war years to become leading lay figures in national communal institutions or in the business world. In his essay 'Anti-Semitism in Britain' written in 1945, George Orwell, arguing against the notion that 'British economic life is dominated by the Jews'—a feature of antisemitic propaganda—noted that, on the contrary, 'they had failed to keep up with the modern tendency towards big amalgamations'. They had 'remained fixed in those trades which are necessarily carried out on a small scale by old fashioned methods'.[12] This needs qualifying, but it is a broadly valid statement.

A Narrow Economic Sector

Despite some additions and some demises, the trades in which Jewish businessmen were occupied were essentially the traditional ones. Moreover, the

range of activities was fairly narrow, the new trades somewhat replacing those
which were of less importance. Tobacco manufacturing, for example, which
had been a significant London Jewish industry in the nineteenth century, now
included only a handful of Jewish firms. The industry was dominated by the
Imperial Tobacco Company which included the two major (non-Jewish) firms,
Wills and Player. As cigarette-smoking increased, three other firms came to be
strong competitors, all Jewish (at least in origin). Godfrey Phillips which had
been a family firm became a public company in the 1920s and absorbed a
number of small companies, some of them Jewish (Abdulla, Marcovitch, and
Cohen, Weenen). Carreras (Bernhard Baron's company—he died in 1929)
moved into cigarette manufacture in 1912 and introduced the famous Craven A
brand in 1921. The third firm was J. Wix & Sons, founded 1901, incorporated
in 1912, its brand name being Kensitas. However, Wix was taken over by the
American Tobacco Company in 1927 and drops out from our story. The firm
of Ardath, founded by Sir Albert Levy (d. 1937), was jointly owned by the
Imperial Tobacco Company and the British American Tobacco Company,
although run more or less autonomously; and two small, independent Jewish
companies were Rothman's and Balkan Sobranie.[13]

In a similar way, but for different reasons, there was a decline in one Jewish
interest, viz., the textile industry, especially the cotton trade. The Lancashire
cotton firms were in one of the hardest hit industries in the country; like the
coal industry it suffered from an extraordinary fall in exports. The Jewish
cotton-merchants of Manchester suffered along with the non-Jewish merchants, and a number of them disappeared.

An approximate indication of the persistence of the traditional trades is given
by a survey which was carried out towards the end of World War II. Its
deficiencies prevent it from being completely reliable, but it is still useful. The
investigation covered the major cities in which lived some 80 per cent of the
Jewish population of Great Britain. Local trade directories were used to list the
firms defined as 'Jewish'; i.e., those which had a majority of Jewish directors
or in which most of the capital or 'control' was in Jewish hands. The word
'firm' was not defined (did a company like Montague Burton count as one firm
or was each of its 500 shops separately recorded?), so the statement that of
some 72,000 firms listed about 11,000 were Jewish is not very helpful. But the
information about the types of economic activity can be used. The most
prominent Jewish trades were the familiar ones—clothing, textiles, drapery,
footwear, jewellery and furniture. Another significant group was food shops,
again a traditional one. The only other kinds, in any numbers, were new
activities of the inter-war years: radio and electrical firms, and cosmetic and
toilet preparation businesses.[14] The fact that one can point to other businesses
such as those for the sale and repair of motor vehicles or—a random
example—an ironmongery shop in a Berkshire village[15] does not in any way
disturb the main conclusion.

Another indication of a limited range arises from a consideration of the Jews in the professions. It is plain, although few statistics are available, that more Jews were becoming doctors, lawyers (solicitors, in particular) and teachers. The professions had different methods of entry and training—teachers went to teacher-training colleges or university education departments, solicitors were articled, barristers became pupils, and medical schools might or might not be university departments—so that published figures relating to Jewish university students do not tell the whole story. It is not surprising for these reasons to read contradictory statements about Jewish professionals. The *Jewish Year Book* of 1937 could speak of a 'marked (some observers thought, a dangerous) concentration on the so-called professions',[16] whereas the war-time survey of firms stated, in passing, 'the participation of Jews in the professions is a limited one'.[17] But two surveys of Jewish university students, undertaken in 1936–37 and 1938–39, provide some minimum information, even if the exclusion of London, the largest university, seriously reduces their value.[18]

They suggest that Jews, comprising about 2 per cent of the student body, were slightly over-represented as compared with the Jewish community's fewer than 1 per cent of the total population. The most important feature was the very high concentration in one faculty: medicine. The Jewish students aiming to become doctors (and dentists) totalled 408 out of what the study called 'a representative group of 768 Jewish students' in 1936–37. The preference for medicine among those Jewish students who were born in Britain was even greater. Of 166 foreign students, in the second survey of 1938–39, only 60 were studying medicine and law; as many as 64 were taking courses in science, engineering and technology, and agriculture.

It is not surprising that medicine should rank so high in student preference to the extent that some students changed to it in mid-course from other faculties. It had, first, high prestige; and, second, the chances of making a living were better than in other professions. Graduate unemployment was real enough in the 1930s, not least in teaching, but also in other professions. Since about half the Jewish students relied on scholarships or other kinds of financial assistance (about the same proportion as non-Jewish students), and therefore did not come from wealthy families, the need to get a job was crucial. Medicine provided the opportunity.

In some cases, graduates did not become professionals but went into family businesses. Michael Goldberg, having studied at Glasgow University, returned to his father's wholesale warehouse in that city and with his brother Ephraim transformed the company into department stores.[19] The sons of Joseph Cohen went to Jesus College, Cambridge, and then into the family business of the Cavendish Woodhouse chain of furniture stores.[20] Lionel Jacobson, having studied jurisprudence at Oxford University, entered his father's business, Jackson the Tailor.[21] Isolated examples like these—in earlier years Simon Marks and Israel Sieff went into Marks & Spencer after graduation—might be counterbalanced by such as Jeremy Raisman of Leeds who was offered a post at Montague Burton but opted to enter the Indian Civil Service.[22] The net effect was probably to reduce the Anglo-Jewish professional segment (and proportionately to emphasise the concentration on medicine).

Small-scale Operation

The relatively restricted range of activities was paralleled by small-scale enterprise. This was obviously true of the independent professions, and it applied too to those in distribution—wholesale or retail—and manufacture. In general, Jewish businessmen were occupied, as manufacturers or traders, in the expanding consumer sector. The women's outerwear industry for example grew in response to the increased purchasing power of women and to changes in their tastes:

> More and more women were wage earners who did not want time-wasting fittings but had enough money to follow fashion. . . . The status symbol aspect of fashion was losing its importance. . . . An era of inexpensive fashion had begun, in which change and variety were more valued than costly impressiveness. Stores and dress shops responded to the need by introducing new, more varied ready-to-wear departments stocked with moderately priced clothes.[23]

While many consumer goods were produced in the growing number of large-scale enterprises—part of a general inter-war trend towards larger enterprises—many were made in small businesses. In a number of industries it was normal to use sub-contractors and this was certainly the case in clothing, which was probably the most important single industry in which Jews were occupied.

It was common for small workshops (and outworkers also) to make the clothes for retail shops or for wholesalers. These customers would use one of two methods. They could send the workshops the cloth ready cut (thereby relieving the sub-contractors of the need to provide working capital for the cloth); or they might use the 'cut, make and trim' method. In this case the workshop would receive cloth and make clothes as required, supplying the trimmings and charging a price that covered the cost of the cloth, the trimmings it supplied and a fixed sum for making. More capital might be required unless the cloth was supplied on credit. Certainly working capital was a major item. The firm of Ellis & Goldstein, founded 1910 as sub-contractors making ladies' outerwear garments, was able to move into manufacturing on its own account at the end of World War I only by obtaining from members of the family the necessary capital for materials and for providing credit to its customers.[24] The ladies' garment industry which expanded rapidly in the 1930s was however composed to a large extent of new, small firms. One of them, Max Radin, started operations in 1932 with four sewing machines bought on hire purchase.

He became a major name soon afterwards and 'developed rapidly in the inexpensive dress trade, in the thirties, introducing Rhona Ray dresses'.[25] Many refugees from Germany and Austria who had been in the industry in those countries were able to open small enterprises. In general quite a number of the important post–World War II firms making women's outerwear garments began in this small way in the 1930s. (In passing it is worth noting that the new fashion of lightweight outerwear was associated with new types of underwear and also the greater use of cosmetics. John Goodenday established the Full-Fashioned Hosiery Co. Ltd.—better known later under the name of Kayser Bondor;[26] and Albert Alberman, a pharmacist, founded Beauté Ltd in 1928, the origin of the Innoxa company.)[27]

Similarly while retail distribution was undergoing a long-term change towards larger enterprises and the proportion of retail sales accruing to independent shops was therefore falling, the independents (those owning less than ten shops) were still responsible for perhaps two-thirds of retail sales on the eve of World War II. Moreover, 'the overwhelming majority' of independents were 'single shops managed by working proprietors'.[28] In a number of ways it was easy to become a shopkeeper and in certain respects easier than in the past. It was always possible to start as a street-seller or market trader (and in some cases a fixed shop would be combined with a market interest). The firm of Tesco Ltd began with its founder, John Cohen, from a tailoring family, selling a variety of cheap goods in the markets after his demobilisation at the end of World War I. He moved into shopkeeping and by 1932 was successful enough to found his company and within six years had 100 cut-price stores.[29]

Cohen and others in certain retail trades had to deploy costing and pricing skills. In a number of trades because of the spread of resale price maintenance—whereby manufacturers fixed the selling price—that skill became less relevant: by the late 1930s about 30 per cent of retail sales were of goods whose prices were fixed in this way. In addition other traditional skills were declining as goods were increasingly pre-packaged. (However in the consumer durable trade technical knowledge of the products was needed.) At the same time hire purchase for the sale of expensive items was available from finance houses, and long credit terms were given by wholesalers. The amount of capital required for shopkeeping was thus not especially great. Although it is not known if the total number of shops increased in this period, it is at least clear, despite the undoubted expansion of the larger firms, that those who wished to become shopkeepers could do so with not too much difficulty.[30] Among those who did were Jews.

The extension of Jewish business activity was by no means a problem-free success story, especially when there was competition with non-Jewish firms. And in industries where the workforce was notoriously under-unionised, relations between employers and employees were not necessarily satisfactory. Of the London clothing trade for example the following has been said:

Before the entry of the Jews in large numbers the distribution side of the industry was handled by non-Jewish City firms. The entry of many Jewish manufacturing and distributing firms, with new methods of selling and display, incurred the displeasure of the old conservative firms, thus giving rise to anti-Jewish feeling, which, however did not openly express itself in any sharp form. It was possible for newcomers to commence business with relatively little capital. The vicissitudes of fashion caused many casualties, and bankruptcy and default were prominent features . . . in this sector of the trade. This presented inevitably a picture of predominantly Jewish malpractice. Because of constant improvements and economies in production and selling methods, considerable price reductions were possible and effected. Although they benefited the consumer, the older established and more conservative sections of the industry resented this tendency as a form of 'price-cutting'. The considerable acceleration in the change of fashions between the wars, and the consequent great depreciation of the value of unsold goods, led, with the new and more energetic firms, to super-profits and high pressure selling methods during the main seasons, with consequent price reductions and bargain sales afterwards. The absence of effective trade unionism also made many apparently or really unpleasant features in the industry possible.[31]

Accusations of price-cutting were also widely asserted in the grocery trade and the British Union of Fascists made much of it in their propaganda among shopkeepers.[32] Anti-Jewish feelings were also expressed in the hat industry partly because a number of London Jewish firms were able to compete strongly by introducing mass production methods and partly because, ironically, the 'newcomers' to the felt-hat industry were not the Jews but the old-established Luton manufacturers. To accommodate changing fashions they moved from the making of straw hats to felt-hat manufacture, thus bringing them into conflict with the London firms.[33]

Two further features of the Jewish aspect of distribution were to do with wholesaling and with larger retail firms. It is likely that on balance the proportion of goods passing through wholesalers fell in the face of direct sales from manufacturer to retailer and even direct to the consumer through door-to-door selling and mail order. (Mail order was a new feature of the period. One of the innovators was Great Universal Stores, which had started in Manchester with Abraham, George and Jack Rose, the three sons of a furniture dealer. It was transformed from a general trading concern using tallymen—at first operating from an attic in the family home—into mail order in the 1920s. In 1930 Isaac Wolfson of Glasgow became its chief buyer and two years later a joint managing director.[34] Mail order sales, however, were a tiny percentage of total retail sales in Britain.) But while wholesaling probably declined relatively, it remained important in a number of trades. The war-time survey already quoted found that of 3,500 Jewish firms in furniture, fur, jewellery and footwear about half were wholesalers.[35]

Large-scale Operation in Traditional Activities

The emphasis so far on small-scale enterprise should not obscure the undoubted fact that there was a general trend in Britain towards larger organisation. The Jewish involvement in this development—outside the new industries, some already mentioned and others to be discussed later—took place in the familiar industries such as clothing manufacture and in some distributive trades.

The general impression from the available evidence is that large-scale enterprises grew as a result of internal growth rather than through mergers and take-overs: one exception was the furniture chain of Cavendish Woodhouse, with seventy-six British shops and ninety in Canada which had originated before 1914 with the purchase of existing firms.[36] More typically Montague Burton, the wholesale bespoke tailors, had opened some 500 shops by the eve of World War II in a feverish expansion programme partly in response to growing demand, partly in order to meet the competition of the equally expansive non-Jewish Fifty Shilling Tailors.[37] A newcomer in that line were the brothers Mick and Nathaniel Horne, who started off in 1919. By 1925 they had opened a chain of retail tailors' shops under the name of John Maxwell. By 1939 they had nearly 100 shops together with four factories.[38] On a smaller scale was Jackson the Tailor, based on Newcastle, which had about thirty shops and two factories.[39]

There was nothing specifically Jewish in this kind of vertical integration. Thus the furniture trade before 1939 was not so structured, the makers and sellers being separate. But wholesale bespoke men's tailoring had developed that way, and H. Samuel made watches and sold them in its 100 or so shops.[40] There were variations, of course. J. Lyons & Co. had begun as caterers but had moved into food manufacture, so much so that while their teashops and restaurants were household names, their manufacturing side became the larger part of their operations. Despite the high degree of integration in the footwear industry the large Jewish company, A. & W. Flatau, did not own shops. Marks & Spencer's variety multiple shops, after some years of hesitation, adopted its long-term policy in the late twenties of selling goods under its own brand name at a maximum price of 5 shillings (to place itself in a different market from Woolworth's, whose maximum price was 6d). It obtained its goods from manufacturers whose output and quality it closely supervised. The company had more than 230 shops by the late 1930s, its effort devoted as much to extending existing stores as to opening new ones.[41]

Nor is it possible to establish why some individual firms became large and others did not, nor why some failed. One of the latter was the retail credit furniture company of Sir Benjamin Drage (Cohen), which was sufficiently expansive to become a public company in the 1920s but was sold in 1937 to Isaac Wolfson after it was making losses.[42]

The names mentioned here do not form a comprehensive list of large Jewish firms. Others could be added: Polikoff's of Hackney was said to be one of the largest clothing firms in London;[43] there were 160 furniture stores of Jay & Campbell (owned by Sir Julien Cahn, better known for the cricketing tours of his own team that he sponsored);[44] Levy & Franks's ran sixty or so public houses, whose reputation was built on its catering facilities, for example.[45] Whatever the total number of large firms and whatever the proportion of the market they held, one conclusion is clear: very few of the large Jewish firms of the 1930s were new creations of the inter-war years. But there were other areas of Jewish business life where the story was different.

Non-traditional and New Industries

Although Jewish economic activities were not widely spread throughout the British economy the earlier mention of Mond and Samuel reminds us that Jews were to be found in other parts of the economy. Some were firms which originated well before 1914 and had in many cases been established by central European immigrants (or their descendants). They included firms in a great variety of activities, and some were very large: General Electric, Shell-Mex, ICI, Unilever. Others were small or medium size: Gestetner, makers of office duplicating equipment; Bovis, in the construction industry; Ward & Goldstone, electrical engineering; Glaxo, makers of food and pharmaceutical products; George Cohen, suppliers, *inter alia*, of a variety of engineering plant and equipment.

It will be noticed that these firms were in the new or expanding sectors of the inter-war years, but Jewish participation in those sectors was generally limited. The sole Jewish involvement in the growing production of motor vehicles was Siegfried Bettman of Coventry. His Triumph motor cycles were successfully used by the army during World War I and production rose to 70 per week and in 1923 he entered car production, although the cycles remained the firm's main business. Indeed, 'car production was always in difficulties and the firm was placed in the hands of the Receiver shortly before the outbreak of the Second World War'. The motor-cycle side was separated from car production in 1936 and made into an independent business, the Triumph Engineering Co.; this was sold to the Birmingham Small Arms Co.[46]

Similarly one does not come across Jews in the burgeoning freight and passenger operating companies (except taxis). However, one of the few pioneer airlines started after World War I was established by Samuel Instone (who had shipping interests) and his son, Alfred. Like other contemporary airlines it was unprofitable and received a government subsidy. In 1924 three such companies, all in the same financial position, were taken over by Imperial Airways which remained in existence until 1940, Sir Samuel Instone being a director.[47] By chance he gets a footnote in labour history in his other role as a colliery proprietor (he was chairman of two colliery companies, Bedwas in South Wales and Askern in Yorkshire). A strike occurred at Bedwas called by the South Wales Miners' Federation in order to get rid of a competing union. Arthur Horner recalls in his memoirs that feeling among the miners towards Instone was high, to the extent that they asked 'whether they could smash the Jewish shops'. His response was that 'if anybody started anti-Jewish activity on this issue I would resign the presidency of the South Wales Miners in protest'.[48]

In addition to the GEC's production of a wide range of electrical equipment, including radios, one other large company in that field was Electrical and Musical Industries Ltd (EMI). This was created in 1931 as a merger between the Gramophone Co. and the Columbia Gramophone Co. in order to concentrate gramophone production under one management. The moving spirits behind this move were Louis Sterling and Alfred Clark. The company and its associates made other electrical goods such as radio equipment and refrigerators.[49] And there were two other, smaller, radio enterprises, associated with the names of Sobell and Thorn. (An earlier figure was Godfrey Isaacs who, on his retirement in 1910 from his father's firm of fruit- and shipbrokers, became managing director of Marconi's Wireless Telegraph Co. He took a leading part 'in the negotiations leading up to the formation of the British Broadcasting Company' [the precursor of the British Broadcasting Corporation] in the early 1920s.[50] He died in 1925 when the radio industry was still in its infancy.) Sobell and Thorn were middle-class immigrants, from Galicia and Austria respectively. Sobell had been in the oil business and in Britain set up a small radio business.[51] Jules Thorn started operations in 1928, taking on the lamp cartel by importing lamps at first and then making them in a factory in Edmonton. In 1936 he entered the radio trade by taking over the established radio firm of Ferguson.[52]

There was much more Jewish involvement in the film and cinema industry, at all levels—the ownership of production companies and of cinemas as well as artistic direction. Sir Michael Balcon (1896–1977) was a pioneer immediately after World War I, when his associates included Oscar Deutsch, a metal merchant, Sol Levy and Charles Moss Woolf. He formed his own production company, Gainsborough Pictures, in 1928.[53] This was one year after the establishment of the Gaumont British Picture Corporation with Isidore Ostrer as president, and his two brothers; Mark, managing director, and Maurice, assistant managing director. (It was a subsidiary of the Metropolis & Bradford Trust Company of which Isidore was chairman and the other brothers directors.) The Ostrers were businessmen with wide interests. Isidore had been a member of the Stock Exchange and became a merchant banker, the firm of Ostrer Brothers being established in 1921. Maurice was associated in the 1930s with Bush Radio Ltd, and also with the wool textile firm of Illingworth, Morris floated in 1921 as Amalgamated Textiles. He remained its chairman until his death in 1975.[54]

It is possible that the establishment in 1928 of both Gainsborough and Gaumont British was a consequence of the 1927 Cinematograph Films Act, which established a minimum quota of British pictures to protect the film industry from being swamped by American productions. It enabled the British industry to survive. The two companies became associated in 1932 and Balcon became production manager for both of them. Five years later he took up the post of executive producer at Ealing Studios where he was responsible for the 'Ealing Comedy' series which were made between 1938 and 1959. And an equally well known producer was Alexander Korda (whose brothers Vincent and Zoltan were also involved in the film industry). They were Hungarians, the sons of an ex-soldier overseer of an estate. Alexander, born 1893, was at first a journalist but went into film-making as early as 1914. After the fall of the post-war revolutionary Bela Kun government to which he was sympathetic, he was arrested and after much travelling arrived in England in 1931.[55]

Gaumont British also owned cinemas (the other combine, Associated British Picture Corporation, was not Jewish). Gaumont British began with about 20 in the late 1920s and had some 350 ten years later, amounting to about 10 per cent of all cinema seats. It also distributed foreign films and owned companies making subsidiary equipment.[56] The only other substantial Jewish cinema name was Oscar Deutsch of Birmingham, who created the Odeon chain of luxury cinemas. He also went into film production but he died in 1941, aged forty-eight, and his interests passed to Joseph Arthur Rank, the Methodist flour-miller, who was emerging as the British film and cinema magnate. In the same year the three Ostrer brothers resigned from Gaumont British, and Rank became its chairman.

In the 1930s there were some 4,400 cinemas of which the two main combines owned over 600.[57] Apart from a few other chains the great majority were independently owned, some by Jews. The father-in-law of Isaac Wolfson owned suburban London cinemas. [58] The father of the Cardiff poet Dannie Abse was part-owner of a cinema in Aberdare.[59] Nat Cohen, the son of an immigrant meat-dealer, bought a cinema in 1932, added six more in the 1930s and went into film distribution.[60] Another was Sidney Lewis Bernstein, whose father had immigrated from Sweden, had owned quarries in Wales and had built cinemas in east London. The young Bernstein (b. 1899), having attended grammar school, started an engineering apprenticeship but by the age of nineteen was in a film distribution office. Later he owned a number of cinemas.[61] No doubt there were others who operated on a fairly small scale.

Jews were also involved in another inter-war entertainments industry. This was the era of the dance halls, and the dance bands included many Jewish musicians and a number of band-leaders: Geraldo, Ambrose, Joe Loss, Harry Roy, Sid Millward, Oscar Rabin and Lou Preager.[62]

Finally, in this section, were the newspaper proprietors and publishers. The ubiquitous Isidore Ostrer owned the *Sunday Referee* for a few years in the 1930s, making losses before selling out to Lord Kemsley's group.[63] The only other newspaper interest, apart from the specifically Jewish communal news-papers, was that of Julius Salter Elias (1873–1946), created Lord Southwood in

1937. His firm, Odhams Press Ltd, was a major publishing concern, producing many magazines and books and also running the Borough Billposting Co. (Odhams was the largest outdoor publicity enterprise in the country). It produced two newspapers: the *People,* which appeared on Sundays, and the *Daily Herald.* This Labour paper was taken over by Odhams in 1930, the Trades Union Congress owning 49 per cent of the shares. Southwood sat in the House of Lords as a Labour peer; but he is somewhat marginal to this narrative. He was Jewish in origin but was not connected with the community. He married a Christian lady and many of his interests were in church matters.[64]

The major Jewish publishing house was Routledge, run by the Franklins, but newcomers included Michael Joseph, Fredric Warburg (who left Routledge for Secker & Warburg, remaining a small unprofitable firm in the 1930s)[65] and Victor Gollancz who set up his publishing firm in 1928. Alongside a general publishing output, the firm produced the Left Book Club series.[66]

This is not the sum total of Jews in 'non-traditional' industries, as the next section on refugees from Nazism demonstrates; nor of newcomers to more familiar activities, whether native born or immigrant. Oswald Michael Stroud (b. 1897), the son of the minister of Bradford's Reform synagogue, established with a friend the woollen textile firm of Stroud, Riley Drummond Ltd.[67]

Among those who left Russia after the 1917 revolution was Evsei Savalievitch Gourvitch whose family had been in the timber trade in Russia for seven generations. Gourvitch had studied and practised as a lawyer in St Petersburg before 1914, and went into the timber trade during World War I. In 1925 he established the Phoenix Timber Co., importing softwood timbers into Britain (thereby joining other Jewish timber firms such as Gliksten's, founded in London in 1875).[68]

Another small group of newcomers were a number of Sephardim from Bokhara and Persia who were in the carpet trade.[69] And there was the special case of the half-dozen Jewish cutlery firms in Sheffield. Lewis, Rose & Co. began in 1922 (later changing its name to Ashberry when it bought up an old-established firm of that name). It employed up to 275 people making high-quality products. Viners, the biggest of this group, originated before 1914. Harrisons made spoon and fork blanks for sale to other firms for finishing, and may have employed up to 100 people. Harris, Miller & Co. started about 1930, with up to 180 workers making cheap cutlery, as did Bernard & Co., established in the 1930s and employing about 120. The last Jewish cutlery businessman was named Smith who bought a firm called Tom Gilpin which had 80 to 100 employees.[70]

Refugees from Nazism

The refugees from Austria, Germany and Czechoslovakia are worthy of a separate section in this discussion: they were the largest group of Jewish immigrants in the inter-war period; they included a high proportion of middle-class people, and, because of their background, often established 'unusual' industries. The intellectuals and professionals among them had diverse experiences. There was a special rescue organisation for intellectuals, scientists and academics, some of whom obtained university posts in Britain,[71] but other professional men were less fortunate, and were more grudgingly received. Lawyers obviously could not readily transfer to the British legal system, and doctors, no matter how highly skilled or experienced, could not practise until they had obtained British qualifications. Among the group, though, were a number of scientists whose arrival led to a marked increase in the absolute number and proportion of Jews among the Fellows of the Royal Society.[72]

Between the onset of Nazism and November 1938 only about 11,000 refugees (not all Jewish) were admitted into Britain when it was still possible to bring over some capital. The government's policy, laid down in 1933, was that refugees should be admitted only if they were not a charge on public funds. One who set up business in Britain even before Hitler's accession was Eric Weiss, born 1908; he had worked at Halle for his uncle Dr Ludwig Weiss, whose company founded in 1924 produced a compound for use in foundries to improve the quality of the product. Eric Weiss's job was to visit the company's agents in various countries and in 1931 he came to England. In that year the German business had to close when the bank in Halle failed and Dr Weiss died and Eric Weiss decided to establish the business in England. His colleague, Dr Kossy Strauss, the firm's chemist, went back to the technical university at Karlsruhe, but came to England shortly after the Nazis took power. Weiss meanwhile advertised for someone willing to invest and almost immediately received a reply from a seventy-year-old man, prepared to invest £250, and the firm was registered in January 1932 as Foundry Services Ltd, with a nominal capital of £500. This was the origin of the Foseco Minsep Company, which by 1939 had expanded so that their expertise was used by the Ministry of Aircraft Production during the war.[73]

In a similar position was the Djanogly family which left Russia after 1917 and established a knitting works in Chemnitz (now Karl-Marx-Stadt). Later they opened a branch sales office in England and subsequently settled to open a factory in 1937 under the name Mansfield Hosiery (now part of their Notting-ham Manufacturing Co.).[74] Altogether it is estimated that by 1938 refugees had started some 250 businesses, providing some 15,000 to 25,000 jobs (the average of 100 employees indicates they were mostly small scale).[75] Many of the refugees had been in the clothing business and some of the 250 were in the same line, but—as with Weiss—more technical enterprises were set up. Mac Goldsmith came to Britain in 1937 and settled in Leicester, establishing a company called Metalastik which produced products using his process for bonding rubber to metal. He had had a car component factory in Germany and in addition to his bonding process had developed an improved clutch which was used extensively in Continental cars.[76]

The great majority of the refugees arrived between November 1938—after the Nazi *Kristallnacht,* when synagogues were burnt and persecution intensified—and the outbreak of war.[77] Some of them set up in business: no numbers are known but there may have been 500 by September 1939; perhaps as many as 80 firms in the fur business were set up in London, established by Jews in that trade from Leipzig. This small proportion of the total refugee number is to be explained by the fact that refugees were permitted to bring from the countries under Nazi control only the minimum of possessions. Thus many refugees took up whatever work they could in a great variety of employments. However, some refugees were more fortunately placed because they could take advantage of the British government's efforts to revitalise the severely depressed industrial regions, through the Special Areas legislation. The intention of this policy was to introduce new industries to the severely depressed areas by a series of inducements, but few British firms were interested. Refugee firms which were willing to provide such employment were welcomed to the extent that advertisements were placed in Continental papers, and British consuls acted as emissaries, explaining the benefits that were available.

As a result, refugee industries were established in a variety of places: the Team Valley Industrial estate in the north-east; the Treforest Industrial estate in South Wales; in Northern Ireland; and in West Cumberland. The numbers must not be exaggerated: the great majority of the refugees settled in London, eschewing the main provincial communities, and the total number of refugee businesses in the Special Areas before the war was fewer than 200. South Wales was the most popular area, followed in order by the north-east, West Cumberland and Northern Ireland.

In most cases the industrialists had to start on a tiny scale. Factories, provided under the legislation, were available, but not other capital. The first arrival on Tyneside was the Great Northern Knitwear Co., which started in February 1938. It used second-hand machinery and obtained some capital from local individuals or firms. While the opening of industries was hugely welcomed in their localities after years of hopeless, severe unemployment, other voices—and not just from the British Union of Fascists—were indignant. David Kirkwood, the Scottish Socialist M.P., objected to the opening of the Great Northern Knitwear works (he emphasised that the founders were both German and Jewish) because it would compete with the depressed Scottish knitwear industry.

The refugees had been largely concentrated in the clothing and textile industries and many therefore took up their old trades; but others had been in the chemical and engineering industries and they too went into similar businesses—Weiss and Goldsmith have already been mentioned, for example. The first refugee industry in northern England was Thomas Mouget & Co. at Middlesbrough (not in the Special Area). This firm specialised in slag and scrap recovery in the steel industry. There were other comparable examples, such as those who established toy-making firms, or who set up new product divisions within British firms and did not establish their own businesses. One of these last was an Austrian named Beck, who was responsible for producing oil seals for the car industry at the Newcastle-upon-Tyne firm of George Angers & Co. (subsequently part of Dunlop). Beck was drowned at sea in 1940, when the ship he and other 'enemy aliens' were sailing in for internment in Canada was torpedoed.

Conclusion

The special case of the refugees apart, the main themes of the inter-war years were two. There was an increase in the number and proportion of Jews who were in some form of business, a growth which was held up by the depression of the 1920s but resumed in the 1930s, especially in the south of the country. Second, the typical unit was small—a retail shop, a workshop, a factory or a wholesale business—and generally within the traditional trades. The professional class was growing and was given a boost by the greater availability of secondary education in the 1930s, but not many entered the professions before the end of that decade. The relatively small number of major industrialists were descendants of the earlier waves of immigration, and it was not yet the turn of the east Europeans to be associated with large enterprises. This was also to come after the war.

14
The Working Class since World War II

A tailor from east London became flyweight boxing champion in the 1970s. He was an immigrant, too, but from Malta. A report in 1978 by the Bethnal Green and Stepney Trades Council, detailing violent attacks on Bengali immigrants in the Tower Hamlets area of east London, noted that most of the 15,000 worked in the clothing industry 'working long hours in the honeycomb of sweatshops covering Aldgate and Whitechapel'.[1] This was once the Jewish district whose clothing-workers, fifty or sixty years ago, were Jews, as were some of the boxers.

A press item of 1978, about a proposed survey of Leeds Jewry stated: 'It is suspected . . . that the Jewish tailor in Leeds is now almost non-existent'.[2] Jews' Free School in the East End of London did not reopen after 1939 and was a casualty of the air raids. In several cities post-war redevelopment destroyed the old property of the inner areas where Jews had lived. Post-war Jewish novels, plays and biographies which are set in the immigrant areas invariably report the past. And one reads of 'the relentless drive of Anglo-Jewry into a middle-class suburban existence' or, succinctly, as the heading of a 1975 article, 'A middle-class community'.[3]

These random images indicate the main lines of development. First, the number of manual workers in the old immigrant trades has fallen drastically. Second there has been an absolute decline in the number of Jewish manual workers of all kinds.[4] The community contains more people in middle-class jobs, notably as self-employed professionals and businessmen. Fourth, most Jews live in the suburbs of the main cities or even further out. To these four can be added another: despite a certain amount of immigration since 1945—displaced persons after the war, from Arab countries and the Indian sub-continent as well as from a variety of other places—it seems likely that the total Jewish population is falling or at best static. The number of Jews marrying in synagogues has fallen, and the number of deaths has exceeded the number of births. The total Anglo-Jewish population is probably no more than 400,000.[5]

Not all these statements are based on systematically gathered information, and some modifications will be suggested in the subsequent discussion. But many of them are easily confirmed by casual observation and familiar knowledge. There has been a massive dispersal of Jews from the old areas to the suburbs. Synagogues and communal institutions in the centres of towns have closed (some having been bombed during the war) while suburban communities have expanded and new ones been created. In Greater London, as Table 13 shows, Jews are to be found living in almost all boroughs with notable concentrations in the north-west (London Boroughs of Brent and Barnet, and beyond) and in the north-east (Hackney and Redbridge).[6] Such places have gained at the expense of a community like West Ham (London Borough of Newham), which had been created originally to reduce East End congestion and which in the 1930s had extended its building to accommodate a growing congregation. Hackney too is losing its Jewish population. The same pattern applies to the provinces. In Liverpool the Jews now live in Childwall and Allerton; in Leeds at Moortown and Alwoodley; Cheadle has become a Jewish suburb of Manchester.

The move to the suburbs has not been confined to the Jews, who form a tiny proportion of the total numbers concerned. The outward emigration of earlier years was hastened by war-time air raids and also by post-war government policy which aimed to disperse people and jobs from congested inner areas. By the 1960s the cities as a whole were losing population. Nor is there anything special about the decline of manual work among the Jews. Since the war in Britain and other advanced industrial countries non-manual employment has grown while the number of manual workers has remained static or even fallen. But it is not the movement of Jews into white-collar jobs that is usually the focus of attention. Two features stand out in the research that has been done, especially in America: a very high rate of upward social mobility, and the large numbers of Jews in business and the professions. American research typically shows that of the groups of immigrants to that country the Jews have experienced faster entries into the higher social strata. Other immigrant Jewish communities—Australia, for example—have followed the same course. In Soviet Russia they have gone into the professions. Many families whose first representative in Britain was a tailor, cabinet-maker, shoe-maker, glazier, pedlar or cap-maker now contain no members of the working class at all. These impressions were given statistical support in the early 1950s in the results of a large-scale investigation sponsored by the *Jewish Chronicle*.[7] Details were obtained from 4,949 individuals, of whom the number of occupied males was 1,586 and occupied women 227. Most were in industry or trade; 342 men and 46 women were professionals. In addition to the fact that the number of women in paid work was small, the most important finding was that three-quarters of the men in trades and half of those in professions were self-employed. One-third of the economically active women were self-employed.

Now, it is unlikely that these figures were a true representation of Anglo-

Jewry at that time. The survey was based on questionnaires distributed by communal organisations: the Representative Councils of Hull and Sheffield, for those cities; the Association of Jewish Ex-Servicemen and Women in other provincial places; and in London by the Ex-Servicemen's Association, the London Jewish Hospital and the staff of the *Jewish Chronicle*. Not only were the respondents not a random sample of the Jewish population, but no replies came from Manchester (the largest provincial community) or from Birmingham; and London was under-represented. Since it is often argued that the smaller provincial communities have a high proportion of self-employed, the results are as expected. The number of those who recorded themselves as self-employed may also have been upgrading themselves—a well-known feature of social surveys.

However, despite the undoubted deficiencies in this survey, later studies of the 1960s and 1970s—by which time there had been more upward social mobility—confirm the existence of a large middle-class component both in the individual communities which were surveyed and in Anglo-Jewry generally.

A study of Edgware (London Borough of Barnet) in the early 1960s, which comprised interviews with 382 Jews, showed that most were in non-manual jobs and as many as 220 (59 per cent) were in social classes I and II; this was even higher than the high proportion of 40 per cent in those classes among the total population of that area. Of the children aged fifteen years and over, 25 per cent were attending university or college and another 13 per cent were preparing to do so. The parents of many of those aged less than fifteen expected them to continue into higher education.[8] The same picture was provided by a much smaller survey, of forty Jews in Wembley (London Borough of Brent). Two-thirds of the heads of households were managers or employers and one in six was a professional, higher than the immediate surrounding population.[9]

It could be argued that a study of Jews in a middle-class district shows them, unsurprisingly, also to be engaged in middle-class occupations, albeit in greater proportions than the local population. But other investigations reinforce the conclusions about upward social mobility. In the small Jewish population of Sheffield (totalling 1,159), the 462 men and women who are at work are overwhelmingly professionals or in business.[10] Even a study of the more working-class borough of Hackney reported that compared with the local population the Jewish residents tended to include a higher proportion of the self-employed. As many as 21 per cent of the Jewish men were in that category compared with 7 per cent for the borough as a whole.[11] The most useful attempt at a comprehensive picture is given in an analysis of the occupations of about 1,200 Jews who died in 1961.[12] Table 14 gives the figures of their social class (based on occupation) and compares them with those of the general population of England and Wales. They show a very clear 'upward' slant: more Jews were in social class I (professionals) and many more in II (certain self-employed occupations, company directors etc.) than in the general population. While the proportion of Jews in social class III (manual and non-manual employees) was about the same, there were fewer in class IV (semi-skilled) and none in class V (unskilled).

This examination of the occupations of Jews who died in 1961 did more than indicate the middle-class economic and social structure of Anglo-Jewry. The survey took account of those who, while buried under Jewish auspices, had not been members of synagogues. Although such people were to be found among all the social classes, they were especially noticeable among the Jews who were not in middle-class occupations. This conclusion was consistent with an earlier report by the same authors who had made estimates of the total Anglo-Jewish population. In that study they found that 39 per cent of Anglo-Jewry were not synagogue members. About one-third of them, they said, 'lived in East London . . . and generally followed working-class occupations.'[13]

This finding was most important for it places a major question mark over generalisations about the economic structure of Anglo-Jewry. Anyone setting out to do a survey of the community has the initial problem of locating its members. With a small provincial group it is possible for everyone—or at least most of them—to be known, so that the 1970s study of Sheffield is probably comprehensive. But in larger communities this degree of coverage is unattainable. Use has to be made of synagogue membership lists and the like; those who do not belong are likely to be missed, and they amount to two Jews out of every five. No wonder that a participant at a 1962 conference on Anglo-Jewry commented, after one lecture, that 'the character of the data presented really meant that the paper should have been entitled "Economic and Social Structure in *Synagogal* Jewry in Great Britain" '.[14] The implication is that the inclusion of those Jews who are organisationally on the peripheries of the community—as was done in the study of the occupations of the 1961 deceased—provides a somewhat different picture from that obtained from a study of middle-class Jews in middle-class suburbs. It is true the occupations of those who died in 1961 confirmed the unusually high proportion of Jews whose occupations placed them in social classes I and II. But at the same time, while there was this very clear imbalance, it is significant that the largest single group was of those who were in social class III—people in skilled manual and lower-level white-collar jobs. And as well as being the largest group in size it was very similar to the proportion for the country as a whole.

The authors of the study rightly commented that the picture it presented

is not one that permits us simplistically to characterize the Jewish population as being predominantly in a single category, such as traders, or 'in the upper middle classes'. On the contrary, it is fairly widely distributed over the class structure.[15]

Only the absence of an unskilled group was, they said, 'remarkable', and reminded them of the Jewish tradition that one of a parent's duties was to teach his son a trade.

This finding, it needs emphasising, is not a picture of a past occupational structure—on the grounds that most of those who died were older and may have entered their occupations many years before they died in 1961. The deaths included people under the age of forty-five, and their occupations were not markedly different from those of the older deceased (Table 14). Slightly more were professionals (class I) and a few less in class III (skilled); but that was all. The survey went further and attempted a description, through a number of statistical calculations based on these death figures, of the occupations of the living Jewish population. Again there was a larger proportion in classes I and II (especially II) but still nearly 50 per cent were in classes III and IV.

It is abundantly clear, therefore, that despite the undoubted changes in Jewish economic life, including the decline of employment in the immigrant trades and a move to middle-class jobs, there remains a substantial working-class element. It is smaller than in the past, certainly; but it still exists.

Perhaps the neglect of this Jewish working class in much post-war discussion is a consequence of changes in the degree of identification with the Jewish community. In the past the anglicisation of earlier immigrant groups was often associated with economic improvement, integration into British society and assimilation through out-marriage. It was the upper and middle classes who left the community. To some extent this still holds: there are many expressions of fears that large numbers of Jewish students may marry non-Jews. But whereas the working-class immigrants from eastern Europe had been religiously or-thodox and had replaced the middle-class losses, nowadays the working class are the ones who opt out by, for example, a lower membership of synagogues. The image of a homogeneous, comfortable, middle-class community requires major modification. This was signalled in a 1978 article in the *Jewish Chronicle*, headed 'Jewish Children without Shoes'. It referred to a recent statement by the headmaster of the JFS Comprehensive School that 'the school sometimes had to buy shoes for children from poverty-stricken families'. Anyone who believed that Jewish poverty was a thing of the past should 'ask anyone who works in a Jewish State-aided school, or for one of the Jewish welfare agencies, or in general social work in one of the areas of high Jewish density such as Hackney or Stamford Hill, or certain areas in Manchester, Liverpool or Leeds'.[16]

The various welfare agencies certainly continue with their work of supplying support and benefits to some of the Jews in need—others rely entirely on the public social services. The charity called 'Food for the Jewish Poor' (estab-lished originally in 1854 as 'Soup Kitchen for the Jewish Poor') was handing out bread and groceries in the early 1970s to some 250 families in the East End of London.[17] At the same period the Jewish Welfare Board—the new name for the Jewish Board of Guardians—was assisting 2,500 elderly people. The Board claimed in 1974, in an appeal for funds, that 'in London and the South-East one in every ten Jewish families come to us for help'.[18] The Norwood Homes for Jewish children were looking after more than one thousand children.[19]

These various problems of poverty or of the need for social assistance of some kind often arise from family disruptions or breakdowns (divorce and illness, for example) and also from the familiar difficulties of a greater number of older people (illness, isolation, as well as lack of income).[20] Perhaps the third major component of poverty in modern Britain—low pay—is less evident, although one favoured Jewish trade, hairdressing, has notoriously low wage-rates. For this reason a description of Jewish social casualties is not central to our theme. We need rather to identify the 'many thousands of Jews in Britain who, while by no means poor, are by no means comfortable either. There is still, for example, a sizeable Jewish working class'.[21] It is important to investigate its components to see why it has survived; for it challenges the generally accepted view of a rapid Jewish move into the self-employed middle class.

That view is normally held about Jews of east European origin. Others may follow different patterns. The long-settled Dutch Jews, the descendants in some cases of the nineteenth-century cigar-makers, were described in the 1960s as having 'been assimilated more into the British working class than any other immigrants to this country'. They were 'not merely English but essentially Cockney'.[22] The grandfather in Alexander Baron's novel *With Hope, Farewell* 'had worked as a fruit-porter in Spitalfields Market, one of the many Jewish porters there who are only distinguished from their Gentile workmates by the fact that they are burlier, their Cockney accents more pronounced, their language more obscene and their capacity for beer greater'.[23]

At the other extreme, in terms of length of residence in Britain, are the more recent arrivals, some of whom have experienced the characteristic occupational downgrading of new immigrants. One group is the 2,000 'Baghdadi' Jews—mainly from India—who came to Britain after Indian independence in 1947. Of the ninety adults whose occupations were recorded, fourteen were unskilled or semi-skilled (in jobs such as railway guard, hospital orderly and postman); eleven were in skilled work, mainly engineering; and thirty were in administrative and white-collar occupations. Fifty-seven sons also included unskilled and semi-skilled (eight); skilled (nineteen); and administrative and white collar (fifteen).[24]

The second group is of the former refugees from Nazism. Many, as we shall see, went into business or the professions, but not all of them. One who came from Czechoslovakia in 1939, worked as a farm labourer and served in the army, settled in Slough and worked as a draughtsman. He became the last mayor of the town before local government reorganisation.[25] Another refugee is a parks superintendent for Ogwr Borough Council in Wales.[26] Others were mentioned in a study of Croydon as working in factories.[27]

Examples like these are known by chance, as are the following details of working-class Jews which happen to get into print. Studies of Jewish students sometimes refer to parental occupations, some of which are working class.[28] They were among those interviewed by the *Jewish Chronicle* about voting intentions at the February 1974 general election.[29] More vaguely—and possibly rhetorically—a shop steward at Vauxhall's car plant at Luton stated, 'we have Christians, Muslims and Jews in the factory'.[30] Individuals who have received publicity include an electrician, a shop steward, who led a strike in a car factory at Coventry;[31] a woman hospital worker who was active in her union's campaign to ban private beds from National Health Service hospitals;[32] as well as a boot- and shoe-worker in Northampton,[33] a hotel chef,[34] a coal-miner,[35] a woman mini-cab driver[36] and a bus conductress.[37]

These occasional examples tell us very little, for they are unlikely to be representative, and those mentioned may well be the only Jews in those occupations. Their uniqueness may sometimes be the reason for their identification in the Jewish newspapers ('how unusual for a Jewish girl to be a bus conductress'). But other information is available to enable us to get some idea of the types of employment Jews have entered. The 1950–52 survey conducted for the *Jewish Chronicle*, however deficient it may be, is a useful starting-point. One hundred and six men in the survey were in manual employment, one-third being in the clothing and furniture trades. The remainder included thirteen in engineering, six in hairdressing and two in building. The seventy-two clerical workers included eight civil servants (another nine being in higher grades), who formed the largest single group, the others being in a wide range of diverse trades and professions. The thirty Jewish women manual workers were in two main groups: fourteen were employed in clothing and drapery and four in domestic service (to whom perhaps can be added the woman described as a manual worker in nursing, and the two in catering). The jobs of the seventy-three women clerical workers were widely distributed and showed no particular pattern.[38]

A few years later, in the mid-1950s, the Jewish Board of Guardians in London arranged 400 apprenticeships for boys. Eight per cent were in electrical, radio and television engineering, 9 per cent in tailoring, and the largest group, 20 per cent, in jewellery and diamonds. Another large group were the 13 per cent who went into hairdressing.[39] More recently, in the 1960s and early 1970s, a regular 15 per cent of those leaving the JFS Comprehensive School in London took up secretarial and clerical occupations. Others went into an 'impressive diversity of jobs . . . from Post Office engineering to radiography, from motor mechanics to stables, from poodle parlours to the Merchant Navy'.[40]

So far, two studies have been published of Jews living in working-class districts. One, in the 1960s, aimed to answer the question, 'whether there is a proletarian base to the Jewish population of contemporary Britain'. The author looked at east London and firmly concluded that it was there. Many of its members, he found, lived in blocks of council flats; in one of the blocks studied over 80 per cent of the inhabitants were Jews, and two such blocks, one in Stepney and one in Hackney, were studied intensively:

> Tailoring and allied trades predominated in Stepney, followed by taxi-driving, and some independent operators such as 'car hire operators' and 'Toastmaster'. Hackney contained a high proportion of tailors who held supervisory positions in clothing firms . . . [and] civil servants (rank never specified but thought to be minor white collar workers).[41]

This small-scale study was succeeded by a larger and more comprehensive survey of the Jews of Hackney, which partly confirmed the earlier findings and partly modified them. Thus of the 30,000 or so Jewish inhabitants of the borough, about 40 per cent were living in low-status council estates or industrial dwellings. But very few were employed in local or national government. The survey confirmed that the largest male group was of skilled manual workers (including a large group of taxi-drivers). While the Jewish men in Hackney were also heavily engaged as owners of small businesses, so that along with taxi-drivers as many as 21 per cent were self-employed (three times the figure for the borough) Jewish employed women followed a similar pattern to that of the females in Hackney. They worked in offices, or were semi-skilled workers in manufacturing and distribution: as fashion workers, sewing machinists and assistants in family shops.[42]

One of the reasons for the lack of information about the Jewish working class is that it is diffused in a variety of occupations and industries. They are not so visible or so concentrated as in the heyday of tailoring and cabinet-making. But one group, the taxi-drivers—of whom it was claimed in the early 1970s, 4,500 were Jewish[43]—do form a distinct social group, whether owner-drivers or employed. Taxi-drivers are organised in their own section of the Transport & General Workers' Union as well as in other associations, including charitable bodies such as the London Taxi Drivers' Fund for Underprivileged Children. The Jews among them were in the news in 1977 when it was reported that Jewish taxi-drivers were boycotting the Dorchester Hotel after it was bought by Arabs.[44]

Whatever the true number of Jewish taxi-drivers—mostly in London but also a few in provincial cities—the trade is a prestige occupation for one segment of Anglo-Jewry. It has been claimed that in Ilford and Hackney the occupation of taxi-driving is the route to 'status, independence, and a comfortable income'.[45] This was put another way at the 1962 conference on modern Anglo-Jewish life, when a speaker referred to Stamford Hill (Borough of Hackney). 'I think you would be surprised to learn how many working class Jews there are in lower clerical jobs, rising in the income groups through, say, hairdressing, into the working *elite* of the taxi driver'.[46] But it would be wrong to think that they live only in the lower-status districts; some, for example, were recorded in the Edgware survey of the early 1960s.[47]

So that while we would expect to find working-class Jews in the old, declining districts such as east London, they are by no means confined to them. They live also in the expanding areas. Ilford, in the London Borough of Redbridge, is one such place, whose Jewish population has grown since the war, especially since the extension to the area in 1947 of the Central Line underground railway. It was said to be 'Britain's fastest growing Jewish community' in the early 1970s with a Jewish population in and around the borough of perhaps 30,000.[48] The *Jewish Chronicle* includes, weekly, a special feature for the community. That newspaper once asked 'Ilford: the new East End?',[49] presumably to indicate that east Londoners were moving there, but the phrase rightly implied more than that. A comprehensive study of the Jews of the area, carried out by the Research Unit of the Jewish Board of Deputies in the mid-1970s, provided solid information.[50] An interim report of the survey noted that 'only a minority of the youngsters go on to higher education. Local parents' aspirations for the children appear to be "post-industrial". More say they want them to be happy, or choose their own way than name a specific career'. There was a wide range of occupations within many different industries—even within the same family—which was roughly similar to the local pattern.

Redbridge Jews are probably more likely to have undergone an apprenticeship than North-East Londoners, and as well as taxi-drivers there are considerable numbers of small businessmen, white-collar workers, engineers, computer operators and skilled craftsmen, particularly in jewellery and printing.

Conclusion

Whether or not a similar picture holds in the larger provincial communities must await comparable, meticulous researches. Perhaps it will be possible to discover why a not inconsiderable section of the Anglo-Jewish population does not, apparently, accord with the stereotype, upwardly socially mobile descendants of lower-class immigrants.

However it does not follow at all that this working class is different in not preferring independent jobs. While it is no longer possible, as it used to be, to refer to an identifiable, compact Jewish economic sector—Jews employing Jews in the traditional trades—for the working class is scattered and more likely to work individually with non-Jews—there is still some clustering. Jobs such as taxi-driving, hairdressing, jewellery, and in distribution either are or can lead to self-employment. Shop assistants for example often work in family shops and can expect to take over in the future. The effects on Jewish employment of the higher, persistent levels of unemployment of the 1970s are not yet known; or of the recrudescence of antisemitism. Perhaps it could result in more Jews opting for self-employment.[51]

15

Business and the Professions since 1945

The furore that greeted Harold Wilson's resignation Honours List in 1976 was only in part the surprised astonishment that a Labour Prime Minister should be rewarding so many businessmen. Several of them were Jews; worse, some had been born abroad and had arrived as refugees from Nazism.[1] A touch of spice for the traditionally xenophobic British. In fact the fairly lengthy post-war list of Jewish peers (mostly life peers) and knights is composed of politicans and various kinds of professionals—academics, scientists, senior civil servants, and judges.[2] Formal honours, though, are merely one index of status and recognition. It is clear that since the war a number of Jews have made their mark in business, some of them creating large organisations, a few of the people being household names. Several biographies have been published, and one book, by Stephen Aris, is devoted to a consideration of them. In it he discusses how they have risen from the ghetto within one or two generations and, echoing Beatrice Webb's inquiry of the 1880s, has sought explanations for this success.[3]

The growth of large-scale organisations has been significant in most western industrial countries but it has gone further in Britain than elsewhere. Aside from the monopolies created by nationalisation, private companies have expanded through their own internal efforts or, especially, by mergers and take-overs. Governments, while encouraging competition—especially in the retail trade—and trying to regulate and control monopolies, have also from time to time been instrumental in creating them, in the private as well as in the public sector. Despite much disenchantment in the 1970s with the post-war obsession with size (so that more is said about the virtues of smallness), the process of aggrandisement has gone on.

Much of this chapter will be concerned therefore with the larger Jewish companies, although small ones will not be neglected. In any case, the story of the great enterprises is by no means confined to the survivors. Within the feverish, periodic flurries of merger activity many Jewish companies have disappeared.[4] Sir Isaac Wolfson's Great Universal Stores acquired, among others, Flatau's footwear-manufacturing concern as well as several chains of furniture stores including Cavendish & Woodhouse, the Times Furnishing

Company, and Jay & Campbell. Lewis's department stores went into Sir Charles Clore's Sears Holdings. Other Jewish firms became part of non-Jewish firms. Bovis, the civil engineering company, having expanded during the post-war period, was taken over by the P. & O. Steam Navigation Co.; Gliksten's timber companies now form part of the International Timber Corporation Ltd; Samuel Montagu's Bank was acquired by the Midland Bank Group; Barnett's Smoked Salmon went into Allied Fisheries;[5] most of the surviving tobacco firms were taken over—only Balkan Sobranie survived within the control of its original family; similarly the few Jewish cutlery firms in Sheffield were absorbed, only Viner's continuing independently.

All of those mentioned were in existence before the war, but the period we are dealing with in this chapter is long enough for more recently established firms to be taken over. Thus the cash-register manufacturers, Gross Brothers, established after the war, became part of the Chubb group.[6] These are the best-known examples, but many other Jewish firms have disappeared through bankruptcy or through the retirement or death of the principals. The turnover among firms is high. A study of the, admittedly special, case of industries established by refugees in the north of England shows that of seventy-six started between 1937 and 1961, as many as twenty-two had closed by 1974 (some having been re-established in other parts of the country, but others of the remaining fifty-four having been acquired by larger firms).[7] It is important to note such changes and in particular the failures, such as the dramatic collapse of John Bloom's washing-machine enterprise (a flamboyant episode in direct selling to the public, in the late 1950s and early 1960s),[8] or William Stern's London house-owning empire which collapsed in 1973–74 when the property-market bubble was pricked,[9] or Sir Eric Miller, another property man, who committed suicide in 1977 when his company's affairs were under investigation.[10]

Small Firms

The concentration in this chapter on the large firms is partly a matter of the availability of information but, more importantly, a reflection of the general trend in British industrial structure since the war. It is necessary, though, to get the picture in perspective. Small and medium-sized firms have continued to exist despite the greater proportions of the market which the large companies have come to operate. Some, while expanding, have remained private, family undertakings: one is Innoxa, the cosmetics company and another is Percy Dalton's peanut concern.[11]

The 'typical' Jewish business (as in Britain generally) is even smaller, to be found among the 800,000 or so firms, half of them being retail shops, which came into the terms of reference of the Bolton Committee on Small Firms which reported in 1971. Every year many thousands of people, foolhardy or enterprising, start up in business—well over 100,000 a year in the 1970s—most

of them small, with unlimited liability.[12] The great majority of Jewish
businessmen—those in the anonymous, statistical columns of social survey
reports—are in this category. They are to be found in a wide range of activities,
in manufacturing and in distribution, including the 'traditional' ones of clothing, footwear, jewellery, leather, timber and foodstuffs, but also in others
such as engineering, chemicals, radio and television, garages, plastics and
printing. One comes across the occasional working farmer. It is remarkable,
though, that clothing has retained its primacy in the post-war period, despite
the introduction of new products. In the Edgware survey of 1963 the largest
individual group of the 434 people recorded was in the clothing and footwear
industry, a total of 119 (27 per cent). The next largest were in the distributive
trades (19 per cent): types of trade were not given. Altogether about one in
three was in clothing, footwear, textiles (nowadays used loosely to include the
handling of finished goods and not confined to the making of cloth), timber,
furniture, leather, leather goods and fur. The proportion in these trades was
probably higher, if we include many of those in distribution. At the same time
8 per cent were in other manufacturing industries such as chemicals and
engineering.[13]

This Edgware classification is industrial, not occupational, and the numbers
include employees as well as employers, but in view of the high proportion of
employers among the Jews of Edgware, about two in five, we can safely use the
figures in the previous paragraph as a rough guide to the types of activity of
small businessmen. (Two qualifications are needed: the figures certainly include some in large concerns; and the emphasis is on men—Jewish women in
Edgware were less economically active than the general population.)

It is easy to understand the persistence of the traditional activities. Children
might enter a family business, for example, and clothing in particular retains
large numbers of small manufacturing enterprises. At the same time, however,
one notes a move into such interests as engineering and chemicals (including
plastics). A mainstay of the struggling literary magazine, the *Jewish Quarterly*,
which commenced in 1953, was an engineering employer. It is possible that a
distinction can be drawn between the descendants of the east European
immigrants and the refugees from Nazism. Although the latter certainly
included a high proportion who had previously been in the clothing industry
(they formed the largest single category among the refugees), others were
experienced in chemicals and engineering. Those who set up in business in
Britain often went into the same kind of activity, and thus were to be found in
what were, among British Jews, relatively unusual industries. Thus the refugee
industries in the north of England[14] included, as well as the expected firms
making furniture, gloves, hosiery and other clothing goods, those making a
variety of products such as metallised paper, aluminium foil, foam cushioning
from plastic waste, ready-mixed mortar, organic chemicals, adhesives and
mechanical handling devices. Typically these firms were small or medium
sized, but a few became large. Marchon Products Ltd in West Cumberland,

which began in 1939 under Frank (later Lord) Schon and a colleague, made its name in the production of detergents as well as chemicals: the firm became part of the Albright & Wilson Group in 1955. Another West Cumberland firm was founded by J. Speiregen, who was born in Russian Poland and lived in France before 1914. (He fought in the British army in World War I and was thus given British nationality.) He was a beret-manufacturer in Paris and opened a similar factory at Cleator Mill in 1937: the use of berets by the British army during World War II gave his firm a boost. After the war the firm moved into general headwear and although its name—Kangol—was particularly associated with berets and caps, it began to produce also safety belts and crash helmets. In 1972 it became part of the American Safety Equipment Corporation, Inc.

These two examples illustrate the transfer to Britain of previous activities: the most dramatic case was the almost total relocation of the fur trade from Leipzig, and one could include too the boost to the diamond trade in Britain caused by the immigration of Amsterdam Jews at the time of the war. The main point being made here is that while many of the ex-refugee industrialists certainly went into new activities, this group was more likely to enter engineering and chemicals than the east Europeans. Jews in Germany, Austria and elsewhere had taken part in those countries' greater emphasis on technical education and they were to be found therefore in industries which used that expertise.

Problems of Definition

The small businesses have the great advantage, in the study of Jewish economic history, of removing one major obstacle. Provided the owner of the business is known to be Jewish his activity will form an unequivocal part of this subject. In the case of large companies there is doubt. Many small firms have no outside shareholders and are run by the owners. Large firms on the other hand have numerous external owners of capital, these days increasingly composed of institutions such as pension funds and insurance companies; often those who control them—the board of directors—may be a tiny minority, holding only a few per cent of the capital. This need not matter for our purposes, if it is known that a particular person—or more than one—has built up the company and is its chairman or managing director, or where the direction is passed down to the next generation in the family. J. Lyons & Co. was one such example of continuing family control.

Difficulties arise, though, in various ways, notably when changes occur in the companies' leadership. In the 1960s Joe Hyman revitalised part of the textile industry as chairman of Viyella International, prominent in the finishing section. In December 1969 he was sacked by the company's board.[15] Presumably that company is part of our story in the 1960s but now (it was absorbed by ICI) it is not. Similarly, Illingworth, Morris became one of the largest companies in the woollen industry when its chairman was Maurice Ostrer, who died in 1975. Thereafter it is not our concern, any more than are firms which were originally founded by Jews but no longer run by them: Shell, ICI, Unilever, Glaxo. It goes without saying that institutions in the public sector are in a different category entirely, for the boards of nationalised industries are appointed by the appropriate government ministers. The first chairman and deputy-chairman of the newly nationalised steel industry, in 1967, were Lord Melchett (a banker) and Dr (later Sir) Monty Finniston (a metallurgist and former academic): Sir Monty later became chairman for a period. Similarly the chairman of the National Coal Board in the 1970s, Sir Derek Ezra, was Jewish, in origin at least.

A second, major, problem arises if one wishes to examine the question: how much of the British economy is—in some sense—in Jewish control, aside from the actual ownership of the capital. This can be divided into two separate considerations. First, to answer it we should need to know more than we do about the inner workings of the companies: who is the *de facto* chief executive? Sir Charles Clore, for example, certainly built up the Sears Holdings conglomerate, but the actual operations of his companies were delegated to others.[16] Second, on a macro-level, we might wish to know how much of an industry or sector is Jewish-controlled, by comparing the output or sales of a company with the appropriate total. While allowing for the uncertainties already mentioned, some indications will be given below; but a word of caution is necessary because so many changes take place, as already noted, when people retire or die or companies change hands. Thus there has been no important Jewish interest in the newspaper industry since the demise of Lord Southwood, but were a Jewish businessman to start one or take one over, that picture would change overnight.

Clearly, given these difficulties, we are really talking about individuals rather than organisations, even though we necessarily have to consider the operations of their institutions.

Chronology and Case Studies

The background to our discussion is the general movement of the British economy. For convenience, four main periods can be identified: the years of war, 1939–45; the post-war austerity period, 1945 to about 1950; the prosperous 1950s and 1960s, culminating in the boom of 1972–73; and the gloomier 1970s. I propose to examine these four periods, introducing illustrative examples.

The war led to the closure of shops and factories because of bombing, the call-up of principals, the curtailment of the manufacture and sale of civilian goods, the compulsory concentration of industry to effect economies and—a special case—the internment in 1940 of refugees among the 'enemy aliens'. (This treatment did not extend to men from Hungary, Poland or Czechoslovakia.) Some of the refugee businesses were re-opened when the men were released; many did not, particularly when the former internees joined the forces. It was during this period that wartime restrictions imposed by the Government under emergency legislation and also problems arising in management and control of individual shops made the furniture trade particularly difficult and hazardous. Furniture sales were at a low level and some of the directors of multiple stores were in the forces.[17] On the other hand because so much of the country's resources were devoted to the war effort, many firms became so engaged. Eric Weiss's Foundry Services Ltd for example produced chemicals for the aircraft and munitions industries. A small company, it needed finance to expand and in 1944 reached an agreement with the old-established Minerals Separation Ltd which took up 20 per cent of the shares. (By 1959 this became 77 per cent.)[18] Moreover it was not impossible to start new companies. André Deutsch, from Hungary, began a publishing company in 1942 under the imprint of Alan Wingate. A newcomer in the engineering field was Emmanuel Kaye, educated at Twickenham Technical College, who founded (with J. R. Sharp) the firm of J. E. Shay Ltd, precision gauge, tool- and instrument-makers. In 1943 they took over Lansing Bagnall & Co. and founded Lansing Bagnall Ltd. Later the company specialised in the manufacture of electric lift trucks, to become the largest European producer of those vehicles.[19]

The post-war years of austerity and rationing, with continuing but gradually alleviating shortages, made it difficult for newcomers to start or to expand; but it was in no way out of the question to do so. Sam and Henry Gross, the sons of a tobacco retailer, began to make cash registers in 1946, designing them and assembling them themselves. In their first year they produced fifty at a loss, but eventually succeeded, becoming a public company in 1965.[20] One man who made radios learned his trade in the army, in the Royal Electrical and Mechanical Engineers. He began in 1946 with £250 demobilisation pay and a loan of £100 from his mother-in-law, making sets 'in a back-street shop (the rent was 15 shillings a week), packed them into a taxi and sold them to shops in the Edgware Road'. It was easy to dispose of them because of the general shortage, and from that beginning he built up Fidelity Radio Ltd. A quarter of a century later, by which time imported radio sets were making big inroads into the domestic market, the company claimed to be the largest British manufacturer of radios.[21]

The war, indeed, provided many people with an introduction to the use of electrical, radio and mechanical equipment which some, who wished to enter business, were able to make use of on their demobilisation. Others changed their jobs because of their war-time experiences. Chaim S. Schreiber, born in Poland in 1918, was an architectural student in Vienna until 1938, when Hitler invaded Austria. In Britain during the war he worked for the Ministry of Aircraft Production working on the development of the Mosquito aircraft, thus becoming interested in engineering in wood. He adapted this after the war and used a patented process for moulding in wood, making cabinets for radios and then for television sets. In 1961 he left this and went into furniture-making.[22]

However, many ex-servicemen went back into their familiar trades. Abe Rosenblatt's career was, in some respects, typical. At the age of twenty-three he had opened a women's clothing manufacturing concern in 1939, under the name of Rexmore Ltd. This closed when he joined the forces and he re-opened it in 1946, using his gratuity as capital.[23] Another example among the ex-refugees was Walter Neurath, born in Vienna in 1903, who came to Britain in 1938. He had been a publisher and in 1949 founded the publishing house of Thames & Hudson, specialising in the production of art books.[24] Similarly the Cohen brothers, on their demobilisation, used the funds from the sale of their furniture chain to buy the old-established furniture firm of Court, which started in 1850 but at the end of the war consisted solely of a small store in Canterbury. By 1950 the new firm had twelve branches and went on to open about three a year during the 1950s, subsequently expanding abroad.[25]

The Cohens are distinguishable from the earlier examples which have been given, for they did not have to rely on demobilisation pay or small family loans to start off. This was the case too of existing companies which were in a financial position to develop. In the post-war period Louis Newmark Ltd had been in existence for nearly a century, beginning as a watch-importing business. After 1945, with government sponsorship and with a view to employing ex-army engineers, the company began to manufacture watches, with the intention of moving into the manufacture of a variety of armament devices. This they did in the 1950s, subsequently giving up the manufacture of watches when the duty on imported watches was removed.[26]

In 1946 Thorn Electrical Industries was still, ten years after it had become a public company, a fairly small firm producing electric lamps and radio sets, but it moved rapidly into making fluorescent tubes, television sets, television tubes, radios and electric-light fittings. Much of this was accomplished through acquisitions of well-known firms such as Ekco-Ensign Electric Ltd and Ultra Radio & Television Ltd.[27]

The reference to take-overs is a convenient point at which to examine the 1950s and 1960s, a new period which saw the growth of giant firms. The significance of the late 1940s was that some of the many new enterprises which started on a shoe-string were to continue and to prosper. The foundations were laid for subsequent development. Others remained small. On the debit side, apart from the failures, was the notorious case of Sidney Stanley (d. 1969). He had been known to the police before the war but efforts to deport him to Poland did not succeed. He came into the news in 1948–49 for his activities as a contact man, a species which emerged as a result of the continuation into peace-time of government regulations and controls. The possibility of corrupt attempts to gain favourable treatment aroused such rumours that a public inquiry under Mr Justice Lynskey was set up. The proceedings and the report tried to distinguish between what Stanley claimed he could do, including his supposed friendships with influential people (which could lead to the granting of licences and permits), and the reality. In effect the inquiry found no more than a few examples of the unwise proferring and acceptance of gifts and hospitality. No great corruption was discovered and no criminal charges were preferred, but one junior minister resigned, as did a former trade union leader holding high office in the new nationalised industries (he had been on the board of the Bank of England and also chairman of the North Western Area of the Electricity Board). However, many of the businessmen witnesses were Jews (they were reported in the press as covering their heads 'in the Jewish fashion' when taking the oath). The stereotype of the unscrupulous Jew undoubtedly aroused some anti-Jewish feelings, especially as the inquiry came soon after the establishment of the State of Israel whose creation was preceded by violent confrontation between the British authorities and the Jews in Palestine.[28]

A Quarter-century of Prosperity

Despite persistently gloomy undercurrents—periodic balance of payments crises, a decreasing share of world trade, complaints of insufficient investment in modern equipment—the 1950s and 1960s were years of unprecedented economic growth. Full employment and rising standards of living were expressed in a greater range of consumer goods, more expenditure on leisure, and an extension of home-ownership. More people owned motor-cars, television sets, a whole range of domestic electrical equipment; large numbers went abroad for their holidays; among the new industries were the making and use of computers and those producing plastic products; and supermarkets expanded to oust the small shopkeepers (who retaliated however by banding together to form buying groups). The debit side included the decline of certain industries and activities—the spread of television reduced live entertainment and films; new materials such as artificial fibres replaced cotton and wool; cheaper imports reduced home production of some commodities; and changes in fashion, while providing opportunities for some firms, led to difficulties for those that could not easily adjust.

Individual Jewish companies and businessmen participated in these developments, in some cases as pioneers. One was Vladimir Raitz, a former journalist, who started the Horizon company for low-cost charter package tours, using at first a war-surplus Dakota aircraft.[29] (Sir) Leon Bagrit (1902–80) organised the first company in Europe devoted to automation, becoming chairman of Elliott-Automation in 1963, having been deputy chairman from 1957 when it was formed.[30] On the other hand the clothing firm of Montague Burton which specialised in men's formal suits was overtaken by the change to more informal clothes and its problems were highlighted in the 1970s when it had to close factories.[31] And the catering and foodstuffs firm of J. Lyons & Co. similarly had to alter in view of the decline of teashops; it changed to a different kind of public catering, but also found itself having to close its Corner Houses, sell hotels, and in 1978 was the object of a take-over bid, having been in difficulties for a number of years.[32]

Although it is not always possible to identify innovators—many competing claims are often made—one can certainly be distinguished. Sir Charles Clore, born in London in 1904, the son of an immigrant textile manufacturer, came into the news in 1953.[33] In February he and his associates took over the old-established firm J. Sears & Co. (True-Form Boot Co.) Ltd, manufacturers of footwear and owners of a string of retail shoe shops. It had begun in 1876 as Freeman, Hardy & Willis Ltd, originally as manufacturers, opened its first shop in 1877 and by World War I had over 400.[34] Clore's take-over was the foundation of Sears Holdings Ltd, a conglomerate company, in a diverse range of activities. Clore, primarily a dealer, began his commercial career in 1924 at the age of twenty, when he purchased, and almost immediately re-sold, the South African film rights of the Tunney-Dempsey world championship boxing contest. In 1928 he bought the derelict skating-rink at Cricklewood in north London and turned it into a successful concern; the following year he bought the Prince of Wales Theatre, hoping to sell it quickly. This property deal did not succeed and he retained it.

Other diverse interests followed and by the end of World War II he had acquired, *inter alia,* a large highland estate in Scotland, a coach-works at Park Royal in London, a firm of hosiery-machine makers in Leicester, a chain of dress shops and a department store in Reading. The last two were sold off in 1949 and in 1951 he purchased the Furness shipbuilding firm at Middlesbrough. The 1953 take-over of Sears brought him to public attention. The novelty of the method was that a direct approach was made to the shareholders with an offer to purchase their shares at a price well above their Stock Exchange value. *The Economist,* discussing the Sears deal, explained what was happening, noting—it should be said—that similar operations were being carried out by other, non-Jewish financiers:

A bid to buy a company's shares at a premium above market prices will be made only if the existing market value of the shares is much lower than it should be—that is to say, if it is well below either the present value of the company's assets or the value to which the bidders think these assets would rise if they were differently employed.[35]

Such take-overs became quite common in the 1950s and the purchaser could use the acquired assets in one of many ways. They could be re-sold at the new, higher value; the least profitable parts could be liquidated and the remainder sold off (the most notorious of such asset-strippers was the non-Jewish firm of Slater Walker);[36] or they could be retained as a going concern. Clore had re-sold some of his acquisitions in earlier years, but the 1953 purchase of Sears became the foundation of his group; to it were added, in subsequent years, a number of other shoe-shop chains, all of which were combined into the British Shoe Corporation in 1956, a subsidiary of Sears Holdings; and such diverse companies as those making knitting machinery, the Scottish Motor Traction Co. (road transport), as well as bookmaking, travel and department stores businesses. The major part of the company's income came from the shoe business, its 1,800 shops being supplied in part by the company's factories, in part by imports. It accounted for some 20 per cent of the total footwear sales in the United Kingdom, highly organised through a computerised warehouse in Leicestershire which aimed to re-stock shops at frequent intervals.[37]

Clore, who retired in 1977, began as a financier and moved into industry and distribution, his companies employing over 50,000 people with a turnover of nearly £1,000 million. These figures might have been larger but for the failure of some of his bids, e.g., his attempt to purchase Watney's brewery and public-house interests. It is plain, through, that the types of industry he entered—there was no pattern to them—were determined by their availability: it would be absurd to find in his shoe business some vestigial link with traditional Jewish economic activities. They were cheap and he bought them; they happened to be in the footwear business.[38] In a different set of circumstances he might have been a major hotelier, caterer or clothing manufacturer. He died in 1979.

Property

Clore was also involved in the property world, and indeed his initial interest in Sears (as well as his earlier activities) are usefully considered in that light. An important feature of the 1953 take-over was the rapid sale ('with the aid of some insurance companies')[39] of many of the freeholds which were then taken on long leases—the method of 'lease-back'. In this way funds were obtained from the sale of the assets, which were released for other purposes.

Much of the discussion in this chapter is about individuals and their companies, but one general field of activity needs separate examination, for property certainly attracted a large Jewish contingent. A study of the phenomenon, published in 1967, listed over 100 men who had been the most successful in it; about two-thirds were Jews.[40] They were especially involved in property development, but one pioneer in this general area of property was an investor rather than a developer. Joseph Aaron Littman, born in 1898, came to Britain from America in the 1920s. He bought his first property in Kilburn in 1927; by 1935 he had acquired whole street blocks of Kilburn High Road with the aid of a loan from the Royal Liver Friendly Society for the then-staggering amount of £1,250,000 for a term of 40 years, at a fixed interest rate of 3¼ per cent. By that time he was reckoned to own, both in Kilburn and elsewhere, well over £3 million worth of property. In the late 1930s he purchased a great deal of property in the West End, particularly in Oxford Street. Much of this was destroyed in war-time air raids. Despite this Littman became the major factor in the London property market immediately after the war. He could certainly be described as the innovator of the lease-back method. He would purchase freeholds, and sell them to insurance companies or pension funds, subject to a lease-back to himself or to a company guaranteed by him, for a term of 99 years at a fixed rent. He engaged in scores of such transactions involving properties worth many millions of pounds, mainly in the West End of London but also in the provinces. At one time he had over sixty companies and found himself running many other businesses (including department stores, West End restaurants, theatres, a car-hire company of chauffeur-driven Rolls Royces, and farming and fishing enterprises) as appendages to his property empire.

> He had an extraordinary shrewdness amounting to a sixth sense about property and gave to the institutions he negotiated with a sense of security based on his known expertise and integrity. This does not, however, disguise the fact that his whole enterprise constituted an enormous gamble, which depended for its success on a continuing rise in property values, at a time of political and economic turmoil, and entailed an outlook on the future that few at that time had the prescience to foresee or the courage to base their enterprise upon.

Littman died while still a relatively young man, in the early 1950s, well before the real boom in property values took place. There was, however, little doubt that in his prime he had been the mentor of the property world, inventing techniques which others used later, with greater effect, in more favourable circumstances.[41]

In the post-war years property was in short supply because of war-time bombing and the absence of new construction during the period of hostilities. Old buildings were at a premium and could be bought for letting on short leases at high rents, they could be refurbished or rebuilt and let at high rents, or after renovation or rebuilding they could be sold off. The possibility of entering this market was high: money for the transactions could normally be obtained from one or other of the financial institutions, especially from insurance companies; and no particular expertise was needed. It was primarily a financial activity, requiring no knowledge of architecture or construction techniques:

> The early property developers were in effect gambling; an activity made all the more exciting by the fact that they were using other people's money. Any number of things could go wrong: the expected demand could fail to materialise; the carefully nurtured tenant on whose income the developer depended could at the last minute change his mind or the equally nurtured local authority could, if the borough's planning officer was feeling liverish that day, refuse the essential planning permission. And any one of these eventualities could spell disaster, threatening the whole elaborately constructed edifice with collapse.[42]

Most important of all 'the key to success was to know where to go to borrow money. The insurance companies were . . . easy sources of cheap long-term loans.'[43]

The other prime prerequisite for property development—apart from the willingness to take a risk—was to know the right time to do it, especially in the 1950s when building restrictions were eased. The lack of specialist expertise for the trade meant that property men came from a variety of backgrounds. Some were already in the field, having been estate agents before the war, including a few who had studied at the College of Estate Management. Jack Cotton, for example, came from a middle-class family and attended public school, opening an estate agent's office in Birmingham.[44] Max Rayne, a tailor's son, began in property after the war, having served in the RAF, when he sub-let a portion of his father's clothing business premises.[45] Maurice Wingate had studied medicine for a time.[45]

This history of the property business included a number of major mergers. One of them, a merger between the property interests of Jack Cotton and Charles Clore 'must rank [as] one of the most ill-fated mergers in post war Britain'.[47] The company, City Centre Properties, was acquired by Sir Harold (later Lord) Samuel, whose company—Land Securities—also took over other property companies to become, by its acquisition in 1969 of the City of London Real Property Company (established in the 1850s), the largest property company in the world.[48] Samuel was one of the property men who remained in that field, but others—Clore, for example—branched out in other interests. Lord Rayne's company, London Merchant Securities, owned most of Carlton's Industries, itself a conglomerate, which made batteries, built houses and distilled Scotch whisky.[49]

It cannot be said that these property and development activities were free from public disquiet, and in the 1970s a halt was called to high-rise residential building, one of the symbols of recent city redevelopment. And the reputation of some of the participants was not enhanced by the Poulson case (a corruption episode as a result of which several people were imprisoned). No Jews were involved in that, but considerable attention was given to the Centre Point office block in London, built by Harry Hyams. This building remained empty for years while its builder sought a tenant. There were others like it, but Centre Point became an issue in local and national politics. [50]

The property men did at least build something. No one ever likes landlords, especially those owning residential property. During the boom of the early 1970s rents rose dramatically to the accompaniement of allegations of the unscrupulous treatment of tenants. Among the landlords so accused were a number of Jews, and in the subsequent publicity the Jewish Board of Deputies condemned 'unethical landlords' (of whatever religion),[51] as did the *Jewish Chronicle*. The Board of Deputies was reported to have 'talked things over with some of the landlords in question and some constructive steps were taken'.[52] Three men in particular were in the news: Osias Freshwater,[53] his son-in-law William Stern (who broke away to form his own group) and Gerson Berger. Each was said to be the largest private landlord in London. Berger's rise was the most spectacular: an inter-war immigrant, he had started as a street-seller, graduating to the manufacture of torch batteries during the war, thereafter investing in property. The obituaries, on his death in 1977, emphasised his Dickensian life-style, for he had lived in a small flat in Hackney.[54]

The stock market collapse in 1974 put an abrupt end to the heroic age of property. For several years activity was at a low level and public opinion turned against urban redevelopment schemes. By then some of the major names had retired or died, and newcomers were sparse.

Industry and Distribution

The property industry has the advantage, in the context of this book, of being relatively compact. Its activities were more or less in one sector and the phenomenon can be allocated to a definable period of time. Moreover, by attracting a number of Jews, it provides another example of clustering, as has been evident throughout Jewish economic history. But an examination of large-scale Jewish business outside property shows it to be of bewildering variety both in types of activity and in approaches and methods. Some have remained entirely or mainly within their original fields; some have become conglomerates. Some have grown largely through mergers, others mainly by internal growth. Some have prospered, others have struggled (while most Jewish businesses, it is necessary to repeat, have remained small). In these matters Jewish companies have been no different from the general run of business. Marks & Spencer, for example, still run by the Sieffs, have remained strictly in retail distribution and have not branched out into manufacture, preferring to rely on independent producers, the quality of whose products they control meticulously. Montague Burton's clothing manufacture and retail stores were faced with two problems: the absence of a clear successor to the founder when he died, and changing fashions. After the death of Sir Montague Burton in 1952 his company purchased the 51 per cent controlling interest in Jackson the Tailor's shops and factories, held by the Jacobson family. The stated reason for the merger was to obtain a more rational distribution of the two complementary sets of menswear stores but, like the contemporaneous Clore operations, it was also a property deal. The property was under-valued and was purchased by Burton for profitable leasing to outsiders. And, especially, the take-over was to buy in managerial experience: Leonard and Sidney Jacobson virtually ran Burton's until 1969.[55]

The histories of three very large companies similarly illustrate the variety of development. Sir Isaac Wolfson's Great Universal Stores, originally a mail order house, expanded through acquisitions and expansions into diverse fields. It remains one of the two main mail order houses, the other being Littlewood's of Liverpool.[55] Great Universal Stores after a hectic period of take-overs, settled down, employing some 40,000 people in four main divisions:

Retail. Mail order; household stores (furniture, wallpapers, electrical goods); multiple shops and stores, mainly selling clothing.

Overseas. Mainly mail order and retail in various countries.

Manufacturing and merchanting. Manufacture of clothing and bedding; importing and exporting; cash-and-carry stores; discount retailing.

Investment, property, finance and travel. Banking; property ownership; travel business.

Thorn Electrical Industries, the second example, was also largely created by one man, Sir Jules Thorn, who began in the electrical field and, as we have seen, moved into radio and television as well as domestic appliances by a number of acquisitions. During the 1960s what had been a steady upward growth was dramatically transformed into a series of purchases which resulted in Thorn's becoming a giant company; the new activities were outside the manufacture of radio, television and lighting. It moved into the retail business in 1961, into the manufacture of gas cookers and fires in 1965, and into engineering in 1967. In 1968 the company's size virtually doubled by the acquisition of the television rental company, Radio Rentals (after an inquiry by the Monopolies Commission).[57] He died in 1980.

The third company, even larger than Thorn's, has a very different history and the General Electric Company is a much transformed descendant of the 'Jewish' organisation whose chairman was Sir Harry Railing from 1943 (after Hugo Hirst's death) until 1957.[58] In the later years of his chairmanship the company was doing badly and in 1961 it merged with Radio & Allied Industries Ltd, one purpose being to obtain the managerial services of Arnold Weinstock. His was a rags-to-riches story. He was from a poor family but had had a university education, and in 1949 married the daughter of Michael Sobell, the pre-war small-scale radio manufacturer. Weinstock joined Sobell in Radio & Allied for the manufacture of radio and television, just as television was expanding (commercial programmes began in 1955). The firm was successful and searched for mergers, ending up with GEC; Weinstock became managing director of both companies' radio and television manufacture and of GEC's domestic appliance side. Within two years he was managing director of GEC. With the Labour government's encouragement GEC acquired Associated Electrical Industries in 1967 and in the following year merged with English Electric, Weinstock remaining managing director. The purpose of these connections was to create a company in the electrical industry efficient enough to compete internationally.

On the other hand, in the process of growth it is possible to discern a recurrent theme. While some men have been brought into existing companies as chief executive or as head of a section of an enterprise—such as Nat Levy, a pre-war cinema-owner on a small scale who, until he retired in 1977, was chairman of EMI Films—the usual pattern is of companies built up by one or more individuals. In the women's clothing trade one can identify Ben Raven of

Raybeck Shops (established in 1947); the Djanogly family, whose pre-war knitting factory was the foundation of the present-day Nottingham Manufacturing Co.; the Laskys of Audiotronics (retail sellers of radio, hi-fi and related products); Kalms of Dixon's Cameras (retail shops selling hi-fi as well as cameras); Sir John Cohen's Tesco stores; the Chinns of the Lex Service Group, originally car-sellers but now in a wide variety of enterprises, including freight transport and the hire of fork-lift trucks and cranes. Among the refugees from Nazism was Arthur Hubert, formerly a metal merchant in Germany. He arrived in 1939 with £1, and after his release in 1941 from internment took a job as a nightwatchman; in 1944 he became a representative for a London scrap-metal merchant and formed his own company, Tom Martin & Co. (Blackburn) Ltd, in 1948. This firm remained in the metal business, processing and merchanting metals and producing zinc and aluminium ingots.[59]

It is not the intention to produce a directory of Jewish business, but one further area needs mentioning—entertainment and related industries. Two of the several regional programme-contracting companies for independent (commercial) television are Granada, based in Lancashire, and Associated Television in the Midlands. The former company grew out of Sidney (later Lord) Bernstein's pre-war cinema interests and the group diversified beyond cinemas and television programmes to encompass television-set rentals (its major income), bingo social clubs, motorway services, book and music publishing, and property. ATV's parent company similarly spread into record-production, film-making, music publishing, theatrical costumiers and theatres. Lord (Lew) Grade was the prime mover in these activities and remained chairman of the parent company when he retired in 1977 at the age of seventy—in accordance with the rules of the Independent Broadcasting Authority—from the chairmanship of ATV Network, the programme company. His brother, Lord Delfont, who came from the same show-business background, became chairman and chief executive of the EMI Films and Theatre Corporation, when EMI took over his company in the 1960s.[60]

An evaluation of these sundry details will help to avoid the appearance of a list of Jewish notabilities, incomplete though it is. An important aspect—already mentioned—is that the history of the Jewish companies has to be considered in relation to their industries' development. For example, in the manufacture of television sets, Thorn's was one of the two dominant companies by the end of the 1960s—the other being Philips. During the 1950s and 1960s the industry rapidly moved towards concentration. In 1954 there were as many as sixty firms making television sets but only eight were in existence in 1968, the reduction being caused to a large extent by mergers. In 1958 the top five companies produced 50 per cent of output and ten years later the top five were responsible for 95 per cent, the two biggest being Thorn (36 per cent) and Philips (with 25 per cent). Part of the history of this industry is the competitive bidding for smaller companies by these two. It is beyond the scope of this book to pursue the question why Philips beat Thorn's in the bid for Pye-Ekco in

1967: if Thorn's had succeeded it might have had over 50 per cent of output. The point is that Thorn's was one of a number of companies in that industry which was characterised by a marked series of mergers and take-overs for a variety of economic factors that applied to them all.[61]

A second feature is that while it is possible to state the industries in which Jewish firms are important—whether because of their individual size (apart from some of those mentioned in the previous pages one can add Ladbroke's in gambling);[62] or in terms of sectors (thus small or large Jewish firms are numerically important in clothing, timber, furniture and other 'traditional' trades)—it is just as necessary to note that large sections of the economy have little interest for Jews. The undoubted widening of Jewish economic activities has not prevented a good proportion of the activities listed in the official Standard Industrial Classification having no Jewish representative or, if there is one, only in a minor capacity.

The 1970s

The quarter-century of prosperity concluded in 1972–74 with a massive Stock Exchange boom, rapidly brought to an end by the rise in oil prices in 1973 and forebodings of doom. The easy monetary conditions of the early 1970s were followed by restriction, high inflation, low economic growth and a fall in real wages. Bankruptcies increased and a rescue operation had to be mounted by the Bank of England to prevent serious trouble after the collapse of 'fringe' banks.

By no means did all parts of the economy suffer difficulties. Property certainly was hard-hit—the 1972–74 boom had resulted in inflated expectations for property—and a number of industries such as clothing began to complain of cheap foreign imports. Other sectors were less troubled. One bright spot was the successful North Sea oil operation whereby the country's dependence on imported fuel was markedly reduced, hugely assisting the balance of payments.

Although it is too soon to pinpoint, from the Jewish angle, any major trends of the 1970s, the decade has already seen the retirement and then death of some of the chief characters: Sir Jules Thorn, Sir John Cohen and Sir Charles Clore, in particular. Their departure raises two questions. Men like these, who have created very large concerns, do not necessarily hand over to their children, following the familiar pattern of the past. Aside from the inability or unwill-ingness of members of the family to do so, large, bureaucratic organisations can seldom be run on kinship connections. It is true that the succeeding chairman has often been a Jewish associate of the recently-retired head, but no great prescience is needed to suggest that firms of this kind may eventually follow such companies as Shell and ICI and depart from the realm of discussion of Jewish business.

Second, does their departure signal an end to the 'heroic' age of entre-preneurship? It is true that during the 1970s, despite the gloom, the number of new, small businesses established each year has increased and some among them will succeed. But it may be that their chances will be less than in the 1950s and 1960s because the conditions for success in those years were special and may not recur. In the Jewish context, however, there is one major considera-tion that will undoubtedly affect the role of Jews in business: a possible reduction in the number wishing to enter it.

The Professions

The prototype immigrant Jewish family of the past, if at all ambitious, would aim, in the first generation, to go into small-scale business. Usually the business would devolve on the children, but the able among them might become doctors or lawyers. Most of these were men, the women going in for teaching or nursing. The move into the professions was delayed by the adverse inter-war conditions, but—this is the significant feature of the post-war years—has speeded up tremendously. This increase is a reflection of greater prosperity, more educational opportunities and an expansion of the profes-sions.

There are many qualitative indications of this growth. The *Jewish Chronicle* regularly publishes a weekly university page, addressed to students, and its 'Situations Vacant' columns often include advertisements for accountants, whereas in the immigration period it carried a weekly 'Jewish Labour News'. Perhaps too we might include the, admittedly highly selective, emigrants to Israel. In the four years 1968–71 a total of 2,600 British Jews went to settle, of whom the occupations of 2,504 are known (the others may have been retired from work, and one ought to exclude 492 students). The two biggest groups, apart from the students, were 892 office staff and 485 in commerce, but there were 254 'medical', 248 teachers and 133 engineers.[63]

Some of the social surveys provide relevant statistics. The figures obtained from a study of people who died in 1961 suggested that as many as 10 per cent of the Jewish population were in social class I (approximately, in the profes-sions);[64] the Edgware survey of the early 1960s discovered that about one in six of the respondents (and about one in four of their children) was a profes-sional;[65] the Sheffield survey ten years later referred to 'the large number of professional occupations—doctors, solicitors, university lecturers. This cate-gory is also increased by the Jewish female members of the work-force, who tend to be employed as teachers, social workers and doctors'.[66] In Sheffield as many as 38 per cent of the men aged 18 to 45 had had a university education, and 26 per cent of the women of that age group.[67] Sheffield has only a small community and its occupational pattern is not likely to be repeated elsewhere; but in view of the great expansion of further and higher education since the early 1960s we can safely assume that even more Jews are experiencing a lengthier educational life, and therefore more will be entering the professions.

Such other numbers as are published are either guesses or are incomplete. The figure of 10,000 Jewish students is bandied about;[68] there are said to be

1,000 Jewish university lecturers, and others in polytechnics and technical colleges.[69] There are said to be 60 full-time social workers,[70] and the Guild of Jewish Journalists claims a membership of 100.[71] Yet notwithstanding the absence of firm data, there is a different distribution of professional jobs. The three types just mentioned—lecturers, social workers and journalists—are one indication; another is the periodic references in the Jewish press to the absence of Jewish nurses. Judging by the Edgware survey of the early 1960s, fewer Jews, proportionately, are entering the traditional occupations of law and medicine. In that study, 'only 22 per cent of the households with professions were qualified in the higher professions (that is, medicine and law): the rest were engineers, accountants, industrial chemists, etc.' The increase in these 'lesser' professions is in line with trends in Britain generally.[72] 'My son the doctor' may well be being replaced by 'My son the accountant, chemist . . .'[73]

Many of these professional people are independent and self-employed, but many are not, and it can be argued that more Jews than is customarily stated are working as employees in what are sometimes large organisations. But a much more important conclusion about the expansion of the Jewish professional class concerns its relationship with business. The Sheffield survey noted that the Jewish men's occupations were broadly of two kinds—professional, and business/management.

> The majority of the sons and grandsons of the early Sheffield Jewish merchants—shop owners, market traders, small factory managers—have continued that mercantile tradition, often enlarging the original business, or branching out into related areas and generally becoming more economically successful. The descendants of the later immigrants, who were mostly self-employed or manual workers, have more often graduated into the professional fields . . .[74]

'The descendants of the later immigrants' are the children and grandchildren of the east Europeans who arrived in the forty or so years before 1914. They are the numerical majority within the community and if recent post-war trends continue, the number of professionals among them will grow.[75] At some point, perhaps, they will overtake the businessmen: it is not likely though that the stereotype image of the commercial Jew will fade.

16
Conclusion

The history of any minority must embrace, as well as its own internal development, the influence of the external world and the interaction between them. By the time Anglo-Jewry appears in the general history of the Jewish people past events had already moulded the attitudes and actions of both Jews and non-Jews. The medieval English Jewry was part of the Ashkenazi world of northern Europe, in whose various states Jews lived at the whim of the rulers. Their economic activities were limited to those they were permitted to perform. They could not join guilds, which controlled entry to the crafts, because they were also Christian fraternities. Restrictions of this kind were a clear and direct influence on Jewish economic activity. Somewhat hazier to establish was the effect of the Jewish religion on attitudes to occupations. As a result of persecution Judaism became inward-looking, and the group in order to survive was bound together behind a barrier of rituals and laws of elaborate meticulousness; some of these were directly concerned with economic behavior, while others were indirectly influential.

External constraints and internal compulsions between them radically affected Jewish economic activity: but it is not easy to decide the relative importance of the various influences.[1] For example, for most of the past 1,000 years, the Jews have been town-dwellers, generally (though by no means entirely) divorced from farming. It can be argued that their absence was due to the religious obligation not to work on the Sabbath day which rendered it hard, if not impossible, to carry out what is often a seven-day activity. Or perhaps the Jews, ever the immigrants and outsiders, could not fit into the social and religious structure of the medieval agrarian system. One explanation for the Jew as moneylender is that the highest ideal was to study the Torah (the basis of Jewish law and religion), but since this required considerable time and energy, an occupation such as moneylending was highly suitable because it did not consume many hours. A moneylender would be in a position to pursue fruitful, pious study. The rabbis, who produced guidance of this kind, similarly argued that a man should teach his son a trade, and preferably a pleasant one. Yet another argument is that the nature of Jewish religious instruction, through questioning and logical argument, was an important developer of Jewish intellectual abilities.

A simple listing of these diverse, possible influences on Jewish attitudes and behaviour is insufficient. There is an obvious qualitative difference between those which were absolutely determinative: the Jewish prohibition of work on a Saturday, or the inability of Jews to join a Christian guild; and those rabbinical opinions which carried prestige but were not binding. It is doubtful if the rabbis' view of Torah study actually directed many into money-lending. It is impossible furthermore to know if religious training heightened Jewish intellectual faculties: the most that can be said with certainty is that the traditional emphasis on education produced a high degree of (male) literacy.

The fact that proof is not readily available about the influence of attitudes on behaviour does not mean that they may not have been extremely important. On the contrary, there is much to be said for the approach of those, notably Max Weber, the pioneer in the study of religious sociology, who investigated the role of religious ideas and beliefs in man's economic life (the converse of the marxist view that religion is part of the superstructure which is economically determined). But it is not to commit the sins of materialism and determinism to argue that, whatever may have been in the minds of the Jews, their actions— and in particular their occupations—were primarily a result of their conditions of life. One example will suffice. The Jew as moneylender is a familiar figure in medieval historiography, so much so that when Max Weber was writing in the early years of the twentieth century he stated that the distinctive economic role of the Jews was in monetary and credit transactions. But considerable research since his time into the position of Jews in many countries shows clearly that they were occupied in numerous jobs (outside those which specifically serviced the religious community)—as printers, goldsmiths, textile workers, tailors and glassblowers, as well as in depressed and degraded trades such as dealing in old clothes and repairing them for resale. In some countries where they were unable to join Christian guilds, they formed Jewish ones.[2] It is a very different world from the largely moneylending medieval English Jewry.

We seldom know the numbers involved, but it has been argued most plausibly that a proper understanding of the economic life of medieval Jewry must take into account the size of the Jewish population in a territory. If the Jews formed a small minority—a few per cent at most, as in England, France, Germany and northern Italy; were excluded from guilds; and often were permitted to reside only if they followed financial and commercial pursuits; then they were necessarily moneylenders and traders. But where larger Jewish communities existed—as in many Mediterranean countries and in eastern Europe after about the year 1400—then a widespread and diverse artisan class came into existence.[3] Concrete factors such as these undoubtedly played a major role in the determination of Jewish economic activity. Jews fitted in where they could: many took up unhygienic jobs such as the handling of furs, despite rabbinical preferences for more suitable types of occupation. But while the lop-sided economic structure of those Jews who lived in a state of oppression and restriction is readily explained, particular Jewish occupational concentrations continued in conditions of greater freedom. Britain was one of the few early countries to provide a liberal environment—others in the seventeenth and eighteenth centuries were Holland and America—where formal limitations on Jewish life were minimal. In countries such as Germany, where the Jews were formally emancipated in the Napoleonic period, there was a dramatic change in Jewish occupations. Petty trading and similar trades rapidly declined and Jews took up more respectable trades, from banking to shopkeeping, as well as in industry.[4] The Jews who came to Britain were emancipated *de facto;* their equality was a result of the growth of religious toleration, of the needs of an expanding economy to be rid of old economic regulations, and the ineffectiveness of guild control.

Explanations for the existence of particular concentrations in the Jewish occupational patterns since the seventeenth century must be based on the prime fact that the community has been built up and reinforced by waves of immigrants. In a very real sense most Jewish immigrants, however different they may have been from each other—Sephardi merchant as against Russian tailor, for example—were individually emancipated when they arrived here. They exchanged a life of restriction or persecution for one of much greater freedom, but the effect on them reflected, in part, their diverse origins. Some of the earliest, the Sephardim of the seventeenth and eighteenth centuries, had escaped from the Inquisition, but many were already accustomed to a much wider world than the narrow confines of medieval ghettoes. The *conversos* among them had taken a full part in Christian religious practices, and, as such, had mixed as equals with the non-Jewish world; and they had come from countries which had a long tradition of international trade and of financial dealings. Some had the ability and the capital to become occupied with the development of Britain's international trade and her financial institutions. Such specialities as the import of diamonds, the handling of precious metals, and dealing in the foreign exchange market must presumably be considered Jewish traditional trades, as legacies of past patterns. In the same way the much greater numbers of Ashkenazim who immigrated in the eighteenth century were often initially pedlars and old-clothes men; these were probably their trades in their previous countries. Moreover, it was an age of domestic economic expansion in which distribution was undertaken by large numbers of middlemen of all kinds. Peddling, requiring little capital or expertise, was an easy trade for poor immigrants to follow, and such regulations as were supposed to regulate it were not strictly administered. The old-clothes men were no doubt continuing with their pre-immigration trade, one of the familiar degraded jobs that Jews did in other countries. There is not much force in the argument that they took it up in London because of the control of entry to the London trades by the City companies. As we have seen, it was not impossible for Jews to be apprenticed and to be shopkeepers: in many trades the companies' control was negligible. A Jew who wished to follow a craft and was prevented from doing so in London could set up in the provinces, where an expanding luxury market provided the opportunity. The major limitations on Jewish craftsmanship were a person's ability and interests, and the availability of employers willing to take on Jewish apprentices.

Similarly the Jewish tobacco-workers of London in the nineteenth century were probably carrying on the employment they had had in Amsterdam and elsewhere, and in which there were Jewish employers. They worked in what, for London, were largish enterprises, and may be considered part of the transformation of the economy of the poorer Jews from petty trading into shopkeeping and paid employment. Jews could readily go into industries where there were Jewish employers and which were small-scale: tailoring and cabinet-making, for example, which were in any case carried on to a great extent in London. That is, while there is evidence that second- and third-generation Jews were entering all manner of occupations and (not excluding the prizefighters, soldiers, sailors, and criminals) producing a rather more 'normal' structure, some special features remained. The suggestion that Jewish employment patterns may be related to the availability of Jewish employers would help to explain the absence of Jews from engineering or dock-working. The association of Jewish worker with Jewish employer would arise either from the employer's preparedness to allow time off for religious occasions or, equally potent, the reality or potentiality of antisemitism. A Jew would feel more comfortable working for a Jew; even if conditions of work were poor he would not be exposed to possible taunts, snubs or outright hostility because he was Jewish. The Jewish working class in the years before the late-nineteenth-century east European immigration did not have a high reputation for religiosity, but they nevertheless remained within the Jewish group, one reason perhaps being the nature of social relationships between Jews and non-Jews.

Yet we must not make too much of the availability of Jewish employers. It is sensible certainly to note that the Jewish magnates of the nineteenth century were in trades such as finance and commerce which provided little direct employment, and that most Jewish shopkeepers were small family businesses with few assistants; between them they could have employed only a few Jews. But Samuda's shipyard in London did not attract Jews to it, and little evidence exists of Jews working for the German-Jewish immigrants in the provincial textile trade, in Nottingham, Bradford, or Dundee. Apart from the London tobacco industry, Jews generally worked in small-scale enterprises, and were not normally to be found in factories. The argument that the Jews had a preference for small workshops, perhaps because they were unused to hierarchical institutions, is seductive; but it is important that throughout the nineteenth century much of British industry remained on a small scale, and especially so in London, where most Jews lived.

A description of the east European immigrants of the late nineteenth and early twentieth centuries is a repetition of a familiar story. They had been conditioned by a virtually medieval environment, a world of separated and mutually hostile groups. The intense religiosity of the Jews was qualified somewhat by exposure to secular ideas, including radical politics, but they retained a culture of their own, which they transferred to their new centres in British cities. It comprised a distinctive religion and language and fear of the Gentile world. Although their very large numbers in the Pale of Settlement had spilled over into a considerable variety of jobs, many flocked into comparatively few occupations and industries. Aside from a few businessmen and professionals, the Jews of eastern Europe were typically pedlars and workers in small workshops, especially in the clothing industry. These trades accompanied their migration to Britain.

Their 'personal' emancipation was not immediate: in many respects the life of a Jewish tailor in Stepney, the Leylands or Strangeways was not very different from his experiences in a Russian town. Their self-imposed isolation as well as poverty worked against them, and one can identify a major distinction between their history and that of the German-Jewish emancipation earlier in the nineteenth century. The German Jews were conscious that in the controversy about the liberalisation of their condition they had to work their passage, to prove their respectability and that they were worthy citizens. But the east European immigrants in Britain felt no such imperatives: the older-established community was already emancipated, and could readily demonstrate their respectability. The Jewish Historical Society of England, formed in 1893, produced academic works which showed that Anglo-Jewry had a long history. The community had been founded in the seventeenth century, not by pedlars or sweated tailors but by merchants, whose 'social condition . . . appears to have been excellent'. According to Lucien Wolf, they were all 'respected merchants' who 'constructed the foundations on which the imposing edifice of English Jewdom [sic] has since been reared'.[5]

The first-generation east European immigrants were too busy surviving to worry about such matters. A few prospered in the immigration period to the extent of being able to send their children to university. Some succumbed to gambling, as Beatrice Webb noticed in her researches of the late 1880s.[6] Others worked hard to improve the life of themselves and their children. Progress was delayed by the inter-war depression although some movement away from manual work was clearly discernible; but a more rapid rush into the middle class had to await the opportunities available in the years of fuller employment for much of the period after 1945.

The romantic success story—from immigrant tailor to business tycoon in three generations—publicised by writers such as Stephen Aris has much validity: the individual examples he gives are true.[7] As a general statement, typical of all Anglo-Jewry, it needs to be qualified, as we have seen. A laconic statement in the annual *Report* for 1975 of the Oxford Jewish Congregation that 'Jewish prisoners in the Oxford Jail were visited whenever a request was made' reminds us that diverse elements make up any community.

Yet although Anglo-Jewry since the resettlement of 1656 has been composed of very different groups of people, a coherent thread unifies the discussion. The history of the Jewish people, in most parts of the world, can be regarded as a case-study in the responses of a group whose life-style has been distorted by their peculiar minority status. Their religious training assisted their intellectual development which could only be brought to fruition when they were freed from restriction. Music and the arts as well as scientific discovery were sometimes the fields in which the newly-released energy flowed. The direction was affected by the interests of the particular society: nineteenth-century Germany paid more attention than did Britain to the arts and to scientific education, for example. The various waves of immigrants who came to Britain occupied different positions in this progress. Some came straight from medieval ghettoes; others had been exposed to freedom before they came. How they developed in Britain depended on their individual personalities, and on the nature of the British environment which surrounded them.

Tables

Table 1   Estimates of the Jewish Population of Britain, 1657–1800

Date	Number
1657	160
1684	414–450
1695	751–853
1730s	6,000
1753	8,000
1790s	20,000–26,000

Sources:

1657	A. S. Diamond, 'The cemetery of the resettlement', *TJHSE*, 19, 1960, pp. 182–86.
1684	L. D. Barnett (ed.), *Bevis Marks Records*, part 1, pp. 16–20. This list of 414 people is increased by Diamond, op. cit., to include Ashkenazim.
1695	A. P. Arnold, 'A list of Jews and their households in London extracted from the Census lists of 1695', *MJHSE*, part 6, 1962, pp. 73–141.
1730s–1790s	V. D. Lipman, 'Sephardi and other Jewish immigrants in England in the eighteenth century', in A. Newman (ed.), *Migration and Settlement*, pp. 37–38. These are contemporary guesses.

Table 2   Estimates of the Number of Jews in Business, 1660–1800

Date	Number	Evidence
1663–81	20–40	Paying Sephardi *imposta*
1695	44	London Census: possessing more than £600 capital
1701	40	Holders of Bank of England stock
1725	54	Holders of Bank of England stock
1753	108	Kent's *Directory*
1770s	150–200 families	

Sources:

1663–81	*Imposta* receipts listed in L. D. Barnett, *El Libro de los Acuerdos*, *passim*.
1695	A. P. Arnold, 'A list of Jews and their households in London extracted from the Census lists of 1695', *MJHSE*, part 6, 1962, pp. 78–101.

1701 and 1725	'Early Jewish holders of Bank of England stock', *MJHSE*, part 6, 1962, pp. 165–66, 169–70. I have excluded women, the deceased, those domiciled in Holland, one minor, and non-Jews wrongly listed.
1753	E. R. Samuel, 'The Jews in English foreign trade—a consideration of the "Philo Patriae" pamphlets of 1753,' in J. M. Shaftesley (ed.), *Remember the Days*, p. 131.
1770s	V. D. Lipman, *Social History of the Jews in England: 1850–1950*, p. 6. No evidence is given for this figure.

Table 3   Estimates of Jewish Population, c. 1850

Region	Town		Estimated population
London			18,000–20,000
Non-industrial			
South-East	Chatham		200
	Canterbury		100
	Sheerness		75
	Dover		50
	Ramsgate		45
South	Portsmouth		300
	Southampton		75
	Brighton		150
South-West	Exeter		175
	Plymouth		200–250
	Falmouth		150
	Penzance		75
West	Bristol		300
	Bath		50
	Cheltenham		75
Midlands	Bedford		20–25
	Cambridge	(closed 1851)	25
	Oxford		50
East Anglia	Ipswich		50
	Norwich		75
	Yarmouth		75
Industrial			
West Midlands	Birmingham		750–1,000
	Coventry		50–100
	Dudley		50–100
	Wolverhampton		50–100
East Midlands	Nottingham		50
Lancashire	Liverpool		2,500
	Manchester		2,000

Yorkshire	Hull	200
	Leeds	100
	Sheffield	50–60
North-East	Newcastle	100
	Sunderland	150
	North Shields	50–100
South Wales	Cardiff	50–100
	Methyr Tydfil	100
	Swansea	100–150
Scotland	Edinburgh	100–150
	Glasgow	150–200
Ireland	Dublin	150–200

Totals	London	18,000–20,000	
	provinces	15,000	
		35,000	

Source:
V. D. Lipman, *Social History of the Jews in England: 1850–1950*, pp. 185–57. The bases of his figures are given in his 'A survey of Anglo-Jewry in 1851', *TJHSE*, 17, 1953, pp. 171–88. The provincial total of 15,000 includes an estimate for wives, children and non-members: these are already incorporated in the London total.

Table 4   Joseph Jacobs's Socio-economic Analysis of London Jewry, c. 1880

Class[a]	Position[b]	Families	Average No. in family	Individuals	
Upper					
A	Professional and retired, W. London	300	4	1,200	
B	Rich merchants, W. London	1,200	4.5	5,400	
					6,600
Middle					
C	Merchants with private houses, N., S. and E. London	800	4.5	3,600	
D	Professions and retired, N., S. and E. London	200	4	800	
E	Shopkeepers, etc.	2,500	5	12,500	
					16,900
Lower					
F	Petty traders[c]	2,750	4	11,000	
G	Servants and assistants[d]	—	—	500	
					11,500

Pauper

H	Board of Guardians, casuals	1,884 ⎤	—	7,911
I	Board of Guardians, chronic	234 ⎦		
J	Other paupers and afflicted	—	—	2,242
K	Russian refugees	—	—	947
				11,100
Total				46,100

Source:

Joseph Jacobs, *Studies in Jewish Statistics, Social, Vital and Anthropometric,* pp. 10–17. I have amended his table on p. 13 in the light of his subsequent revision of the figures. There is a discussion of this analysis in V. D. Lipman, *Social History of the Jews in England: 1850–1950,* pp. 75 ff.

[a]He thought classes A–D were 'probable'; H–K were 'certain'; 'and only E–G about which there can be any serious departure from the actual state of the population'.

[b]'Merchants' apparently means those engaged in business in the City. 'Professionals' includes barristers and schoolmasters (the latter, who were generally not well paid, are surprisingly in his category A).

[c]This table does not identify workers in paid employment, except, by implication, those in the pauper classes. However, later in the book, Jacobs clearly shows that his class F included many workers (pp. 38–40): these are the workers who never applied to the Board of Guardians or ceased to apply.

[d]Class G were those employed 'in the families' of those above poverty, presumably as *domestic* servants.

Table 5   Rothschild Capital, 1815–75

Date	Total (£)[a]	Nathan Mayer Rothschild's holding (£)
1815	136,000	90,000
1818	1,772,000	500,000
1825	4,082,000	1,075,000
1828	4,338,333	1,128,000
1863[b]	22,312,864	
1875	34,358,562	6,509,208 (London house)

Source:

1815–28, Bertrand Gille, *Histoire de la Maison Rothschild,* vol. I, p. 458; 1863–75, ibid., vol. II, p. 571.

[a]The first four figures are notional, as their roundness suggests (Gille, vol. I, p. 458: 'La législation de l'époque permet de ne pas fixer un capital défini pour une maison de banque. Le capital qui figure sur les livres ne constitue qu'une notion compatable, non un chiffre absolu').

[b]The 1863 figure is based on information at the liquidation of the Naples house, and is a multiplicand of the Naples Rothschild and his proportion of the firm's total.

Table 6   Jewish Migration, 1881–1914

Country of emigration	Number of migrants	Total
Russia	1,950,000	
Austria-Hungary	450,000	
Romania	150,000	
Other countries	200,000	
		2,750,000
Country of admission		
United States	2,036,000	
Europe	350,000	
Other countries outside Europe and the United States	400,000	
		2,786,000

Source:
Arieh Tartakower, *In Search of Home and Freedom,* pp. 30–31. These figures include some estimates, as the different totals imply.

Table 7   Numbers of Applicants to the Jewish Board of Guardians, by Type of Occupation, Selected Years, 1882–1912

1	2	3	4	5	6	7	8	9
Year	Total occupied[a]	Tailor-ing	Boot- and shoe- making	Hawkers, etc.	General dealers	Tobacco	Glaziers	Wood-working
1882	1,588	438	187	257	108	146	118	54
1892	2,834	926	466	316	151	146	75	160
1902	2,874	725	600	363	214	93	31	163
1912	1,829	683	342	289	166	39	5	132

Source:
V. D. Lipman, *A Century of Social Service,* p. 84.

[a]The 'total occupied' does not include other applicants who were without occupations, who were usually women and old men. Other occupations of less importance are not given.

Table 8   Membership of Principal Jewish Trade Unions, 1892–1901

Union and date of foundation	1892	1893	1894	1895	1896	1897	1898	1899	1900	1901
Tailors										
International Journeymen Tailors', Machinists' and Pressers' Union (1882)	107	155	118	87	559	70	30	a	—	—
United Capmakers' Union (1889)	252	235	69	215	149	130	116	115	—	144[b]
United Ladies Tailoresses' and Mantle Makers' Union (1891)	250	450	392	375	459	550	461	351	316	325
Independent Tailors', Machinists' and Pressers' Union (1893)	—	272	124	492	504	259	468	a	—	—
Leeds Jewish Tailors', Machinists' and Pressers' Union (1893)	—	30	152	510	1,130	1,210	1,055	1,150	1,150	1,100
Military and Uniform Tailors' and Tailoresses' Union (1896)	—	—	—	—	130	180	150	80	121	60
Manchester Jewish Tailors', Machinists' and Pressers' Union (1896)	—	—	—	—	200	896	1,211	1,000	900	628
Cabinet-makers										
Independent Cabinet Makers' Association (1895)	—	—	—	228	283	180	154	228	317	328
Food and tobacco										
International Bakers Union (1892)	50	65	70	110	77	78	96	124	63	109
Amalgamated Cigarette-makers' and Tobacco Cutters' Union (1897)	—	—	—	—	—	143	147	157	185	112
Boot- and shoe-makers										
London Sew-Round Trade and Sick Benefit Society (1893)	—	59	159	149	50	49	48	40	27	27
Leeds Jewish Slipper Makers', Rivetters' and Finishers' Union (1894)	—	57	159	149	50	90	26	150	100	c

Source:
Annual Reports of the Registrar of Friendly Societies *(PP)*. Details for London Jewish unions were extracted and printed (inaccurately) by Georg Halpern, *Die Jüdischen Arbeiter in London*, pp. 66–68, together with those for short-lived unions.

[a]Amalgamated in 1898 to form the London Tailors', Machinists' and Pressers' Union.
[b]Newly organized in 1901.
[c]Dissolved 1901.

Table 9   Synagogue Membership, Greater London, by Boroughs, 1930 (per cent)

Boroughs		Per cent
East London		
Stepney and City	42.7	
Bethnal Green	3.2	
Shoreditch	0.3	
Poplar	1.2	
Hackney	9.6	
Stoke Newington	1.1	
		58.1
Outer East London		
East and West Ham	2.0	
Leyton and Walthamstow	0.5	
Barking, Becontree and Ilford	0.5	
		3.0
North and North West London		
Islington	2.9	
Hampstead and Willesden	5.3	
Hornsey, Tottenham, Southgate, Hendon, Finchley and Wembley	3.6	
		11.8
West London		
Westminster, Holborn and St Pancras	7.6	
St Marylebone, Paddington and Kensington	12.5	
Chelsea, Fulham, Hammersmith, Ealing and Acton	2.4	
		22.5
South London		
Southwark and Bermondsey	1.2	
Deptford, Woolwich, Lewisham and Camberwell	1.0	
Lambeth and Battersea	1.8	
		4.0
Outer South London		
Richmond, Surbiton, Kingston and Croydon	0.6	
		0.6
Total		100.0

Source:
H. Llewellyn Smith (ed.), *New Survey of London Life and Labour,* vol. VI, p. 296.

The boroughs (county, metropolitan and municipal, as they were before local government reorganization of the 1960s and 1970s) were grouped, in the original publication, because 'members may come from adjoining boroughs'. Sometimes they lived some distance away. Of the 594 seat-holders (male and female) of the West Ham District Synagogue in 1935, 20 lived outside the immediate area, 2 of them as far away as Laindon in Essex, 1 at Sidcup, Kent, and 1 at Brighton, Sussex. West Ham District Synagogue, *Order of Service at the Re-consecration,* 16 June 1935.

Table 10   Occupations of London Entrants, aged 14–20, into Jewish Friendly Societies, 1913 and 1930 (per cent)

Occupations	Male 1913		Male 1930		Female 1913		Female 1930	
Clothing								
Dress-makers, embroiderers	—		—		7.9		28.3	
Furriers	5.5		10.2		8.8		5.7	
Hat- and cap-makers, milliners	4.4		0.3		9.2		12.7	
Tailors, pressers	46.6		22.8		39.8		9.1	
Underwear- and corset-makers	—		—		4.6		—	
Boot- and shoe-makers	2.7	59.2	0.3	33.6	1.9	72.2	—	55.8
Furniture		11.2		15.5		0.2		0.1
Transport		—		0.1		—		—
Clerks, shop assistants								
Clerks, typists	6.5		9.2		9.4		24.0	
Salesmen, shop assistants, travellers	3.8	10.3	20.1	29.3	1.9	11.3	17.3	41.3
Personal service								
Domestic workers, waiters, waitresses		—		0.1		0.7		—
Miscellaneous								
Cigarette- and cigar-workers	2.0		0.1		13.6		0.3	
Hairdressers	5.5		9.3		0.7		1.3	
Metal-workers, electricians	0.7		3.0		—		—	
Musicians	—		0.4		—		—	
Printers	2.0		1.2		—		0.4	
Leather-workers	—		0.7		—		0.3	
Jewellers	2.4		0.7		—		—	
Warehousemen, packers	2.0		1.5		0.5		0.4	
Others	4.7	19.3	4.5	21.4	0.8	15.6	0.1	2.8
Totals		100.0		100.0		100.0		100.0

Source:
H. Llewellyn Smith (ed.), *New Survey of London Life and Labour*, vol. VI, p. 295 (absolute figures are not given).

Table 11   Parental Occupations of Pupils at Liverpool Jewish School, 1910–1939 (per cent)

Occupation	1910–11	1927–28	1936–39
Cabinet-makers	23.3	33.0	21.2
Tailoring	32.0	23.0	21.2
Craftsmen	9.3	5.0	9.6
Manual workers	3.3	7.0	5.8
Travellers	6.0	3.0	9.6
Distributive trades	18.8	16.0	9.6
Manufacturers	2.7	—	—
Teachers/ministers	3.3	2.0	1.9
Property agents	—	4.0	—
Clerical workers	—	1.0	—
Seafarers	—	—	7.6
Deceased	1.3	7.0	13.5
Totals	100.0	101.0	100.0

Source:
Cyril Hershon, 'The Evolution of Jewish Elementary Education in England with Special Reference to Liverpool', unpublished Ph.D. thesis, University of Sheffield, 1973, Table 17.

Note. Absolute figures are not given, neither is the definition of 'craftsmen' or 'manual workers'. I take it that the former must have been in a variety of skilled jobs outside furniture and tailoring, and that manual work here means unskilled work outside those two industries.

Table 12   Distribution of Estimated Jewish Population of Great Britain, 1960–65

South-East		
Greater London	280,000	
Brighton and Hove	7,500	
Southend and Westcliff	4,500	
		292,000
North		
Glasgow	13,400	
Manchester	36,000	
Leeds	19,400	
Liverpool	7,500	
		76,300
Midlands		
Birmingham	6,300	
		6,300
Sub-total: major urban centres		374,600
Other provincial centres		35,400
Grand total		410,000

Source:
S. J. Prais, 'Synagogue statistics and the Jewish population of Great Britain: 1900–70', *Jew. J. Sociol.*, 14(2), December 1972, p. 217.

Table 13   Estimated Jewish Population of Greater London, by London Boroughs, 1970

Inner London		Outer London	
North and East		*North and West*	
Tower Hamlets and City	15,700	Enfield	11,400
Hackney	41,100	Barnet	58,900
Camden	14,400	Brent	20,200
Islington	1,100	Harrow	14,400
West and South-West		*West*	
Westminster	24,600	Ealing	2,500
Kensington and Chelsea	4,500	Hounslow	800
Hammersmith	2,600	Hillingdon	900
South		*South*	
Lambeth	5,600	Kingston	1,400
Lewisham	2,100	Merton	1,900
Wandsworth	1,700	Richmond	1,300
Greenwich	700	Sutton	900
Southwark	300	Croydon	1,000
Total Inner London	114,400	Bromley	700
		Bexley	—
Outer London		Total Outer London	158,600
North and East		Grand Total	273,000
Newham	4,200		
Waltham Forest	8,900		
Redbridge	18,900		
Barking	1,100		
Havering	1,600		
Haringey	7,600		

Source:
S. J. Prais, 'Synagogue statistics and the Jewish population of Great Britain: 1900–70', *Jew. J. Sociol.*, 14(2), December 1972, p. 222.

Table 14   Social Class Structure of Anglo-Jewry, and the General Population, 1961, by Age Groups (per cent)

Social class	Jews	General population	Jews		General population	
			15–44	45–74	15–44	45–74
I Professional	4	2	7	3	3	2
II Intermediate	34	14	32	32	13	15
III Skilled	46	46	41	45	48	44
IV Partly skilled	14	22	16	17	20	23
V Unskilled	—	13	—	—	. 12	14
Unoccupied and unclassified	3	3	4	3	4	2
Totals	101	100	100	100	100	100

Source:
S. J. Prais and M. Schmool, 'The social-class structure of Anglo-Jewry: 1961', *Jew. J. Sociol.*, 17(1), June 1975, pp. 8, 10.

Abbreviations

AJR	Association of Jewish Refugees
JC	*Jewish Chronicle*
MJHSE	*Miscellanies of the Jewish Historical Society of England* (parts 1–6 were published separately; part 7 and onwards published with *TJHSE*)
TJHSE	*Transactions of the Jewish Historical Society of England*

Notes

Introduction   The Earlier Communities

1. P. Hyams, 'The Jewish minority in mediaeval England, 1066–1290', *J. Jew. Studies,* 25, 1974, p. 271. S. Applebaum, 'Were there Jews in Roman Britain?', *TJHSE,* 17, 1953, pp. 189–205, reviews the evidence for the earlier period.

2. R. Chazan, *Medieval Jewry in Northern France: A Political and Social History,* pp. 24–29.

3. R. B. Dobson, *The Jews of Medieval York and the Massacre of 1190,* p. 5.

4. Chazan, op. cit., p. 50.

5. Cecil Roth, *A History of the Jews in England,* p. 4; H. G. Richardson, *The English Jewry under Angevin Kings,* chap. 1, 'The Settlement'.

6. V. D. Lipman, 'The anatomy of medieval Anglo-Jewry', *TJHSE,* 21, 1968, pp. 64–65, and *The Jews of Medieval Norwich,* pp. 36–38.

7. L. Hyman, *The Jews of Ireland: From Earliest Times to the Year 1910,* pp. 1–5.

8. C. Roth, op. cit., pp. 276–78 for a list.

9. Dobson, op. cit., p. 16.

10. Ibid., pp. 7–8. For an excellent, up-to-date summary, see R. B. Dobson, 'The decline and expulsion of the medieval Jews of York', *TJHSE,* 26, 1979, pp. 34–52.

11. I. Epstein, 'Pre-expulsion England in the Responsa', *TJHSE,* 14, 1940, pp. 187–205; A. Owen, 'The references to England in the Responsa of Rabbi Meir ben Baruch of Rothenburg: 1215–1293', *TJHSE,* 17, 1953, pp. 73–78.

12. Lipman, *Norwich,* p. 65.

13. Richardson, op. cit., p. 115.

14. Lipman, *Norwich,* chap. 6, 'The Family of Jurnet'.

15. Cecil Roth, 'Elijah of London: The most illustrious English Jew of the middle ages', *TJHSE,* 15, 1946, pp. 29–62.

16. Cecil Roth, *The Intellectual Activities of Medieval English Jewry.*

17. C. Roth, 'Elijah of London', pp. 40–41.

18. Richardson, op. cit., chap. 3, 'The King's Borrowings'.

19. P. Elman, 'Jewish finance in thirteenth-century England', *TJHSE,* 16, 1952, pp. 93–94; Lipman, *Norwich,* pp. 93–94.

20. Richardson, op. cit., p. 108.

21. Lipman, *Norwich,* pp. 78–81; Richardson, op. cit., pp. 25–27; Dobson, *Jews of Medieval York,* p. 7 n.23.

22. Lipman, *Norwich,* p. 48.

23. Lipman, 'Anatomy of medieval Anglo-Jewry', pp. 74–75. The recently-published 'Accounts of receipts from Jews in the Tower of London 1275–8', in H. G. Richardson (ed.), *Calendar of the Plea Rolls of the Exchequer of the Jews,* pp. 148–94, gives some information about the lesser Jews but not their occupations.

24. Chazan, op. cit., pp. 15–18.

25. M. Adler, 'Benedict the gildsman of Winchester', *MJHSE*, part 4, 1942, pp. 1–8.

26. M. Mate, 'The indebtedness of Canterbury Cathedral priory 1215–95', *Econ. Hist. Rev.* 26(2), 1973, pp. 183–97.

27. Ibid., p. 185.

28. By a similar process of interpretation of texts, some Jews lent to other Jews at interest, despite biblical prohibitions. If the loan was not repaid on time, it was fictitiously re-lent to a non-Jew at interest; A. M. Fuss, 'Inter-Jewish loans in pre-expulsion England', *Jew. Quart. Rev.*, 65, 1975, pp. 229–45.

29. C. N. L. Brooke assisted by G. Keir, *London 800–1216: The Shaping of a City*, pp. 222–33, analyses the money market for the previous century in terms of: (a) richer Jews of London; (b) Christian usurers; (c) the Knights Templar. Other references to Christian moneylenders are in Richardson, op. cit., pp. 50–60.

30. C. Roth, *Jews in England*, chap. 3; P. Elman, 'Jewish finance in thirteenth-century England with special reference to royal taxation', *Bull. Inst. Hist. Res.*, 15, 1938, pp. 112–13. Also Elman, 'The economic causes of the expulsion of the Jews in 1290', *Econ. Hist. Rev.*, 7, 1937, pp. 145–54 (see pp. 153–54 for details of Jewish tallages 1221–87).

31. Lipman, *Norwich*, pp. 162–68; Richardson, op. cit., pp. 106–7, 229–30.

32. Richardson, op. cit., pp. 217–23.

33. Ibid., p. 229.

34. R. W. Kaeuper, *Bankers to the Crown: The Riccardi of Lucca and Edward I*, p. 225.

35. Richardson, op. cit., pp. 225–31 for details of the Gascony expulsion. He opposes the view of Elman, in 'Economic causes of the expulsion', that Italian financiers took the place of the English Jews. Hyams, op. cit., p. 263 n.63, briefly criticises Richardson's brusque dismissal of Elman's argument.

36. Among the many relevant studies on the history of Jewish-Christian relations, one of the most interesting is J. Katz, *Exclusiveness and Tolerance: Studies in Jewish-Gentile Relations in Medieval and Modern Times*. References to more recent literature are given in Hyams, op. cit.

37. Thus Jews would be affected adversely in periods of social and political turmoil, as is shown in G. A. Williams, *Medieval London: From Commune to Capital*. See also R. B. Pugh, *Imprisonment in Medieval England*, for suggestions about the greater likelihood of Jews being imprisoned.

38. Hyams, op. cit., p. 278.

39. C. Roth, *Jews in England*, p. 9. The most recent discussion of this episode is by Lipman, *Norwich*, pp. 49–57.

40. Dobson, *Jews of Medieval York*, p. 48. His study is the fullest account of these events.

41. J. C. Holt, *The Northerners: A Study in the Reign of King John*, p. 165.

42. For recent discussions see Hyams, op. cit., and G. I. Langmuir, 'The Jews and the archives of Angevin England: reflections on medieval anti-semitism', *Traditio*, 19, 1963, pp. 183–244.

43. Chazan, op. cit., pp. 183–84. The newly-arrived English Jews were ordered in 1291 to be expelled from France, but some stayed after that date.

44. Cecil Roth, 'Sir Edward Brampton', *TJHSE*, 16, 1952, pp. 121–27.

45. A. McKay, 'Popular movements and pogroms in fifteenth century Castile', *Past & Present*, no. 55, May 1972, p. 45.

46. Ibid., p.35, for a list of violent outbursts.

47. Ibid., p. 62; see also P. Wolff, 'The 1391 pogrom in Spain: Social crisis or not?', *Past & Present*, no. 50, February 1971, pp. 4–18.

48. F. Braudel, *The Mediterranean and the Mediterranean World in the Age of Philip II*, vol. I, p. 415: 'Proof of the overpopulation of Mediterranean Europe . . . is the frequent expulsions of the Jews'.

49. R. Highfield (ed.), *Spain in the Fifteenth Century:1369–1516*, p. 256 (Eng. trans. of extract from J. C. Vivens, *Historia Economia de Espana)*. The debate continues; S. H. Haliczer, 'The

Castilian urban patriciate and the Jewish expulsions of 1480–92', *Amer. Hist. Rev.*, 78(1), 1973, pp. 35–58, concludes that antisemitism was not a major cause.

50. There is no comprehensive history of this period of Sephardi history, least of all the economic aspects of *converso* life. Two important studies are Hermann Kellenbenz, 'Sephardim an der unteren Elbe: ihre wirtschaftliche und politische Bedeutung vom Ende des 16 bis zum Beginn des 18 Jahrhunderts', *Vierteljahrschrift für Sozial- und Wirtschaftsgeschichte* (Wiesbaden), 40, 1958; H. I. Bloom, *The Economic Activities of the Jews of Amsterdam in the Seventeenth and Eighteenth Centuries*. See also R. D. Barnett (ed.), *The Sephardi Heritage*.

51. A. Schischa, 'Spanish Jews in London in 1494', *MJHSE*, part 9, 1975, pp. 214–15.

52. L. Wolf, 'Jews in Tudor England', in his *Essays in Jewish History*, pp. 73–90.

53. Cecil Roth, 'The middle period of Anglo-Jewish history (1290–1655) reconsidered', *TJHSE*, 19, 1960, pp. 6–7, corrects the version given by Wolf, op. cit., pp. 82–83.

54. Wolf, op. cit., pp. 84–89; Cecil Roth, 'The case of Thomas Fernandes before the Lisbon Inquisition, 1556', *MJHSE*, part 2, 1935, pp. 32–56.

55. L. Wolf, 'Jews in Elizabethan England', *TJHSE*, 11, 1928, pp. 1–91. This pioneering work remains the basis of knowledge on the subject. A useful subsequent article is C. J. Sisson, 'A colony of Jews in Shakespeare's London', *Essays by Members of the English Association*, 22, 1938, pp. 38–51. The most recent general statement, incorporating research done since Wolf's article, is by Roth, 'The middle period . . . reconsidered'.

56. Wolf, 'Jews in Elizabethan England', p. 19; see pp. 33–35 for a list of names.

57. Ibid., p. 21.

58. Ibid., pp. 21–22; also p. 7 for a deposition by a Spanish ex-prisoner of war of 1588 who gave the names of eight Portuguese in London: 'it is public and notorious in London, that by race they are all Jews, and it is notorious that in their own homes they live as such observing their Jewish rites.'

59. Wolf, 'Jews in Elizabethan England', *passim*; Conyers Read, *Mr Secretary Walsingham and the Policy of Queen Elizabeth*, vol. III, pp. 125–26, 292; John Gwyer, 'The case of Dr Lopez', *TJHSE*, 16, 1952, pp. 163–84.

60. E. R. Samuel, 'Portuguese Jews in Jacobean London', *TJHSE*, 18, 1958, pp. 171–230; Roth, *Jews in England*, pp. 144, 283–84.

61. It is quite clear that apart from Carvajal the London *conversos* of 1656 were very recent arrivals, as is shown by the earliest dates of residence given in M. Woolf, 'Foreign trade of London Jews in the seventeenth century', *TJHSE*, 24, 1975, pp. 38–58: all were in the 1650s. The only other references to Jews in London relate to the 1640s: an Amsterdam firm transacted business with Francisco Lopes d'Azevedo alias Abraham Farar (presumably the Dutch firm's London agent); Bloom, op. cit., p. 106. A vague reference occurs to Dutch Jews being brought over in 1643 to assist in the export of English goods, presumably a temporary residence; *Cal. State Papers Venetian*, 26, 1642–43, p. 252. Apart from one or two converts to Christianity, this is the sum total of evidence of Jews or *conversos* in England before the 1650s, and it is hard to think that, apart from Carvajal and his entourage, any 'group' was holding Jewish religious services.

1 Readmission, 1656

1. Christopher Hill, *Society and Puritanism in Pre-revolutionary England*, p. 204.

2. H. Fisch, *Jerusalem and Albion*; M. Fixler, *Milton and the Kingdoms of God*.

3. S. R. Gardiner, *History of the Commonwealth and Protectorate: 1649–1656*, vol. IV, p. 11 n.1, refers to a meeting of Jews in June 1655, who appear to have to have a Judaising sect.

4. The standard work is L. Wolf (ed.), *Menasseh ben Israel's Mission to Oliver Cromwell*. Some of this has been superseded by later research. The most recent general statement is by Cecil Roth, *A History of the Jews in England*, pp. 149–54.

5. P. Toon, 'The latter-day glory', in P. Toon (ed.), *Puritans, the Millennium and the Future of Israel: Puritan Eschatology, 1600 to 1660*, p. 25.

6. Among relevant writings are W. M. Lambert, *Godly Rule: Politics and Religion, 1603–60*, and B. S. Capp, *The Fifth Monarchy Men*.

7. H. R. Trevor-Roper, *Religion, the Reformation and Social Change*, pp. 246–47.

8. Based on Ismar Schorsch, 'From messianism to Realpolitik: Menasseh ben Israel and the readmission of the Jews to England', *Proceedings of the American Academy for Jewish Research*, vol. 45, 1978, pp. 187–208. I am grateful to Dean Schorsch for allowing me to see a manuscript copy of his article before it was published. The traditional story is in Wolf, op. cit., and in C. Roth, 'The resettlement of the Jews in England', in V. D. Lipman (ed.), *Three Centuries of Anglo-Jewish History*, pp. 1–25.

9. The petitions and related documents are printed in L. Wolf, 'American elements in the resettlement', *TJHSE*, 3, 1899, pp. 88–93.

10. Wolf, *Menasseh ben Israel's Mission*, p. xxxix.

11. Ibid.; this reprints the pamphlet.

12. W. C. Abbott, *The Writings and Speeches of Oliver Cromwell*, vol. IV, p. 52.

13. Ibid., pp. 51–52.

14. Ibid., p. 53.

15. Roth, 'Resettlement', p. 11.

16. This is Roth's view in 'Resettlement'.

17. A. S. Diamond, 'The cemetery of the resettlement', *TJHSE*, 19, 1960, p. 166. The discussion on pp. 163–70 leads persuasively to the conclusion that no written licence was granted. For the synagogue see W. S. Samuel, 'The first London synagogue of the resettlement', *TJHSE*, 10, 1924, pp. 1–147, in which he established the date of the first Sephardi synagogue as 1656 (the present building at Bevis Marks was opened in 1701). Without this knowledge, so excellent a study as H. S. Q. Henriques, *The Jews and the English Law*, could argue that the events of 1655–56 left unchanged the position of the Jews in England (pp. 94–114, 122–25), and they could not worship openly before about 1663. Thus while he knew that the burial ground dated from 1657, he concluded that any burials with a Jewish religious ceremony must have been observed with strict secrecy.

18. Fixler, op. cit., p. 241. I am grateful to Dr Bernard Capp for his suggestions about the decline of millenarianism and the growth of opposition to the readmission idea.

19. There are many factual mistakes even in recent books; e.g., Antonia Fraser, *Cromwell: Our Chief of Men*, pp. 558–68, refers to a pre-admission synagogue, but this was in fact the post-admission house of worship. She refers to *converso* groups in Dover and York: there was none. Similarly Abbott, op. cit., vol. 4, pp. 18–19, writes of 'considerable numbers of them [Jews] in London and no doubt elsewhere in the British Isles'. There were very few, and none outside London. M. James, *Social Problems and Policy during the Puritan Revolution*, pp. 188–92, has a section based on Wolf and on Werner Sombart. It is out of date and inaccurate.

20. Wolf, *Menasseh ben Israel's Mission*, pp. xxviii–xxxvii for 'Cromwell's policy'; E. F. Heckscher, *Mercantilism*, vol. II, pp. 305–7.

21. M. P. Ashley, *Financial and Commercial Policy under the Cromwellian Protectorate*, p. 3.

22. Abbott, op. cit., vol. IV, pp. 18–19; Toon, op. cit., p. 121.

23. Wolf, *Menasseh ben Israel's Mission*, p. xxx. The original source is *Cal. State Papers Venetian*, 26, 1642–43, p. 252.

24. Christopher Hill, *Antichrist in Seventeenth Century England*, p. 115.

25. R. S. Paul, *The Lord Protector: Religion and Politics in the Life of Oliver Cromwell*, p. 331; M. P. Ashley, *The Greatness of Oliver Cromwell*, p. 288; A. Woolrych, 'The English revolution: an introduction', in E. W. Ives (ed.), *The English Revolution: 1600–1660*, pp. 29–32; Woolrych, 'Puritanism, politics and society', ibid., pp. 95–99.

26. H. N. Brailsford, *The Levellers and the English Revolution*, p. 395.

27. See the controversy on mercantilism in D. C. Coleman (ed.), *Revisions in Mercantilism*; also D. Patinkin, 'Mercantilism and the readmission of the Jews to England', *Jew. Soc. Stud.*, 7, 1946, pp. 161–78.

28. John Thurloe, *A Collection of Papers containing Authentic Memorials of the English Affairs from 1638 to the Restoration,* vol. IV, pp. 308, 333.

29. Wolf, 'American elements', p. 86.

30. Abbott, op. cit., vol. IV, p. 55.

31. R. D. Barnett, 'The correspondence of the Mahamad of the Spanish and Portuguese congregation of London during the seventeenth and eighteenth centuries', *TJHSE,* 20, 1964, p. 2.

32. This is suggested by H. S. Q. Henriques, op. cit., pp. 146, 149.

33. L. D. Barnett (ed.), *Bevis Marks Records,* part I, pp. 7–9; H. S. Q. Henriques, op. cit., pp. 147–48.

34. L. D. Barnett, op. cit., p. 9.

35. Ibid.

36. H. S. Q. Henriques, op. cit., pp. 148–49.

37. L. D. Barnett, op. cit., pp. 10–11; Henriques, op. cit., pp. 149–50.

38. L. D. Barnett, op. cit., pp. 13–15; Henriques, op. cit., pp. 152–54.

39. H. S. Q. Henriques, op. cit., pp. 13–17, 167.

40. C. Roth, *Jews in England,* p. 188. A proposal came before the Commons in 1689 to raise £100,000 in taxes from the Jews, one of a series of measures to provide funds for the prosecution of the war in Ireland and against France. But the proposition was dropped; T. B. Macaulay, *The History of England from the Accession of James the Second,* vol. III, pp. 497–98.

41. *Cal. S. P. Ven.,* 33, 1661–64, pp. 11, 120, 123 (the quotations are from p. 123). Also *Cal. State Papers Domestic,* 1661–62, pp. 241, 290, 611 (relating to his dealings and his sojourn in the Fleet prison).

42. F. Ashe Lincoln, 'The non-Christian oath in English law', *TJHSE,* 16, 1952, pp. 73–76; Henriques, op. cit., pp. 177–89.

43. C. Roth, *Jews in England,* pp. 216–23, 289; T. W. Perry, *Public Opinion, Propaganda and Politics in Eighteenth Century England: A Study of the Jew Bill of 1753.*

2   Merchants and Brokers: The Commercial and Financial Revolutions

1. T. S. Ashton, *An Economic History of England: The Eighteenth Century,* p. 1; and see P. G. M. Dickson, *The Financial Revolution in England: A Study in the Development of Public Credit, 1688–1756,* chaps. 1 and 2, for an excellent discussion of the background. There are useful studies of overseas trade in W. E. Minchinton (ed.), *The Growth of English Overseas Trade in the 17th and 18th Centuries,* notably two articles by Ralph Davis: 'English foreign trade, 1660–1700', pp. 78–98, and 'English foreign trade, 1700–1774', pp. 99–120.

2. L. Wolf, *Essays in Jewish History,* p. 131.

3. H. Beinart, 'The Jews in the Canary Islands: A re-evaluation', *TJHSE,* 25, 1977, pp. 48–86, has details of several mid-seventeenth-century *conversos* in Britain.

4. Dorothy K. Clark, 'A restoration goldsmith-banking house: the Vine on Lombard Street', in *Essays in Modern English History in Honor of Wilbur Cortez Abbott,* pp. 20–21.

5. M. Woolf, 'Foreign trade of London Jews in the seventeenth century', *TJHSE,* 24, 1975, pp. 38–58.

6. Ibid., p. 48.

7. Ibid., p. 50.

8. Ibid., p. 51.

9. Ibid.

10. J. R. Marcus, *The Colonial American Jew: 1492–1776,* vol. I, pp. 95–97.

11. In the period 1651 to 1700, of 6,500 naturalisations in Britain and the colonies, 190 were of Jews; J. M. Ross, 'Naturalisation of Jews in England', *TJHSE,* 24, 1975, p. 71. The names, and other details, are in W. S. Samuel, 'A list of persons endenizened and naturalised: 1609–1799', *MJHSE,* part 7, 1970, pp. 111–44. For the Jews in Barbados and Jamaica see Marcus, op. cit., vol. I, pp. 100–103; W. S. Samuel, 'Review of the Jewish colonists in Barbados in the year 1680',

TJHSE, 13, 1936, pp. 1–111; P. F. Campbell, 'The merchants and traders of Barbados', *J. Barbados Museum and Hist. Soc.*, 34(2), 1972, pp. 94–96.

12. *Journals of the House of Commons*, 8, 1660–67, p. 441; L. A. Harper, *The English Navigation Laws*, pp. 59ff.

13. G. Yogev, *Diamonds and Corals: Anglo-Dutch Jews and Eighteenth-Century Trade*, p. 63. This excellent work is the basis of much of the discussion in this chapter. See Samuel, op. cit., pp. 24–25, for the Mendes brothers.

14. Yogev, op. cit., chaps. 5 and 6, takes the story up to the 1720s.

15. L. D. Barnett (ed.), *El Libro de los Acuerdos*, pp. 1, 24.

16. Yogev, op. cit., pp. 287–88 n.20, lists thirteen traders, but one of them (p. 84) lived in Venice.

17. W. J. Fischel, 'The Jewish merchant-colony in Madras (Fort St George) during the 17th and 18th centuries', *J. Econ. and Soc. Hist. of the Orient*, 3, 1960, pp. 78–107, 175–95.

18. A. S. Diamond, 'The community of the re-settlement, 1656–1684: a social survey', *TJHSE*, 24, 1975, pp. 137 n.28, 147 n.83 and p. 146 for a general statement about jewellers. See also the names of Jews in E. R. Samuel, 'Sir Francis Child's jewellery business', *Three Banks Rev.*, no. 113, 1977, p. 53 (although this refers to a date later in the century).

19. Wolf, *Essays in Jewish History*, p. 133; also Dudley Abrahams, 'Jew brokers of the City of London', *MJHSE*, part 3, 1937, pp. 80–94.

20. Dickson, op. cit., p. 486.

21. Diamond, op. cit., pp. 146–47.

22. *Cal. State Papers Domestic*, 71, 1672, p. 210. One of those who immigrated because of this invitation was Solomon de Medina; O. K. Rabinowicz, *Sir Solomon de Medina*, chap. 1.

23. Charles Wilson, 'New introduction' to W. A. Cunningham, *Alien Immigrants in England*, p. xv.

24. Diamond, op. cit., pp. 147–49.

25. The standard work is H. S. Q. Henriques, *The Jews and the English Law*.

26. For example, W. A. Cunningham, *The Growth of English Industry and Commerce in Modern Times*, p. 327; E. T. Powell, *The Evolution of the Money Market*, p. 90.

27. J. R. Kellett, 'The breakdown of gild and corporation control over the handicraft and retail trade in London', *Econ. Hist. Rev.*, 10(3), 1958, pp. 381–94; W. F. Kahl, 'Apprenticeship and the freedom of the London livery companies: 1690–1750', *Guildhall Miscellany*, 1(7), 1956, pp. 16–20, notes the decline in apprenticeship.

28. Charles Wilson, *Anglo-Dutch Commerce and Finance in the Eighteenth Century*, p. 28.

29. Sonia L. Lipman, 'Judith Montefiore—first lady of Anglo-Jewry', *TJHSE*, 21, 1968, p. 289, for Montefiore (he was also in the diamond-coral trade to a small extent; Yogev, op. cit., pp. 144–45); pp. 288 and 302 n. 7, for Cohen (in 1778 he was one of three Jewish merchants who organised the ring for the purchase of 'damaged' cloth; Yogev, op. cit., p. 75).

30. Yogev, op. cit., p. 144. This section is based on his chaps. 6–9.

31. English Jews are not mentioned as trading to the Levant in the various studies of the company: G. Ambrose, 'The Levant company mainly from 1640–1753', unpublished B. Litt. thesis, University of Oxford, 1935; A. C. Wood, *A History of the Levant Company*; Ralph Davis, *Aleppo and Devonshire Square: English Traders in the Levant in the Eighteenth Century*. There were interlopers, but they did not trade directly between London and the east, rather on one of the two legs of the route—London-Leghorn, Leghorn-Turkey. Jewish merchants of Leghorn were among those in this illicit system; Ambrose, op. cit., pp. 239–40; *Journal of the Commissioner for Trade and Plantations*, 1704–1708/9, p. 203. The parliamentary debate is in *Parliamentary History*, 13, 1744, cols. 895–96.

32. Yogev, op. cit., 65.

33. A. Levy, 'The origins of Scottish Jewry', *TJHSE*, 19, 1960, p. 146.

34. J. M. Price, 'Joshua Johnson in London, 1771–1775: credit and commercial organization in

the British Chesapeake trade', in A. Whiteman, J. S. Bromley and P. G. M. Dickson (eds), *Statesmen, Scholars and Merchants,* pp. 173–74.

35. L. Hershowitz, 'Some aspects of the New York Jewish merchant in colonial trade', in A. Newman (ed.), *Migration and Settlement,* pp. 101–17. The list of freemen of the city of New York which he prints shows that after 1740 only eight were described as merchants. The majority had occupations such as tailor, goldsmith, watch-maker. There are many documents relating to Aaron Lopez in 'Commerce of Rhode Island', *Massachussetts Hist. Soc. Collections,* 7th series, 59 and 60, 1914 and 1915. He was one of the few considerable Jewish merchant-shippers, but according to this material had little trade with Britain.

36. Marcus, op. cit., vol. II, pp. 640–41; also Yogev, op. cit., pp. 64–66.

37. Yogev, op. cit., p. 63.

38. Ibid., p. 30.

39. Ibid., p. 35.

40. H. E. S. Fisher, *The Portugal Trade: A Study in Anglo-Portuguese Commerce, 1700–1770,* p. 55. Cf. L. S. Sutherland, *A London Merchant: 1695–1774,* appendix 3, pp. 138–39, for a list of sixty-three London Portugal merchants; none is Jewish.

41. The main source is Yogev, op. cit., pp. 42–46.

42. E. R. Samuel, 'The Jews in English foreign trade—a consideration of the "Philo Patriae" pamphlets of 1753', in J. M. Shaftesley (ed.), *Remember the Days,* pp. 123–43, for a discussion and extracts from the pamphlets. The second of them, 'Further considerations on the Act to permit persons professing the Jewish religion, to be naturalised by Parliament', contains details of Jewish commerce.

43. Yogev, op. cit., appendix A, p. 331.

44. Ibid., pp. 46–49.

45. Ibid., pp. 38–42 for information about bullion imports. He thinks that Jewish merchants may have switched from gold to diamond imports from the 1730s.

46. Yogev, op. cit., part 3, has a full account based on the firm's documents, housed at the Public Record Office.

47. As Yogev, op. cit., pp. 213–15, suggests.

48. M. Woolf, 'Eighteenth-century London Jewish shipowners', *MJHSE,* part 9, 1975, pp. 198–204.

49. For example: De Paba *v.* Ludlow, *English Reports,* 92, 1720, p. 1112; Da Costa *v.* Firth, *English Reports,* 98, 1766, pp. 24–26; Da Costa *v.* Newnham, *English Reports,* 100, 1788, pp. 219–23. Also W. S. Samuel, 'Tentative list of Jewish underwriting members of Lloyd's (from some time prior to 1800 until the year 1901)', *MJHSE,* part 5, 1948, pp. 176–92.

50. E. R. Samuel, 'The Jews in English foreign trade', p. 133.

51. Yogev, op. cit., pp. 15–21 for a discussion.

52. Quoted in M. F. Modder, *The Jew in the Literature of England to the End of the 19th Century,* p. 65. Chap. 4 has other eighteenth-century examples.

53. Rabinowicz, op. cit., for a biography of Medina. Also L. Hyman, *The Jews of Ireland: From Earliest Times to the Year 1910,* pp. 19–20.

54. Charles Rubens, 'Joseph Cortissos and the War of the Spanish Succession', *TJHSE,* 24, 1975, pp. 114–33.

55. For Prado and da Costa see A. M. Hyamson, *The Sephardim of England,* p. 103. For Franks, Norman Baker, *Government and Contractors: The British Treasury and War Supplies,* chap.9, 'The contractors'.

56. L. B. Namier, *The Structure of Politics at the Accession of George III,* pp. 47–49.

57. 'Early Jewish holders of Bank of England stock (1694–1725)', *MJHSE,* part 6, 1962, pp. 143–74.

58. Charles Wilson, 'New Introduction', to Cunningham, op. cit., p. xvii.

59. L. S. Sutherland, 'Samson Gideon and the reduction of interest, 1749–50', *Econ. Hist. Rev.,* 16 (1–2), 1946, pp. 15–29; ibid., 'Samson Gideon: eighteenth-century Jewish financier', *TJHSE,*

17, 1953, pp. 79–90; ibid., *The City of London and the Devonshire-Pitt Administration: 1756–71;* Dickson, op. cit., pp. 34, 222–28, 230–36.

60. M. Woolf, 'Joseph Salvador: 1716–1786', *TJHSE,* 21, 1968, pp. 104–37.

61. Between 1708 and 1755 there were 854 sworn brokers, of whom 43 also dealt in shares, Dickson, op. cit., p. 494. The author notes that Moses Hart (leader of the Ashkenazi community) was a sworn broker who dealt in shares.

62. This section is based on Dickson, op. cit., chap. 20; also E. V. Morgan and W. A. Thomas, *The Stock Exchange;* L. Wolf, op. cit., pp. 117–36.

63. Dickson, op. cit., p. 494, for a reference from the 1760s that only one-third of stockbrokers were sworn brokers, and p. 518 for a Jew named Mustaphia who operated as a broker, although not admitted as one.

64. Ibid., pp. 498, 513–14.

65. J. H. Clapham, *The Bank of England: A History,* vol. I, pp. 132–41; Yogev, op. cit., pp. 51–53.

66. Ashton, op. cit., p. 190.

67. Ibid., pp. 188–96, for a description of the eighteenth-century foreign exchange market.

68. H. Hamilton, 'The failure of the Ayr bank, 1772', *Econ. Hist. Rev.,* 8(3), 1956, pp. 405–17; C. Wilson, *Anglo-Dutch Commerce,* p. 178; H. I. Bloom, *The Economic Activities of the Jews of Amsterdam in the Seventeenth and Eighteenth Centuries,* pp. 200–201.

69. Yogev, op. cit., pp. 260–63.

70. C. Wilson, *Anglo-Dutch Commerce,* p. 116.

71. R. D. Barnett, 'The travels of Moses Cassuto', in Shaftesley, op. cit., p. 103.

72. C. Wilson, *Anglo-Dutch Commerce,* p. 117. See his appendices B, C and D, which give the names of Dutch buyers and their London agents. However, as mentioned earlier, London Jews had Christian correspondents in Cadiz and there are other examples of, for example, Jews having Christian partners.

73. A. H. John, 'Insurance investment and the London money market of the 18th century', *Economica,* 20, 1953, p. 140.

3 The Jews of the 'Other' London

1. Wolf, 'Crypto-Jews under the Commonwealth', *TJHSE,* 1, 1895, p. 87.

2. M. Woolf, 'Foreign trade of London Jews in the seventeenth century', *TJHSE,* 24, 1975, p. 43 (Manuel Perera).

3. Wolf, op. cit., p. 87.

4. George Rudé, *Hanoverian London: 1714–1808,* p. 83; chap. 5 is on 'The "other" London'. The fullest account of these segments of the Anglo-Jewish community is in T. M. Endelman, *The Jews of Georgian England, 1714–1830,* especially chaps. 5, 6 and 7.

5. A. S. Diamond, 'The community of the resettlement, 1656–1684: a social survey', *TJHSE,* 24, 1975, pp. 147–48; L. Wolf, *Essays in Jewish History,* p. 193, gives the same proportion of one-quarter for 1690.

6. L. D. Barnett (ed.), *El Libro de los Acuerdos,* pp. xx, 28; L. D. Barnett (ed.), *Bevis Marks Records,* part 1, p. 29 n.3.

7. L. D. Barnett, *El Libro,* p. 28.

8. Wolf, *Essays,* p. 123.

9. This view seems to have originated from ibid., pp. 123–24.

10. Israel Abrahams, 'Passes issued to Jews in the period 1689 to 1696', *MJHSE,* part 1, pp. 24–33.

11. R. D. Barnett, 'The correspondence of the Mahamad of the Spanish and Portuguese congregation of London during the seventeenth and eighteenth centuries', *TJHSE,* 20, 1964, pp. 3–4.

12. Ibid., p. 4.

13. A. S. Diamond, 'Problems of the London Sephardi community, 1720–33', *TJHSE*, 21, 1968, pp. 60–61.

14. R. D. Barnett, 'Dr Samuel Nunes Ribeiro and the settlement of Georgia', in A. Newman (ed.), *Migration and Settlement*, pp. 82–89, 94–100.

15. M. Dorothy George, *London Life in the Eighteenth Century*, p. 127. Cordosa was born in Amsterdam and his name suggests that he was a Sephardi.

16. A. M. Hyamson, *The Sephardim of England*, p. 169.

17. Barnett, *El Libro*, p. 22; L. D. Barnett, 'First record of the Hebra Guemilut Hasadim, London, 1678', *TJHSE*, 10, 1924, pp. 258–60.

18. Hyamson, op. cit., pp. 94–95. The rules of the girls' school are on p. 85 n.1.

19. A. Rubens, *Anglo-Jewish Portraits*, pp. 119–23.

20. Hyamson, op. cit., pp. 84–85.

21. A. Schischa, 'Reb Salmen London: immigrant, emigrant, migrant', in Newman (ed.), op. cit., p. 19, shows that the earliest London Ashkenazi charitable and fraternal society dates from 1702, not, as was previously thought, 1761.

22. B. A. Fersht, 'The earliest Jewish friendly society in England, Rodphea Shalom', *MJHSE*, part 2, 1935, pp. 90–98. Also V. D. Lipman, *Social History of the Jews in England: 1850–1950*, pp. 50–53.

23. S. Stein, 'Some Ashkenazi charities in London at the end of the eighteenth and the beginning of the nineteenth centuries', *TJHSE*, 20, 1964, pp. 70–71.

24. Cecil Roth, 'Educational abuses and reforms in Hanoverian England', in his *Essays and Portraits in Anglo-Jewish History*, p. 220.

25. Stein, op. cit.; S. S. Levin, 'The origins of the Jews' Free School', *TJHSE*, 19, 1960, pp. 97–114.

26. V. D. Lipman, 'Sephardi and other Jewish immigrants in England in the eighteenth century', in Newman (ed.), op. cit., p. 40; Raphael Mahler, *A History of Modern Jewry: 1780–1815*, especially pp. 129–40 (Germany) and 279–91 (Poland); M. A. Shulvass, *From East to West: The Westward Migration of Jews from Eastern Europe during the Seventeenth and Eighteenth Centuries*.

27. George, op. cit., p. 360 n.60.

28. Ibid., p. 127.

29. Cecil Roth, *A History of the Jews in England*, pp. 235–36.

30. E. P. Thompson, 'Eighteenth century crime, popular movements and social control', *Bull. Soc. Study Labour Hist.*, no. 25, 1972, p. 10.

31. Barnett, *El Libro*, p. 112 (parenthesis in original); Hyamson, op. cit., p. 181.

32. Gerald Howson, *Thief-Taker General: The Rise and Fall of Jonathan Wild, passim*.

33. *Gentleman's Magazine*, 14, 1744, p. 104. Cordosa was executed for 'breaking out of Newgate', the other three for burglary.

34. L. Radzinowicz, *A History of the English Criminal Law and Its Administration from 1750*, vol. III, pp. 48–49; 'Vagrant Jews concerned with crime', *Cal. Home Office Reports of the Reign of George III: 1770–1772*, 1881, pp. 335–58.

35. A recent study is W. J. Shelton, *English Hunger and Social Disorders: A Study of Social Conflict during the First Decade of George III's Reign*. Also George Rudé, *Wilkes and Liberty*.

36. Richard Cobb, *Paris and Its Provinces, 1792–1802*.

37. Shulvass, op. cit., has details.

38. Daniel Mendoza, *The Memoirs of the Life of Daniel Mendoza*. See the edition edited by Paul Magriel. Endelman, op. cit., chap. 6, 'Pickpockets and pugilists'.

39. John Ford, *Prizefighting: The Art of Regency Boximania*, p. 36.

40. A. Rubens, 'The Jews of the Parish of St James, Duke's Place, in the City of London', in J. M. Shaftesley (ed.), *Remember the Days*, p. 186. He gives examples of Jews in receipt of poor relief.

41. A. Rubens, 'Portrait of Anglo-Jewry (1656–1836)', *TJHSE*, 19, 1960, p. 18.

42. J. S. Levi and G. F. J. Bergman, *Australian Genesis: Jewish Convicts and Settlers, 1788–1850*, p. 10.

43. J. J. Tobias, *Prince of Fences: The Life and Crimes of Ikey Solomons*. In fact, as Levi and Bergman, op. cit., show, the usual crime for which Jews were sentenced was theft.

44. Radzinowicz, op. cit., especially chap. 3, 'Patrick Colquhoun: his life and writings'.

45. Op. cit., *Letters on the Present State of the Jewish Poor in the Metropolis*.

46. Walter Harrison, *A New and Universal History, Description and Survey of the Cities of London and Westminster*, p. 549.

47. R. D. Barnett, 'Anglo-Jewry in the eighteenth century', in V. D. Lipman (ed.), *Three Centuries of Anglo-Jewish History*, p. 61.

48. Lipman, *Social History*, p. 13.

49. Barnett, *El Libro*, pp. 83–84.

50. Barnett, *Bevis Marks Records*, part I, pp. 16–20.

51. A. P. Arnold, 'A list of Jews and their households in London, extracted from the Census lists of 1695', *MJHSE*, part 6, 1962, pp. 73–141. See the discussion in Table 1 in chap. 2 for the compiler's allocation of those whose names he has selected as Jewish ('certain and probable' and 'doubtful'). He suggests that there were eight 'certain and probable' domestic servants and another eight 'doubtful' ones, one 'doubtful' apprentice and a 'doubtful' barber.

52. Hyamson, op. cit., p. 179. The Jewish merchants in Madras had Ashkenazi servants; G. Yogev, *Diamonds and Corals*, pp. 167–68.

53. Cecil Roth, *History of the Great Synagogue*, p. 70. Lists of names are in Cecil Roth, 'The membership of the Great Synagogue, London, to 1791', *MJHSE*, part 6, 1962, pp. 175–85.

54. R. D. Barnett, 'The travels of Moses Cassuto', in Shaftesley, op. cit., p. 103: 'The Jews have Protestants in their employ as maid-servants, waiters, servants, and coachmen, even as wet-nurses.'

55. Wolf, *Essays*, p. 195.

56. *Gentleman's Magazine*, 51, 1781, p. 595.

57. Lipman, in Newman (ed.), op. cit., p. 55. Polly Levi, a Jewess, was a servant of Lord George Gordon, a convert to Judaism, when he was in prison in the 1790s. Christopher Hibbert, *King Mob*, p. 185.

58. George, op. cit., p. 360 n.4.

59. Roth, 'Membership of the Great Synagogue', *passim*.

60. Arthur Barnett, *The Western Synagogue through Two Centuries (1761–1961)*, p. 21.

61. Ibid., pp. 30–31.

62. Ibid., pp. 41, 42, 46–48.

63. Ibid., p. 296.

64. I am grateful to Raphael Samuel for this information.

65. The Aliens list is printed in Newman, op. cit., pp. 47–58.

66. George, op. cit., p. 360 n.4. Henry Solomons, the father of Ikey Solomons, was a glass-engraver; Tobias, op. cit., pp. 2–3.

67. See the names extracted from F. J. Britten, *Old Clocks and Watches and their Makers*, in A. Rubens, 'Early Anglo-Jewish artists', *TJHSE*, 14, 1940, pp. 126–29.

68. E.g., Rubens, 'Jews of St James', pp. 202–3.

69. Rubens, *Anglo–Jewish Portraits*, pp. 119–23.

70. Roth, *Jews in England*, p. 291.

71. 'Apprentices of Great Britain: 1710–1773', *MJHSE*, part 7, 1970, pp. 145–57.

72. Hyamson, op. cit., p. 209.

73. Mendoza, op. cit., chap. 1. Endelman, op. cit., pp. 188–90, for some comments on apprenticeship. He notes that the fees required were high, thus reducing the numbers able to take out indentures.

74. A. Rubens, 'Jews and the English stage: 1667–1850', *TJHSE*, 24, 1975, pp. 151–70.

75. Wolf, *Essays*, p. 26.

76. George, op. cit., pp. 159–60.

77. G. H. Whitehill (ed.), *Bevis Marks Records*, part 3. This consists of extracts from the marriage contracts and of the civil marriage registers for the period 1837–1901; see especially p. 10.

78. Ibid., p. 13.

79. Thus Endelman, op. cit., p. 189, mentions the existence of Jewish artisans but much of his evidence about the lower-class Jews comes from the records of court cases and the craftsmen are less represented in them.

4   The Provinces, before the Railways

1. Millicent Rose, *The East End of London*, p. 41.

2. Rachel Daiches-Dubens, 'Eighteenth century Anglo-Jewry in and around Richmond, Surrey', *TJHSE*, 18, 1958, pp. 143–69; H. F. Finberg, 'Jewish residents in eighteenth-century Twickenham', *TJHSE*, 16, 1952, pp. 129–35. Other eighteenth-century places of residence near London, noted by V. D. Lipman, 'The rise of Jewish suburbia', *TJHSE*, 21, 1968, pp. 79–80, include Isleworth, Leyton, Morden, Mortlake, Roehampton, Stamford Hill, Stanmore, Stoke Newington, Teddington, Totteridge and Watford.

3. Cecil Roth, 'Jews in Oxford after 1290', *Oxoniensia*, 15, 1950, pp. 63–80; Edinburgh, see below; Dublin and other Irish towns, L. Hyman, *The Jews of Ireland: From Earliest Times to the Year 1910;* Ewell and Worcester (Sarah Athias and Samuel de Paz), 'Early Jewish holders of Bank of England stock (1694–1725)', *MJHSE*, part 6, 1962, pp. 146, 160.

4. The basic book is Cecil Roth, *The Rise of Provincial Jewry*, but more recent research is incorporated into this chapter. The best analysis is V. D. Lipman, 'The origins of provincial Anglo-Jewry', in A. Newman (ed.), 'Provincial Jewry in Victorian Britain'; Lipman's article includes a description and criticism of the discussion by Lucien Wolf which had held sway since it appeared in the early years of the century.

5. Alan Everitt, 'The food market of the English town', *Third International Conference on Economic History*, vol. I, p. 57.

6. L. D. Barnett (ed.), *El Libro de los Acuerdos*, p. 3, The Dublin community, noted in the early chap. of Hyman, op. cit., had mostly disappeared by 1730.

7. A. Levy, 'The origins of Scottish Jewry', *TJHSE*, 19, 1960, p. 137.

8. Cecil Roth, 'The membership of the Great Synagogue, London, to 1791', *MJHSE*, part 6, 1962, pp. 175–85.

9. E. Newman, 'Some new facts about the Portsmouth Jewish community', *TJHSE*, 17, 1953, pp. 251–68. The register is transcribed in translation on pp. 263–68.

10. Roth, *Provincial Jewry*, pp. 17–18.

11. *Leeds Intelligencer*, 11 April 1769, quoted in G. D. Lumb (ed.), 'Extracts from the "Leeds Intelligence" and the "Leeds Mercury" 1769–1776', *Pub. Thoresby Soc.*, 38, 1937, p. 3. 'Merchant' might mean anything. The news item cryptically refers to a projected meeting of creditors at Halifax, 'which will defeat the iniquitous Intention of certain Jews and other pretended Creditors'.

12. G. D. Guttentag, 'The beginnings of the Newcastle Jewish community', *TJHSE*, 25, 1977, pp. 4–5.

13. Roth, *Provincial Jewry*, p. 18.

14. David Spector, 'The Jews of Brighton, 1770–1900', *TJHSE*, 22, 1970, p. 42.

15. Lucien Wolf, *Essays in Jewish History*, p. 139 n.2.

16. *Gentleman's Magazine*, 1754, p. 44; ibid., 1760, p. 413.

17. Wolf, op. cit., p. 139 n.3.

18. Cecil Roth, 'The Portsmouth community and its historical background', *TJHSE*, 13, 1936, pp. 161–62.

19. H. P. Stokes, *Studies in Anglo-Jewish History*, p. 229 n.3. He says there were several such occasions.

20. *Gentleman's Magazine*, 1815, p. 376, quoted Roth, *Provincial Jewry*, p. 67.

21. Israel Finestein, 'The Jews of Hull: 1770–1870'. I am grateful to Judge Finestein for showing me a copy of his unpublished MS.

22. Roth, *Provincial Jewry*, pp. 74–75. A foreign visitor to Britain met Jewish pedlars in Bath and Bristol and in Pontypool and other Welsh villages; J. Rumney, 'Anglo-Jewry as seen through foreign eyes (1730–1830)', *TJHSE*, 13, 1936, p. 336.

23. Maurice Myers, 'Calendars of the coaching days', *TJHSE*, 5, 1908, pp. 219–25.

24. Israel J. Solomon, *Records of My Family*.

25. Henry Mayhew, *London Labour and the London Poor*, vol. I, p. 454.

26. An obscure reference on p. 113 suggests they were cousins of George Jessel, later Sir George, Master of the Rolls.

27. Cecil Roth, 'The Jew peddler—an 18th-century rural character', in his *Essays and Portraits in Anglo-Jewish History*, p. 132.

28. Alan Everitt, 'The county community', in E. W. Ives (ed.), *The English Revolution: 1600–1660*, pp. 59–61.

29. Relevant literature includes: R. B. Westerfield, *Middlemen in English Business, Particularly between 1660 and 1760;* Dorothy Davis, *A History of Shopping,* chap. 11, 'The Man with the Pack'; P. Mantoux, *The Industrial Revolution in the Eighteenth Century,* pp. 108–12; G. W. Daniels, *The Early English Cotton Industry,* p. 65 (for 'The Society of Travelling Scotchmen of Bridgnorth'); T. C. Smout, *A History of the Scottish People: 1560–1830,* p. 385 (for linen drapers: 'the occupation, often in Glasgow called "English merchant", was traditionally one in which a man of small means could start on a peddling trade'); J. H. Clapham, *An Economic History of Modern Britain: The Early Railway Age, 1820–1850,* pp. 219ff.; R. Lawton, 'The population of Liverpool in the mid-nineteenth century', *Trans. Hist. Soc. Lancs. and Cheshire,* 107, 1955, p. 97: the wives of dock-workers, mostly of Irish origin, 'swelled the "trade" sections in such occupations as "orange dealer".'

30. T. S. Ashton, *Economic Fluctuations in England: 1700–1800,* p. 10.

31. Eileen Cavanagh Davies, 'A chronological synopsis and index to Oxfordshire items in "Jackson's Oxford Journal", 1753–1780', 1967, unpublished MS, Bodleian Library, Oxford, R. Top. 731; Roth, 'Jews in Oxford', p. 75.

32. Z. Josephs, 'Jewish glass-makers', *TJHSE*, 25, 1977, p. 109.

33. M. Lissack, *Jewish Perseverance, or the Jew, at Home and Abroad: An Autobiography,* p. 80; see his obituary, *JC*, 18 January 1895, p. 11. The firm set up in business in London, probably in the 1880s, as wine merchants. See *JC*, 30 March 1883, p. 7, for a reference to J. M. Lissack Jnr leaving Bedford for London. That newspaper regularly carried notices by the company advertising its wine.

34. Alex M. Jacob, 'The Jews of Falmouth: 1740–1860', *TJHSE*, 17, 1953, pp. 63–72. Further details are in A. P. Joseph, 'Jewry of south-west England and some of its Australian connections', *TJHSE*, 24, 1975, pp. 24–37.

35. Bill Williams, *The Making of Manchester Jewry: 1740–1875,* p. 5.

36. Ibid.

37. Ibid., p. 8.

38. Roth, *Provincial Jewry,* p. 22.

39. 'Social acclimatization of Jews in eighteenth and nineteenth century Devon', in Roger Burt (ed.), *Industry and Society in the South-West,* pp. 62–63. However, a statement in a book of 1809 about Portsmouth implies perhaps a higher status for Jews there. 'Jew shopmen, taylors, and drapers jostle Christian pawnbrokers, watch-jobbers, and trinket merchants'; anon., *History of Portsmouth,* p. 8, quoted in Roth, 'Portsmouth', p. 163.

40. Many more people mentioned in the book have no occupation allocated to them. There is no way of knowing whether those with occupations are representative, but the constant repetition, from a variety of sources, of the same trades, is impressive evidence.

41. For Liverpool, see B. L. Benas, 'Records of the Jews in Liverpool', *Trans. Hist. Soc. Lancs. and Cheshire,* 51, 1901, pp. 45–84. Details of artists and engravers are in A. Rubens, 'Early

Anglo-Jewish artists', *TJHSE*, 14, 1940, pp. 91–129, and his 'Francis Town of Bond Street (1738–1826) and his family, with further notes on early Anglo-Jewish artists', *TJHSE*, 18, 1958, pp. 89–111. See also 'List of Jewish goldsmiths' in Rubens, 'Early artists', pp. 124–26 (it is not known if all those listed were Jews). For watch- and clock-makers see H. Miles Brown, *Cornish Clocks and Clockmakers*, pp. 70–71. Rubens, 'Early artists', appendix 2, is a list of Jewish watch- and clock-makers, sixteen being in the provinces. Roth, *Provincial Jewry*, mentions fourteen by name, of whom only seven are in Rubens's list. Many of these are identified by name, but other sources confirm they are Jews. It is possible there were more: G. H. Baillie, *Watchmakers and Clockmakers of the World*, contains many 'Jewish' names—Abrahams, Cohen, Samuel, Solomon and others—but I have not thought it useful to select them. We know neither that they were Jews nor that they actually made clocks and watches.

42. Roth, *Provincial Jewry*, index of names. These are examples only. There are others in the book.

43. V. D. Lipman, 'The Plymouth Aliens list 1798 and 1803', *MJHSE*, part 6, 1962, pp. 187–94; also, 'Sephardi and other Jewish immigrants in England in the eighteenth century', in A. Newman (ed.), *Migration and Settlement*, pp. 47–58.

44. B. Susser, *An Account of the Old Jewish Cemetery on Plymouth Hoe*, mentions a number of these.

45. S. Jones, 'Blood Red Roses: the supply of merchant seamen in the nineteenth century', *Mariner's Mirror*, 58(4), 1972, p. 436.

46. Jacob, op. cit., p. 69.

47. Roth, 'Portsmouth', p. 164.

48. I. S. Meisels, 'The Jewish congregation of Portsmouth (1766–1842)', *TJHSE*, 6, 1912, pp. 112–13.

49. P. 12.

50. P. 414.

51. See a list of navy agents in Roth, 'Portsmouth', pp. 183–87.

52. Jacob, op. cit., p. 69.

53. Susser, 'Social acclimatization of Jews', has pertinent comments on this subject.

54. Arthur Barnett, *The Western Synagogue through Two Centuries (1761–1961)*, pp. 118–19.

55. Cecil Roth, 'An eighteenth-century Jewish community in Colchester', *AJA Quarterly*, 3(2), 1957, p. 24. This article contains random notes on Jews in other provincial places.

56. Based on Josephs, 'Jewish glass-makers'. See also D. E. C. Eversley, in Victoria County History, *Warwickshire*, vol. 7, 1964, pp. 88, 105–6.

57. S. J. Prais, 'The development of Birmingham Jewry', *Jewish Monthly*, 2(11), 1949, pp. 665–79. *Wrightson's New Triennial Directory of Birmingham*, 1818, contains a number of possible Jewish names; e.g., Levi Aaron, watch-maker and pawnbroker; Abraham Abraham, factor; Abraham Solomon, M.D.; Moses Solomon, jeweller and pencil-maker.

58. Susser, *An Account of the Old Jewish Cemetery*, p. 17.

59. L. S. Pressnell, *Country Banking in the Industrial Revolution*, pp. 14, 37, 45. The subsequent analysis is based on this work. The only Jew mentioned in John Hughes, *Liverpool Banks and Bankers: 1760–1837*, is Barned (p. 34). Joseph Daltera (pp. 140–42) might have been Jewish, but it is unlikely. His son, also Joseph, was an attorney and notary but he is not mentioned in E. R. Samuel, 'Anglo-Jewish notaries and scriveners', *TJHSE*, 17, 1953, pp. 113–59. For Phillips, see *Dictionary of Welsh Biography down to 1940*, p. 761.

60. Roth, 'Colchester', p. 25.

61. Susser, *An Account of the Old Jewish Cemetery*, p. 26 (Nathan), p. 8 (Joseph).

5   The Middle Class: Industry, 1800–80

1. A. Newman (ed.), 'Provincial Jewry in Victorian Britain', *s.v.* Birmingham, gives 752; B. Williams, *The Making of Manchester Jewry: 1740–1875*, p. 356, gives 1,092.

2. The details of emancipation are given in H. S. Q. Henriques, *The Jews and the English law.*

3. Cecil Roth, 'The Jews in the English universities', *MJHSE,* part 4, 1942, pp. 102–15.

4. Newman, op. cit., includes a number of accounts of provincial communities.

5. P. G. Hall, *The Industries of London since 1861;* G. Stedman Jones, *Outcast London: A Study in the Relationship between Classes in Victorian Society;* F. Sheppard, *London, 1808–1870: The Infernal Wen;* F. Bédarida, 'Londres au milieu du XIXe siècle', *Annales,* 23(2), 1968, pp. 268–95.

6. C. C. Aronsfeld, 'German Jews in Victorian England', *Leo Baeck Year Book,* 7, 1962, pp. 312–29.

7. Robert Henriques, *Marcus Samuel, First Viscount Bearsted and Founder of the 'Shell' Trading and Transport Company; 1853–1927,* pp. 24–25.

8. S. M. Gollancz, *Biographical Sketches and Selected Verses,* p. 129.

9. V. D. Lipman, 'The age of emancipation: 1815–1880', in V. D. Lipman (ed.), *Three Centuries of Anglo-Jewish History,* pp. 86–87, for details of private schools. Also L. Hyman, 'Hyman Hurwitz: the first Anglo-Jewish professor', *TJHSE,* 21, 1968, p. 232.

10. Israel Finestein, *A Short History of Anglo-Jewry,* pp. 110–11; C. E. Cassell, 'The West Metropolitan Jewish school: 1845–1897', *TJHSE,* 19, 1960, pp. 124–28; A. M. Hyamson, *Jews' College, London: 1855–1955.*

11. Williams, op. cit., p. 330.

12. Ibid., pp. 25, 26, 336, 405.

13. P. L. S. Quinn, 'The Jewish schooling systems of London, 1656–1956', unpublished Ph.D. thesis, University of London, 1958, pp. 278–79, 430ff.

14. Arthur Barnett, 'Sussex Hall: the first Anglo-Jewish venture in popular education', *TJHSE,* 19, 1960, p. 77.

15. Williams, op. cit., p. 206.

16. Josephine Kamm, *Indicative Past: A Hundred Years of the Girls' Public Day School Trust,* p. 55. As Quinn shows, op. cit., 'The education of the wealthy Jewish girl', pp. 430ff., very few of this class got an education in the nineteenth century.

17. Viscount Samuel, *Memoirs,* p. 4. Quinn, op. cit., pp. 436–37, notes that some London schools, including Sir John Cass and Cowper Street schools, engaged teachers of Hebrew and Judaism in order to attract Jewish pupils.

18. Alexander Carlebach, 'The Rev. Dr Joseph Chotzner', *TJHSE,* 21, 1968, pp. 266–67; C. H. L. Emanuel, 'The Jewish House at Harrow: some recollections of the 'eighties', *JC,* 29 September 1938; A. I. Polack, 'Clifton and Anglo-Jewry', in N. G. L. Hammond (ed.), *Centenary Essays on Clifton College,* pp. 51–71.

19. *From a Biography of Myself,* p. ix. The *Jewish Chronicle,* 20 March 1874, referred to a Henriques serving in the Royal Artillery, and mentioned two commissioned officers named Leverson, and another, a Montefiore—a sum total of four.

20. V. D. Lipman, 'The rise of Jewish suburbia', *TJHSE,* 21, 1968, p. 78.

21. Williams, op. cit., p. 86.

22. Lipman, 'Rise of Jewish suburbia', for details; see also his 'Social topography of a London congregation: the Bayswater synagogue: 1863–1963', *Jew. J. Sociol.,* 6(1), July 1964, pp. 69–74. For a general statement about the relationship between the development of transport in London and areas of settlement according to social class, see Harold Pollins, 'Transport lines and social divisions', in Centre for Urban Studies (ed.), *London: Aspects of Change,* pp. 29–61.

23. Williams, op. cit., pp. 72–73, 85–86, 125–26, 298, 310.

24. Tova Benski, 'Glasgow', in Newman, 'Provincial Jewry'.

25. Williams, op. cit., pp. 358–60.

26. H. Perkin, *The Origins of Modern English Society: 1780–1880,* p. 71; also A. Raistrick, *Quakers in Science and Industry.* Other recent contributions are K. Samuelsson, *Religion and Economic Action,* and T. Burns and S. B. Saul (eds), *Social Theory and Social Change.*

27. T. S. Ashton and J. Sykes, *The Coal Industry of the Eighteenth Century,* pp. 1–6; A. R.

Griffin, *Mining in the East Midlands: 1550–1947*, part 1, chap. 2; J. H. Morris and L. J. Williams, *The South Wales Coal Industry: 1841–1875*, pp. 125ff.

28. T. S. Ashton, *Iron and Steel in the Industrial Revolution*, pp. 211–13. He also notes that many were Quakers.

29. F. Crouzet, 'Capital formation in Great Britain during the Industrial Revolution', in F. Crouzet (ed.), *Capital Formation in the Industrial Revolution*, pp. 162–222; Charlotte Erickson, *British Industrialists: Steel and Hosiery, 1850–1950*, especially chap. 4, 'Social Origins of the Nottingham Hosiers'.

30. For Jonassohn see Arnold Levy, *History of the Sunderland Jewish Community: 1755–1955*, chap. 5. The mining engineer was named Veiner and he contributed towards the improvement of the Sunderland synagogue. For Isaac, see Griffin, op. cit., pp. 104–5, and 'Tory's first Jewish M.P.', *JC*, 1 March 1974. For Ellis, see Arthur Barnett, *The Western Synagogue through Two Centuries*, pp. 89–90.

31. Jean Lindsay, *A History of the North Wales Slate Industry*, p. 84.

32. S. Pollard, 'The decline of shipbuilding on the Thames', *Econ. Hist. Rev.*, 3(1), 1950, pp. 72–89; Charles Hadfield, *Atmospheric Railways*. Another engineer was Nathan Defries, who invented a 'monster Gas Meter for the House of Lords'; *JC*, 9 February 1849, reprinted in W. Frankel, *Friday Nights: A 'Jewish Chronicle' Anthology: 1841–1971*, p. 247.

33. Dennis Rebbeck, 'The history of iron shipbuilding on the Queen's Island up to July, 1874', unpublished Ph.D. thesis, The Queen's University, Belfast, 1950; Hyman, Jews of Ireland, p. 209. Also P. L. Robertson, 'Shipping and shipbuilding: the case of William Denny and Brothers', *Business Hist.*, 16(1), 1974, p. 36.

34. For Martin Samuelson, see J. M. Bellamy, 'A Hull shipbuilding firm: the history of C. & W. Earle and Earle's Shipbuilding and Engineering Company Ltd.', *Business Hist.*, 6, 1963, p. 29. There are many references to Sir Bernhard Samuelson in *Cake and Cockhorse*, the journal of the Banbury Historical Society, for which turn he was M.P.

35. L. Girard, *La Politique des travaux publiques du Second Empire*; Bertrand Gille, *Histoire de la Maison Rothschild*; B. Ratcliffe, 'The origins of the Paris-Saint Germain railway', *J. Transport Hist.*, 1(4), 1972, pp. 197–219, and 2(1), 1973, pp. 20–40.

36. Harold Pollins, 'The Jews' role in the early British railways', *Jew. Soc. Stud.*, 15(1), 1953, pp. 53–62. For general background see Harold Pollins, *Britain's Railways: An Industrial History*, and M. C. Reed, *Investment in Railways in Britain, 1820–1844: A Study in the Development of the Capital Market*.

37. For the origins of the Rothschild family see R. Ehrenberg, *Grosse Vermoegen: ihre Entstehung und ihre Bedeutung: Fugger-Rothschild-Krupp*; C. W. Berghoeffer, *Meyer Amschel Rothschild: der Gründer des Rothschildschen Bankhauses*. The best account of Nathan Mayer's early years in England is S. D. Chapman, *The Foundation of the English Rothschilds: N. M. Rothschild as a Textile Merchant, 1799–1811*, which is based on the firm's archives. (This is virtually identical with Dr Chapman's article, with the same title, in *Textile Hist.*, 8, 1977, pp. 99–115.)

38. S. D. Chapman, 'The international houses: the continental contribution to British commerce: 1800–1860', *J. European Econ. Hist.*, 6(1), 1977, pp. 5–48, for a general statement on foreign firms, Jewish and non-Jewish, in Britain.

39. Arthur Schuster, *Biographical Fragments*, pp. 4–5. The family had been importers of English cotton goods.

40. Williams, op. cit., p. 22.

41. S. D. Chapman, *The Cotton Industry in the Industrial Revolution*, pp. 48–49. A more specialised study, which Chapman uses in his briefer survey, is M. M. Edwards, *The Growth of the British Cotton Trade: 1780–1815*.

42. Williams, op. cit., p. 81.

43. D. C. M. Platt, 'Further objections to an "Imperialism of Free Trade"': 1830–60', *Econ. Hist. Rev.*, 26(1), 1973, pp. 86–87.

44. A. M. Hyamson, *The Sephardim of England*, pp. 358–59. The first President of the congregation was Isaac D. Belisha, grandfather of Leslie Hore-Belisha, the National Liberal Cabinet Minister of the 1930s. Also Williams, op. cit., pp. 319–42.

45. Williams, op. cit., pp. 23–24.

46. Ibid., p. 82.

47. Ibid., p. 87.

48. Ibid., p. 360.

49. F. E. Hyde, B. B. Parkinson and S. Marriner, 'The cotton broker and the rise of the Liverpool cotton market', *Econ. Hist. Rev.*, 8(1), 1955, pp. 75–83. The names are printed in T. Ellison, *The Cotton Trade of Great Britain*, p. 171 (for the earliest brokers), p. 182 (for the ninety firms which formed the Liverpool Cotton Brokers' Association on its foundation in 1841), and pp. 352–55 (for the members of the Association on its amalgamation with the Liverpool Cotton Exchange in the 1880s). None of them appears to be Jewish.

50. Arthur Behrend, *Portrait of a Family Firm*. The firm's records were lost during air raids in World War II, and the early history is not known. The first Behrend to join the firm did so in 1835, but he had been a shipbroker on his own before then.

51. E. M. Sigsworth, *Black Dyke Mills: A History*, p. 66, which quotes *Sir Jacob Behrens: 1806–1889*, a privately printed memoir. For the general financial background see A. J. Topham, 'The credit structure of the West Riding wool-textile industry in the 19th century', unpublished M. A. thesis, University of Leeds, 1953.

52. Sigsworth, op. cit., pp. 64ff. He refers to their 'holding meetings of their Schillerverein, sending their sons to fight for the Fatherland in the Franco-Prussian war'.

53. A. R. Rollin, 'The Jewish contribution to the British textile industry: "builders of Bradford" ', *TJHSE*, 17, 1960, pp. 45–51; Robert Speaight, *William Rothenstein: The Portrait of an Artist in His Own Time*.

54. D. E. Varley, *A History of the Midland Counties Lace Manufacturers' Association: 1915–1958*, p. 86. His statements and those in J. D. Chambers, 'Victorian Nottingham', *Trans. Thoroton Soc. of Nottingham*, 63, 1959, pp. 4–5, are based on the researches of C. C. Aronsfeld, 'Nottingham's lace pioneers', *Nottingham Guardian Journal*, 19 and 20 April 1954. The other names given are Moritz Jacoby, Jacob Weinberg (founder of Simon, May & Co.), Bernard Stiebel, Josef Neuberg, Moritz Dann, L. Jacobsen, Fleirsheim, Feilmann & Co., Liepmann, Kohn & Co., Lowenstein, Polack & Co., and Albert Cahn.

55. R. A. Church, *Economic and Social Change in a Midland Town: Victorian Nottingham, 1815–1900*, pp. 76–77, 352, 363, 371.

56. C. C. Aronsfeld, 'German Jews in Dundee', *JC*, 20 November 1953 and 'German Jews in Ireland', *AJR Information*, December 1953; Hyman, *Jews of Ireland*, pp. 204–8, who refers also to other Jewish linen firms in Belfast and Dundee.

57. J. M. Cohen, *Life of Ludwig Mond*; S. Koss, *Sir John Brunner: Radical Plutocrat;* W. J. Reader, *Imperial Chemical Industries: A History*, vol. I: *The Forerunners, 1870–1926*, especially chap. 3, 'Alkali in Cheshire'. See also R. H. Kargon, *Science in Victorian Manchester: Enterprise and Expertise*, for references to Jewish scientists.

58. C. C. Aronsfeld, 'Great Jewish chemists', *Jewish Telegraph*, 18 December 1953; Paul H. Emden, *Jews of Britain*, p. 276.

59. Emden, op. cit., pp. 254–55.

60. A. Rive, 'The consumption of tobacco since 1600', *Econ. Hist.* (supplement to *Econ. J.*), 1, 1926, p. 64.

61. D. J. Richardson, 'The history of the catering industry with special reference to the development of J. Lyons and Co. Ltd. to 1939', unpublished Ph. D. thesis, University of Kent at Canterbury, 1970, for Salmon & Gluckstein; Emden, op. cit., pp. 548–49.

62. *Tobacco Times*, 23 March 1895, p. 36. This trade journal contains a number of references to Jewish manufacturers and merchants.

63. C. Booth (ed.), *Life and Labour of the People in London*, vol. IV. pp. 220–21.

64. B. W. E. Alford, *W. D. & H. O. Wills and the Development of the U. K. Tobacco Industry: 1786–1965*, p. 130. For Jewish manufacturers in Dublin see Hyman, *Jews of Ireland*, pp. 133, 144, 245, 247.

65. Alford, op. cit., p. 130. Booth, op. cit., p. 221, noted that the earlier differentiation between Jewish cigar-makers and Gentile cigarette-makers no longer held in the 1880s. Some details of a firm of wholesale cigar merchants and pipe manufacturers are in Gilbert Frankau, *Self-Portrait: A Novel of His Own Life*, pp. 16, 24, 99.

66. 12 July 1867, p. 2.

67. E.g., Nathan Harris, cap-maker, and David Soman, boot- and shoe-maker in the 1830s in Norwich: Henry Levine, *The Norwich Hebrew Congregation, 1840–1960: A Short History*, pp. 5–6.

68. Fourth Report of the Children's Employment Commission, *PP*, 1865, 20, p. xxxiv.

69. Asa Briggs, *Friends of the People: The Centenary History of Lewis's*, pp. 30, 43. The illustration of the workshop, opposite p. 111, includes a statement—in an advertisement—that the firm employed 600 workmen in 1880.

70. *JC*, 1 March 1901, obituary notice; Levine, op. cit., pp. 17–19.

71. Samuel Flatau, *A. & W. Flatau & Co. Ltd.*, *Henry Playfair Ltd.*, *Metropolitan Boot Co. Ltd.: Foundation and History, 120 Years*, Guildhall Library.

72. P. K. Newman, 'The early London clothing trades', *Oxf. Econ. Papers*, 4(2), 1952, pp. 243–51.

73. *The Times*, 15 December 1843, editorial.

74. E. P. Thompson and E. Yeo (eds), *The Unknown Mayhew*, p. 150.

75. Newman, op. cit.; Williams, op. cit., pp. 69–71.

76. Thompson and Yeo, op. cit., p. 236.

77. Williams, op. cit., pp. 69–71.

78. *The Times*, 31 October 1843, p. 3.

79. Thompson and Yeo, op. cit., p. 41.

80. For Moses see F. Boase, *Modern British Biography*, vol. II, p. 750 (*s.v.*, Isaac Moses Marsden, d. 1884). The Hyam business was founded by Hyam Hyam, who began at Bury St Edmunds and then moved to Colchester. His various sons, except for Simon, opened their own businesses—Benjamin in Manchester, for example. Samuel went to Birmingham about 1836 and opened a business in Leeds a few years later before coming to Oxford Street in London in 1849 (see his obituary in *JC*, 8 May 1891, p. 9). The youngest son, who changed his name to Halford, went into his father's business (obituary, *JC*, 29 March 1901, p. 10). Other details are to be found in 'Prospectus of Hyam & Co. (1900) Ltd.', Bodleian Library, Oxford, 232865 b 4; Williams, op. cit., pp. 67–69, 113–15.

81. Williams, op. cit., p. 69.

82. Ibid., p. 68.

83. Ibid., p. 115. Also Briggs, op. cit., pp. 28–29; Hyman, *Jews of Ireland*, p. 137.

84. 27 October 1843, p. 4. The lawsuit was reported on 26 October.

85. *The Times*, 31 October 1843, p. 3.

86. *Northern Star*, 24 February 1844.

87. [J. Burn], *Commercial Enterprise and Social Progress*, p. 56.

88. W. H. Chaloner, 'The birth of modern Manchester', in C. F. Carter (ed.), *Manchester and Its Region*, p. 141.

89. Joan Thomas, 'A history of the Leeds clothing industry', *Yorks. Bulletin of Econ. and Soc. Research*, Occasional Paper no. 1, 1955, p. 14, lists twenty-one firms in 1881, very few of which were Jewish. See also Joseph Buckman, 'The economic and social history of alien immigrants to Leeds: 1880–1914', unpublished Ph.D. thesis, University of Strathclyde, 1968, chap. 1, for early Jewish firms.

6 Trade, Finance and the Professions, 1800–80

1. J. B. Jefferys, *Retail Trading in Britain: 1850–1950*, pp. 1ff.
2. A. Newman (ed.), 'Provincial Jewry in Victorian Britain', *s.v.* Hull.
3. A. Temple Patterson, *A History of Southampton: 1700–1914*, vol. II: *The Beginnings of Modern Southampton: 1836–1867*, p. 41.
4. Jefferys, op. cit., p. 416.
5. Gwen Hart, *A History of Cheltenham*, p. 239. The occupations of eleven Jewish residents are given. The others were a surgeon-dentist, the owner of the Fleece Hotel, two pawnbrokers, and a book-seller. The eleventh was a 'Gentleman'.
6. Bill Williams, *The Making of Manchester Jewry: 1740–1875*, p. 113.
7. Ibid., p. 359. Nine of the twenty-four food shops were run by women.
8. Newman, op. cit., *s.v.* Brighton.
9. Ibid., *s.v.* Birmingham.
10. Williams, op. cit., pp. 33, 359.
11. Select Committee on the Observance of the Sabbath Day, *PP*, 1831–32, 7, q. 445.
12. J. S. Levi and G. F. J. Bergman, *Australian Genesis: Jewish Convicts and Settlers, 1788–1850*, p. 11.
13. Henry Mayhew, *London Labour and the London Poor*, vol. I, pp. 106–7, 'How the street-Irish supplanted the street-Jews in the orange trade'.
14. Select Committee on Sunday Trading (Metropolis), *PP*, 1847, 9, q. 1250. Mayhew, op. cit., vol. II, pp. 26ff., describes the Old Clothes Exchange, as well as another belonging to the Jewish firm of Levy & Simmons.
15. Select Committee on Sunday Trading, q. 1251.
16. Mayhew, op. cit., vol. I, pp. 86–91. Also Select Committee on the Observance of the Sabbath Day, qq. 2177–79, for an earlier reference.
17. *Studies in Jewish Statistics, Social, Vital and Anthropometric*. His first guess was 3,000 (p. 13) and he reduced this to 2,500 (p. 17). The analysis based on the *Post Office Directory* is on pp. 33–38, the number of 'tradesmen' being on p. 35.
18. Some details about wholesaling are in Jefferys, op. cit., pp. 10–14, 381–82. He notes the problem of making generalisations about a diverse system. Also Dorothy Davis, *A History of Shopping*, pp. 256ff. For the Faudel-Phillips family see Paul H. Emden, *Jews of Britain*, pp. 218–22.
19. Warren Tute, *The Grey Top Hat: The Story of Moss Bros of Covent Garden*.
20. Williams, op. cit., p. 119.
21. Ibid., p. 358.
22. A possible total for the number of shops can be established from the assessments under the Inhabited Houses Duty, using shops of a value of £20 or more. The average for the years 1879–82, in England and Wales, was 86 per 10,000 population. London's population was just under 4.25 million, giving about 37,000 shops. For the calculations see Jefferys, op. cit., p. 15 n.1. This method probably underestimates the number of shops, as Jefferys points out. In that case the Jewish proportion would be smaller.
23. W. B. Whitaker, *Victorian and Edwardian Shopworkers*, has many examples. Brian Harrison, 'The Sunday trading riots of 1855', *Hist. J.*, 8(2), pp. 219–45, has only one reference to Jews. Neither is there any mention of them in the section on Sunday trading in J. M. Wigley, 'Nineteenth century English sabbatarianism: a study of a religious, political and social phenomenon', unpublished Ph.D. thesis, University of Sheffield, 1972, pp. 253ff., but they are referred to in the Select Committee on Sunday Trading (Metropolis), *PP*, 1847, 9, qq. 421, 1086, 1088.
24. For histories of distribution see, in addition to Jefferys, op. cit., and Davis, op. cit., Alison Adburgham, *Shops and Shopping 1800–1914: Where, and in What Manner the Well-Dressed Englishwoman Bought Her Clothes;* Julia Hood and B. S. Yamey, 'The middle-class co-operative retailing societies in London, 1864–1900', *Oxf. Econ. Papers*, 9(3), 1957, pp. 309–22.

25. B. L. Benas, 'Records of the Jews in Liverpool', *Trans. Hist. Soc. Lancs. and Cheshire*, 51, 1901, pp. 75–76.

26. Arthur Behrend, *Portrait of a Family Firm, passim*.

27. Newman, op. cit., *s.v.* Birmingham and Bristol.

28. Jacobs, op. cit., pp. 35–38. The wholesale cigar merchants, J. Frankau & Co., was founded in 1837 to import leeches from France and changed to importing sponges before entering the tobacco business. Gilbert Frankau, *Self-Portrait*, pp. 2, 53.

29. Robert Henriques, *Marcus Samuel, First Viscount Bearsted and Founder of the 'Shell' Transport and Trading Company: 1853–1927*. The quotation is on p. 61. The pre-oil era is described in chap. 1 and 2. Also F. E. Hyde, *Far Eastern Trade: 1860–1914*.

30. Based on David Landes, *Bankers and Pashas*, chap. 1. See also M. G. Buist, *At Spes non Fracta: Hope & Co., 1770–1815, Merchant Bankers and Diplomats at Work;* R. Tilly, 'Germany 1815–1870', in R. Cameron (ed.), *Banking in the Early Stages of Industrialisation;* J. P. Wechsberg, *The Merchant Bankers;* H. Kupferberg, *The Mendelssohns;* David Farrer, *The Warburgs*.

31. S. D. Chapman, *The Foundation of the English Rothschilds: N. M. Rothschild as a Textile Merchant, 1799–1811*, p. 20.

32. Details are in J. H. Clapham, 'Loans and subsidies in time of war: 1793–1814', *Econ. J.*, 22, 1917, pp. 495–501; Paul H. Emden, 'The brothers Goldsmid and the financing of the Napoleonic Wars', *TJHSE*, 14, 1940, pp. 225–46; S. R. Cope, 'The Goldsmids and the development of the London money market during the Napoleonic Wars', *Economica*, 9, 1942, pp. 180–206; K. Helleiner, *The Imperial Loans;* J. M. Sherwig, *Guineas and Gunpowder: British Foreign Aid in the Wars with France, 1793–1815*. The stockjobber and economist, David Ricardo, was also a contractor. He married a Quaker in 1792 and thereafter was not associated with the Jewish community.

33. S. D. Chapman, 'The international houses: the continental contribution to British commerce: 1800–1860', *J. European Econ. Hist.*, 6(1), 1977, p. 12. For other non-Jewish immigrant merchant bankers see Emden, *Jews of Britain*, p. 497. For Walter Boyd, see J. H. Clapham, *The Bank of England: A History*, vol. II, pp. 16ff.

34. The main source for the Herries-Rothschild relationship is Edward Herries, *Memoirs of the Public Life of John S. Herries;* other details are in Sherwig, op. cit. The export of gold guineas by Nathan to his brother James apparently began in 1811, and is described by Bertrand Gille, *Histoire de la Maison Rothschild*, vol. I, pp. 45ff., and by F. Crouzet, *L'Economie britannique et le blocus continental (1806–1813)*, p. 842 n.80.

35. Landes, op. cit., p. 12.

36. Helleiner, op. cit., has full details of the loans.

37. R. W. Hidy, *The House of Baring in American Trade and Finance*, p. 54.

38. Chapman, *Foundation of the English Rothschilds*, p. 20.

39. Ronald Palin, *Rothschild Relish*, p. 27.

40. Lucien Wolf first published his refutation in newspaper articles in 1909 and 1913 (reprinted in his *Essays in Jewish History*, pp. 276–86). Other recent writers follow Wolf: Elizabeth Longford, *Wellington: Pillar of State*, pp. 7–8; Virginia Cowles, *The Rothschilds: A Family of Fortune*, pp. 47–50, which contains a few more details. But the old version is given in Hamish MacRae and Frances Cairncross, *Capital City: London as a Financial Centre*, p. 55n. The story was popularised by John Reeves, *The Rothschilds: the Financial Rulers of Nations*, pp. 169–75, a book rightly dismissed as worthless by Wolf, op. cit., p. 279, but surprisingly praised by Gille, op. cit., vol. I, p. 9.

41. This is true even of such a good writer as L. H. Jenks, *The Migration of British Capital to 1875*, e.g., p. 44.

42. This is not to deny that the Rothschilds certainly did engage in arbitrage operations between London, Paris and Berlin, for which their excellent intelligence service was crucial. See Fritz Stern, *Gold and Iron: Bismarck, Bleichröder, and the Building of the German Empire*, p. 7.

43. Clapham, *Bank of England*, vol. II, pp. 80–81, 95, 117, 143–44, 280, for sundry details. G. Walshe, *Recent Trends in Monopoly in Great Britain*, pp. 82–83.

44. Hidy, op. cit., p. 125.

45. Charles Buxton (ed.), *Memoirs of Sir Thomas Fowell Buxton*, p. 289.

46. Emden, *Jews of Britain*, pp. 171–74, for the Alliance Assurance Co., which corrects earlier versions about its formation; ibid. p. 108 (Canal Co.); and p. 112 (Owen). For the last of these, see *The Life of Robert Owen, Written by Himself*, pp. 182–83 and 211.

47. R. S. Sayers, *Gilletts in the London Money Market: 1867–1967*, pp. 40ff. These are the only figures given for this period.

48. *Lombard Street: A Description of the Money Market*, p. 203.

49. Emden, *Jews of Britain*, pp. 107ff., 228–36, 495–501. Also his *Money Powers of Europe*, *passim*.

50. Pp. 421–44.

51. *JC*, 29 March 1972.

52. E. V. Morgan and W. A. Thomas, *The Stock Exchange*, pp. 103–4, based on Jenks, op. cit., appendix C. The latter notes, p. 280, that his figures were not exhaustive and did not, for example, include funds raised privately. They would not cover, therefore, the money channelled by Scottish solicitors to Australia, altogether outside the scope of the London money market; J. D. Bailey, 'Australian borrowing in Scotland in the nineteenth century', *Econ. Hist. Rev.*, 12(2), 1959, pp. 268–79.

53. L. Hyman, *The Jews of Ireland: From Earliest Times to the Year 1910*, pp. 103–4, for Gotheimer. P. L. Cottrell, 'Investment banking in England: case study of the International Financial Society', unpublished Ph.D. thesis, University of Hull, 1974, an examination of one field in which a few Jews were involved. Some parts of the thesis have been published: 'The financial sector and economic growth: England in the nineteenth century', *Int. J. Econ. and Soc. Hist.*, 1, 1972, pp. 64–84; 'London financiers and Austria, 1863–75: the Anglo-Austrian Bank', *Business Hist.*, 11, 1969, pp. 106–19; 'Anglo-French financial co-operation', *J. European Econ. Hist.*, 3(1), 1974, pp. 54–84.

54. Emden, *Jews of Britain*, pp. 495–501.

55. Op. cit., pp. 16–28. He qualifies some of his argument on pp. 28–32.

56. Dolores Greenberg, 'Yankee financiers and the establishment of trans-Atlantic partnerships: a re-examination', *Business Hist.*, 16(1), 1974, p. 34. She criticises, *inter alia*, the view expressed by B. E. Supple, 'A business elite: German-Jewish bankers in nineteenth century New York', *Business Hist. Rev.*, 31, 1957, pp. 157–76.

57. R. E. Cameron, 'French financiers and Italian unity: the Cavourian decade', *Amer. Hist. Rev.*, 62(3), 1957, p. 565.

58. R. E. Cameron, 'Papal finance and the temporal power: 1815–1871', *Church Hist.*, 26(2), 1957, pp. 4, 7.

59. D. C. M. Platt, *Finance, Trade and Politics in British Foreign Policy: 1815–1914*, p. 42.

60. There are many references to the association between Disraeli and the Rothschilds in W. F. Monypenny and G. E. Buckle, *The Life of Benjamin Disraeli, Earl of Beaconsfield*. The relatively few in Agatha Ramm, *The Political Correspondence of Mr Gladstone and Lord Granville: 1876–1886*—to take one example—show that they had much less to do with Gladstone. Lord Rothschild, *'You Have It Madam': The Purchase, in 1875, of Suez Canal Shares by Disraeli and Baron Lionel de Rothschild*.

61. *The History of 'The Times'*, vol. II: *The Tradition Established, 1841–1884*, pp. 332–33; W. F. F. Grace, 'Russia and *The Times* in 1863 and 1873', *Camb. Hist. J.*, 1(1), 1923, p. 95.

62. Op. cit., vol. II, especially the chapter 'Les hommes', pp. 591–616. Unfortunately this volume, which covers the period 1848–70, has very little on the London House.

63. Ramm, op. cit., vol. II, p. 302.

64. Evelyn Sharp, *Hertha Ayrton*.

65. V. D. Lipman, *A Century of Social Service, 1859–1959*, pp. 1—3: the chairman, Ephraim

Alex, was a dentist, Algernon Edward Sydney was a solicitor and Jacob Waley was the barrister and economist.

66. For the offspring of wealthy families in the legal profession see Israel Finestein, 'Sir George Jessel: 1824–1883', *TJHSE*, 18, 1958, pp. 243–83; Lord Justice Cohen, 'Levi Barent Cohen and some of his descendants', *TJHSE*, 16, 1952, pp. 11–23; A. L. Goodhart, *Five Jewish Lawyers of the Common Law*; B. B. Benas, 'Jacob Waley (1818–1873)', *TJHSE*, 18, 1958, pp. 41–52.

67. Jacobs, op. cit., p. 37.

68. Williams, op. cit., p. 359.

69. Newman, op. cit., *s.v.* Birmingham, Bristol and Swansea. Z. Josephs, *Birmingham Jewry, 1749–1914*, chap. 5, 'The Professions'.

70. C. P. Hershon, 'Genesis of a Jewish day school', in Newman, op. cit.

71. 24 July 1874.

72. Newman, op. cit., *s.v.* Birmingham and Manchester. Williams, op. cit., p. 359.

73. Hyman, *Jews of Ireland*, chap. 18, 'Dublin Jews in the Liberal Professions (1830–1900)'; Newman, op. cit., *s.v.* Swansea. J. Wilson, *A History of the Durham Miners' Association: 1870–1904*, refers to I. Isaacs of Sunderland, who acted as solicitor to the Association and was clerk to the Castle Eden magistrates.

74. M. Hyman Isaacs, 'John Isaacs—actor, and his family', *Jewish Monthly*, 3(4), 1949, pp. 239–44.

75. A. Tropp, *The Schoolteachers, passim,* but especially pp. 94–95, 147–50, for the social origins of teachers. There were said to be twenty-two Jewish schoolteachers in the 1840s: *J. Stat. Soc.*, 6, 1843, pp. 213–14.

7   The Working Population, 1800–80

1. *Jewish Fate and Future*, p. 135.

2. Asher I. Myers (comp.), *The Jewish Directory for 1874*, p. 130.

3. 10 October 1845, reprinted in W. Frankel, *Friday Nights: A 'Jewish Chronicle' Anthology, 1841–1971*, pp. 3–4.

4. L. Loewe (ed.), *Diaries of Sir Moses and Lady Montefiore*, vol. I, pp. 75, 80. Cf. a police report of 1831 of the same district: 'Inhabited by Jews who are very dirty, the Place is seldom cleansed by Scavengers, and all sorts of Filth may be seen all day in the Street'; Public Record Office, PC 1/114, 22 July 1831 (supplied by Raphael Samuel).

5. C. H. L. Emanuel, *A Century and a Half of Jewish History, Extracted from the Minute Books of the London Committee of Deputies of the British Jews*, pp. 56–57.

6. B. Susser (ed.), 'Statistical accounts of all the congregations in the British Empire 5606/1845', in A. Newman (ed.), 'Provincial Jewry in Victorian Britain'. Also Miriam Anne Steiner, 'Philanthropic activity and organization in the Manchester Jewish community: 1867–1914', unpublished M.A. thesis, University of Manchester, 1974. Other details about Manchester are in Bill Williams, *The Making of Manchester Jewry*.

7. L. Hyman, *The Jews of Ireland: From Earliest Times to the Year 1910*, p. 158.

8. *JC*, 25 December 1857, p. 13.

9. Ibid., 8 February 1867, p. 5. A letter in the previous week's issue referred to a twelve-year-old Leeds girl named Hyams who, along with two non-Jewish girls, stole from a shop. The writer proposed the establishment of a Jewish reformatory.

10. [Cecil Roth], *'Jewish Chronicle' 1841–1941: A Century of Newspaper History*, p. 5.

11. V. D. Lipman, *A Century of Social Service, 1859–1959: The Jewish Board of Guardians*, pp. 13–20, and *Social History of the Jews in England: 1850–1950*, pp. 52–53, for a list of charitable organisations. Israel Finestein, 'Anglo-Jewish opinion during the struggle for emancipation (1828–1858)', *TJHSE*, 20, 1964, p. 127, speaks of more than fifty charities 'judging by contemporary reports in the Jewish press'. For Jews and the Poor Law see Lipman, *Social Service*, pp. 10–13,

and A. Rubens, 'The Jews of the Parish of St James, Duke's Place, in the City of London', in J. M. Shaftesley (ed.), *Remember the Days,* p. 186. For private charity see [Roth], op. cit., pp. 19, 49.

12. G. Best, *Mid-Victorian Britain: 1851–75,* p. 121.

13. 'Degraded': Twelfth Report of the London Society for Promoting Christianity among the Jews, quoted in S. S. Levin, 'The origins of the Jews' Free School', *TJHSE,* 19, 1960, p. 113; 'almost bordering on barbarism': Report of the House Committee of the Jews' Hospital, August 1830 (referring to earlier years); quoted in E. S. Conway, 'The origins of the Jewish Orphanage', *TJHSE,* 22, 1970, p. 56; 'moral and social degradation': letter to the *Voice of Jacob,* 22 December 1843, quoted in Arthur Barnett, 'Sussex Hall: the first Anglo-Jewish venture in popular education', *TJHSE,* 19, 1960, p. 66.

14. P. L. S. Quinn, 'The Jewish schooling systems of London: 1656–1956', unpublished Ph.D. thesis, University of London, 1958, p. 256.

15. 20 October 1854, quoted in Finestein, op. cit., pp. 128–29.

16. Lipman, *Social History,* pp. 45–49; Quinn, op. cit.; C. P. Hershon, 'The evolution of Jewish elementary education in England with special reference to Liverpool', unpublished Ph.D. thesis, University of Sheffield, 1973; Arthur Barnett, *The Western Synagogue through Two Centuries (1761–1961),* chap. 10, 'The Westminster Jews' Free School'.

17. *JC,* 18 March 1859, p. 5.

18. Lipman, *Social Service,* p. 34; also Barnett, op. cit., chap. 11, 'Social and Philanthropic Activities'. The *Jewish Chronicle,* 12 January 1872, noted the large number of poor London Jews living outside the East End in such places as Saffron Hill, the Strand, Seven Dials and 'especially' Soho. It noted too the poor who lived in the prosperous districts of Bayswater, Chelsea and Westminster.

19. Colquhoun, *A Treatise on Indigence,* quoted in M. E. Rose, *The English Poor Law: 1780–1930,* p. 47.

20. Quoted in Lipman, *Social Service,* pp. 5–6.

21. Raphael Mahler, *A History of Modern Jewry: 1780–1815,* p. 78, gives a Jewish population of 24,000 in Amsterdam at the end of the eighteenth century; ibid., pp. 79–81, for a brief description of economic conditions of Dutch Jews at that period.

22. A. R. Rollin, 'Russo-Jewish immigrants in England before 1881', *TJHSE,* 21, 1968, pp. 202–13. Also Mieczyslaw Paskiowicz, 'Aliens' certificates in the Public Record Office: Polonica (1826–1852)', *Antemurale,* 19, 1975, pp. 159–263, prints the names of some 3,000 Poles who entered Britain, including many with Jewish names.

23. Emanuel, op. cit., pp. 75, 79. For the general background, see A. Chouraqui, *Les Juifs d'Afrique du Nord,* especially pp. 91–98.

24. A. M. Hyamson, *The Sephardim of England,* pp. 332, 334. No figures are given. Cf. the statement made by the vice-president of the Western Jewish Philanthropic Society, that the foreign poor came to Britain to get charity 'in order to save the donors the trouble of sending it'; Barnett, op. cit., p. 138.

25. *PP,* 1840, 23, p. 112, quoted in Lipman, *Social History,* p. 31.

26. Op. cit., vol. I, pp. 106–7. There are other examples in his book.

27. Lipman, *Social Service,* p. 18.

28. Levin, op. cit., pp. 108–9.

29. Lipman, *Social History,* p. 31. His source is *JC,* 13 June 1851.

30. S. Stein, 'Some Ashkenazi charities in London at the end of the eighteenth and the beginning of the nineteenth centuries', *TJHSE,* 20, 1964, p. 77; also A. Highmore, *Philanthropia Metropolitana: A View of the Charitable Institutions Established in or near London Chiefly during the Last Twelve Years,* pp. 276–79.

31. Quinn, op. cit., pp. 321ff. for pupil-teachers, and p. 327 for girls as domestic servants.

32. Ibid., p. 192b.

33. Ibid., pp. 184–94, for contemporary criticisms of residential apprentice training.

34. See the excellent analysis in D. C. Coleman, *The Domestic System in Industry.*

35. E. P. Thompson, *The Making of the English Working Class*, pp. 251, 258.

36. Tailors: 'Report by Dr Edward Smith on the Sanitary Circumstances of Tailors in London', appendix 12 to 6th Report of the Medical Officer of Health to the Privy Council, *PP*, 1863, 28, p. 416; footwear: P. G. Hall, 'The East London footwear industry: an industrial quarter in decline', *East London Papers*, 5(1), 1962, pp. 3–21; furniture: J. Leonard Oliver, 'The East London furniture industry', *East London Papers*, 4(2), 1961, p. 96. Also F. Sheppard, *London, 1808–1870: the Infernal Wen*, pp. 168–74.

37. Lipman, *Social Service*, pp. 67–69.

38. G. H. Whitehill (ed.), *Bevis Marks Records*, part 3, p. 10.

39. Joseph Jacobs, *Studies in Jewish Statistics, Social, Vital and Anthropometric*, pp. 39–40.

40. Lipman, *Social Service*, p. 84.

41. Op. cit., vol. I, p. 442.

42. Second Report of the Children's Employment Commission, *PP*, 1843, 15, appendix 1, F 278; Fourth Report of the Children's Employment Commission, *PP*, 1865, 20, pp. 80–93; Report of the Factory and Workshop Acts Commission, *PP*, 1876, 30, q. 1068.

43. *Seventy Years of Life and Labor*, chap. 1.

44. Harold Pollins, 'Jews on strike', *JC*, 4 January 1974. Perhaps the earliest reference to a Jewish trade unionist, and one of some temporary importance, was in the preceding decade. Samuel Jacobs, a cabinet-maker, was secretary of the Bristol branch of the Cabinet Makers' Society, secretary of the United Trades of Bristol, and then a 'roving missionary' of the National United Trades Association and based in Scotland. For the recent resurrection of this man, and his place in labour history, see Michael A. Shepherd, 'The origins and incidence of the term "Labour aristocracy" ', *Bull, Soc. Study Lab. Hist.*, no. 37, 1978, pp. 51–55.

45. Report of the Factory and Workshop Acts Commission, appendix D, pp. 145–46, and qq. 3856–88; also Report of the Inspectors of Factories, *PP*, 1868–69, 16, p. 10; J. M. Wigley, 'Nineteenth century English sabbatarianism: a study of a religious, political and social phenomenon', unpublished Ph.D. thesis, University of Sheffield, 1972, pp. 252–53. The relevant statutes were: Factory Acts Extension Act, 1867, 30 & 31 Vict., c. 103; Workshop Regulation Act, 1867, 30 & 31 Vict., c. 146; an Act for Exempting Persons Professing the Jewish Religion from Penalties in Respect of Young Persons and Females Professing the said Religion Working on Sundays, 1871, 34 Vict., c. 19.

46. Jacobs, op. cit., p. 39.

47. Factory and Workshop Acts Commission, q. 3863.

48. L. P. Gartner, *The Jewish Immigrant in England: 1870–1914*, p. 73.

49. Op. cit., pp. 39–40.

50. J. S. Levi and G. F. J. Bergman, *Australian Genesis: Jewish Convicts and Settlers, 1788–1850, passim*, especially, pp. 10–11, 16, 62. 'Veteran cabby', *JC*, 4 June 1971; ibid., 22 January 1858, re Solomon Hyam Levy, deceased, an officer of Wellclose Square court. Levi and Bergman, op. cit., p. 68, state that the low-ranking office of bailiff was 'an office which Jews occupied quite frequently in London, perhaps because it was a first step up from the degraded trades in which many had had to find a living. The early issues of *Punch*, of the 1840s and 1850s, always depict a bailiff with caricatured Jewish features.'

51. Whitehill, op. cit., from which these details are taken. From time to time middle-class women suggested that working-class Jewish girls take up domestic and similar work, the argument being, sometimes, that a diversification from the needle trades was desirable. See *Jewish Record*, 24 June 1870, p. 9, and 1 July 1870, p. 3, regarding a proposal for a laundry to be staffed by Jewish girls. It was established in the spring in 1871 at Denmark Gardens, Kilburn (*JC*, 29 September 1871, p. 2). Also, *JC*, 30 January 1885, pp. 6–7, for two letters regarding Jewesses as domestic servants, one of them being a spirited response from 'A Jewish Working Girl' (a feather-maker, and member of the Jewish Working Men's Club).

52. Oppenheim: Report of the Factory and Workshop Acts Commission, q. 3888; Report of the Inspectors of Factories, *PP*, 1876, 16, pp. 88–89.

53. Alan Fox, *A History of the National Union of Boot and Shoe Operatives: 1874–1957*, p. 18. This refers to 1878.

54. Williams, op. cit., pp. 358–60.

55. Newman, op. cit., for Birmingham and Brighton.

56. Hyman, op. cit., p. 158.

57. *Hull Packet*, 20 February 1857, re 'Sjouquist', a 'poor Jew' from Sheffield (supplied by Raphael Samuel).

58. Weinberg's evidence to the Factory and Workshop Acts Commission is ambiguous (qq. 7889–7913). He said he would like to employ 'Jewish operatives, if I had them, on Sundays till 2 o'clock'; but he also answered 'Very few' to the question: 'Do you employ many Jews?'

59. Williams, op. cit., pp. 35–38, 87.

60. Alexander Behr, 'Isidor Gerstenberg (1821–1876): founder of the Council of Foreign Bondholders', *TJHSE*, 17, 1953, pp. 207–13; Williams, op. cit., pp. 35–36, 87.

61. B. Shillman, *A Short History of the Jews in Ireland*, p. 88.

62. Clerical work for women, especially in the civil service, certainly expanded during this period. In 1851 there were only 15 women clerks in England and Wales but by 1881 there were nearly 6,000; R. Silverstone, 'Office work for women: an historical review', *Business Hist.*, 17(1), 1976, pp. 98–110.

8 The Transformation of Anglo-Jewry, 1880–1914

1. A. R. Rollin, 'Russo-Jewish immigrants in England before 1881', *TJHSE*, 21, 1968, pp. 202–13; Israel Finestein, 'The Jews of Hull: 1770–1870'; Ernest Krausz, *Leeds Jewry: Its History and Social Structure*, pp. 4–5; Birmingham Jewish Local History Study Group, 'A portrait of Birmingham Jewry in 1851', in A. Newman (ed.), 'Provincial Jewry in Victorian Britain'.

2. V. D. Lipman, *Social History of the Jews in England: 1850–1950*, pp. 65–66, and *A Century of Social Service, 1859–1959: The Jewish Board of Guardians*, Table I, pp. 276ff. One reason for the drop in the number of Dutch applicants to the Board of Guardians was the creation in 1875 of the Netherlands Benevolent Society which assisted distressed persons of Dutch nationality in Britain, irrespective of creed. Loans could be received, but grants were payable in certain circumstances. In the 1890s it was reported that a high proportion of the applicants were Jews and the Society's president issued an appeal for support from well-to-do Dutch Jews in London. *JC*, 7 April 1893, p. 15, describes the Society and mentions the appeal.

3. Finestein, op. cit., for information on immigration through Hull; Rosalind O'Brien, 'The establishment of the Jewish minority in Leeds', unpublished Ph.D. thesis, University of Bristol, 1975, p. 96, for marriage statistics.

4. O'Brien, op. cit., p. 99, quoting a guess by a witness to the Select Committee on Emigration and Immigration (Foreigners), 1889.

5. L. P. Gartner, 'North Atlantic Jewry', in A. Newman (ed.), *Migration and Settlement*, p. 121. The figures are based on the statistics in Lipman, *Social Service*, Tables 1 and 2, pp. 276–85, 290–91.

6. L. P. Gartner, *The Jewish Immigrant in England: 1870–1914*, pp. 24–30.

7. L. Saipe (ed.), *Leeds Tercentenary Celebration of the Resettlement of the Jews in the British Isles*, p. 24.

8. L. P. Gartner, 'Notes on the statistics of Jewish immigration to England: 1870–1914', *Jew. Soc. Stud.*, 22(2), 1960, pp. 97–102; and *The Jewish Immigrant in England*; J. A. Garrard, *The English and Immigration*, appendix 1; B. Gainer, *The Alien Invasion: The Origins of the Aliens Act of 1905*, chaps. 1 and 2; Lipman, *Social History*, chap. 5.

9. Brinley Thomas, *Migration and Economic Growth*, p. 224.

10. Isaac Deutscher, *The Prophet Armed: Leon Trotsky, 1879–1921*; Jacob Lvavi, 'Jewish

agricultural settlement in the USSR', *Soviet Jewish Affairs*, 1, 1971, p. 91: by the end of the Tsarist regime the Jewish agricultural population was about 55,000.

11. See the analysis in Ezra Mendelsohn, *Class Struggle in the Pale: The Formative Years of the Jewish Workers' Movement in Tsarist Russia*, chap. 1, 'The Jewish Proletariat'.

12. David Patterson, *The Hebrew Novel in Czarist Russia*, p. 132. This monograph studies eighteen novels published between 1868 and 1888. The novels which combine 'an attractive tale with didactic ideas and social criticism' (p. 220) are useful sources on the life of Jews in eastern Europe. Descriptions are also to be found in recently-published autobiographies: Nahum Goldman, *Memories;* Myer Weisgal, *So Far;* Golda Meir, *My Life.*

13. John Morley, *The Life of Richard Cobden*, p. 451.

14. There are differences of opinion about the causes of the emigration. L. P. Gartner, 'Immigration and the formation of American Jewry: 1840–1925', in H. H. Ben-Sasson and S. Ettinger (eds), *Jewish Society Through the Ages*, p. 304, states 'it would be an error to take pogroms as the main cause of emigration'. He instances the case of Galicia which had perhaps the highest rate of emigration but whose Jews were emancipated in 1867 and experienced no pogroms. However, Arieh Tartakower, *In Search of Home and Freedom*, p. 33, while emphasising the economic pressures, argues that 'it played a far larger role in the case of the non-Jews', and considers Galicia an exceptional circumstance.

15. Lionel Kochan, *The Making of Modern Russia*, p. 197. L. Wolf (ed.), *The Legal Sufferings of the Jews in Russia*, gives an account of the legal and administrative restrictions. A useful statement is by Leonard Schapiro, 'The Russian background of the Anglo-American Jewish immigration', *TJHSE*, 20, 1964, pp. 215–31.

16. Rose Odle, *Salt of Our Youth*, p. 10; Selig Brodetsky, *Memoirs: From Ghetto to Israel*, p. 39.

17. Mendelsohn, op. cit., p. 14 n.4.

18. Brodetsky, op. cit., pp. 15–16. See also the story by Sholom Aleichem, 'We steal across the frontier', in his *The Adventures of Mottel the Cantor's Son* (trans. Tamara Kahana), pp. 114–25.

19. Gartner, 'North Atlantic Jewry', p. 121.

20. Tartakower, op. cit., p. 35.

21. A. S. Redford and L. S. Russell, *The History of Local Government in Manchester*, vol. III, pp. 127–28.

22. Edward Cadbury, M. C. Matheson and G. Shann, *Women's Work and Wages: A Phase of Life in an Industrial City*, pp. 97–98.

23. 11th ed., 1914, p. 185 (the book was first published in 1905).

24. Gartner, *Jewish Immigrant in England*, pp. 229–31.

25. J. J. Tobias, 'Police-immigrant relations in England: 1880–1910', *New Community*, 3(3), 1974, pp. 211–14, and *Crime and Industrial Society in the Nineteenth Century*, pp. 150–51.

26. For a recent discussion and review of the literature see Colin Holmes, 'In search of Sidney Street', *Bull. Soc. Study Lab. Hist.*, 29, 1974, pp. 70–77, referring especially to Donald Rumbelow, *The Houndsditch Murders and the Siege of Sidney Street.* Jewish radical movements are discussed in W. J. Fishman, *East End Jewish Radicals: 1875–1914.* The Sidney Street affair is on pp. 287–93.

27. *Fourscore Years*, p. 212. The many recent descriptions of immigrant life in Britain include Gartner, *Jewish Immigrant in England;* Fishman, op. cit.; John Woodeson, *Mark Gertler: Biography of a Painter, 1891–1939;* M. Donbrow, *They Docked at Newcastle.*

28. L. Hyman, *The Jews of Ireland: From Earliest Times to the Year 1910*, chap. 25, especially pp. 212–17; 'Pogrom: Limerick 1904', *Nusight* (Dublin), May 1970, pp. 25–28; G. Alderman, 'The anti-Jewish riots of August 1911 in South Wales', *Welsh Hist. Rev.*, 6(2), 1972, pp. 190–200, and 'Into the vortex: South Wales Jewry before 1914', in Newman, 'Provincial Jewry in Victorian Britain'.

29. Alderman, 'Anti-Jewish riots', p. 190.

30. Gartner, *Jewish Immigrant In England*, pp. 16–17.

31. G. Stedman Jones, *Outcast London: A Study in the Relationship between Classes in Victorian Society,* p. 215, and chap. 11, 'The Housing Crisis of the 1880s'.

32. Lipman, *Social History,* pp. 94–97.

33. Asa Briggs, *Victorian Cities,* pp. 338–39.

34. Ibid., p. 340.

35. Op. cit., p. 1.

36. G. R. Searle, *The Quest for National Efficiency: A Study in British Politics and Political Thought, 1899–1914,* p. 54.

37. Among recent discussions are Bernard Semmel, *Imperialism and Social Reform: English Social-Imperial Thought, 1894–1914;* D. A. Hamer, *Liberal Politics in the Age of Gladstone and Rosebery: A Study in Leadership and Policy.*

38. Quoted in Gainer, op. cit., p. 141. See his chap. 6, 'Free Trade in Paupers'.

39. See Gainer, op. cit., chap. 8, 'The Struggle for the Aliens Act'; Garrard, op. cit., chap. 3, 'How the Act was Passed'; Israel Finestein, 'Jewish immigration in British party politics in the 1890s', in Newman, *Migration and Settlement,* pp. 128–45.

40. K. O. Morgan, *Wales in British Politics: 1868–1922;* P. F. Clarke, *Lancashire and the New Liberalism.*

41. E.g., Chaim Bermant, *Troubled Eden: An Anatomy of British Jewry,* pp. 22–25, but he notes, pp. 25–26, 'important mitigating circumstances'.

42. Tartakower, op. cit., p. 12.

43. To take one example, Kevin O'Connor, *The Irish in Britain.*

9 The Immigrant Trades, 1880–1914

1. This is the best-documented period of Anglo-Jewish history, and the numerous contemporary inquiries and reports have been well examined and analysed in a number of studies. I have used these works, which often contain full bibliographical sources, and have not given many detailed references to contemporary material. Undoubtedly the best monograph is L. P. Gartner, *The Jewish Immigrant in England: 1870–1914,* especially chap. 3; V. D. Lipman, *Social History of the Jews in England: 1850–1950,* chap. 5, 6, and 7, and *A Century of Social Service, 1859–1959: The Jewish Board of Guardians,* chaps. 3 and 4, are both important. J. A. Garrard, *The English and Immigration, 1880–1910,* and B. A. Gainer, *The Alien Invasion,* have relevant material. E. H. Hunt, *Regional Wage Variations in Great Britain: 1850–1914,* pp. 305–23, analyses the data on Jewish wages in London. G. Stedman Jones, *Outcast London,* as well as providing an excellent discussion of the late nineteenth-century London background, has information on the Jews. Leeds is well covered in three unpublished works: Joseph Buckman, 'The economic and social history of alien immigrants to Leeds, 1880–1914', unpublished Ph.D. thesis, University of Strathclyde, 1968; June Hendrick, 'The tailoresses in the ready-made clothing industry in Leeds, 1889–1899: a study in labour failure', unpublished M.A. thesis, University of Warwick, 1970; Rosalind O'Brien, 'The establishment of the Jewish minority in Leeds', unpublished Ph.D. thesis, University of Bristol, 1975. Some information is included in A. Newman (ed.), 'Provincial Jewry in Victorian Britain'.

2. Malcolm Slowe, 'The foundation of Aldershot synagogue', in Newman, op. cit., quoting *JC,* 8 and 15 September 1882; C. H. L. Emanuel, *A Century and a Half of Jewish History,* pp. 117, 119, 150.

3. Arnold Levy, *History of the Sunderland Jewish Community,* p. 123.

4. See the description in, for example, David Patterson, *The Hebrew Novel in Czarist Russia,* pp. 148–51.

5. Buckman, op. cit., pp. 33–34, and chap. 7, 'The Jewish Footwear Trade'; Robert H. Sherard, *The White Slaves of England,* chap. 3, 'The Slipper-makers and Tailors of Leeds'.

6. C. Booth (ed.), *The Life and Labour of the People in London,* vol. V, 1895, p. 386, 'in

Whitechapel, several Jews are entering the trade'. *JC*, 8 March 1901, p. 27, noted that whereas in the past a few Jewish workers were scattered in the English workshops, now Jews employed Jews and a Jewish branch of the Amalgamated Tinplate Workers' Union had been formed. This may have been a newly-formed version of the Hebrew Iron and Tin Plate Workers' Union of 1898; Georg Halpern, *Die Jüdischen Arbeiter in London*, p. 68.

7. Obituary notice, *Guardian*, 1 February 1974.

8. Gartner, op. cit., pp. 183–86; W. J. Fishman, *East End Jewish Radicals: 1875–1914*, pp. 58–60.

9. Halpern, op. cit., p. 68.

10. G. Alderman, 'Into the vortex: South Wales Jewry before 1914', in Newman, op. cit., n.p., n. 12.

11. *The Times*, 3 September 1903; *JC*, 4, 11, 18 September 1903. Emanuel, op. cit., refers to attacks on Jewish miners at Dowlais, but dates it as 1904. This might be the same 1903 incident.

12. 18 April 1873.

13. Garrard, op. cit., p. 114.

14. H. Llewellyn Smith (ed.), *New Survey of London Life and Labour*, vol. VI, 1934, p. 295, shows that 10 per cent of the boys and 11 per cent of the girls were in these occupations; no absolute figures are given. Occupations of youth club members similarly do not identify the sections of the community to which they belonged. The 164 members in 1903 of the Butler Street Girls' Club, Spitalfields, included only nine clerical workers and shop assistants, as well as twenty-five 'helping at home'. As many as 110 of the 129 manual workers were in the clothing trade. Surprisingly, of the 203 members of the Brady Boys' Club in 1908, 51 were in white-collar jobs (mostly clerks) but clothing occupied 55 and cabinet-making 13; others were in a wide range of occupations. In any case the membership of the clubs may not have been representative of East End Jewish youth, and too much should not be made of the figures; Sidney Bunt, *Jewish Youth Work in Britain*, pp. 43–44.

15. G. H. Whitehill (ed.), *Bevis Marks Records*, part 3, *passin*.

16. Report of the Inspector of Factories, *PP*, 1880, 14, p. 88; Booth, op. cit., vol. VI, 1896, p. 10.

17. E. G. Howarth and M. Wilson, *West Ham: A Study in Social and Industrial Problems*, p. 166. This area of East London became the site of many noxious and unpleasant industries in the later nineteenth century.

18. Millicent Rose, *The East End of London*, pp. 139–40: 'not even the Rosemary Lane Irish would tolerate the dreadful conditions in the industry'. She is referring to a period before the transfer of the industry from the East End to West Ham.

19. Booth, op. cit., vol. VI, 1896, pp. 136–37.

20. Gartner, op. cit., pp. 57–58. The figures are from the *Annual Reports* of the Shelter for 1895–96, 1899–1900, 1901–2, 1903–4 and 1907–8. Gartner gives the boot- and shoe-makers' percentage wrongly as 9.

21. O'Brien, op. cit., p. 41.

22. Hunt, op. cit., p. 314.

23. A. Newman, *Leicester Hebrew Congregation: A Centenary Record*, p. 9.

24. Gartner, op. cit., p. 24.

25. Ibid., pp. 63–64.

26. Quoted in Hunt, op. cit., p. 323.

27. Booth, op. cit., vol. VII, 1896, p. 36 (see p. 25 for age distribution).

28. J. G. Dony, *A History of the Straw Hat Industry*, p. 120.

29. Hunt, op. cit., p. 321.

30. The following description is based on Buckman, op. cit., chap. 2, 'The Leeds Clothing Industry: 1880–1914', and chap. 4, 'The Jewish Tailoring Trade'.

31. Joan Thomas, 'A history of the Leeds clothing industry', *Yorks. Bull. of Econ. and Soc. Research*, Occasional Paper no. 1, p. 12. The figures, from the decennial Population Census, are

approximate, since they exclude homeworkers. The age range of those included varied from Census to Census.

32. Buckman, op. cit., pp. 34–35 and chap. 7, 'The Jewish Footwear Trade'; Sherard, op. cit., chap. 3, 'The Slipper-makers and Tailors of Leeds'.

33. Hunt, op. cit., p. 312. Jews were also involved in the box-making industry, one of the first four sweated industries to have their wages determined by the negotiating machinery established under the Trade Boards Act of 1909. The Male and Female Cardboard Box Makers' Union was formed in 1900, and comprised 133 members, of whom 79 were women (Halpern, op. cit., p. 68). The industry, of some 30,000 to 40,000 workers, consisted largely of unmarried women workers; the 15 per cent of the workforce who were men normally cut out the cardboard, but in the Jewish workshops the men were often employed in making-up as well as cutting; M. E. Bulkley, *The Establishment of Legal Minimum Rates in the Boxmaking Industry under the Trade Boards Act of 1909*, pp. 1ff.

34. Beatrice Webb, *My Apprenticeship*, p. 331. A good, recent discussion is in Gainer, op. cit., chap. 2 and 5.

35. Joseph Buckman, 'Evolution of the alien economy of Leeds: 1880–1914', unpublished paper for the Urban History Group conference, Leeds, April 1975. The original sources include the annual *Reports*, from 1908, of the Leeds School Medical Officer, and Physical Examination of Men of Military Age, 1917–18: Medical Boards' Report, *PP*, 1920, 26, p. 105; *JC*, 29 July 1910.

36. Stedman Jones, op. cit., p. 42.

37. Ibid., p. 43.

38. Buckman, 'Economic and social history of alien immigrants' pp. 352, 397–402.

39. The wage statistics are published and discussed in Gartner, op. cit., pp. 95–99; Lipman, *Social History*, pp. 110–11; Thomas, op. cit., pp. 27–29; and especially Hunt, op. cit., pp. 305–23.

40. Thomas, op. cit., p. 35. R. H. Tawney, *The Establishment of Minimum Rates in the Tailoring Industry under the Trade Boards Act of 1909*, for a general study of the effects of the Act on the clothing industry.

41. Robert Roberts, *The Classic Slum*, pp. 136–37.

42. 'The Jewish community (East London)', in Booth, op. cit., vol. III, 1892, pp. 166–91.

43. Fishman, op. cit., pp. 140–41, for references in the 1880s to gambling in Leeds and London.

44. Webb, *My Apprenticeship*, p. 333.

45. Israel Sieff, *Memoirs*, chap. 1, for details of the family background.

46. Goronwy Rees, *St Michael: A History of Marks and Spencer*, chaps. 1 and 2.

10 Jewish Trade Unionism, 1870–1914

1. Roy B. Helfgott, 'Trade unionism among the Jewish garment workers of Britain and the United States', *Labor Hist.*, 2(2), 1961, p. 204.

2. H. A. Clegg, A. Fox and A. F. Thompson, *A History of British Trade Unions since 1889*, vol. 1: *1889–1910*, for example, has a handful of references as does A. Fox, *A History of the National Union of Boot and Shoe Operatives:1874–1957*. The official history of the National Union of Tailors and Garment Workers (Margaret Stewart and Leslie Hunter, *The Needle Is Threaded*) has much material on Jews but is not a very satisfactory study.

3. Georg Halpern, *Die Jüdischen Arbeiter in London*, chap. 5, 'Stellung der jüdischen Arbeiter zur Gewerksvereinfrage'; V. D. Lipman, *Social History of the Jews in England:1850–1950*, pp. 116–19; Shirley Lerner, 'The history of the United Clothing Workers' Union: a case study of social disorganization', unpublished Ph.D. thesis, University of London, 1956; L. P. Gartner, *The Jewish Immigrant in England:1870–1914*, pp. 117–40; J. A. Garrard, *The English and Immigration:1880–1910*, pp. 166–73. The more sympathetic account in W. J. Fishman, *East End Jewish Radicals:1875–1914*, only slightly amends the story.

4. H. G. Swift, *A History of Postal Agitation*, p. 106.

5. H. Collins and C. Abramsky, *Karl Marx and the British Labour Movement*, index, 'Cigar Makers'. Their delegate was J. Cohn.

6. For the London unions of the 1870s see P. Elman, 'The beginnings of the Jewish trade union movement in England', *TJHSE*, 17, 1953, pp. 53–62, and Fishman, op. cit., chap. 4. Nora Levin, *Jewish Socialist Movements: 1871–1917*, chap. 4 for Lieberman.

7. See Chimen Abramsky, 'The Jewish labour movement: some historiographical problems', *Soviet Jewish Affairs*, 1, 1971, pp. 45–51; M. Mishkinsky, 'The Jewish labour movement and European socialism', in H. H. Ben-Sasson and S. Ettinger (eds), *Jewish Society through the Ages*, pp. 284–96. As Abramsky's article demonstrates, there is a vast literature in many languages.

8. 23 June 1876, quoted in Fishman, op. cit., p. 112.

9. 8 September 1876, quoted in Fishman, op. cit., p. 119.

10. The events in Leeds are described in Joseph Buckman, 'Alien working-class response: the Leeds Jewish tailors, 1880–1914', in K. Lunn (ed.), *Hosts, Immigrants and Minorities*, pp. 222–62 (which covers the whole period of this chapter); and more specifically in Colin Holmes, 'The Leeds Jewish tailors' strikes of 1885 and 1888', *Yorks. Arch. J.*, 45, 1973, pp. 158–66.

11. Fishman, op. cit., p. 137.

12. Gartner, op. cit., p. 117.

13. *Agudat Poalim Yehudim b'Anglia (Jewish Unions in England)*, pp. 1–11. This reprints the rules of five unions for the period 1886–90.

14. E. Aves, 'The furniture trade', in C. Booth (ed.), *Life and Labour of the People in London*, vol. IV, 1893, pp. 209–10. Gartner, op. cit., p. 120, quoting reports of 1887, prematurely writes it off.

15. *Agudat Poalim Yehudim b'Anglia*, pp. 48–62.

16. Bill Williams, 'The beginnings of Jewish trade unionism in Manchester, 1889–1891', in Lunn, op. cit., pp. 263–307.

17. This account of the Leeds strike of 1888 is based on Buckman, op. cit., and on Holmes, op. cit.

18. E. P. Thompson, 'Homage to Tom Maguire', in Asa Briggs and John Saville (eds), *Essays in Labour History*, p. 297.

19. The fullest account is in Fishman, op. cit., pp. 134ff.

20. Williams, op. cit.

21. *Agudat Poalim Yehudim b'Anglia*, pp. 64–81.

22. The synagogue parade is described in Gartner, op. cit., pp. 115–17 and in Fishman, op. cit., pp. 164–69. Extracts from a scrapbook kept by Lyons, now in the possession of the National Union of Tailors and Garment Workers, were printed in *JC*, 12 March 1971 and in the union's monthly journal, the *Garment Worker* (issues of April 1971, including a reprint of the March 1889 leaflet, May and September 1971).

23. The 1889 strike is narrated in Gartner, op. cit., pp. 122–26 and in Fishman, op. cit., pp. 169–79, both based largely on reports in the *Arbeiter Freint*. See also A. R. Rollin, 'A Jewish tailors' strike of 60 years ago', *JC*, 14 October 1949, p. 19. The strike balance sheet is printed in Report of the Strikes and Lock-outs of 1889, *PP*, 1890, 119, pp. 124–25, and reprinted in Fishman, op. cit., appendix 2. The Amalgamated Society of Boot and Shoe Makers was the new name of the old craft union, the Amalgamated Cordwainers' Society, from which the National Union of Boot and Shoe Operatives broke away in the 1870s.

24. A. B. Levy, *East End Story*, pp. 90–91.

25. The proposed East London Federation is described in Fishman, op. cit., pp. 183–84 and the stick-makers' strike on pp. 185–86.

26. The strike is in Fox, op. cit., chap. 12 but with no mention of Jews. See also Gartner, op. cit., p. 128.

27. Buckman, op. cit.

28. Quoted in Garrard, op. cit., p. 167.

29. Minutes of Evidence, Group C, Royal Commission on Labour, *PP*, 1892, 26, part 2, qq. 20047ff. The quotation is from q. 20058. The Jews were said to be not very skilled.

30. Halpern, op. cit., for these details.

31. R. Hyman, *The Workers' Union*, p. 18.

32. Report on the Strikes and Lock-outs . . . in 1901, *PP*, 1902, pp. xxiii–xxxiv, 12–13.

33. 22 March 1901, p. 31.

34. The Cardiff union is mentioned in the Reports of the Registrar of Friendly Societies which appeared annually in *PP*. Halpern, op. cit., p. 71, states that in April 1901 the boot and shoe union had 1,600 members, but by November of that year only 51 remained. The union certainly disappeared after the dispute, but no union, then or now, would be likely to be so efficient as to know its membership figures at such frequent intervals.

35. Membership figures in Clegg, Fox and Thompson, op. cit., p. 83; see their chaps. 2, 3 and 4 for a detailed review of this period of trade union history. Also E. J. Hobsbawm, 'General labour unions in Great Britain:1889–1914', *Econ. Hist. Rev.*, 1(2 and 3), 1949, pp. 123–42.

36. John Saville, 'Trade unions and free labour: the background to the Taff Vale decision', in Briggs and Saville (eds), op. cit., p. 319.

37. Fishman, op. cit., pp. 201–3.

38. Based on Buckman, op. cit.

39. Royal Commission on Alien Immigration, *PP*, 1903, 9, q. 14111 (Lyons); q. 21085 (Policoff); 20524 (Solomons).

40. The *Cigarette-Maker*, July to December 1906, is at the British Library Newspaper Library.

41. 7 February 1906, quoted in Lipman, op. cit., p. 279; also ibid., pp. 285–86.

42. Clegg, Fox and Thompson, op. cit., pp. 441–42.

44. R. Rocker, *The London Years*, pp. 218–25; *Board of Trade Labour Gazette*, June 1912, p. 260, and July 1912, p. 315. R. A. Leeson, *Strike: A Live History, 1887–1971* p. 47, prints a recently-conducted interview with a survivor of the strike.

45. S. and B. Webb, *Industrial Democracy*, p. 127 n. 1, for a reference to Jewish branches of the National Union of Boot and Shoe Operatives. The Royal Commission on Alien Immigration was told (qq. 20525–26) that there had been two such branches but they had disappeared because the Jewish workers had been badly treated in certain workshops and been forced to leave. The Hebrew Cabinet Makers' Union of 1887 was absorbed in 1893 by the Alliance Cabinet Makers' Association, in which it continued as a 'Hebrew' branch. The Amalgamated Society of Tailors had Jewish branches in several towns—Newcastle and Sheffield, for example.

46. Figures are in the annual Reports of the Registrar of Friendly Societies.

47. Royal Commission on Alien Immigration, qq. 13965–69.

48. P. Thompson, *Socialists, Liberals and Labour: The Struggle for London, 1885-1914*, p. 39, gives figures of trade union membership in London.

49. This is one of the themes in Joel Seidman, *The Needle Trades*, on the early history of the American clothing unions.

11   Business and the Professions in the Era of Immigration

1. V. D. Lipman, 'The development of London Jewry', in S. S. Levin (ed.), *A Century of Anglo-Jewish Life: 1870–1970*, p. 50.

2. V. D. Lipman, 'The rise of Jewish suburbia', *TJHSE*, 21, 1968, pp. 78–103. Also A. Newman, *The United Synagogue: 1870–1970*, chap. 5, 'The Growth of London Jewry'.

3. Tova Benski, 'Glasgow', in A. Newman (ed.), 'Provincial Jewry in Victorian Britain'; also A. Levy, *The Origins of Glasgow Jewry: 1812–1895*.

4. *Memoirs*, p. 17. Cheetham was still a popular area; Kingsley Martin, *Harold Laski (1893–1950): A Biographical Memoir*, chap. 1, for the family of a cotton-shipper who lived there. Southport also became a middle-class settlement; Pat Hodess, 'Southport's golden years', *JC*, 10 September 1976, p. 21.

5. B. A. Kosmin and N. Grizzard, 'The Jewish dead in the Great War as an indicator for Anglo-Jewish demography and class stratification in 1914,' Research Unit, Board of Deputies of British Jews, duplicated. I am indebted to the authors for permission to use their paper, which is to be published in *MJHSE*. The source of their material is M. Adler (ed.), *The British Jewry Book of Honour.*

6. R. M. Fox, *Smoky Crusade,* pp. 18, 25–26, 58, 67.

7. Bill Williams, 'Power and poverty in Manchester Jewry', *JC,* 14 October 1977, p. 19.

8. Thea Vigne and A. Howkins, 'The small shopkeeper in industrial and market towns', in G. Crossick (ed.), *The Lower Middle Classes in Britain: 1870–1914,* pp. 187–88.

9. Fritz Stern, *Gold and Iron: Bismarck, Bleichröder, and the Building of the German Empire.*

10. Cecil Roth, 'The court Jews of Edwardian England,' in his *Essays and Portraits in Anglo-Jewish History,* pp. 282–94. J. Camplin, *The Rise of the Plutocrats: Wealth and Power in Edwardian England.*

11. S. G. Checkland, 'The mind of the City: 1870–1914', *Oxf. Econ. Papers,* 9(3), 1957, p. 263.

12. Paul H. Emden, *Money Powers of Europe,* and *Jews of Britain* contain much useful material.

13. R. R. James, *Rosebery: A Biography of Archibald Philip, Fifth Earl of Rosebery,* pp. 78–88.

14. Kurt Grunwald, ' "Windsor-Cassel"—the last court Jew', *Leo Baeck Year Book,* 14, 1969, pp. 119–64.

15. Emden, *Jews of Britain,* for these details. Also T. C. Barker and M. Robbins, *A History of London Transport,* vol. II, pp. 70–74 (and index).

16. *Imperialism: A Study,* pp. 56–57. Since then there has been considerable discussion on the validity of the analysis. For a symposium containing a variety of views see Roger Owen and Bob Sutcliffe (eds), *Studies in the Theory of Imperialism.*

17. For example, see Christopher Hollis, *The Mind of Chesterton,* pp. 127–40. For the Marconi affair, see Frances Donaldson, *The Marconi Scandal,* and W. P. Jolly, *Marconi.*

18. Herbert Feis, *Europe: The World's Banker, 1870–1914.*

19. Stern, op. cit., chap. 14, 'Rumania: the Triumph of Expediency'. C. C. Aronsfeld, 'Jewish bankers and the Tsar', *Contemporary Rev.,* 224, March 1974, pp. 127–33, and 'Unfavoured nation', *JC,* 26 April 1974.

20. Emden, *Jews of Britain,* pp. 533–34.

21. Based on Robert Henriques, *Marcus Samuel, First Viscount Bearsted and Founder of the 'Shell" Transport and Trading Company: 1853–1927,* and *Sir Robert Waley Cohen, 1877–1952: A Biography.* See also F. C. Gerretson, *History of the Royal Dutch;* and Marian Jack, 'The purchase of the British government's shares in the British Petroleum Company: 1912–1914,' *Past & Present,* no. 39, April 1968, pp. 139–68, for some extra details.

22. D. J. Richardson, 'The history of the catering industry, with special reference to the development of J. Lyons and Co. Ltd. to 1939', unpublished Ph.D. thesis, University of Kent at Canterbury, 1970; B. W. E. Alford, *W. D. & H. O. Wills and the Development of the U. K. Tobacco Industry: 1768–1965;* H. W. MacRosty, *The Trust Movement in British Industry,* chap. 9.

23. Emden, op. cit., pp. 491–95; and pp. 518–19 for other small Jewish companies. The statement by Cecil Roth, *A Short History of the Jewish People,* p. 393, that the Jewish immigrants 'captured the cigarette-making industry, previously an American monopoly' is nonsense.

24. M. E. Bulkley, *The Establishment of Legal Minimum Rates in the Boxmaking Industry under the Trade Boards Act of 1909,* p. 3 refers to 'Jewish workshops'.

25. A. R. Rollin, 'Russo-Jewish immigrants in England before 1881', *TJHSE,* 21, 1968, p. 21.

26. Elizabeth Ewing, *History of Twentieth Century Fashion,* pp. 51–52. The former developed into the Harella company, and two sons created the Windsmoor company. Not all the pioneers were long-term successes. For the story of an immigrant who flourished but ended in bankruptcy (partly because of his persistent gambling), see Sharon Wallach, ' "Life was one big speculation": the story of Frank Peterman, a pioneer in the fashion industry', *JC* Colour Magazine, 23 November 1979, pp. 85–86.

27. 'A résumé of the life, business and social activities of Mr. Samuel Goldstein', unpublished MS., 1968. I am grateful to Mr William Goldstein, deputy chairman of Ellis & Goldstein (Holdings) Ltd for supplying a copy of this account written by Samuel Goldstein.

28. The firm of L. S. & J. Sussman Ltd was founded about 1900 (information from Mr N. Sussman).

29. *JC*, 28 April 1978, p. 19. The company is Shubette of London Ltd.

30. J. Gliksten began as a cabinet-maker in 1875; International Timber Corporation, *Report and Accounts* for 1975, has a brief reference to its origins.

31. This section is based on J. B. Jefferys, *Retail Trading in Britain: 1850–1950*, chap. 13.

32. Max Newman, 'Tottenham over five decades', *JC*, 11 June 1976, p. 13; Samuel Flatau, *A. & W. Flatau & Co. Ltd., Henry Playfair Ltd., Metropolitan Boot Co. Ltd.: Foundation and History, 120 Years*, Guildhall Library, pam. 8625.

33. Jefferys, op. cit., pp. 67, 416.

34. E. Lipson, 'The Brights of Market Place', *Trans. Hunter Arch. Soc.*, 6, 1950, pp. 117–25.

35. I am grateful to Mr David Brown for much information about the history of Jews in Sheffield, especially of the cutlery industry.

36. *One Hundred Years, 1834–1934: George Cohen Sons & Co. Ltd.*, Guildhall Library, London, SL 69/1.

37. Bill Williams, *The Making of Manchester Jewry: 1740–1875*, pp. 127, 394.

38. K. Richardson, *Twentieth-Century Coventry*, pp. 36–37; H. Louis and B. Carrie, *The Story of Triumph Motor Cycles;* Bettman gets a brief mention in A. E. Harrison, 'The competitiveness of the British cycle industry: 1890–1914', *Econ. Hist. Rev.*, 22, 1969, pp. 287–303.

39. Robert Jones and Oliver Marriott, *Anatomy of a Merger: A History of GEC, AEI, and English Electric*, especially chap. 4, 'Lord Hirst of GEC'.

40. Victoria County History, *Essex*, vol. 6, 1973, p. 80.

41. Sir Harry Jephcott, *The First Fifty Years: An Account of the Early Life of Joseph Edward Nathan and the First Fifty Years of his Merchandise Business that Eventually became the Glaxo Group.* I am grateful to the late Sir Harry for showing me a copy of this privately printed book.

42. Charles Wilson, *The History of Unilever*, especially vol. II. Peter Mathias, *Retailing Revolution: A History of Multiple Retailing in the Food Trades based upon the Allied Suppliers Group of Companies*, for a discussion of the competition between van den Berghs and (the non-Jewish) Jurgens to obtain outlets for their margarine in the multiple food shops.

43. He was a member of the Salmon and Gluckstein families. For the company see *Stock Exchange Year Book* (annual).

44. W. B. Proudfoot, *The Origin of Stencil Duplicating*.

45. Raphael Tuck (1821–1900) was born in East Prussia and came to London in 1866. See his obituary in *Jewish World*, 23 March 1900, p. 407; *Jewish Guardian*, 4 January 1925, p. 15, for the jubilee of Elkin & Co.

46. F. A. Mumby, *The House of Routledge: 1834–1934*, pp. 148–49. Cecil A. Franklin joined the firm in 1906 and became managing director in 1912. For Stallybrass, see Emden, *Jews of Britain*, p. 120 n. 1.

47. Emden, *Jews of Britain*, pp. 357–63.

48. Harold Hobson, Phillip Knightley and Leonard Russell, *The Pearl of Days: An Intimate Memoir of 'The Sunday Times', 1822–1972*, pp. xv, 51–58.

49. Victor Gollancz, *My Dear Timothy*, pp. 34, 81–82. A brief account of a clothing business is in M. C. McKenna, *Myra Hess: A Portrait*, pp. 3–4, 53–55. It ended in bankruptcy in 1911.

50. D. J. Richardson, op. cit., and 'J. Lyons & Co. Ltd.: caterers and food manufacturers, 1894 to 1939', in D. J. Oddy and D. S. Miller (eds), *The Making of the Modern British Diet*, pp. 161–72.

51. Information from Mr H. C. Franks, a grandson of one of the founders.

52. L. Hyman, *The Jews of Ireland from Earliest Times to the Year 1910*, pp, 160–61.

53. L. Olsover, 'North-East England', in A. Newman (ed.), 'Provincial Jewry'.

54. L. Olsover, 'Middlesbrough'.

55. G. Havenhand, *Nation of Shopkeepers,* pp. 66–68.

56. Information from Mr E. N. Cohen, a son of Mr Joseph Cohen. The latter arrived in Dublin from Lithuania in 1889 at the age of seventeen and at first was a pedlar.

57. Stephen Aris, *Jews in Business,* pp. 136–37.

58. F. M. Musgrave, *The Migratory Elite,* p. 10, notes the significance of the 'Local' examinations in this respect.

59. C. H. L. Emanuel, *A Century and a Half of Jewish History,* pp. 73–74.

60. Ibid., p. 118, Cambridge; p. 123, Oxford.

61. Ibid., pp. 121, 132, 135, 143, 145, 164 and 168.

62. Ibid., p. 184.

63. Ibid., pp. 137, 141, 156, 157–58, 177, 179, 181, 182. Also pp. 170 and 175 for references to teaching, the Post Office and a Medical Officer of Health.

64. Israel Cohen, 'The economic activities of modern Jewry', *Econ. J.,* 24, 1914, especially pp. 55–56.

65. *JC,* 22 April 1904, p. 10.

66. Adler, op. cit., p. 189, Royal Navy; pp. 516–17, RAMC; p. 610, addenda.

67. *JC,* 22 December 1905, p. 19.

68. A. M. Hyamson, 'Plan of a dictionary of Anglo-Jewish biography', in *Anglo-Jewish Notabilities: Their Arms and Testamentary Dispositions,* pp. 1–73. More specific information is in Hyman, op. cit., chap. 18, which deals with Irish Jews in the liberal professions, and in G. H. Whitehill (ed.), *Bevis Marks Records,* part 3, which contains the names of some 440 Sephardi bridegrooms who were married during the period 1881–1901. Fifteen of them were professionals: a solicitor, a notary public, three teachers, three professors of music, a professor of history (Charles Gross), a professor of chemistry (Raphael Meldola), two doctors and three journalists. An interesting biographical account is in Norman Bentwich, *My Seventy-seven Years: An Account of My Life and Times, 1883–1960,* chap. 1.

69. Edward Jamilly, 'Anglo-Jewish architects, and architecture in the 18th and 19th centuries', *TJHSE,* 18, 1958, pp. 127–41, and 'Synagogue art and architecture', in Levin, op. cit., pp. 75–91.

70. For Sir Landon Ronald see his books: *Variations on a Personal Theme* and *Myself and Others.* For Charles Kensington Salaman, see Malcolm Charles Salaman, 'My father and I: happy memories of two long lives', *Synagogue Rev.,* 11, 1951, pp. 321–29.

71. See, for example, John Woodeson, *Mark Gertler: Biography of a Painter, 1891–1939;* Joseph Cohen, *Journey to the Trenches: The Life of Isaac Rosenberg;* Jean Moorcroft Wilson, *Isaac Rosenberg: Poet and Painter;* Jean Liddiard, *Isaac Rosenberg: The Half Used Life.* The novelists included Amy Levy, Israel Zangwill and Samuel Gordon.

72. *JC,* 18 October 1974, obituary of Blok; 16 January 1976, obituary of Henriques.

73. M. D. Brown, *David Salomons House: Catalogue of Mementoes,* p. v. The book includes details of his various patents and publications.

74. Stella Wills, 'The Anglo-Jewish contribution to the education movement for women in the nineteenth century', *TJHSE,* 17, 1953, pp. 269–81, has some useful points; Evelyn Sharp, *Hertha Ayrton, 1854–1923: A Memoir.*

75. Helen Bentwich, *If I Forget Thee: Some Chapters of Autobiography, 1912–1920,* pp. 1–11.

76. Ronald Fletcher (ed.), *The Science of Society and the Unity of Mankind* (a collection of essays on Ginsberg); Selig Brodetsky, *Memoirs: From Ghetto to Israel.*

77. Vera Weizmann, *The Impossible Takes Longer,* p. 41.

78. Julia Namier, *Lewis Namier: A Biography.*

79. One woman academic was Edith Morley, 1875–1964, who became eventually Professor of English Literature at Reading University. She was the daughter of a Jewish dental surgeon, but she formally ceased adherence to Judaism when she was twenty-one; *The Times,* 21 January 1964, obituary.

12 The Working Class in the Inter-war Years

1. For a discussion of these figures see Hannah Neustatter, 'Demographic and other statistical aspects of Anglo-Jewry', in M. Freedman (ed.), *A Minority in Britain*, pp. 55–108, and appendix 2, pp. 260–62. The Sephardi immigrants are noted in A. M. Hyamson, *The Sephardim of England*, pp. 412–13 and in H. Llewellyn Smith (ed.), *New Survey of London Life and Labour*, vol. VI, p. 270.

2. A. J. Sherman, *Island Refuge: Britain and Refugees from the Third Reich, 1933–1939;* Austin Stevens, *The Dispossessed: German Refugees in Britain.*

3. A. Newman, *The United Synagogue: 1870–1970*, pp. 216–17.

4. H. S. Levin and S. S. Levin, *Jubilee at Finchley: The Story of a Congregation*, pp. 2–3, 26. For other references see A. A. Jackson, *Semi-Detached London*, pp. 82–83, 269–70.

5. Elaine Larsen, 'Death of a district', *JC* Colour Magazine, 26 November 1969, p. 73.

6. E. Krausz, *Leeds Jewry: Its History and Social Structure*, pp. 22–26.

7. As many as 85,000 in the 1930s: V. D. Lipman, *Social History of the Jews in England: 1850–1950*, pp. 168–69 and 'The development of London Jewry', in S. S. Levin (ed.), *A Century of Anglo-Jewish Life: 1870–1970*, pp. 52–53.

8. Llewellyn Smith, op. cit., vol. VI, p. 287.

9. V. D. Lipman, *A Century of Social Service*, chap. 5, 'The Growth of Social Services (1914–1939)'.

10. *Journey through a Small Planet*, p. 92 (Penguin ed., 1976, pp. 79–80).

11. *Taxi!*, p. 15, and his *The Woman from Bessarabia*, p. 54. See a note about a Liverpool taxi-driver, born in Russia in 1900, arrived Liverpool 1914, and became a taxi-driver in 1923, having been a tailor and a soldier; *JC*, 26 October 1973, p. 39. Other reminiscences of the Jewish Orphanage are in David Nathan, 'They asked for more—and got it: the story of Norwood', *JC* Colour Magazine, 22 November 1974, pp. 68–75.

12. *What Nobody Told the Foreman*, p. 81. Also his *I Was One of the Unemployed*. See in addition a comparable account by another cabinet-maker; Paul Martinson, 'Cabinet Maker', in *Working Lives*, vol. I: *1905–1945: A People's Autobiography of Hackney*, pp. 96–105.

13. Frank Butler, *A History of Boxing in Britain*, pp. 148–52 (Lewis), 162–64 (Berg), 177–78 (Phillips); Brian Glanville, 'Reunion in Windmill Street', *JC* Colour Magazine, 22 November 1968, pp. 47–50; *JC*, 2 November 1973 (Moss) and 27 January 1978 (Cannons). The first Jewish private soldier to be killed in World War I, formerly a Leeds postal worker, had been an army boxing champion in 1907; Paul H. Emden, *Jews of Britain*, p. 448.

14. A. B. Levy, *East End Story*, pp. 15–16. One of the twenty Jewish road-sweepers of Stepney in the late 1940s had been so employed since the 1920s. He was of Dutch-Jewish origin.

15. Michael Wallach, 'How "greeners" came to the valley', *JC* Colour Magazine, 28 November 1975, p. 25.

16. S. P. Dobbs, *The Clothing Workers of Great Britain*, pp. 37, 49.

17. Vol. VI, p. 295.

18. Ibid.

19. Ibid., vol. II, pp. 218–19.

20. C. P. Hershon, 'The evolution of Jewish elementary education in England with special reference to Liverpool', unpublished Ph.D. thesis, University of Sheffield, 1973, Table 18.

21. Llewellyn Smith, op. cit., vol. II, p. 213.

22. P. G. Hall, 'The East London footwear industry: an industrial quarter in decline', *East London Papers*, 5(1), 1962, pp. 20–21.

23. Dobbs, op. cit., pp. 165–66.

24. Llewellyn Smith, op. cit., vol. II, pp. 26, 280. The clothing industry is there defined widely, to include, for example, the making of headgear and of artificial flowers, as well as the main manufacture of outerwear and underclothing.

25. Elizabeth Ewing, *History of Twentieth Century Fashion*, p. 132. The figure comes originally from Margaret Wray, *The Women's Outerwear Industry*.

26. Board of Trade, *Working Party Reports: Furniture*, pp. 45–46. The statistical material is discussed on pp. 45–52.

27. Dobbs, op. cit., p. 200.

28. Larsen, op. cit., p. 73. Dobbs, op. cit., has much useful contemporary material. See, *inter alia*, 'Mark Simons—tailor', in *Working Lives*, vol. I: *1905–1945: A People's Autobiography of Hackney*, pp. 70–74; and Willy Goldman's stories: *East End My Cradle* and *A Saint in the Making*.

29. Joan Thomas, 'A history of the Leeds clothing industry', *Yorks. Bull. of Econ. and Soc. Research*, Occasional Paper no. 1, 1955, pp. 56–57. Dobbs, op. cit., p. 23, noted that 'in most factories owned by Gentiles, it is usual, if Jews are employed, to provide one room for Jews and one for Gentiles, the view being taken that the two races will not mix.'

30. Information from Mr Ronald Hurst.

31. Flann Campbell, 'East London grammar schools', *East London Papers* 1(2), 1958, p. 3 n.2. He mentions three other schools each with between 16 and 27 per cent of Jewish pupils. Also G. Alderman, *The History of Hackney Downs School, formerly the Grocers' Company School*, pp. 42, 79, for references to Jewish pupils.

32. Neustatter, op. cit., p. 132. The comparable figure for England and Wales was 16 per cent.

33. Two women who spent their working lives employed by the railways were Mrs Sylvia Morris of Leeds (*JC*, 5 April 1974, p. 46, obituary), Miss Frances Levy (*JC*, 14 January 1977, p. 17). Ashley Smith's novel, *You Forget so Quickly*, describes the effect of the 1938 Munich crisis on the Jewish and non-Jewish staff members of an East End Borough. Also Levy, op. cit., p. 16. In the late 1940s, sixty-two of Stepney Borough's office staff were Jews.

34. See chap. 3, n.62.

35. Lipman, op. cit., p. 171. The Board's industrial work is described on pp. 170–72. Apprenticeship statistics are on pp. 287 and 289.

36. *JC*, 16 May 1975, p. 31, obituary.

37. Ibid., 11 February 1922.

38. Leon Samuels, 'The Jewish labour movement', *Jew. Quart.*, 11(3), 1956, pp. 35–36.

39. Llewellyn Smith, op. cit., vol. V, pp. 47–48.

40. R. A. Leeson, *Strike: A Live History*, pp. 133–34.

41. Dobbs, op. cit., p. 126. His chap. 6 is a useful account of clothing trade unionism in the 1920s.

42. Margaret Stewart and Leslie Hunter, *The Needle Is Threaded*, especially chaps. 17 and 19.

43. Ibid., chap. 18; S. W. Lerner, *Breakaway Unions and the Small Trade Union*, pp. 85–143; also L. J. MacFarlane, *The British Communist Party: Its Origin and Development until 1929*, pp. 258–60. Leeson, op. cit., pp. 116–19, for some reminiscences by E. Mofshovitz, an organiser for the breakaway union.

44. Stewart and Hunter, op. cit., pp. 200–202.

45. Ibid., p. 181.

46. Ibid., p. 199.

47. Dobbs, op. cit., p. 46.

48. Sheila Cunnison, *Wages and Work Allocation: A Study of Social Relations in a Garment Workshop*, p. 26. This section is based on pp. 24–28.

13 Business and the Professions in the Inter-war Years

1. 'Anglo-Jewry under George V, 1910–1936', *Jewish Year Book*, 5697–98 (1937), p. 370.

2. Ibid., p. 369.

3. Robert Henriques, *Marcus Samuel, First Viscount Bearsted and Founder of the 'Shell' Transport and Trading Company: 1853–1927*; A. E. C. Hare, *The Anthracite Coal Industry of the*

Swansea District, pp. 42ff.; W. J. Reader, *Imperial Chemical Industries: A History,* vol. I: *The Forerunners, 1870–1926.*

4. Robert Jones and Oliver Marriott, *Anatomy of a Merger: A History of GEC, AEI, and English Electric,* chaps. 4, 5 and 9.

5. Charles Wilson, *The History of Unilever,* vol. II, part 4.

6. D. J. Richardson, 'J. Lyons & Co. Ltd.: caterers and food manufacturers, 1894 to 1939', in D. J. Oddy and D. S. Miller (eds), *The Making of the Modern British Diet,* pp. 161–72.

7. See T. Balogh, *Studies in Financial Organisation, passim.*

8. Paul H. Emden, *Jews of Britain,* pp. 344–47. Some members of these families moved out of banking. Dr Richard Seligman established the Aluminium Plant & Vessel Co. in 1910 to exploit the first British patent for welding aluminium. He married a Roman Catholic; his son, Sir Peter Seligman, recently chairman of APV Holdings, is a member of the Church of England. Neither is included, therefore, in our discussion of Jews in industry (even though the *Jewish Chronicle* listed Sir Peter in its identification of Jews in the 1978 New Year's Honours List).

9. Ibid., p. 542.

10. R. Palin, *Rothschild Relish.*

11. E. Beddington-Behrens, *Look Back, Look Forward,* chap. 7, has some references to Jewish City personalities of the 1930s.

12. George Orwell, 'Anti-semitism in Britain', in his *England Your England, and Other Essays,* p. 68. The essay was first published in the *Contemporary Jewish Record* in 1945.

13. B. W. E. Alford, *W. D. & H. O. Wills and the Development of the U.K. Tobacco Industry,* pp. 334–35, 345. The book contains other references to some of these companies.

14. N. Barou, *The Jews in Work and Trade: A World Survey,* pp. 4–11, originally published in the *Bulletin* of the Trades Advisory Council. The names in the local directories were identified by Trades Advisory Council members in the relevant districts. Although their knowledge was extensive, they could not overcome the permanent difficulty of establishing whether a particular firm was Jewish. Fringe Jews and those in 'unusual' industries were probably unknown to them.

15. *JC,* 26 April 1974, obituary of S. Leverton. The family's ironmongery shop still continues, in Oxford.

16. 'Anglo-Jewry under George V . . .', p. 370.

17. Barou, op. cit., p. 7.

18. G. D. M. Block, 'Jewish students at the universities of Great Britain and Ireland—excluding London, 1936–1939', *Sociol. Rev.,* 34(3 and 4), 1942, pp. 183–97.

19. G. Havenhand, *Nation of Shopkeepers,* pp. 107–9. Information from Mr Mark Goldberg, managing director.

20. Information from Mr E. N. Cohen, chairman of Courts (Furnishers) Ltd.

21. Havenhand, op. cit., p. 150; *JC,* 3 March 1978, obituary.

22. *JC,* 24 March 1978, obituary of Sir Jeremy Raisman.

23. Elizabeth Ewing, *History of Twentieth Century Fasion,* p. 119; see generally chap. 6, 'Developments in Fashion Manufacture between the Wars, 1918–1939'. Also Margaret Wray, *The Women's Outerwear Industry.*

24. 'A résumé of the life, business and social activities of Mr Samuel Goldstein'.

25. Ewing, op. cit., p. 126. This book contains useful accounts of a number of firms, some of them Jewish.

26. W. Branch Johnson, *Hertfordshire,* p. 214. *Stock Exchange Year Book.*

27. *JC,* 10 October 1971, obituary of Albert Alberman. It remains a private company but information about it is filed at Companies House.

28. S. Pollard, *The Development of the British Economy,* p. 182. See accounts of Jewish shopkeeping life in R. Waterman, *A Family of Shopkeepers,* and Z. Marenbon, *Don't Blow Out the Candle: A Liverpool Childhood of the Twenties.*

29. M. Corina, *Pile It High and Sell It Cheap: The Authorised Biography of Sir John Cohen, Founder of Tesco.* The father in Waterman, op. cit., sells in the markets while the mother looks

after the shop. In Evelyn Cowan, *Spring Remembered: A Scottish Jewish Childhood*, pp. 21ff., there is a description of peddling in Scotland in the late 1920s.

30. J. B. Jefferys, *Retail Trading in Britain: 1850–1950*, the standard work on the subject. Also Pollard, op. cit., pp. 175–83.

31. D. B. Halpern, 'Jews in Britain's economy: IV', *Jew. Quart.*, 18, 1957, p. 37. He also states that in 1930 of 14,000 clothing establishments in London ('including furs, dry-cleaning, repairs etc.'), 8,000 were Jewish. The basis of these figures is not given.

32. M. Freedman, 'Jews in the society of Britain', in M. Freedman (ed.), *A Minority in Britain*, pp. 213–16.

33. J. G. Dony, *History of the Straw Hat Industry*, pp. 171–75, and 'The hat industry', in H. A. Silverman (ed.), *Studies in Industrial Organization*, pp. 155–98.

34. S. Aris, *The Jews in Business*, pp. 131ff.

35. Barou, op. cit., p. 7.

36. Information from Mr E. N. Cohen. Jefferys, op. cit., p. 424.

37. Aris, op. cit., p. 106. The expansion programme led to acute financial problems; Beddington-Behrens, op. cit., pp. 86–89.

38. *JC*, 3 December 1976, obituary of N. Horne. Jefferys, op. cit., p. 304.

39. Havenhand, op. cit., p. 152.

40. Ibid., p. 194; Jefferys, op. cit., p. 416. It was a private business until 1952. Gilbert Edgar, chairman from 1935 to 1978, was a descendant of the founders. See his obituary in *The Times*, 13 April 1978, and *JC*, 31 March 1978.

41. Goronwy Rees, *St Michael: A History of Marks and Spencer*, pp. 70–124. It became a public company in 1926.

42. Aris, op. cit., pp. 136–38.

43. S. W. Lerner, *Breakaway Unions and the Small Trade Union*, p. 120.

44. Aris, op. cit., pp. 122–23.

45. Information from Mr H. C. Franks.

46. K. Richardson, *Twentieth-Century Coventry*, pp. 36–37.

47. E. Birkhead, 'The financial failure of British air transport companies: 1919–24', *J. Transport Hist.*, 4(3), 1960, pp. 133–45.

48. A. Horner, *Incorrigible Rebel*, pp. 150–51.

49. A. Plummer, *New British Industries in the Twentieth Century*, p. 49.

50. A. Briggs, *The History of Broadcasting in the United Kingdom*: vol. I, *The Birth of Broadcasting*, p. 32; *Who's Who*.

51. Jones and Marriott, p. 241.

52. Information from Thorn Electrical Industries Ltd.

53. M. Balcon, *Michael Balcon Presents . . . A Lifetime of Films*; Charles Barr, *Ealing Studios*; *The Times*, 18 October 1977, obituary of Sir Michael Balcon.

54. Emden, op. cit., pp. 540–41; information from Mr B. Ostrer; Beddington-Behrens, op. cit., p. 83; *Stock Exchange Year Book* (s.v. Illingworth, Morris).

55. Karol Kulik, *Alexander Korda: The Man Who Could Work Miracles*.

56. Plummer, op. cit., pp. 327–31.

57. Ibid., pp. 325, 328.

58. Aris, op. cit., p. 129.

59. D. Abse, *A Poet in the Family*, pp. 56, 72.

60. *Guardian*, 17 November 1973, p. 9, profile of Nat Cohen.

61. *JC*, 1 February 1974, p. 11, profile of Lord Bernstein.

62. Albert McCarthy, *The Dance Band Era*; S. Colin, *And the Bands Played On*; *JC*, 17 December 1971, obituary of Syd Fay; ibid., 20 October 1971, article on Sidney Lipton; ibid., 10 May 1974, obituary of Geraldo. Among other Jews in the wide field of entertainment and music were comedians such as Bud Flanagan and Ernie Lotinga, pianists such as Myra Hess and Solomon, and Louis Levy, the conductor.

63. Emden, op. cit., p. 540.

64. R. J. Minney, *Viscount Southwood.*

65. F. Warburg, *All Authors Are Equal: The Publishing Life of Fredric Warburg, 1936–1971.*

66. Sheila Hodges, *Gollancz: The Story of a Publishing House, 1928–1978; The Times,* 9 February 1967, obituary of Sir Victor Gollancz. See also the autobiography of another publisher, originally a journalist; Mark Goulden, *Mark My Words!*

67. *JC,* 27 May 1977, p. 10, profile of Oswald Stroud, It became a public company in 1954. Also in the textile trade was (Sir) Nicholas Sekers, an immigrant from Hungary, who established a silk-weaving enterprise in Whitehaven in 1937; *JC,* 14 July 1972, obituary.

68. Information from Mr A. Gourvitch, chairman and managing director of the Phoenix Timber Co., nephew of the founder. An important figure in the trade was Sir Archibald, son of Rev. Isidore Harris. Sir Archibald was timber controller at the Ministry of Supply during World War II; *JC,* 6 August 1971, obituary.

69. Michael Freedland, 'New roots for old', *JC,* 15 April 1977, p. 19, a profile of the Persian Jewish community in London.

70. Information from Mr David Brown, a director of Lewis, Rose & Co. for forty years until the firm was sold in 1969 to Spear & Jackson.

71. Norman Bentwich, *The Rescue and Achievement of Refugee Scholars: The Story of Displaced Scholars and Scientists, 1933–1952;* Lord Robbins, *Autobiography of an Economist,* pp. 143–44; Walter Adams, 'The refugee scholars of the 1930s', *Pol. Quart.,* 39(1), 1968, pp. 7–14.

72. R. N. Salaman, 'The Jewish Fellows of the Royal Society', *MJHSE,* part 5, 1948, pp. 171–72.

73. Foseco Minsep Ltd, *History of Foseco: 1931–1969;* 'Foseco, 1932–1957: an era of enterprise', unpublished history of the company. I am grateful to Sir Eric Weiss for lending me a copy of this MS.

74. Information from Mr H. Djanogly, chairman of the Nottingham Manufacturing Co. Ltd.

75. H. Loebl, 'Government-financed factories and the establishment of industries by refugees in the Special Areas of the North of England 1937–1961', unpublished M.Phil. thesis, University of Durham, 1978, p. 121.

76. *JC,* 23 July 1971; *The Sunday Times,* 5 March 1978, p. 59. The company was eventually absorbed by the Dunlop group in 1968.

77. The rest of this section is based on Loebl, op. cit.; *Britain's New Citizens: The Story of the Refugees from Germany and Austria* (Tenth Anniversary Publication of the Association of Jewish Refugees in Great Britain), pp. 25ff.; L. Simmonds, 'From Germany with honour', *JC* Colour Magazine, 26 November 1976, pp. 46–56.

14 The Working Class since World War II

1. Reported in *The Times,* 25 September 1978, p. 2.

2. *JC,* 27 January 1978, p. 8.

3. G. Alderman, 'Not quite British: the political attitudes of Anglo-Jewry', in Ivor Crewe (ed.), *British Political Sociology Yearbook,* vol. II, p. 196; V. D. and S. L. Lipman, 'A middle-class community', *JC* Colour Magazine, 28 November 1975, pp. 74–76. This is a useful brief statement of main trends since 1945.

4. Thus we can ignore the special cases of those young Jews who trained in Britain as agricultural workers in preparation for emigration to Israel, and the war-time conscripts to the coal mines.

5. S. J. Prais and M. Schmool, 'The size and structure of the Anglo-Jewish population: 1960–65', *Jew. J. Sociol.,* 10(1), 1968, pp. 15–34. This reduced to 410,000 the commonly accepted figure of 450,000. It has probably fallen since the 1960s. Prais and Schmool, 'Statistics of Milah [circumcision] and the Jewish birth-rate', ibid., 12(2), 1970, pp. 187–93; 'The fertility of Jewish

families in Britain: 1971', ibid., 15(2), 1973, pp. 189–203. Also, B. A. Kosmin, 'What's happening to us?' *JC*, 9 September 1977, p. 57.

6. S. J. Prais, 'Synagogue statistics and the Jewish population of Great Britain: 1900–70', *Jew. J. Sociol.*, 14(2), 1972, p. 222, for estimates for each London borough. More recent expansions in the outer areas have been reported at Borehamwood and Elstree (*JC*, 11 February 1977, p. 17); at Belmont (ibid., 1 April 1977, p. 10); and Pinner (ibid., 24 June 1977, p. 5). One estimate of the Jewish population of the East End in the early 1970s puts it at 8,000, and falling, *JC*, 16 January 1976, p. 9.

7. This was reported in H. Neustatter, 'Demographic and other statistical aspects of Anglo-Jewry', in M. Freedman (ed.), *A Minority in Britain*, pp. 66, 124–30; ibid., pp. 254–57 for statistical tables.

8. Ernest Krausz, 'The Edgware survey: occupation and social class', *Jew. J. Sociol.*, 11(1), 1969, Table 1. This article is based on his 'A sociological field study of Jewish suburban life in Edgware 1962–3 with special reference to minority identification', unpublished Ph.D. thesis, University of London, 1965.

9. Gerald Cromer, 'Intermarriage and communal survival in a London suburb', *Jew, J. Sociol.* 16 (2), 1974, p. 156, based on his 'A comparison of Jewish and non-Jewish family life with special reference to inter-generational relations', unpublished Ph.D. thesis, University of Nottingham, 1973; see especially pp. 115–31.

10. B. A. Kosmin, M. Bauer and N. Grizzard, *Steel City Jews*, pp. 20–23.

11. B. A. Kosmin and N. Grizzard, *Jews in an Inner London Borough*, pp. 25–30.

12. S. J. Prais and M. Schmool, 'The social-class structure of Anglo-Jewry: 1961', *Jew. J. Sociol.*, 17(1), 1975, pp. 5–15.

13. Prais and Schmool, 'Size and structure . . .', p. 11.

14. J. Gould and S. Esh (eds), *Jewish Life in Modern Britain*, p. 37. It was a comment on a paper by Ernest Krausz, 'The economic and social structure of Anglo-Jewry', ibid. pp. 27–34.

15. Prais and Schmool, 'Social-class structure . . .', p. 8.

16. *JC*, 31 March 1978, p. 22.

17. *JC* Supplement, 24 September 1971, p. 1.

19. Ibid., 3 October 1974, p. 7. In 1978 the paper reported an increase in the number of families whose children were being supported; ibid., 13 January 1978, p. 8.

20. See, *inter alia*, *JC*, 4 March 1977, p. 5 ('middle class poverty'), and p. 17, 'What can we do about grandpa?'

21. Ibid., 31 March 1978, p. 22.

22. Gould and Esh (eds), op. cit., p. 183.

23. P. 48. See also the comments on Dutch Jews in Ralph Finn, *No Tears in Aldgate*, pp. 17–18.

24. Paul Gottlieb, 'Social mobility of the Jewish immigrant', unpublished M.Phil. thesis, University of Nottingham, 1970, pp. 240–45; also Sonia Ladsky, 'Refugees from the Raj', *JC*, 17 June 1977, p. 23.

25. *JC*, 15 June 1973, p. 15.

26. Ibid., 21 February 1975, p. 19.

27. Sheila Patterson, *Immigrants in Industry*, pp. 336, 340, 343.

28. Union of Liberal and Progressive Synagogues, *Jewish Students: A Question of Identity*, p. 6, which mentions as examples the occupations of diamond-cutter and taxi-driver; also E. J. de Kadt, 'Locating minority group members: two British surveys of Jewish university students.', *Jew. J. Sociol.*, 6 (1), 1964, p. 35.

29. *JC*, 15 and 24 February 1974.

30. *The Times*, 18 January 1977.

31. *The Observer*, 30 September 1973, p. 19.

32. *JC*, 12 July 1974, p. 19.

33. Sam Allen, 'Live and let live', *New Epoch*, Ruskin College magazine, 1965, pp. 32–33.

34. *JC* Colour Magazine, 23 November 1973, p. 25.

35. *JC,* 5 April 1974, p. 21.

36. Ibid., 23 January 1976, pp. 22–23.

37. Ibid.

38. Freedman (ed.), op. cit., pp. 254–57.

39. Lipman and Lipman, op. cit., p. 76.

40. Ibid.

41. J. W. Carrier, 'A Jewish proletariat', in M. Mindlin and Chaim Bermant (eds), *Explorations: An Annual on Jewish Themes,* pp. 120–40.

42. Kosmin and Grizzard, op. cit., pp. 29–30.

43. Carole Field, 'Taxi!—the Jews behind the wheel', *JC* Colour Magazine, 30 April 1971, pp. 14–20; also June Rose, 'A Jewish "Mayhew" ', in Mindlin and Bermant (eds), op. cit., pp. 115–17.

44. *Daily Mirror,* 29 June 1976, p. 11.

45. Field, op. cit., p. 14.

46. Gould and Esh (eds), op. cit., p. 40.

47. Krausz, 'Edgware survey', p. 80.

48. Enid Grizzard and Peter Marsh, 'Ilford: profile of a community,' *JC* Colour Magazine, 26 November 1971, p. 28. The more systematic survey which was carried out a few years later suggested a figure of 35,000, B. A. Kosmin, 'The face of Jewish suburbia', *JC,* 14 July 1978, p. 21.

49. Grizzard and Marsh, op. cit., front cover of magazine.

50. Kosmin, 'The face of Jewish suburbia', *JC,* 14 July 1978, pp. 21, 29; and 21 July 1978, p. 17.

51. Rising unemployment was recorded by, for example, the Sabbath Observance Employment Bureau, *JC,* 13 August 1976, p. 12, but the numbers were small, as were those of allegations of discrimination against Jews in employment which were referred to the Trades Advisory Council. Only eighteen were received between January 1975 and December 1977; ibid., 31 March 1978, p. 7.

15   Business and the Professions since 1945

1. Andrew Roth, *Harold Wilson: Yorkshire Walter Mitty,* has a relevant discussion.

2. Published each year in the *Jewish Year Book.*

3. *The Jews in Business.*

4. Many of the details given in this chapter are taken from published company Reports and Accounts as well as from direct contact with some of the people involved. Other useful information is available in published reports such as those of the Monopolies and Mergers Commission and the Commission on Industrial Relations. Case study material is given in P. E. Hart, M. A. Utton and G. Walshe, *Mergers and Concentration in British Industry* and in G. Walshe, *Recent Trends in Monopoly in Great Britain.* Most of these data refer to public companies, but private companies are required to submit to the Department of Trade and Industry certain information which is publicly available.

5. In 1974. *The Sunday Times,* 11 December 1977, p. 61.

6. M. Persoff, 'A name that registers: a profile of the Gross brothers', *JC* Business Efficiency Supplement, 1 October 1971, p. vi. This appeared when the firm was still independent.

7. H. Loebl, 'Government-financed factories and the establishment of industries by refugees in the special areas of the North of England 1937–1961', unpublished M. Phil. thesis, University of Durham, 1978, *passim.* This study contains case studies of many of the firms.

8. John Bloom, *It's No Sin to Make a Profit;* A. Robertson, 'Its bloom is shed', in his *The Lessons of Failure,* pp. 72–81.

9. 'How Stern made and lost those easy millions', *The Sunday Times,* 4 June 1978, p. 62.

10. The newspapers were full of this story. See, for example, *The Times,* 23 September 1977, obituary; *Observer,* 25 September 1977, p. 2.

11. *JC,* 17 January 1975, p. 19.

12. 'Life and survival of the little man', *Guardian*, 13 January 1978, p. 14, has annual statistics.

13. E. Krausz, 'The Edgware survey: occupation and social class', *Jew. J. Sociol.*, 11(1), 1969, p. 78.

14. Details in Loebl, op. cit.

15. Aris, *The Jews in Business*, p. 18; *The Economist*, 13 December 1969, pp. 62–63.

16. *The Sunday Times*, 11 December 1977, p. 71: 'a good delegator', contrasting him with Jack Cotton, the property developer, in discussing why their merger was not a success. Also *Observer*, 8 September 1974, in an article 'Pieces of folk Clore': 'having once found people who can mind his millions, he has sensibly left them to go on minding'.

17. Aris, op. cit., pp. 139–41; information from Mr E. N. Cohen.

18. 'Foseco 1932–1957: an era of enterprise', unpublished, pp. 40–57.

19. Information from Sir Emmanuel Kaye; *Who's Who*.

20. Persoff, op. cit.

21. 'Mister Fidelity', *JC* Audio-visual Supplement, 20 July 1973, p. iv.

22. Information from Mr C. S. Schreiber.

23. Information from Mr A. Rosenblatt.

24. *The Times*, 27 September 1967, obituary. A pre-1938 associate in Vienna, Harry Fischer, established with a colleague the Marlborough Fine Arts Gallery after the war; *The Times*, 15 April 1977, obituary.

25. Information from Mr E. N. Cohen.

26. Information from Mr H. Newmark.

27. Information from Thorn Electrical Industries Ltd.

28. John Gross, 'The Lynskey Tribunal', in M. Sissons and P. French (eds), *The Age of Austerity*, pp. 255–75, a useful summary and discussion.

29. *JC*, 5 October 1973, p. 31.

30. *Who's Who*.

31. Newspaper headlines encapsulated the problems: 'Gone for a Burton', *The Sunday Times*, 28 November 1976, p. 55, and 'Coming apart at the seams', ibid., 15 May 1977, p. 63. But the company began to make profits soon afterwards.

32. 'The agony of J. Lyons', *The Sunday Times*, 31 October 1976, p. 55, analyses the difficulties which led to the take-over bid two years later.

33. Goronwy Rees, 'The multi-millionaires: 3. Pioneer of the take-over: Charles Clore', *The Sunday Times* Magazine Section, 24 January 1960, pp. 11–12. I am grateful to Mr Leonard Sainer, a long-term associate of Sir Charles Clore and his successor as chairman of Sears Holdings, for drawing my attention to this article. See also *JC*, 3 August 1979, p. 12, for obituary of Sir Charles Clore.

34. Information from BSC (Footwear) Ltd.

35. 14 February 1953, p. 433.

36. Charles Raw, *Slater Walker: An Investigation of a Financial Phenomenon*.

37. *The Observer*, 4 July 1976, p. 12.

38. See Robert Heller's comments in the *Observer*, 8 September 1974, where he argues that Clore's companies progressed by opportunism and that Clore 'never dreamt of going into footwear until he found shoe shops were cheap today, cheaper than yesterday'.

39. *The Economist*, 18 September 1954, 'Mr Clore clears the decks'; also ibid,. 25 September 1954, p. 1,006.

40. Oliver Marriott, *The Property Boom*. I am grateful to Mr Edward Erdman for providing much useful data on the property world.

41. Information from Mr L. T. S. Littman; *The Times*, 27 August 1953, p. 8, and 24 September 1953, p. 3; Marriott, op. cit., pp. 45–46; Littman *v.* Barron, *Reports of Tax Cases*, vol. 33 (1950–52), 1953, pp. 373–413, gives some details of his property dealings.

42. Aris, op. cit., p. 202.

43. Raw, op. cit., p. 41.

44. *The Times*, 23 March 1964, obituary.

45. Aris, op. cit., pp. 191–92, 195–96; 'Sir Max Rayne',*JC* Property Supplement, 25 June 1971, pp. viii–ix; 'The cultured man of property', *Observer*, 25 July 1971. He had just been appointed chairman of the National Theatre.

46. *JC*, 10 November 1972, p. 33, obituary. His property firm is now part of the Wimpey construction group.

47. *The Sunday Times*, 11 December 1977, p. 71.

48. *The Economist*, 11 January 1969, p. 73, which qualifies this by including the word 'probably'.

49. *The Sunday Times*, 30 April 1978, p. 72, when Carlton Industries was the subject of a bid by Hawker Siddeley.

50. 'Everyone's wild about Harry', *The Observer*, 2 July 1972, p. 9.

51. *JC*, 23 June 1972, p. 7. Also ibid., 12 May 1972, p. 24, editorial.

52. Ibid., 13 April 1973, p. 28.

53. The conduct of his group was raised in parliament by a Jewish MP;*JC*, 19 November 1971, p. 19; the matter was taken up by the Trades Advisory Council; ibid., 26 November 1971, p. 6. See also a profile of Freshwater in ibid., 26 May 1972, p. 10.

54. 'The elusive tycoon',*JC*, 9 March 1973, p. 15; 'Death of an unknown property emperor', *The Sunday Times*, 25 September 1977, p. 72; 'Pauper millionaire', *Daily Express*, 22 September 1977, p. 7.

55. *The Economist*, 11 July 1953, p. 126.

56. In 1977 Great Universal Stores claimed to have one-third of the mail order business, Littlewood's having a little less; *Daily Mail*, 13 October 1977, p. 37. Despite expansion, mail order business accounts for only a few per cent of consumer sales in the U.K.

57. Hart, Utton and Walshe, op. cit., pp. 43–48; Monopolies Commission, *Thorn Electrical Industries Ltd and Radio Rentals Ltd*.

58. Based on Robert Jones and Oliver Marriott, *Anatomy of a Merger: A History of GEC, AEI, and English Electric*, which has full references. For an acerbic profile of Sir Arnold Weinstock, see *New Statesman*, 26 September 1975, pp. 359–60: 'The dedicated calculating machine'. He was created a life peer in 1980.

59. The information in this paragraph comes from the respective companies' Reports and Accounts. See also M. Corina, *Pile It High and Sell It Cheap,* for Tesco; S. Kalisch, *A Builder of Judaism: The Story of Arthur Hubert and his Family; The Observer,* 30 April 1972, p. 16, for Hubert. Its turnover in the 1970s of some £20 million classifies it as a medium-sized company.

60. There is plenty of material on the Grade brothers. On Lord Grade, for example, 'The mogul of mass taste', *The Sunday Times* Colour Magazine, 5 December 1971, pp. 33–34, and 'Britain's showbiz Mr Big', *The Observer* Colour Magazine, 4 December 1973, pp. 43–47. For Lord Delfont; 'Impresario royal',*JC*, 13 October 1972, p. 16.

61. Hart, Utton and Walshe, op. cit., pp. 43–48.

62. *The Observer* Colour Magazine, 17 September 1972, pp. 24–26. Max Stein, a bookmaker, took over Ladbroke's in 1956, his nephew Cyril Stein becoming managing director. The company extended into hotels and catering.

63. *JC*, 1 September 1972, p. 9.

64. S. J. Prais and M. Schmool, 'The social-class structure of Anglo-Jewry: 1961', *Jew. J. Sociol.*, 17 (1), 1975, p. 11.

65. Krausz, op. cit., p. 84.

66. B. A. Kosmin, M. Bauer and N. Grizzard, *Steel City Jews*, p. 20.

67. Ibid., p. 23.

68. *JC*, B'nai B'rith Hillel Foundation Supplement, 29 December 1972, p. ii.

69. *JC*, 13 May 1977, p. 5; ibid., 5 August 1977, p. 4.

70. Ibid., 17 December 1971, p. 24.

71. Ibid., 27 April 1973, p. 9. This is not likely to be the total number of Jewish journalists.

72. Krausz, op. cit., p. 79.

73. 'My son the youth worker' was the heading of a news item in the *Jewish Chronicle*, 17 December 1971, p. 24.

74. Kosmin, Bauer and Grizzard, op. cit., p. 22.

75. Given the cut-back in teacher training in the mid-1970s in view of the country's falling birth-rate, the number of Jews entering teaching will undoubtedly fall.

16   *Conclusion*

1. Max Weber argued that the nature of the Jewish religion was particularly influential. See his *Ancient Judaism*, and *The Sociology of Religion*. A useful summary and brief criticism of Weber's ideas is by I. Schiper, 'Max Weber on the sociological basis of the Jewish religion', *Jew. J. Sociol.*, 1(2), 1959, pp. 250–60. Important factual material which corrects and amends Weber's empirical propositions is in M. Wischnitzer, *A History of Jewish Crafts and Guilds*, especially Werner J. Cahnman, 'Introduction: role and significance of the Jewish artisan class', pp. xiii–xxvii.

2. Wischnitzer, op. cit., is an important source.

3. Cahnman, op. cit., p. xvi.

4. See the brief excellent article by David S. Landes, 'The Jewish merchant: typology and stereotypology in Germany', *Leo Baeck Year Book*, 19, 1974, pp. 11–23; also Werner J. Cahnman, 'Village and small-town Jews in Germany—a typological study', ibid., pp. 107–30.

5. Lucien Wolf, 'Crypto-Jews under the Commonwealth', *TJHSE*, 1, 1895, pp. 73–75.

6. See p. 150 above.

7. *The Jews in Business*.

Bibliography

Bibliographies

The following have not been referred to directly but are worth including as helpful guides to the literature:

Roth, Cecil, *Magna Bibliotheca Anglo-Judaica: A Bibliographical Guide to Anglo-Jewish History*, London, 1937.
Lehmann, Ruth P., *Nova Bibliotheca Anglo-Judaica: A Bibliographical Guide to Anglo-Jewish History, 1937-1960*, London, 1961.
Lehmann, Ruth P., *Anglo-Jewish Bibliography: 1937–1970*, London, 1973.

Unpublished

Alderman, G., 'Into the vortex: South Wales Jewry before 1914', in A. Newman (ed.), 'Provincial Jewry in Victorian Britain', 1975, n. p.
Ambrose, G., 'The Levant company mainly from 1640–1753', unpublished B. Litt. thesis, University of Oxford, 1935.
Benski, Tova, 'Glasgow', in A. Newman (ed.), 'Provincial Jewry in Victorian Britain', 1975, n. p.
Birmingham Jewish Local History Study Group, 'A portrait of Birmingham Jewry in 1851', in A. Newman (ed.), 'Provincial Jewry in Victorian Britain', 1975, n. p.
Buckman, Joseph, 'Evolution of the alien economy of Leeds: 1880–1914', paper for the Urban History Group conference, Leeds, 1975.
Buckman, Joseph, 'The economic and social history of alien immigrants to Leeds: 1880–1914', unpublished Ph. D. thesis, University of Strathclyde, 1968.
Cottrell, P. L., 'Investment banking in England: case study of the International Financial Society', unpublished Ph. D. thesis, University of Hull, 1974.
Cromer, Gerald, 'A comparison of Jewish and non-Jewish family life with special reference to inter-generational relations', unpublished Ph. D. thesis, University of Nottingham, 1973.
Davies, Eileen Cavanagh, 'A chronological synopsis and index to Oxfordshire items in "Jackson's Oxford Journal", 1753–1780', Bodleian Library, Oxford, R. Top. 731.
Finestein, Israel, 'The Jews of Hull: 1770–1870'.
'Foseco, 1932–1957: an era of enterprise', unpublished history of Foseco Minsep Ltd.
Gottlieb, Paul, 'Social mobility of the Jewish immigrant', unpublished M. Phil. thesis, University of Nottingham, 1970.

Hendrick, June, 'The tailoresses in the ready-made clothing industry in Leeds, 1889–1899: a study in labour failure', unpublished M. A. thesis, University of Warwick, 1970.

Hershon, C. P., 'Genesis of a Jewish day school', in A. Newman (ed.), 'Provincial Jewry in Victorian Britain', 1975, n. p.

Hershon, C. P., 'The evolution of Jewish elementary education in England with special reference to Liverpool', unpublished Ph. D. thesis, University of Sheffield, 1973.

Kosmin, B. A., and N. Grizzard, 'The Jewish dead in the Great War as an indicator for Anglo-Jewish demography and class stratification in 1914', Research Unit, Board of Deputies of British Jews, 1974.

Krausz, Ernest, 'A sociological field study of Jewish suburban life in Edgware 1962–63 with special reference to minority identification', unpublished Ph. D. thesis, University of London, 1965.

Lerner, Shirley, 'The history of the United Clothing Workers' Union: a case study of social disorganization', unpublished Ph. D. thesis, University of London, 1956.

Lipman, V. D., 'The origins of provincial Anglo-Jewry', in A. Newman (ed.), 'Provincial Jewry in Victorian Britain', 1975, n. p.

Loebl, H., 'Government-financed factories and the establishment of industries by refugees in the Special Areas of the North of England 1937–1961', unpublished M. Phil. thesis, University of Durham, 1978.

Newman, A. (ed.), 'Provincial Jewry in Victorian Britain': papers for a conference at University College London convened by the Jewish Historical Society of England, 6 July 1975, n. p.

O'Brien, Rosalind, 'The establishment of the Jewish minority in Leeds', unpublished Ph. D. thesis, University of Bristol, 1975.

Olsover, L., 'Middlesbrough', in A. Newman (ed.), 'Provincial Jewry in Victorian Britain', 1975, n. p.

Olsover, L., 'North-East England', in A. Newman (ed.), 'Provincial Jewry in Victorian Britain', 1975, n. p.

'Prospectus of Hyam & Co. (1900) Ltd.', Bodleian Library, Oxford, 232865 b 4.

Quinn, P. L. S., 'The Jewish schooling systems of London: 1656–1956', unpublished Ph. D. thesis, University of London, 1958.

Rebbeck, Dennis, 'The history of iron shipbuilding on the Queen's Island up to July, 1874', unpublished Ph. D. thesis, The Queen's University, Belfast, 1950.

'A résumé of the life, business and social activities of Mr Samuel Goldstein', unpublished MS, 1968.

Richardson, D. J., 'The history of the catering industry, with special reference to the development of J. Lyons and Co. Ltd. to 1939', unpublished Ph. D. thesis, University of Kent at Canterbury, 1970.

Slowe, Malcolm, 'The foundation of Aldershot synagogue', in A. Newman (ed.), 'Provincial Jewry in Victorian Britain', 1975, n. p.

Steiner, Miriam Anne, 'Philanthropic activity and organization in the Manchester Jewish community: 1867–1914', unpublished M. A. thesis, University of Manchester, 1974.

Susser, Bernard (ed.), 'Statistical accounts of all the congregations in the British Empire 5606/1845', in A. Newman (ed.), 'Provincial Jewry in Victorian Britain', 1975, n. p.

Topham, A. J., 'The credit structure of the West Riding wool-textile industry in the 19th century', unpublished M. A. thesis, University of Leeds, 1953.

Wigley, J. M. 'Nineteenth century English sabbatarianism: a study of a religious, political and social phenomenon', unpublished Ph. D. thesis, University of Sheffield, 1972.

Parliamentary Papers

Select Committee on the Observance of the Sabbath Day, *PP*, 1831–32, 7.
Report on Handloom Weavers, *PP*, 1840, 23.
Second Report of the Children's Employment Commission, *PP*, 1843, 15.
Select Committee on Sunday Trading (Metropolis), *PP*, 1847, 9.
'Report by Dr Edward Smith on the sanitary circumstances of tailors in London', appendix 12 to 6th Report of the Medical Officer of the Privy Council, *PP*, 1863, 28.
Fourth Report of the Children's Employment Commission, *PP*, 1865, 20.
Report of the Inspectors of Factories, *PP*, 1868–69, 16.
Report of the Factory and Workshop Acts Commission, *PP*, 1876, 30.
Report of the Inspectors of Factories, *PP*, 1876, 16.
Report of the Inspectors of Factories, *PP*, 1880, 14.
Minutes of Evidence, Royal Commission on Labour, Group C, *PP*, 1892, 36, part 2.
Royal Commission on Alien Immigration, *PP*, 1903, 9.
Physical Examination of Men of Military Age, 1917–18: Medical Boards' Report, *PP*, 1920, 26.

Books and Articles

Abbott, W. C., *The Writings and Speeches of Oliver Cromwell*, vol. IV, Cambridge, Mass., 1947.
Abrahams, Dudley, 'Jew brokers of the City of London', MJHSE, part 3, 1937, pp. 80–94.
Abrahams, Israel, 'Passes issued to Jews in the period 1689 to 1696', *MJHSE*, part 1, 1925, pp. 24–33.
Abramsky, Chimen, 'The Jewish labour movement: some historiographical problems', *Soviet Jewish Affairs*, 1, 1971, pp. 45–51.
Abse, D., *A Poet in the Family*, London, 1974.
Adams, Walter, 'The refugee scholars of the 1930s', *Pol. Quart.*, 39(1), 1968, pp. 7–14.
Adburgham, Alison, *Shops and Shopping 1800–1914: Where, and in What Manner the Well-Dressed Englishwoman Bought her Clothes*, London, 1964.
Adler, M. (ed.), *The British Jewry Book of Honour*, London, 1922.
Adler, M., 'Benedict the gildsman of Winchester', *MJHSE*, part 4, 1942, pp. 1–8.
'The agony of J. Lyons', *The Sunday Times*, 31 October 1976, p. 55.
Agudot Poalim Yehudim B'Anglia (Taknonim, 1886–1890) (Jewish Unions in England [Rules, 1886–1890], Jerusalem, 1967.
Alderman, G., 'The anti-Jewish riots of August 1911 in South Wales', *Welsh Hist. Rev.*, 6(2), 1972, pp. 190–200.
Alderman, G., *The History of Hackney Downs School, formerly the Grocers' Company School*, London, 1972.
Alderman, G., 'Not quite British: the political attitudes of Anglo-Jewry', in Ivor Crewe (ed.), *British Political Sociology Yearbook*, vol. II, London 1975, pp. 188–211.
Aleichem, Sholom, *The Adventures of Mottel the Cantor's Son* (trans. Tamara Kahana), London and New York, 1958.
Alford, B. W. E., *W. D. & H. O. Wills and the Development of the U. K. Tobacco Industry: 1786–1965*, London, 1973.
Allen, Sam, 'Live and let live', *New Epoch*, Ruskin College magazine, 1965, pp. 32–33.
Anglo-Jewish Notabilities: Their Arms and Testamentary Dispositions, London, 1949.
'Anglo-Jewry under George V, 1910–1936', *Jewish Year Book*, 5697–98 (1937).

Anon., *History of Portsmouth*, 1809.

Applebaum, S., 'Were there Jews in Roman Britain?', *TJHSE*, 17, 1953, pp. 189–205.

Aris, S., *The Jews in Business*, London, 1970.

Arnold, A. P., 'A list of Jews and their households in London, extracted from the Census lists of 1695', *MJHSE*, part 6, 1962, pp. 73–141.

Arnold, A. P., 'Apprentices of Great Britain, 1710–1773', *MJHSE* part 7, 1970, pp. 145–57.

Aronsfeld, C. C., 'German Jews in Dundee', *JC*, 20 November 1953.

Aronsfeld, C. C., 'German Jews in Ireland', *AJR Information*, December 1953.

Aronsfeld, C. C., 'Great Jewish chemists', *Jewish Telegraph*, 18 December 1953.

Aronsfeld, C. C., 'Nottingham's lace pioneers', *Nottingham Guardian Journal*, 19 and 20 April 1954.

Aronsfeld, C. C., 'German Jews in Victorian England', *Year Book of the Leo Baeck Institute*, 7, 1962, pp. 312–29.

Aronsfeld, C. C., 'Jewish bankers and the Tsar', *Contemporary Rev.*, 224, March 1974, pp. 127–33.

Aronsfeld, C. C., 'Unfavoured nation', *JC*, 26 April 1974.

Ashley, M. P., *Financial and Commercial Policy under the Cromwellian Protectorate*, London, 1934.

Ashley, M. P., *The Greatness of Oliver Cromwell*, London, 1957.

Ashton, T. S., *An Economic History of England: The Eighteenth Century*, London, 1955.

Ashton, T. S., *Economic Fluctuations in England: 1700–1800*, Oxford, 1959.

Ashton, T. S., *Iron and Steel in the Industrial Revolution*, 3rd ed., Manchester, 1963.

Ashton, T. S., and J. Sykes, *The Coal Industry of the Eighteenth Century*, Manchester, 1929.

Aves, E., 'The furniture trade', in C. Booth (ed.), *Life and Labour of the People in London*, IV, 1893, pp. 157–218.

Bagehot, W., *Lombard Street: A Description of the Money Market*, 14th ed., London, 1915.

Bailey, J. D., 'Australian borrowing in Scotland in the nineteenth century', *Econ. Hist. Rev.*, 12(2), 1959, pp. 268–79.

Baillie, G. H., *Watchmakers and Clockmakers of the World*, 2nd ed., London, 1947.

Baker, Norman, *Government and Contractors: The British Treasury and War Supplies*, London, 1971.

Balcon, M., *Michael Balcon Presents . . . A Lifetime of Films*, London, 1969.

Balogh, T., *Studies in Financial Organisation*, Cambridge, 1947.

Barker, T. C., and M. Robbins, *A History of London Transport*, vol. II; *The Twentieth Century to 1970*, London, 1974.

Barnett, Arthur, 'Sussex Hall: the first Anglo-Jewish venture in popular education', *TJHSE*, 19, 1960, pp. 65–79.

Barnett, Arthur, *The Western Synagogue Through Two Centuries (1761–1961)*, London, 1961.

Barnett, L. D., 'First record of the Hebra Guemilut Hasadim, London, 1678', *TJHSE*, 10, 1924, pp. 258–60.

Barnett, L. D. (ed.), *El Libro de los Acuerdos: Being the Records and Accompts of the Spanish and Portuguese Synagogue of London from 1663 to 1681*, Oxford, 1931.

Barnett, L. D. (ed.), *Bevis Marks Records*, part 1, London, 1940.

Barnett, R. D., 'The travels of Moses Cassuto', in J. M. Shaftesley (ed.), *Remember the Days*, London, 1961, pp. 73–121.

Barnett, R. D., 'The correspondence of the Mahamad of the Spanish and Portuguese congregation of London during the seventeenth and eighteenth centuries', *TJHSE*, 20, 1964, pp. 1–50.

Barnett, R. D., 'Anglo-Jewry in the eighteenth century', in V.D. Lipman (ed.), *Three Centuries of Anglo-Jewish History*, London, 1971, pp. 45–68.

Barnett, R. D., 'Dr Samuel Nunes Ribeiro and the settlement of Georgia', in A. Newman (ed.), *Migration and Settlement*, London, 1971, pp. 63–100.

Barnett, R. D. (ed.), *The Sephardi Heritage*, London, 1972.

Baron, Alexander, *With Hope, Farewell*, London, 1952.

Barou, N., *The Jews in Work and Trade: A World Survey*, London, 1948.

Barr, Charles, *Ealing Studios*, London and Newton Abbot, 1977.

Bédarida, F., 'Londres au milieu du XIXe siècle', *Annales*, 23(2), 1968, pp. 268–95.

Beddington-Behrens, E., *Look Back, Look Forward*, London, 1963.

Behr, Alexander, 'Isidor Gerstenberg (1821–1876): founder of the Council of Foreign Bondholders', *TJHSE*, 17, 1953, pp. 207–13.

Behrend, Arthur, *Portrait of a Family Firm: Bahr, Behrend & Co.: 1793–1945*, Liverpool, 1970.

Beinart, H., 'The Jews in the Canary Islands: a re-evaluation', *TJHSE*, 25, 1977, pp. 48–86.

Bellamy, J. M., 'A Hull shipbuilding firm: the history of C. & W. Earle and Earle's Shipbuilding and Engineering Company Ltd.', *Business Hist.*, 6, 1963.

Ben-Sasson, H. H., and S. Ettinger (eds), *Jewish Society through the Ages*, London, 1971.

Benas, B. B., 'Jacob Waley (1818–1873)', *TJHSE*, 18, 1958, pp. 41–52.

Benas, B. L., 'Records of the Jews in Liverpool', *Trans. Hist. Soc. Lancs. and Cheshire*, 51, 1901, pp. 45–84.

Bentwich, Helen, *If I Forget Thee: Some Chapters of Autobiography, 1912–1920*, London, 1973.

Bentwich, Norman, *The Rescue and Achievement of Refugee Scholars: The Story of Displaced Scholars and Scientists, 1933–1952*, The Hague, 1953.

Bentwich, Norman, *My Seventy-seven Years: An Account of My Life and Times, 1883–1960*, London, 1962.

Berghoeffer, C. W., *Meyer Amschel Rothschild: der Gründer des Rothschildschen Bankhauses*, Frankfurt, 1922.

Bermant, Chaim, *Troubled Eden: An Anatomy of British Jewry*, London, 1969.

Bermant, Chaim, *The Cousinhood*, London, 1971.

Best, G., *Mid-Victorian Britain: 1851–75*, London, 1971.

Birkhead, E., 'The financial failure of British air transport companies: 1919–24', *J. Transport Hist.*, 4(3), 1960, pp. 133–45.

Block, G. D. M., 'Jewish students at the universities of Great Britain and Ireland— excluding London, 1936–1939', *Sociol. Rev.*, 34(3 and 4), 1942, pp. 183–97.

Bloom, H. I., *The Economic Activities of the Jews of Amsterdam in the Seventeenth and Eighteenth Centuries*, 1937, reprinted Port Washington, New York and London, 1969.

Bloom, John, *It's No Sin to Make a Profit*, London, 1971.

Board of Trade, *Working Party Report: Furniture*, London, 1946.

Boase, F., *Modern English Biography*, 2 vols, 2nd ed., London, 1965.

Booth, C. (ed.), *Life and Labour of the People in London*, 1889–1903.

Brailsford, H. N., *The Levellers and the English Revolution*, London, 1961.

Braudel, F., *The Mediterranean and the Mediterranean World in the Age of Philip II*, vol. I, London, 1972.

Briggs, Asa, *Friends of the People: The Centenary History of Lewis's*, London, 1956.

Briggs, Asa, *The History of Broadcasting in the United Kingdom*, vol. I; *The Birth of Broadcasting*, London, 1961.

Briggs, Asa, *Victorian Cities*, London, 1963.

Briggs, Asa and John Saville (eds.), *Essays in Labour History*, London, 1960.

Britain's New Citizens: The Story of the Refugees from Germany and Austria (Tenth Anniversary Publication of the Association of Jewish Refugees in Great Britain), London, 1951.

'Britain's showbiz Mr Big', *The Observer* Colour Magazine, 4 December 1973, pp. 43–47.

Brodetsky, Selig, *Memoirs: From Ghetto to Israel*, London, 1960.

Brooke, C. N. L., assisted by G. Keir, *London 800–1216: The Shaping of a City*, London, 1975.

Brotz, Howard M., 'The outlines of Jewish society in London', in M. Freedman (ed.), *A Minority in Britain*, London, 1955, pp. 137–97.

Brown, H. Miles, *Cornish Clocks and Clockmakers*, Newton Abbot, 1961.

Brown, M. D., *David Salomons House: Catalogue of Mementoes*, London, 1968.

Buckman, Joseph, 'Alien working-class response: the Leeds Jewish tailors, 1880–1914', in K. Lunn (ed.), *Hosts, Immigrants and Minorities: Historical Responses to Newcomers in British Society 1870–1914*, London, 1980, pp. 222–62.

Buist, M. G., *At Spes Non Fracta: Hope & Co., 1770–1815, Merchant Bankers and Diplomats at Work*, The Hague, 1974.

Bulkley, M. E., *The Establishment of Legal Minimum Rates in the Boxmaking Industry under the Trade Boards Act of 1909*, London, 1915.

Bull, G., and A. Vice, *Bid for Power*, London, 1958.

Bunt, Sidney, *Jewish Youth Work in Britain: Past, Present and Future*, London, 1975.

[Burn, J.], *Commercial Enterprise and Social Progress*, London, 1858.

Burnett, A., *Knave of Clubs*, London, 1963.

Burns, T., and S. B. Saul (eds), *Social Theory and Social Change*, London, 1967.

Burt, Roger (ed.), *Industry and Society in the South-West*, Exeter, 1970.

Butler, Frank, A *History of Boxing in Britain*, London, 1972.

Buxton, Charles (ed.), *Memoirs of Sir Thomas Fowell Buxton*, 3rd ed., London, 1849.

Cadbury, Edward, M. C. Matheson and G. Shann, *Women's Work and Wages: A Phase of Life in an Industrial City*, London, 1906.

Cahnman, Werner J., 'Introduction: role and significance of the Jewish artisan class', in M. Wischnitzer, *A History of Jewish Crafts and Guilds*, New York, 1965, pp. xiii–xxvii.

Cahnman, Werner J., 'Village and small-town Jews in Germany—a typological study', *Year Book of the Leo Baeck Institute*, 19, 1974, pp. 107–30.

Cameron, R. (ed.), *Banking in the Early Stages of Industrialisation*, New York, 1967.

Cameron, R. E., 'French financiers and Italian unity: the Cavourian decade', *Amer. Hist. Rev.*, 62(3), 1957, pp. 552–69.

Cameron, R. E., 'Papal finance and the temporal power: 1815–1871', *Church Hist.*, 26(2), 1957, pp. 3–13.

Campbell, Flann, 'East London grammar schools', *East London Papers*, 1(2), 1958, pp. 3–14.

Campbell, P. F., 'The merchants and traders of Barbados', *J. Barbados Museum and Hist. Soc.*, 34(2), 1972, pp. 94–96.

Camplin, J., *The Rise of the Plutocrats: Wealth and Power in Edwardian England*, London, 1978.

Capp, B. S., *The Fifth Monarchy Men*, London, 1972.

Carlebach, Alexander, 'The Rev. Dr Joseph Chotzner', *TJHSE*, 21, 1968, pp. 261–73.

Carrier, J. W., 'A Jewish proletariat', in M. Mindlin and Chaim Bermant (eds), *Explorations: An Annual on Jewish Themes*, London, 1967, pp. 120–40.

Carter, C. F. (ed.), *Manchester and Its Region*, Manchester, 1962.

Cassell, C. E., 'The West Metropolitan Jewish School: 1845–1897', *TJHSE*, 19, 1960, pp. 115–28.

Centre for Urban Studies (ed.), *London: Aspects of Change*, London, 1964.

Chaloner, W. H., 'The birth of modern Manchester', in C. F. Carter (ed.), *Manchester and its Region*, Manchester, 1962, pp. 131–46.

Chambers, J. D., 'Victorian Nottingham', *Trans. Thoroton Soc. of Nottingham*, 63, 1959, pp. 1–23.

Chapman, S. D., *The Cotton Industry in the Industrial Revolution*, London, 1972.

Chapman, S. D., *The Foundation of the English Rothschilds: N. M. Rothschild as a Textile Merchant, 1799–1811*, London, 1977.

Chapman, S. D., 'The international houses: the continental contribution to British commerce: 1800–1860', *J. European Econ. Hist.*, 6(1), 1977, pp. 5–48.

Chazan, R., *Medieval Jewry in Northern France: A Political and Social History*, Baltimore and London, 1973.

Checkland, S. G., 'The mind of the City: 1870–1914', *Oxf. Econ. Papers*, 9(3), 1957, pp. 261–78.

Chouraqui, A., *Les Juifs d'Afrique du Nord*, Paris, 1952.

Church, R. A., *Economic and Social Change in a Midland Town: Victorian Nottingham, 1815–1900*, London, 1966.

Clapham, J. H., 'Loans and subsidies in time of war: 1793–1814', *Econ. J.*, 22, 1917, pp. 495–501.

Clapham, J. H., *An Economic History of Modern Britain: The Early Railway Age, 1820–1850*, 2nd ed., Cambridge, 1930.

Clapham, J. H., *The Bank of England: A History*, 2 vols, London, 1944.

Clark, Dorothy K., 'A restoration goldsmith-banking house: the Vine on Lombard Street', in *Essays in Modern English History in Honor of Wilbur Cortez Abbott*, Cambridge, Mass., 1941, pp. 3–47.

Clarke, P. F., *Lancashire and the New Liberalism*, London, 1971.

Clegg, H. A., A. Fox and A. F. Thompson, *A History of British Trade Unions since 1889*, vol. I: *1889–1910*, Oxford, 1964.

Cobb, Richard, *Paris and its Provinces: 1792–1802*, London, 1975.

Cohen, Israel, 'The economic activities of modern Jewry', *Econ. J.*, 24, 1914, pp. 41–56.

Cohen, J. M., *Life of Ludwig Mond*, London, 1956.

Cohen, Joseph, *Journey to the Trenches: The Life of Isaac Rosenberg*, London, 1975.

Cohen, Lord Justice, 'Levi Barent Cohen and some of his descendants', *TJHSE*, 16, 1952, pp. 11–23.

Cohen, Max, *I Was One of the Unemployed*, London, 1945.

Cohen, Max, *What Nobody Told the Foreman*, London, 1953.

Coleman, D. C. (ed.), *Revisions in Mercantilism*, London, 1969.

Coleman, D. C., *The Domestic System in Industry*, Historical Association, Aids for Teachers, London, 1960.

Colin, S., *And the Bands Played On*, London, 1977.

Collins, H.; and C. Abramsky, *Karl Marx and the British Labour Movement*, London, 1965.

Colquhoun, P., *A Treatise on Indigence*, London, 1806.

Colquhoun, P., *A Treatise on the Police of the Metropolis*, London, 1795.

'Coming apart at the seams', *Sunday Times*, 15 May 1977, p. 63.

'Commerce of Rhode Island', *Massachussetts Hist. Soc. Collections*, 7th series, 59 and 60, 1914 and 1915.

Conway, E. S., 'The origins of the Jewish Orphanage', *TJHSE*, 22, 1970, pp. 53–66.

Cope, S. R., 'The Goldsmids and the development of the London money market during the Napoleonic Wars', *Economica*, 9, 1942, pp. 180–206.

Corina, Maurice, *Pile It High and Sell It Cheap: The Authorised Biography of Sir John Cohen, Founder of Tesco*, London, 1971.

Cottrell, P. L., 'London financiers and Austria, 1863–75: the Anglo-Austrian Bank', *Business Hist.*, 11, 1969, pp. 106–19.

Cottrell, P. L., 'The financial sector and economic growth: England in the nineteenth century', *Int. J. Econ. and Soc. Hist.*, 1, 1972, pp. 64–84.

Cottrell, P. L., 'Anglo-French financial co-operation', *J. European Econ. Hist.*, 3(1), 1974, pp. 54–86.

Coulton, G. G., *Fourscore Years*, Cambridge, 1944.

Cowan, Evelyn, *Spring Remembered: A Scottish Jewish Childhood*, Edinburgh, 1974.

Cowles, Virginia, *The Rothschilds: A Family of Fortune*, London, 1973.

Crewe, Ivor (ed.), *British Political Sociology Yearbook*, vol. II, London, 1975.

Cromer, Gerald, 'Intermarriage and communal survival in a London suburb', *Jew. J. Sociol.*, 16(2), December 1974, pp. 155–69.

Crossick, G. (ed.), *The Lower Middle Classes in Britain, 1870–1914*, London, 1977.

Crouzet, F., *L'Economie britannique et le blocus continental (1806–1813)*, Paris, 1958.

Crouzet, F. (ed.), *Capital Formation in the Industrial Revolution*, London, 1972.

Crouzet, F., 'Capital formation in Great Britain during the Industrial Revolution', in F. Crouzet (ed.), *Capital Formation in the Industrial Revolution*, London, 1972, pp. 162–222.

'The cultured man of property', *The Observer*, 25 July 1971.

Cunningham, W. A., *The Growth of English Industry and Commerce in Modern Times*, 4th ed., London, 1907.

Cunningham, W. A., *Alien Immigrants in England*, 2nd ed., London, 1969.

Cunnison, Sheila, *Wages and Work Allocation: A Study of Social Relationships in a Garment Workshop*, London, 1966.

Daiches-Dubens, Rachel, 'Eighteenth century Anglo-Jewry in and around Richmond, Surrey', *TJHSE*, 18, 1958, pp. 143–69.

Daniels, G. W., *The Early English Cotton Industry*, Manchester, 1920.

Davis, Dorothy, *A History of Shopping*, London, 1966.

Davis, Ralph, *Aleppo and Devonshire Square: English Traders in the Levant in the Eighteenth Century*, London, 1967.

Davis, Ralph, 'English foreign trade: 1660–1700', in W. E. Minchinton (ed.), *The Growth of English Overseas Trade in the 17th and 18th Centuries*, London, 1969, pp. 78–98.

Davis, Ralph, 'English foreign trade: 1700–1774', in W. E. Minchinton (ed.), *The Growth of English Overseas Trade in the 17th and 18th Centuries*, London, 1969, pp. 99–120.

de Kadt, E. J., 'Locating minority group members: two British surveys of Jewish university students', *Jew. J. Sociol.*, 6(1), 1964, pp. 30–51.

'Death of an unknown property emperor', *The Sunday Times*, 25 September 1977, p. 72.

Deutscher, Isaac, *The Prophet Armed: Leon Trotsky, 1879–1921*, London, 1970.

Diamond, A. S., 'The cemetery of the resettlement', *TJHSE*, 19, 1960, pp. 163–90.

Diamond, A. S., 'Problems of the London Sephardi community, 1720–33', *TJHSE*, 21, 1968, pp. 39–63.

Diamond, A. S., 'The community of the re-settlement, 1656–1684: a social survey', *TJHSE*, 24, 1975, pp. 134–50.

Dickson, P. G. M., *The Financial Revolution in England: A Study in the Development of Public Credit, 1688–1756*, London, 1967.

Dictionary of Welsh Biography down to 1940, London, 1959.

Dobbs, S. P., *The Clothing Workers of Great Britain,* London, 1928.

Dobson, R. B., *The Jews of Medieval York and the Massacre of 1190,* Borthwick Papers no. 45, University of York, 1974.

Dobson, R. B., 'The decline and expulsion of the medieval Jews of York', *TJHSE,* 26, 1979, pp. 34–52.

Donaldson, Frances, *The Marconi Scandal,* London, 1962.

Donbrow, M., *They Docked at Newcastle,* Jerusalem, 1972.

Dony, J. G., *A History of the Straw Hat Industry,* Luton, 1942.

Dony, J. G., 'The hat industry', in H. A. Silverman (ed.), *Studies in Industrial Organization,* London, 1946, pp. 155–98.

'Early Jewish holders of Bank of England stock (1694–1725)', *MJHSE,* part 6, 1962, pp. 143–74.

Edwards, M. M., *The Growth of the British Cotton Trade: 1780–1815,* Manchester, 1967.

Ehrenberg, R., *Grosse Vermoegen: ihre Entstehung und ihre Bedeutung: Fugger-Rothschild-Krupp,* Berlin, 1905.

Ellison, T., *The Cotton Trade of Great Britain,* 1886, reprinted London, 1968.

Elman, P., 'The economic causes of the expulsion of the Jews in 1290', *Econ. Hist. Rev.,* 7, 1937, pp. 145–54.

Elman, P., 'Jewish finance in thirteenth-century England with special reference to royal taxation', *Bull. Inst. Hist. Res.,* 15, 1938, pp.112–13.

Elman, P., 'Jewish finance in thirteenth-century England', *TJHSE,* 16, 1952, pp. 89–96.

Elman, P., 'The beginnings of the Jewish trade union movement in England', *TJHSE,* 17, 1953, pp. 53–62.

'The elusive tycoon', *JC,* 9 March 1973, p. 15.

Emanuel, C. H. L., *A Century and a Half of Jewish History, Extracted from the Minute Books of the London Committee of Deputies of the British Jews,* London, 1910.

Emanuel, C. H. L., 'The Jewish House at Harrow: some recollections of the 'eighties', *JC,* 29 September 1938.

Emden, Paul H., *Money Powers of Europe in the Nineteenth and Twentieth Centuries,* London, 1937.

Emden, Paul H., 'The brothers Goldsmid and the financing of the Napoleonic Wars', *TJHSE,* 1940, pp. 225–46.

Emden, Paul H., *Jews of Britain,* London, [1944?].

Endelman, Todd M., *The Jews of Georgian England, 1714–1830: Tradition and Change in a Liberal Society,* Philadelphia, 1979.

Epstein, I., 'Pre-expulsion England in the Responsa', *TJHSE,* 14, 1940, pp. 187–205.

Erickson, Charlotte, *British Industrialists: Steel and Hosiery, 1850–1950,* Cambridge, 1959.

Essays in Modern English History in Honor of Wilbur Cortez Abbott. Cambridge, Mass., 1941.

Everitt, Alan, 'The county community', in E. W. Ives (ed.), *The English Revolution:1600–1660,* London, 1968, pp. 59–61.

Everitt, Alan, 'The food market of the English town, 1660–1760', *Third International Conference on Economic History,* vol. I, Paris, 1968, pp. 57–71.

'Everyone's wild about Harry', *The Observer,* 2 July 1972, p. 9.

Ewing, Elizabeth, *History of Twentiety Century Fashion,* London, 1974.

Farrer, David, *The Warburgs,* London, 1975.

Feis, Herbert, *Europe: the World's Banker, 1870–1914,* New Haven, Conn., 1930.

Fersht, B. A., 'The earliest Jewish friendly society in England, Rodphea Shalom', *MJHSE,* part 2, 1935, pp. 90–98.

Field, Carole, 'Taxi!—the Jews behind the wheel', *JC* Colour Magazine, 30 April 1971, pp. 14–20.

Finberg, H. F., 'Jewish residents in eighteenth-century Twickenham', *TJHSE*, 16, 1952, pp. 129–35.

Finestein, Israel, *A Short History of Anglo-Jewry*, London, 1957.

Finestein, Israel, 'Sir George Jessel: 1824–1883', *TJHSE*, 18, 1958, pp. 243–83.

Finestein, Israel, 'Anglo-Jewish opinion during the struggle for emancipation (1828–1858)', *TJHSE*, 20, 1964, pp. 113–43.

Finestein, Israel, 'Jewish immigration in British party politics in the 1890s', in A. Newman (ed.), *Migration and Settlement*, London, 1971, pp. 128–45.

Finn, Ralph, *No Tears in Aldgate*, London, 1963.

Fisch, H., *Jerusalem and Albion*, London, 1964.

Fischel, W. J., 'The Jewish merchant-colony in Madras (Fort St George) during the 17th and 18th centuries', *J. Econ. and Soc. Hist. of the Orient*, 3, 1960, pp. 78–107, 175–95.

Fisher, H. E. S., *The Portugal Trade: A Study in Anglo-Portuguese Commerce, 1700–1770*, London, 1971.

Fishman, W. J. *East End Jewish Radicals: 1875–1914*, London, 1975.

Fixler, M., *Milton and the Kingdoms of God*, London, 1964.

Flatau, Samuel, *A. & W. Flatau & Co. Ltd., Henry Playfair Ltd., Metropolitan Boot Co. Ltd.: Foundation and History, 120 Years*, London, 1948, Guildhall Library, Pam. 8625.

Fletcher, Ronald (ed.), *The Science of Society and the Unity of Mankind*, London, 1974.

Ford, John, *Prizefighting: The Art of Regency Boximania*, Newton Abbot, 1971.

Foseco Minsep Ltd, *History of Foseco: 1931–1969*, privately printed, 1974.

Fox, Alan, *A History of the National Union of Boot and Shoe Operatives: 1874–1957*, Oxford, 1958.

Fox, R. M., *Smoky Crusade*, London, 1937.

Frankau, Gilbert, *Self-Portrait: A Novel of His Own Life*, London, 1940.

Frankel, W., *Friday Nights: A 'Jewish Chronicle' Anthology, 1841–1971*, London, 1973.

Fraser, Antonia, *Cromwell: Our Chief of Men*, London, 1973.

Freedland, Michael, 'New roots for old', *JC* 15 April 1977, p. 19.

Freedman, M. (ed.), *A Minority in Britain*, London, 1955.

Freedman, M., 'Jews in the society of Britain', in M. Freedman (ed.), *A Minority in Britain*, London, 1955, pp. 201–42.

Fuss, A. M., 'Inter-Jewish loans in pre-expulsion England', *Jew. Quart. Rev.*, 65, 1975, pp. 229–45.

Gainer, B. A., *The Alien Invasion: The Origins of the Aliens Act of 1905*, London, 1972.

Gardiner, S. R., *History of the Commonwealth and Protectorate: 1649–1656*, 4 vols, reprinted New York, 1965.

Garrard, J. A., *The English and Immigration: A Comparative Study of the Jewish Influx, 1880–1910*, London, 1971.

Gartner, L. P., 'Notes on the statistics of Jewish immigration to England: 1870–1914', *Jew. Soc. Stud.*, 22(2), 1960, pp. 97–102.

Gartner, L. P., 'Immigration and the formation of American Jewry: 1840–1925', in H. H. Ben-Sasson and S. Ettinger (eds), *Jewish Society through the Ages*, London, 1971, pp. 297–312.

Gartner, L. P., 'North Atlantic Jewry', in A. Newman (ed.), *Migration and Settlement*, London, 1971, pp. 118–27.

Gartner, L. P., *The Jewish Immigrant in England: 1870–1914*, 1960, reprinted London, 1973.

George, M. Dorothy, *London Life in the Eighteenth Century,* 3rd ed., London, 1951.

Gerretson, F. C., *History of the Royal Dutch,* 4 vols, Leiden, 1953–57.

Gille, Bertrand, *Histoire de la Maison Rothschild,* vol. I: *Des origines à 1848,* Geneva, 1965; vol. II, *1848–1870,* Geneva, 1967.

Girard, L., *La Politique des travaux publiques du Second Empire,* Paris, 1952.

Glanville, Brian, 'Reunion in Windmill Street', *JC* Colour Magazine, 22 November 1968, pp. 47–50.

Goldman, W., *East End My Cradle,* London, 1940.

Goldman, W., *A Saint in the Making,* London, 1951.

Goldman, Nahum, *Memories,* London, 1970.

Gollancz, S. M., *Biographical Sketches and Selected Verses,* London, 1930.

Gollancz, Victor, *My Dear Timothy,* London, 1952.

Gompers, S., *Seventy Years of Life and Labor,* New York, 1925.

'Gone for a Burton', *Sunday Times,* 28 November 1976, p. 55.

Goodhart, A. L., *Five Jewish Lawyers of the Common Law,* London, 1949.

Gould, J. and S. Esh (eds.), *Jewish Life in Modern Britain,* London, 1964.

Goulden, Mark, *Mark My Words!* London, 1978.

Grace, W. F. F., 'Russia and *The Times* in 1863 and 1873', *Camb. Hist. J.,* 1(1), 1923, pp. 95–102.

Greenberg, Dolores, 'Yankee financiers and the establishment of trans-Atlantic partnerships: a re-examination', *Business Hist.,* 16(1), 1974, pp. 17–35.

Griffin, A. R., *Mining in the East Midlands: 1550–1947,* London, 1971.

Grizzard, Enid, and Peter Marsh, 'Ilford: profile of a community', *JC* Colour Magazine, 26 November 1971.

Gross, John, 'The Lynskey Tribunal', in M. Sissons and P. French (eds), *The Age of Austerity,* London, 1963, pp. 255–75.

Grunwald, Kurt, '"Windsor-Cassel"—the last court Jew', *Year Book of the Leo Baeck Institute,* 14, 1969, pp. 119–64.

Guttentag, G. D., 'The beginnings of the Newcastle Jewish community', *TJHSE,* 25, 1977, pp. 1–24.

Gwyer, John, 'The case of Dr Lopez', *TJHSE,* 16, 1952, pp. 163–84.

Hadfield, Charles, *Atmospheric Railways,* Newton Abbot, 1967.

Haliczer, S. H., 'The Castilian urban patriciate and the Jewish expulsions of 1480–92', *Amer. Hist. Rev.,* 78(1), 1973, pp. 35–58.

Hall, P. G., 'The East London footwear industry: an industrial quarter in decline', *East London Papers,* 5(1), 1962, pp. 3–21.

Hall, P. G., *The Industries of London since 1861,* London, 1962.

Halpern, D. B., 'Jews in Britain's economy: IV', *Jew. Quart.,* 18, 1957, pp. 36–40.

Halpern, Georg, *Die Jüdischen Arbeiter in London,* Stuttgart and Berlin, 1903.

Hamer, D. A., *Liberal Politics in the Age of Gladstone and Rosebery: A Study in Leadership and Policy,* London, 1972.

Hamilton, H., 'The failure of the Ayr bank, 1772', *Econ. Hist. Rev.,* 8(3), 1956, pp. 405–17.

Hammond, N. G. L., *Centenary Essays on Clifton College,* Bristol, 1962.

Hare, A. E. C., *The Anthracite Coal Industry of the Swansea District,* Swansea, 1940.

Harper, L. A. *The English Navigation Laws,* New York, 1939.

Harrison, A. E., 'The competitiveness of the British cycle industry: 1890–1914' *Econ. Hist. Rev.,* 22, 1969, pp. 287–303.

Harrison, Brian, 'The Sunday trading riots of 1855', *Hist. J.,* 8(2), 1965, pp. 219–45.

Harrison, Walter, *A New and Universal History, Description and Survey of the Cities of London and Westminster,* London, 1770.

Hart, Gwen, *A History of Cheltenham,* Leicester, 1965.

Hart, P. E., M. A. Utton and G. Walshe, *Mergers and Concentration in British Industry*, London, 1973.

Havenhand, Greville, *Nation of Shopkeepers*, London, 1970.

Heckscher, E. F., *Mercantilism*, 2 vols, London, 1935.

Helfgott, Roy B., 'Trade unionism among the Jewish garment workers of Britain and the United States', *Labor Hist.*, 2(2), 1961, pp. 202–14.

Helleiner, K., *The Imperial Loans*, Oxford, 1965.

Heller, Robert, 'Pieces of folk Clore', *The Observer*, 8 September 1974.

Henriques, H. S. Q., *The Jews and the English Law*, Oxford, 1908.

Henriques, Roberts, *Marcus Samuel, First Viscount Bearsted and Founder of the 'Shell' Transport and Trading Company: 1853–1927*, London, 1960.

Henriques, Robert, *Sir Robert Waley Cohen, 1877–1952: A Biography*, London, 1966.

Henriques, Robert, *From a Biography of Myself*, London, 1969.

Herries, Edward, *Memoirs of the Public Life of John S. Herries*, London, 1880.

Hershowitz, L., 'Some aspects of the New York Jewish merchant in colonial trade', in A. Newman (ed.), *Migration and Settlement*, London, 1971, pp. 101–17.

Hibbert, Christopher, *King Mob: The Story of Lord George Gordon and the Riots of 1780*, London, 1958.

Hidy, R. W., *The House of Baring in American Trade and Finance*, Cambridge, Mass., 1949.

Highfield, R. (ed.), *Spain in the Fifteenth Century: 1369–1516*, London, 1972.

Highmore, A., *Philanthropia Metropolitana: A View of the Charitable Institutions Established in or near London Chiefly during the Last Twelve Years*, London, 1822.

Hill, Christopher, *Society and Puritanism in Pre-Revolutionary England*, London, 1964.

Hill, Christopher, *Antichrist in Seventeenth Century England*, London, 1971.

Hindley, Charles, *The Life and Adventures of a Cheap Jack: By One of the Fraternity*, London, 1876.

The History of 'The Times', vol. II: *The Tradition Established, 1841–1884*, London, 1939.

Hobsbawm, E. J., 'General labour unions in Great Britain: 1889–1914', *Econ. Hist. Rev.*, 1(2 and 3), 1949, pp. 123–42.

Hobson, Harold, Phillip Knightley and Leonard Russell, *The Pearl of Days: An Intimate Memoir of 'The Sunday Times', 1822–1972*, London, 1972.

Hobson, J. A., *Imperialism: A Study*, 3rd ed., London, 1938.

Hodess, Pat, 'Southport's golden years', *JC*, 10 September 1976, p. 21.

Hodges, Sheila, *Gollancz: The Story of a Publishing House, 1928–1978*, London, 1978.

Hollis, Christopher, *The Mind of Chesterton*, London, 1970.

Holmes, Colin, 'The Leeds Jewish tailors' strikes of 1885 and 1888', *Yorks. Arch. J.*, 45, 1973, pp. 158–66.

Holmes, Colin, 'In search of Sidney Street', *Bull. Soc. Study Lab. Hist.*, 29, 1974, pp. 70–77.

Holmes, Colin, *Anti-Semitism in British Society: 1876–1939*, London, 1979.

Holt, J. C., *The Northerners: A Study in the Reign of King John*, Oxford, 1961.

Hood, Julia, and B. S. Yamey, 'The middle-class co-operative retailing societies in London: 1864–1900', *Oxf. Econ. Papers*, 9(3), 1957, pp. 309–22.

Horner, A., *Incorrigible Rebel*, London, 1960.

'How Stern made and lost those easy millions', *The Sunday Times*, 4 June 1978, p. 62.

Howarth, E. G., and M. Wilson, *West Ham: A Study in Social and Industrial Problems*, London, 1907

Howson, Gerald, *Thief-taker General: The Rise and Fall of Jonathan Wild*, London, 1970.

Hughes, John, *Liverpool Banks and Bankers: 1760–1937*, Liverpool, 1906.

Hunt, E. H., *Regional Wage Variations in Great Britain: 1850–1914*, Oxford, 1973.

Hyams, P., 'The Jewish minority in mediaeval England, 1066–1290', *J. Jew. Studies*, 25, 1974, pp. 270–93.

Hyamson, A. M., 'Plan of a dictionary of Anglo-Jewish biography', in *Anglo-Jewish Notabilities: Their Arms and Testamentary Dispositions*, London, 1949, pp. 1–73.

Hyamson, A. M., *The Sephardim of England*, London, 1951.

Hyamson, A. M., *Jews' College, London: 1855–1955*, London, 1955.

Hyde, F. E., B. B. Parkinson and S. Marriner, 'The cotton broker and the rise of the Liverpool cotton market', *Econ. Hist. Rev.*, 8(1), 1955, pp. 75–83.

Hyde, F. E., *Far Eastern Trade: 1860–1914*, London, 1973.

Hyman, L., 'Hyman Hurwitz: the first Anglo-Jewish professor', *TJHSE*, 21, 1968, pp. 232–42.

Hyman, L., *The Jews of Ireland: From Earliest Times to the Year 1910*, London and Jerusalem, 1972.

Hyman, R., *The Workers' Union*, London, 1971.

'Impresario royal', *JC*, 13 October 1972, p. 16.

Isaacs, M. Hyman, 'John Isaacs—actor, and his family', *Jewish Monthly*, 3(4), 1949, pp. 239–44.

Ives, E. W. (ed.), *The English Revolution: 1600–1660*, London, 1968.

Jack, Marian, 'The purchase of the British government's shares in the British Petroleum Company: 1912–1914', *Past & Present*, no. 39, April 1968, pp. 139–68.

Jackson, A. A., *Semi-Detached London: Suburban Development, Life and Transport, 1900–1939*, London, 1973.

Jacob, Alex. M., 'The Jews of Falmouth: 1740–1860', *TJHSE*, 17, 1953, pp. 63–72.

Jacobs, Joseph, *Studies in Jewish Statistics, Social, Vital and Anthropometric*, London, 1891.

James, M., *Social Problems and Policy during the Puritan Revolution*, 1930, reprinted London, 1966.

James, R. R., *Rosebery: A Biography of Archibald Philip, Fifth Earl of Rosebery*, London, 1963.

Jamilly, Edward, 'Anglo-Jewish architects and architecture in the 18th and 19th centuries', *TJHSE*, 18, 1958, pp. 127–41.

Jamilly, Edward, 'Synagogue art and architecture', in S. S. Levin (ed.), *A Century of Anglo-Jewish Life: 1870–1970*, London, 1973, pp. 75–91.

Jefferys, J. B., *Retail Trading in Britain: 1850–1950*, London, 1954.

Jenks, L. H., *The Migration of British Capital to 1875*, 1927, reprinted, London, 1963.

Jephcott, Sir Harry, *The First Fifty Years: an Account of the Early Life of Joseph Edward Nathan and the First Fifty Years of His Merchandise Business that Eventually Became the Glaxo Group*, privately printed, London, 1969.

John, A. H., 'Insurance investment and the London money market of the 18th century', *Economica*, 20, 1953, pp. 137–61.

Johnson, W. Branch, *Hertfordshire*, London, 1970.

Jolly, W. P., *Marconi*, London, 1972.

Jones, G. Stedman, *Outcast London: A Study in the Relationship between Classes in Victorian Society*, London, 1971.

Jones, Robert, and Oliver Marriott, *Anatomy of a Merger: A History of GEC, AEI and English Electric*, London, 1970.

Jones, S., 'Blood Red Roses: the supply of merchant seamen in the nineteenth century', *Mariner's Mirror*, 58(4), 1972, pp. 429–42.

Joseph, A. P., 'Jewry of south-west England and some of its Australian connections', *TJHSE*, 24, 1975, pp. 24–37.

Josephs, Z., 'Jewish glass-makers', *TJHSE*, 25, 1977, pp. 107–19.

Josephs, Z., *Birmingham Jewry, 1749–1914*, Birmingham, 1980.

Kaeuper, R. W., *Bankers to the Crown: The Riccardi of Lucca and Edward I*, Princeton, N. J., 1973.

Kahl, W. F., 'Apprenticeship and the freedom of the London livery companies: 1690–1750', *Guildhall Miscellany*, 1(7), 1956, pp. 16–20.

Kalisch, S., *A Builder of Judaism: The Story of Arthur Hubert and His Family*, Manchester, 1978.

Kamm, Josephine, *Indicative Past: A Hundred Years of the Girls' Public Day School Trust*, London, 1971.

Kargon, R. H., *Science in Victorian Manchester: Enterprise and Expertise*, Manchester, 1977.

Katz, J., *Exclusiveness and Tolerance: Studies in Jewish-Gentile Relations in Medieval and Modern Times*, London, 1961.

Kellenbenz, Hermann, 'Sephardim an der unteren Elbe: ihre wirtschaftliche und politische Bedeutung vom Ende des 16 bis zum Beginn des 18 Jahrhunderts', *Vierteljahrschrift für Sozial- und Wirtschaftsgeschichte* (Wiesbaden), 40, 1958.

Kellett, J. R., 'The breakdown of gild and corporation control over the handicraft and retail trade in London', *Econ. Hist. Rev.*, 10(3), 1958, pp. 381–94.

Kochan, Lionel, *The Making of Modern Russia*, Harmondsworth, 1963.

Kosmin, B. A., 'What's happening to us?', *JC*, 9 September 1977, p. 57.

Kosmin, B. A., 'The face of Jewish suburbia', *JC*, 14 July 1978, pp. 21, 29; and 21 July 1978, p. 17.

Kosmin, B. A., M. Bauer and N. Grizzard, *Steel City Jews*, London, 1976.

Kosmin, B. A., and N. Grizzard, *Jews in an Inner London Borough: A Study of the Jewish Population of the London Borough of Hackney Based on the 1971 Census*, London, 1975.

Koss, S., *Sir John Brunner: Radical Plutocrat*, Cambridge, 1970.

Krausz, Ernest, 'The economic and social structure of Anglo-Jewry', in J. Gould and S. Esh (eds), *Jewish Life in Modern Britain*, London, 1964, pp. 27–34.

Krausz, Ernest, *Leeds Jewry: Its History and Social Structure*, Cambridge, 1964.

Krausz, Ernest, 'The Edgware survey: occupation and social class', *Jew. J. Sociol.*, 11(1), 1969, pp. 75–95.

Kulik, Karol, *Alexander Korda: The Man Who Could Work Miracles*, London, 1975.

Kupferberg, H., *The Mendelssohns*, London, 1972.

Ladsky, Sonia, 'Refugees from the Raj', *JC*, 17 June 1977, p. 23.

Lambert, W. M., *Godly Rule: Politics and Religion, 1603–60*, London, 1969.

Landes, David, *Bankers and Pashas*, London, 1958.

Landes, David, 'The Jewish merchant: typology and stereotypology in Germany', *Year Book of the Leo Baeck Institute*, 19, 1974, pp. 11–23.

Langmuir, G. I., 'The Jews and the archives of Angevin England: reflections on medieval anti-semitism', *Traditio*, 19, 1963, pp. 183–244.

Larsen, Elaine, 'Death of a district', *JC* Colour Magazine, 28 November 1969, pp. 70–76.

Lawton, R., 'The population of Liverpool in the mid-nineteenth century', *Trans. Hist. Soc. Lancs. and Cheshire*, 107, 1955, pp. 89–120.

Leeson, R. A., *Strike: A Live History, 1887–1971*, London, 1973.

Lerner, S. W., *Breakaway Unions and the Small Trade Union*, London, 1961.

Levi, J. S., and G. F. J. Bergman, *Australian Genesis: Jewish Convicts and Settlers, 1788–1850*, London, 1974.

Levin, H. S., and S. S. Levin, *Jubilee at Finchley: The Story of a Congregation*, London, 1976.

Levin, Nora, *Jewish Socialist Movements: 1871–1917*, London, 1978.

Levin, S. S., 'The origins of the Jews' Free School', *TJHSE*, 19, 1960, pp. 97–114.

Levin, S. S. (ed.), *A Century of Anglo-Jewish Life: 1870–1970*, London, 1973.

Levine, Henry, *The Norwich Hebrew Congregation, 1840–1960: A Short History*, Norwich, 1961.

Levinson, Maurice, *Taxi!*, London, 1963.

Levinson, Maurice, *The Woman from Bessarabia*, London, 1964.

Levy, A., *The Origins of Glasgow Jewry: 1812–1895*, Glasgow, 1949.

Levy, A., 'The origins of Scottish Jewry', *TJHSE*, 19, 1960, pp. 129–62.

Levy, Arnold, *History of the Sunderland Jewish Community: 1755–1955*, London, 1956.

Levy, A. B., *East End Story*, London, 1950.

Lewis, Michael, *A Social History of the Navy*, London, 1960.

Liddiard, Jean, *Isaac Rosenberg: The Half Used Life*, London, 1975.

'Life and survival of the little man', *Guardian*, 13 January 1978, p. 14.

The Life of Robert Owen, Written by Himself, orig. pub. 1857, intro. by John Butt, London, 1971.

Lincoln, F. Ashe, 'The non-Christian oath in English law', *TJHSE*, 16, 1952, pp. 73–76.

Lindsay, Jean, *A History of the North Wales Slate Industry*, Newton Abbot, 1974.

Lipman, Sonia L., 'Judith Montefiore—first lady of Anglo-Jewry', *TJHSE*, 21, 1968, pp. 287–303.

Lipman, V. D., *Social History of the Jews in England: 1850–1950*, London, 1954.

Lipman, V. D., *A Century of Social Service, 1859–1959: The Jewish Board of Guardians*, London, 1959.

Lipman, V. D., 'A survey of Anglo-Jewry in 1851', *TJHSE*, 17, 1960, pp. 171–88.

Lipman, V. D., 'The age of emancipation: 1815–1880', in V. D. Lipman (ed.), *Three Centuries of Anglo-Jewish History*, London, 1961, pp. 69–106.

Lipman, V. D. (ed.), *Three Centuries of Anglo-Jewish History*, London, 1961.

Lipman, V. D., 'The Plymouth Aliens list 1798 and 1803', *MJHSE*, part 6, 1962, pp. 187–94.

Lipman, V. D., 'Social topography of a London congregation: the Bayswater synagogue: 1863–1963', *Jew. J. Sociol.*, 6(1), 1964, pp. 69–74.

Lipman, V. D., *The Jews of Medieval Norwich*, London, 1967.

Lipman, V. D., 'The anatomy of medieval Anglo-Jewry', *TJHSE*, 21, 1968, pp. 64–77.

Lipman, V. D., 'The rise of Jewish suburbia', *TJHSE*, 21, 1968, pp. 78–103.

Lipman, V. D., 'Sephardi and other Jewish immigrants in England in the eighteenth century', in A. Newman (ed.), *Migration and Settlement*, London, 1971, pp. 37–62.

Lipman, V. D., 'The development of London Jewry', in S. S. Levin (ed.), *A Century of Anglo-Jewish Life: 1870–1970*, London, 1973, pp. 43–56.

Lipman, V. D., and S. L. Lipman, 'A middle-class community', *JC* Colour Magazine, 28 November 1975, pp. 74–76.

Lipson, E., 'The Brights of Market Place', *Trans. Hunter Arch. Soc.*, 6, 1950, pp. 117–25.

Lissack, M., *Jewish Perseverance, or the Jew, at Home and Abroad: an Autobiography*, London, 1851.

Litvinoff, Emanuel, *Journey through a Small Planet*, London, 1972.

Loewe, L. (ed.), *Diaries of Sir Moses and Lady Montefiore*, 2 vols, London, 1890.

Longford, Elizabeth, *Wellington: Pillar of State*, London, 1972.

Louis, H., and B. Carrie, *The Story of Triumph Motor Cycles*, London, 1975.

Lumb, G. D. (ed.), 'Extracts from the "Leeds Intelligencer" and the "Leeds Mercury" 1769–1766', *Pub. Thoresby Soc.*, 38, 1937, pp. 1–189.

Lunn, K. (ed.), *Hosts, Immigrants and Minorities: Historical Responses to Newcomers in British Society 1870–1914*, London, 1980.

Lvavi, Joseph, 'Jewish agricultural settlement in the USSR', *Soviet Jewish Affairs*, 1, 1971.

Macaulay, T. B., *The History of England from the Accession of James the Second*, vol. III, London, 1855.

McCarthy, Albert, *The Dance Band Era*, London, 1972.

MacFarlane, L. J., *The British Communist Party: Its Origin and Development until 1929*, London, 1966.

McKay, A., 'Popular movements and pogroms in fifteenth century Castile', *Past & Present*, no. 55, May 1972, pp. 33–67.

McKenna, M., *Myra Hess: A Portrait*, London, 1976.

MacRae, Hamish, and Frances Cairncross, *Capital City: London as a Financial Centre*, London, 1973.

MacRosty, H. W., *The Trust Movement in British Industry*, London, 1907.

Mahler, Raphael, *A History of Modern Jewry: 1780–1815*, London, 1971.

Mantoux, P., *The Industrial Revolution in the Eighteenth Century*, rev. ed., London, 1961.

Marcus, J. R., *The Colonial American Jew: 1492–1776*, 3 vols, Detroit, 1970.

'Mark Simons—tailor', in *Working Lives*, vol. I: *1905–1945; A People's Autobiography of Hackney*, London, n.d., pp. 70–74.

Marenbon, Z., *Don't Blow Out the Candle: A Liverpool Childhood of the Twenties*, London, 1973.

Marriott, Oliver, *The Property Boom*, London, 1967.

Martin, Kingsley, *Harold Laski (1893–1950): A Biographical Memoir*, London, 1953.

Mate, M., 'The indebtedness of Canterbury Cathedral priory 1215–95', *Econ. Hist. Rev.* 26(2), 1973, pp. 183–97.

Mathias, Peter, *Retailing Revolution: A History of Multiple Retailing in the Food Trades Based upon the Allied Suppliers Group of Companies*, London, 1967.

Mayhew, Henry, *London Labour and the London Poor*, 3 vols, London, 1851; 4 vols, London, 1861.

Meir, Golda, *My Life*, London, 1975.

Meisels, I. S., 'The Jewish congregation of Portsmouth (1766–1842)', *TJHSE*, 6, 1912, pp. 111–27.

Menasseh ben Israel, *Mikveh Israel: Hoc Est Spes Israelis*, Amsterdam, 1650; Eng. trans. by Moses Wall, London, 1650; 2nd ed., London 1651; reprinted London, 1652.

Menasseh ben Israel, *To His Highnesse the Lord Protector of the Commonwealthe of England, Scotland and Ireland, the Humble Addresses of Menasseh ben Israel, a divine, and doctor of physick, in behalfe of the Jewish nation*, London, 1655.

Mendelsohn, Ezra, *Class Struggle in the Pale: The Formative Years of the Jewish Workers' Movement in Tsarist Russia*, Cambridge, 1970.

Mendoza, Daniel, *The Memoirs of the Life of Daniel Mendoza*, ed. Paul Magriel, London, 1951.

Minchinton, W. E. (ed.), *The Growth of English Overseas Trade in the 17th and 18th Centuries*, London, 1969.

Mindlin, M., and Chaim Bermant (eds), *Explorations: An Annual on Jewish Themes*, London, 1967.

Minney, R. J., *Viscount Southwood*, London, 1954.

Mishkinsky, M., 'The Jewish labour movement and European socialism', in H. H. Ben-Sasson and S. Ettinger (eds), *Jewish Society through the Ages*, London, 1971, pp. 284–96.

'Mister Fidelity', *JC*, Audio-visual Supplement, 20 July 1973, p. iv.

Modder, M. F., *The Jew in the Literature of England to the End of the 19th Century*, Philadelphia, 1939.

'The mogul of mass taste', *Sunday Times* Colour Magazine, 5 December 1971, pp. 33–34.

Money, Leo Chiozza, *Riches and Poverty*, 11th ed., London, 1911.

Monopolies Commission, *Thorn Electrical Industries Ltd and Radio Rentals Ltd*, HC 318, London, 1968.

Monypenny, W. F., and G. E. Buckle, *The Life of Benjamin Disraeli, Earl of Beaconsfield*, 6 vols, London, 1910–20.

Morgan, E. V., and W. A., Thomas, *The Stock Exchange*, London, 1962.

Morgan, K. O., *Wales in British Politics: 1868–1922*, Cardiff, 1970.

Morley, John, *The Life of Richard Cobden*, 14th ed., London, 1910.

Morris, J. H., and L. J. Williams, *The South Wales Coal Industry: 1841–1875*, Cardiff, 1958.

Moses, E. & Son, *The Growth of an Important Branch of British Industry*, London, 1860.

Mumby, F. A., *The House of Routledge: 1834–1934*, London, 1934.

Musgrave, F. M., *The Migratory Elite*, London, 1963.

'My son the youth worker', *JC*, 17 December 1971, p. 24.

Myers, Asher I. (comp.), *The Jewish Directory for 1874*, London, 1874.

Myers, Maurice, 'Calendars of the coaching days', *TJHSE*, 5, 1908, pp. 219–25.

Namier, Julia, *Lewis Namier: A Biography*, London, 1971.

Namier, L. B., *The Structure of Politics at the Accession of George III*, 2nd ed., London, 1957.

Nathan, David, 'They asked for more—and got it: the story of Norwood', *JC* Colour Magazine, 22 November 1974, pp. 68–75.

National Union of Conservative and Constitutional Associations, *The Case against Radicalism*, London, 1909.

Neustatter, Hannah, 'Demographic and other statistical aspects of Anglo-Jewry', in M. Freedman (ed.), *A Minority in Britain*, London, 1955, pp. 55–133.

Newman, A., *Leicester Hebrew Congregation: A Centenary Record*, Leicester, 1974.

Newman, A. (ed.), *Migration and Settlement*, London, 1971.

Newman, A., *The United Synagogue: 1870–1970*, London, 1977.

Newman, E., 'Some new facts about the Portsmouth Jewish community', *TJHSE*, 17, 1953, pp. 251–68.

Newman, Max, 'Tottenham over five decades', *JC*, 11 June 1976, p. 13.

Newman, P. K., 'The early London clothing trades', *Oxf. Econ. Papers*, 4(2), 1952, pp. 243–51.

O'Connor, Kevin, *The Irish in Britain*, London, 1972.

Oddy, D. J. and D. S. Miller (eds), *The Making of the Modern British Diet*, London, 1976.

Odle, Rose, *Salt of Our Youth*, Penzance, 1972.

Oliver, J. Leonard, 'The East London furniture industry', *East London Papers*, 4(2), 1961, pp. 88–101.

One Hundred Years, 1834–1934: George Cohen Sons & Co. Ltd., privately published, London, 1934, Guildhall Library, London, SL 69/1.

Orwell, George, 'Anti-semitism in Britain', in his *England Your England, and Other Essays*, London 1953, pp. 68–80.

Owen, A., 'The references to England in the Responsa of Rabbi Meir ben Baruch of Rothenburg: 1215–1293', *TJHSE*, 17, 1953, pp. 73–78.

Owen, Roger, and Bob Sutcliffe (eds), *Studies in the Theory of Imperialism*, London, 1972.

Palin, Ronald, *Rothschild Relish*, London, 1970.

Paskiewicz, Mieczyslaw, 'Aliens' certificates in the Public Record Office: Polonica (1826–1852)', *Antemurale*, 19, 1975, pp. 159–263.

Patinkin, D., 'Mercantilism and the readmission of the Jews to England', *Jew. Soc. Stud.*, 7, 1946, pp. 161–78.

Patterson, David, *The Hebrew Novel in Czarist Russia*, Edinburgh, 1964.

Patterson, Sheila, *Immigrants in Industry*, London, 1968.

'Paul Martinson—cabinet maker', in *Working Lives*, vol. 1: *1905–1945: A People's Autobiography of Hackney*, pp. 96–105, London, n.d., pp. 96–105.

Paul, R. S., *The Lord Protector: Religion and Politics in the Life of Oliver Cromwell*, London, 1955.

'Pauper millionaire', *Daily Express*, 22 September 1977, p. 7.

Perkin, H., *The Origins of Modern English Society: 1782–1880*, London, 1969.

Perry, T. W., *Public Opinion, Propaganda and Politics in Eighteenth Century England: A Study of the Jew Bill of 1753*, Cambridge, Mass., 1962.

Persoff, M., 'A name that registers: a profile of the Gross brothers', *JC* Business Efficiency Supplement, 1 October 1971, p. vi.

Platt, D. C. M., *Finance, Trade and Politics in British Foreign Policy: 1815–1914*, London, 1968.

Platt, D. C. M., 'Further objections to an "Imperialism of Free Trade": 1830–60', *Econ. Hist. Rev.*, 26(1), 1973, pp. 77–91.

Plummer, A., *New British Industries in the Twentieth Century*, London, 1937.

'Pogrom: Limerick 1904', *Nusight* (Dublin), May 1970, pp. 25–28.

Polack, A. I., 'Clifton and Anglo-Jewry', in N. G. L. Hammond (ed.), *Centenary Essays on Clifton College*, Bristol, 1962, pp. 51–71.

Pollard, S., *The Development of the British Economy: 1914–1967*, London, 1969.

Pollard, S., 'The decline of shipbuilding on the Thames', *Econ. Hist. Rev.*, 3(1), 1950, pp. 72–89.

Pollins, Harold, *Britain's Railways: An Industrial History*, Newton Abbot, 1971.

Pollins, Harold, 'Jews on strike', *JC*, 4 January 1974.

Pollins, Harold, 'The Jews' role in the early British railways', *Jew. Soc. Stud.*, 15(1), 1953, pp. 53–62.

Pollins, Harold, 'Transport Lines and social divisions', in Centre for Urban Studies (ed.), *London: Aspects of Change*, London, 1964, pp. 29–61.

Powell, E. T., *The Evolution of the Money Market*, London, 1916.

Prais, S. J., 'The development of Birmingham Jewry', *Jewish Monthly*, 2(11), 1949, pp. 665–79.

Prais, S. J., 'Synagogue statistics and the Jewish population of Great Britain: 1900–70', *Jew. J. Sociol.*, 14(2), 1972, pp. 215–28.

Prais, S. J., 'The fertility of Jewish families in Britain: 1971', *Jew. J. Sociol.*, 15(2), 1973, pp. 189–203.

Prais, S. J., 'Not enough children', *JC*, 18 January 1974, p. 10.

Prais, S. J. and M. Schmool, 'The size and structure of the Anglo-Jewish population: 1960–65', *Jew. J. Sociol.*, 10(1), 1968, pp. 15–34.

Prais, S. J. and M. Schmool, 'Statistics of Milah and the Jewish birth-rate', *Jew. J. Sociol.*, 12(2), 1970, pp. 187–93.

Prais, S. J., and M. Schmool, 'The social-class structure of Anglo-Jewry: 1961', *Jew. J. Sociol.*, 17(1), 1975, pp. 5–15.

Pressnell, L. S., *Country Banking in the Industrial Revolution*, Oxford, 1956.

Price, J. M., 'Joshua Johnson in London, 1771–1775: credit and commercial organization in the British Chesapeake trade', in A. Whiteman, J. S. Bromley and P. G. M. Dickson (eds.), *Statesmen, Scholars and Merchants: Essays in Eighteenth-Century History Presented to Dame Lucy Sutherland*, London, 1973.

Proudfoot, W. B., *The Origin of Stencil Duplicating*, London, 1972.

Pugh, R. B., *Imprisonment in Medieval England*, Cambridge, 1968.

Rabinowicz, O. K., *Sir Solomon de Medina*, London, 1974.

Radzinowicz, L., *A History of the English Criminal Law and Its Administration from 1750*, vol. III, London, 1956.

Raistrick, A., *Quakers in Science and Industry*, 1950, reprinted Newton Abbot, 1969.

Ramm, Agatha, *The Political Correspondence of Mr Gladstone and Lord Granville: 1876–1886*, 2 vols, Oxford, 1962.

Ratcliffe, B., 'The origins of the Paris–Saint-Germain railway', *J. Transport Hist.*, 1(4), 1972, pp. 197–219, and 2(1), 1973, pp. 20–40.

Raw, Charles, *Slater Walker: An Investigation of a Financial Phenomenon*, London, 1977.

Read, Conyers, *Mr Secretary Walsingham and the Policy of Queen Elizabeth*, Oxford, 1925.

Reader, W. J., *Imperial Chemical Industries: A History*, vol. I: *The Forerunners, 1870–1926*, London, 1970.

Redford, A. S., and L. S. Russell, *The History of Local Government in Manchester*, vol. III, London, 1940.

Reed, M. C., *Investment in Railways in Britain, 1820–1844: A Study in the Development of the Capital Market*, London, 1975.

Rees, Goronwy, 'The multi-millionaires: 3. Pioneer of the take-over: Charles Clore', *Sunday Times* Magazine Section, 24 January 1960, pp. 11–12.

Rees, Goronwy, *St Michael: A History of Marks and Spencer*, London, 1969.

Reeves, John, *The Rothschilds: The Financial Rulers of Nations*, London, 1887.

Richardson, D. J., 'J. Lyons & Co. Ltd.: caterers and food manufacturers, 1894 to 1939', in D. J. Oddy and D. S. Miller (eds), *The Making of the Modern British Diet*, London, 1976, pp. 161–72.

Richardson, H. G., *The English Jewry under Angevin Kings*, London, 1960.

Richardson, H. G. (ed.), *Calendar of the Plea Rolls of the Exchequer of the Jews*, vol. IV, London, 1972.

Richardson, K., *Twentieth-Century Coventry*, London, 1972.

Rive, A., 'The consumption of tobacco since 1600', *Econ. Hist.* (supplement to *Econ. J.*), 1, 1926, pp. 57–75.

Robbins, Lord, *Autobiography of an Economist*, London 1971.

Roberts, Robert, *The Classic Slum*, Manchester, 1971.

Robertson, A., 'Its bloom is shed', in A. Robertson, *The Lessons of Failure*, London, 1974, pp. 72–81.

Robertson, P. L., 'Shipping and shipbuilding: the case of William Denny and Brothers', *Business Hist.*, 16(l), 974, pp. 36–47.

Rocker, R., *The London Years*, London, 1956.

Rollin, A. R., 'A Jewish tailors' strike of 60 years ago', *JC*, 14 October 1949, p. 19.

Rollin, A. R., 'The Jewish contribution to the British textile industry: "builders of Bradford"', *TJHSE*, 17, 1960, pp. 45–51.

Rollin, A. R., 'Russo-Jewish immigrants in England before 1881', *TJHSE*, 21, 1968, pp. 202–13.

Ronald, Sir Landon, *Variations on a Personal Theme*, London, 1922.

Ronald, Sir Landon, *Myself and Others*, London, 1931.

Rose, June, 'A Jewish "Mayhew"', in M. Mindlin and Chaim Bermant (eds), *Explorations: An Annual on Jewish Themes*, London, 1967, pp. 107–19.

Rose, M. E., *The English Poor Law: 1780–1930*, Newton Abbot, 1971.

Rose, Millicent, *The East End of London*, London, 1951.

Ross, J. M., 'Naturalisation of Jews in England', *TJHSE*, 24, 1975, pp. 59–72.

Roth, Andrew, *Harold Wilson: Yorkshire Walter Mitty*, London, 1978.

Roth, Cecil, 'The case of Thomas Fernandes before the Lisbon Inquisition, 1556', *MJHSE*, part 2, 1935, pp. 32-56.

Roth, Cecil, 'The Portsmouth community and its historical background', *TJHSE*, 13, 1936, pp. 157–87.

Roth, Cecil, 'The Jews in the English universities', *MJHSE*, part 4, 1942, pp. 102–15.

Roth, Cecil, 'Elijah of London: the most illustrious English Jew of the middle ages', *TJHSE*, 15, 1946, pp. 29–62.

Roth, Cecil, *The Intellectual Activities of Medieval English Jewry*, Brit. Acad. Supplemental Papers, no. 8, London, 1949.

[Roth, Cecil], *'Jewish Chronicle' 1841–1941: A Century of Newspaper History*, London, 1949.

Roth, Cecil, *History of the Great Synagogue*, London, 1950.

Roth, Cecil, 'Jews in Oxford after 1290', *Oxoniensia*, 15, 1950, pp. 63–80.

Roth, Cecil, *The Rise of Provincial Jewry*, London, 1950.

Roth, Cecil, 'Sir Edward Brampton', *TJHSE*, 16, 1952, pp. 121–27.

Roth, Cecil, 'An eighteenth-century Jewish community in Colchester', *AJA Quarterly*, 3(2), 1957, pp. 22–25.

Roth, Cecil, 'The middle period of Anglo-Jewish history (1290–1655) reconsidered', *TJHSE*, 19, 1960, pp. 1–12.

Roth, Cecil, 'The resettlement of the Jews in England', in V. D. Lipman (ed.), *Three Centuries of Anglo-Jewish History*, London, 1961, pp. 1–25.

Roth, Cecil, *Essays and Portraits in Anglo-Jewish History*, Philadelphia, 1962.

Roth, Cecil, 'Educational abuses and reforms in Hanoverian England', in C. Roth, *Essays and Portraits in Anglo-Jewis History*, Philadelphia, 1962, pp. 219-31.

Roth, Cecil, 'The Jew peddler—an 18th-century rural character', in C. Roth, *Essays and Portraits in Anglo-Jewish History*, Philadelphia, 1962, pp. 130–38.

Roth, Cecil, 'The membership of the Great Synagogue, London, to 1791', *MJHSE*, part 6, 1962, pp. 175-85.

Roth, Cecil, *A History of the Jews in England*, 3rd ed., London, 1964.

Roth, Cecil, *A Short History of the Jewish People*, rev. ed., London, 1969.

Rothschild, Lord, *'You Have It Madam': The Purchase, in 1875, of Suez Canal Shares by Disraeli and Baron Lionel de Rothschild*, London, 1980.

Rubens, A., *Anglo-Jewish Portraits*, London, 1935.

Rubens, A., 'Early Anglo-Jewish artists', *TJHSE*, 14, 1940, pp. 91–129.

Rubens, A., 'Francis Town of Bond Street (1738–1826) and his family, with further notes on early Anglo-Jewish artists', *TJHSE*, 18, 1958, pp. 89–111.

Rubens, A., 'Portrait of Anglo-Jewry (1656-1836)', *TJHSE*, 19, 1960, pp. 13–52.

Rubens, A., 'The Jews of the parish of St James, Duke's Place, in the City of London', in J. M. Shaftesley (ed.), *Remember the Days*, London, 1966, pp. 181–205.

Rubens, A., 'Jews and the English stage: 1667–1850', *TJHSE*, 24, 1975, pp. 151–70.

Rubens, Charles, 'Joseph Cortissos and the war of the Spanish Succession', *TJHSE*, 24, 1975, pp. 114–33.

Rudé, George, *Wilkes and Liberty*, Oxford, 1962.

Rudé George, *Hanoverian London: 1714–1808*, London, 1971.

Rumbelow, Donald, *The Houndsditch Murders and the Siege of Sidney Street*, London, 1973.

Rumney, J., 'Anglo-Jewry as seen through foreign eyes (1730–1830)', *TJHSE*, 13, 1936, pp. 323–40.

Ruppin, A., *Jewish Fate and Future*, London, 1940.

Saipe, L. (ed.), *Leeds Tercentenary Celebration of the resettlement of the Jews in the British Isles*, Leeds, 1956.

Salaman, Malcolm Charles, 'My father and I: happy memories of two long lives', *Synagogue Rev.*, 11, 1951, pp. 321–29.

Salaman, R. N., 'The Jewish Fellows of the Royal Society', *MJHSE*, part 5, 1948, pp. 146–75.

Samuel, E. R., 'Anglo-Jewish notaries and scriveners', *TJHSE*, 17, 1953, pp. 113–59.

Samuel, E. R., 'Portuguese Jews in Jacobean London', *TJHSE*, 18, 1958, pp. 171–230.

Samuel, E. R., 'The Jews in English foreign trade—a consideration of the "Philo Patriae" pamphlets of 1753', in J. M. Shaftesley (ed.), *Remember the Days*, London, 1966, pp. 123–43.

Samuel, E. R., 'Sir Francis Child's jewellery business', *Three Banks Rev.*, no. 113, 1977, pp. 43–55.

Samuel, Viscount, *Memoirs*, London, 1945.

Samuel, W. S., 'The first London synagogue of the resettlement', *TJHSE*, 10, 1924, pp. 1–147.

Samuel, W. S. 'Review of the Jewish colonists in Barbados in the year 1680', *TJHSE*, 13, 1936, pp. 1–111.

Samuel, W. S., 'Tentative list of Jewish underwriting members of Lloyd's (from some time prior to 1800 until the year 1901)', *MJHSE*, part 5, 1948, pp. 176–92.

Samuel, W. S., 'A list of Jewish persons endenizened and naturalised: 1609–1799', *MJHSE*, part 7, 1970, pp. 111–44.

Samuels, Leon, 'The Jewish labour movement', *Jew. Quart.*, 11(3), 1956, pp. 35–36.

Samuelsson, K., *Religion and Economic Action*, London, 1961.

Sanger, 'Lord' George, *Seventy Years a Showman*, London, [1900?].

Saville, John, 'Trade unions and free labour: the background to the Taff Vale decision', in Asa Briggs and John Saville (eds), *Essays in Labour History*, London, 1960, pp. 317–50.

Sayers, R. S., *Gilletts in the London Money Market: 1867–1967*, London, 1968.

Schapiro, Leonard, 'The Russian background of the Anglo-American Jewish immigration', *TJHSE*, 20, 1964, pp. 215–31.

Schiper, I., 'Max Weber on the sociological basis of the Jewish religion', *Jew. J. Sociol.*, 1(2), 1959, pp. 250–60.

Schischa, A., 'Reb Salmen London: immigrant, emigrant, migrant', in A. Newman (ed.), *Migration and Settlement*, London, 1971, pp. 14–36.

Schischa, A., 'Spanish Jews in London in 1494', *MJHSE*, part 9, 1975, pp. 214–15.

Schorsch, Ismar, 'From messianism to Realpolitik: Menasseh ben Israel and the readmission of the Jews of England', *Proc. Amer. Acad. for Jewish Research*, vol. 45, 1978, pp. 187–208.

Schuster, Arthur, *Biographical Fragments*, London, 1932.

Searle, G. R., *The Quest for National Efficiency: A Study in British Politics and Political Thought, 1899–1914*, Oxford, 1971.

Seidman, Joel, *The Needle Trades*, New York, 1942.

Semmel, Bernard, *Imperialism and Social Reform: English Social-Imperial Thought, 1895–1914*, London, 1960.

Shaftesley, J. M. (ed.), *Remember the Days*, London, 1966.

Sharp, Evelyn, *Hertha Ayrton, 1854–1923: A Memoir*, London, 1926.

Shepherd, Michael A., 'The origins and incidence of the term "Labour aristocracy" ', *Bull. Soc. Study Lab. Hist.*, no. 37, 1978, pp. 51–67.

Shelton, W. J., *English Hunger and Social Disorders: A Study of Social Conflict during the First Decade of George III's Reign*, London, 1973.

Sheppard, F., *London, 1808–1870: The Infernal Wen*, London, 1971.

Sherard, Robert H., *The White Slaves of England*, London, 1897.

Sherman, A. J., *Island Refuge: Britain and the Refugees from the Third Reich, 1933–1939*, London, 1973.

Sherwig, J. M., *Guineas and Gunpowder: British Foreign Aid in the Wars with France, 1793–1815*, Cambridge, Mass., 1969.

Shillman, B., *A Short History of the Jews in Ireland*, Dublin, 1945.

Shulvass, M. A., *From East to West: The Westward Migration of Jews from Eastern Europe during the Seventeenth and Eighteenth Centuries*, Detroit, 1971.

Sieff, Israel, *Memoirs*, London, 1970.

Sigsworth, E. M., *Black Dyke Mills: A History*, Liverpool, 1958.

Silverman, H. A. (ed.), *Studies in Industrial Organization*, London, 1946.

Silverstone, R., 'Office work for women: an historical review', *Business Hist.*, 17(1), 1976, pp. 98–110.

Simmonds, L., 'From Germany with honour', *JC* Colour Magazine, 26 November 1976, pp. 46–56.

Sir Jacob Behrens: 1806–1889, privately printed, 1925.

'Sir Max Rayne', *JC* Property Supplement, 25 June 1971, pp. viii–ix.

Sisson, C. J., 'A colony of Jews in Shakespeare's London', *Essays by Members of the English Association*, 22, 1938, pp. 38–51.

Sissons, M., and P. French (eds), *The Age of Austerity*, London, 1963.

Smith, Ashley, *You Forget So Quickly*, London, 1946.

Smith, H. Llewellyn (ed.), *New Survey of London Life and Labour*, 9 vols, London, 1930–35.

Smout, T. C., *A History of the Scottish People: 1560–1830*, London, 1969.

Solomon, Israel J., *Records of My Family*, New York, 1887.

Soref, H., 'A demographic revolution', *JC*, 15 March 1952.

Speaight, Robert, *William Rothenstein: The Portrait of an Artist in His Own Time*, London, 1962.

Spector, David, 'The Jews of Brighton, 1770–1900', *TJHSE*, 22, 1970, pp. 42–52.

Spenser, Edward, *An Epistle to the Learned Menasseh ben Israel, in Answer to his, Dedicated to the Parliament*, London, 1650.

Stein, S., 'Some Ashkenazi charities in London at the end of the eighteenth and the beginning of the nineteenth centuries', *TJHSE*, 20, 1964, pp. 63–81.

Stern, Fritz, *Gold and Iron: Bismarck, Bleichröder, and the Building of the German Empire*, New York, 1977.

Stevens, Austin, *The Dispossessed: German Refugees in Britain*, London, 1975.

Stewart, Margaret, and Leslie Hunter, *The Needle Is Threaded*, London, 1964.

Stokes, H. P., *Studies in Anglo-Jewish History*, Edinburgh, 1913.

Supple, B. E., 'A Business elite: German-Jewish bankers in nineteenth century New York', *Business Hist. Rev.*, 31, 1957, pp. 157–76.

Susser, B., *An Account of the Old Jewish Cemetery on Plymouth Hoe*, Plymouth, 1975.

Susser, B., 'Social acclimatization of Jews in eighteenth and nineteenth century Devon', in Roger Burt (ed.), *Industry and Society in the South-West*, Exeter, 1970, pp. 51–69.

Sutherland, L. S., 'Samson Gideon and the reduction of interest, 1749–50', *Econ. Hist. Rev.*, 16(1–2), 1946, pp. 15–29.

Sutherland, L. S., 'Samson Gideon: eighteenth-century Jewish financier', *TJHSE*, 17, 1953, pp. 79–90.

Sutherland, L. S., *The City of London and the Devonshire-Pitt Administration: 1756–71*, Raleigh Lecture on History, Brit. Academy, 1960.

Sutherland, L. S., *A London Merchant: 1695–1774*, 1933, reprinted London, 1962.

Swift, H. G., *A History of Postal Agitation*, rev. ed., Manchester and London, 1929.

Tartakower, Arieh, *In Search of Home and Freedom*, London, 1958.

Tawney, R. H., *The Establishment of Minimum Rates in the Tailoring Industry Under the Trade Boards Act of 1909*, London, 1915.

Temple Patterson, A., *A History of Southampton 1700–1914*, vol. II: *The Beginnings of Modern Southampton: 1836–1867*, Southampton Records Series, vol. 14, 1971.

Thomas, Brinley, *Migration and Economic Growth*, London, 1954.

Thomas, Joan, 'A history of the Leeds clothing industry', *York. Bull. of Econ. and Soc. Research*, Occasional Paper no. 1, 1955.

Thompson, E. P., 'Homage to Tom Maguire', in Asa Briggs and John Saville (eds), *Essays in Labour History*, London, 1960, pp. 276–316.

Thompson, E. P., *The Making of the English Working Class*, London, 1963.

Thompson, E. P., 'Eighteenth century crime, popular movements and social control', *Bull. Soc. Study Labour Hist.*, no. 25, 1972, pp. 9–11.

Thompson, E. P., and Eileen Yeo (eds), *The Unknown Mayhew*, Harmondsworth, 1973.

Thompson, P., *Socialists, Liberals and Labour: The Struggle for London, 1885–1914*, London, 1967.

Thurloe, John, *A Collection of Papers Containing Authentic Memorials of the English Affairs from 1638 to the Restoration*, vol. IV, London, 1742.

Tilly, R., 'Germany 1815–1870', in R. Cameron (ed.), *Banking in the Early Stages of Industrialisation*, New York, 1967.

Tobias, J. J., *Crime and Industrial Society in the Nineteenth Century*, Harmondsworth, 1972.

Tobias, J. J., 'Police-immigrant relations in England: 1800–1910', *New Community*, 3(3), 1974, pp. 211–14.

Tobias, J. J., *Prince of Fences: The Life and Crimes of Ikey Solomons*, London, 1974.

Toon, P. (ed.), *Puritans, the Millennium and the Future of Israel: Puritan Eschatology, 1600 to 1660*, Cambridge and London, 1970.

Toon, P., 'The latter-day glory', in P. Toon (ed.), *Puritans, the Millennium and the Future of Israel: Puritan Eschatology, 1600 to 1660*, Cambridge and London, 1970, pp. 23–41.

'Tory's first Jewish M. P.', *JC*, 1 March 1974.

Tovey, D'Bloissiers, *Anglia Judaica: Or the History and Antiquities of the Jews in England*, Oxford, 1738.

Trevor-Roper, H. R., *Religion, the Reformation and Social Change*, 2nd ed., London, 1972.

Trollope, Anthony, *The Way We Live Now*, London, 1875.

Tropp, A., *The Schoolteachers*, London, 1957.

Tute, Warren, *The Grey Top Hat: The Story of Moss Bros of Covent Garden*, London, 1961.

Union of Liberal and Progressive Synagogues, *Jewish Students: A Question of Identity*, London, 1974.

'Vagrant Jews concerned with crime', *Cal. Home Office Reports of the Reign of George III: 1770–1772*, 1881, pp. 355–58.

Van Oven, Joshua, *Letters on the Present State of the Jewish Poor in the Metropolis*, London, 1802.

Varley, D. E., *A History of the Midland Counties Lace Manufacturers' Association: 1915–1958*, Long Eaton, 1959.

'Veteran cabby', *JC*, 4 June 1971.

Victoria County History, *Essex*, vol. 6, London, 1973.

Victoria County History, *Warwickshire*, vol. 7, London, 1964.

Vigne, Thea, and A. Howkins, 'The small shopkeeper in industrial and market towns', in G. Crossick (ed.), *The Lower Middle Classes in Britain: 1870–1914*, London, 1977, pp. 184–209.

Wallach, Michael, 'How "greeners" came to the valley', *JC* Colour Magazine, 28 November 1975, pp. 28–34.

Wallach, Sharon, ' "Life was one big speculation": the story of Frank Peterman, a pioneer in the fashion industry', *JC* Colour Magazine, 23 November 1979, pp. 85–86.

Walshe, G., *Recent Trends in Monopoly in Great Britain*, London, 1974.

Warburg, F., *All Authors are Equal: The Publishing Life of Fredric Warburg, 1936–1971*, London, 1973.

Waterman, R., *A Family of Shopkeepers*, London, 1973.

Webb, Beatrice, 'The Jewish community (East London)', in C. Booth (ed.), *The Life and Labour of the People in London*, vol. III, London, 1893, pp. 166–91.

Webb, Beatrice, *My Apprenticeship*, London, 1926.

Webb, S. and B., *Industrial Democracy*, London, 1902.

Weber, Max, *Ancient Judaism*, trans. and ed. by H. H. Gerth and D. Martindale, Chicago, 1952.

Weber, Max, *The Sociology of Religion*, Eng. trans. of 4th ed., London, 1963.

Wechsberg, J. P., *The Merchant Bankers*, London, 1967.

Weisgal, Myer, *So Far*, London, 1972.

Weizmann, Vera, *The Impossible Takes Longer*, London, 1967.

West Ham District Synagogue, *Order of Service at the Re-consecration*, 16 June 1935.

Westerfield, R. B., *Middlemen in English Business, Particularly between 1660 and 1760*, 1915, reprinted Newton Abbot, 1969.

Whitaker, W. B., *Victorian and Edwardian Shopworkers*, Newton Abbot, 1973.

Whitehill, G. H. (ed.), *Bevis Marks Records*, part 3, London, 1973.

Whiteman, A. J. S. Bromley and P. G. M. Dickson (eds), *Statesmen, Scholars and Merchants: Essays in Eighteenth-Century History Presented to Dame Lucy Sutherland*, London, 1973.

Williams, Bill, *The Making of Manchester Jewry: 1740–1815*, Manchester, 1976.

Williams, Bill, 'Power and poverty in Manchester Jewry', *JC*, 14 October 1977, p. 19.

Williams, Bill, 'The beginnings of Jewish trade unionism in Manchester, 1889–1891', in K. Lunn (ed.), *Hosts, Immigrants and Minorities, Historical Responses to Newcomers in British Society 1870–1914*, London, 1980.

Williams, G. A. *Medieval London: From Commune to Capital*, London, 1963.

Wills, Stella, 'The Anglo-Jewish contribution to the education movement for women in the nineteenth century', *TJHSE*, 17, 1953, pp. 269–81.

Wilson, Charles, *Anglo-Dutch Commerce and Finance in the Eighteenth Century*, 1941, reprinted Cambridge, 1966.

Wilson, Charles, *The History of Unilever*, 2 vols, Cambridge, 1954.

Wilson, J., *A History of the Durham Miners' Association: 1870–1904*, Durham, 1907.

Wilson, Jean Moorcroft, *Isaac Rosenberg: Poet and Painter*, London, 1975.

Wischnitzer, M., *A History of Jewish Crafts and Guilds*, New York, 1965.

Wolf, Lucien, 'Crypto-Jews under the Commonwealth', *TJHSE*, 1, 1895, pp. 55–85.

Wolf, Lucien, 'American elements in the resettlement', *TJHSE*, 3, 1899, pp. 85–93.

Wolf, Lucien (ed.), *Menasseh ben Israel's Mission to Oliver Cromwell*, London, 1901.

Wolf, Lucien (ed.), *The Legal Sufferings of the Jews in Russia*, London, 1912.

Wolf, Lucien, 'Jews in Elizabethan England', *TJHSE*, 11, 1928, pp. 1–91.

Wolf, Lucien, *Essays in Jewish History*, London, 1934.

Wolf, Lucien, 'Jews in Tudor England', in L. Wolf, *Essays in Jewish History*, London, 1934, pp. 73–90.

Wolff, P., 'The 1391 pogrom in Spain: social crisis or not?', *Past & Present*, no. 50, February 1971, pp. 4–18.

Wood, A. C., *A History of the Levant Company*, London, 1935.

Woodeson, John, *Mark Gertler: Biography of a Painter, 1891–1939*, London, 1972.

Woolf, M., 'Eighteenth-century London Jewish shipowners', *MJHSE*, part 9, 1975, pp. 198–204.
Woolf, M., 'Foreign trade of London Jews in the seventeenth century', *TJHSE*, 24, 1975, pp. 38–58.
Woolf, M., 'Joseph Salvador: 1716–1786', *TJHSE*, 21, 1968, pp. 104–37.
Woolrych, A., 'Puritanism, politics and society', in E. W. Ives (ed.), *The English Revolution: 1600–1660*, London, 1968, pp. 95–99.
Woolrych, A., 'The English revolution: an introduction', in E. W. Ives (ed.), *The English Revolution: 1600–1660*, London, 1968, pp. 29–32.
Working Lives, vol. 1: *1905–1945: A People's Autobiography of Hackney*, London, n.d.
Wray, Margaret, *The Women's Outerwear Industry*, London, 1957.
Wrightson's New Triennial Directory of Birmingham, 1818, reprinted Newcastle-upon-Tyne, 1970.
Yogev, G., *Diamonds and Corals: Anglo-Dutch Jews and Eighteenth-Century Trade*, Leicester, 1978.

Glossary

Ascama (Heb.)	Article of the constitution of the Sephardi synagogue
Ashkenazi (pl. -m) (Heb.)	Jew(s) from northern and central Europe
Greeners	Newly-arrived immigrants
Imposta (Port.)	Contributions paid by member of Sephardi synagogue, based on income
Landsman (Yid.)	Immigrant from the same district
Mahamad (Heb.)	Executive officers of the Sephardi synagogue
Responsa	Rabbinical answers to questions
Sedacca (Heb.)	'Charity' (Sephardi pronunciation). General funds of the Sephardi synagogue
Sephardi (pl. -m)	Jew(s) originating from Spain and Portugal
Shlimazel (Yid.)	Simpleton
Shtetl (Yid.)	Small town or village
Talmud Torah (Heb.)	'Study of the Law'. Used for school for teaching religious subjects
Torah (Heb.)	'Law'; body of Jewish religious knowledge
Vest	Waistcoat
Yeshivot (pl.) (Heb.)	Religious seminaries; advanced teaching
Yomtovim (pl.) (Yid.)	Holy days

Index